Relabeling in Language Genesis

Relabeling in Language Genesis

CLAIRE LEFEBVRE

Oxford University Press is a department of the University of Oxford.
It furthers the University's objective of excellence in research, scholarship,
and education by publishing worldwide.

Oxford New York
Auckland Cape Town Dar es Salaam Hong Kong Karachi
Kuala Lumpur Madrid Melbourne Mexico City Nairobi
New Delhi Shanghai Taipei Toronto

With offices in
Argentina Austria Brazil Chile Czech Republic France Greece
Guatemala Hungary Italy Japan Poland Portugal Singapore
South Korea Switzerland Thailand Turkey Ukraine Vietnam

Oxford is a registered trade mark of Oxford University Press
in the UK and certain other countries.

Published in the United States of America by
Oxford University Press
198 Madison Avenue, New York, NY 10016

Library of Congress Cataloging-in-Publication Data
Lefebvre, Claire.
  Relabeling in language genesis / Claire Lefebvre.
    p. cm.
 Summary: "This book presents a coherent picture of the progress that has been made in research
on relabeling over the last 15 years" — Provided by publisher.
  Includes bibliographical references and indexes.
  ISBN 978–0–19–994531–3 (paperback) — ISBN 978–0–19–994529–0 (hardcover) —
ISBN 978–0–19–020120–3 (ebook) 1. Languages in contact. 2. Creole dialects.
3. Bilingualism. 4. Second language acquisition. 5. Construction grammar. I. Title.
  P130.5.L43 2014
  417'.22—dc23
                              2014018508

9 8 7 6 5 4 3 2 1

Printed in the United States of America on acid-free paper

There is nothing important that comes easy.
Shimon Peres

To my grandchildren Olivier and Edouard
May they find their passion

CONTENTS

Preface   ix
List of Abbreviations   x

CHAPTER 1   Introduction   1

CHAPTER 2   Relabeling: A Central Process in Language Contact/
Genesis   9

CHAPTER 3   The Relabeling-Based Theory of Creole Genesis   31

CHAPTER 4   Relabeling in Two Different Theories of the Lexicon   103
Renée Lambert-Brétière and Claire Lefebvre

CHAPTER 5   Relabeling and Word Order: A Construction Grammar
Perspective   139
Claire Lefebvre and Renée Lambert-Brétière

CHAPTER 6   Relabeling Options: On Some Differences Between
Haitian and Saramaccan   164

CHAPTER 7   Relabeling and the Contribution of the Superstrate
Languages to Creoles   177

CHAPTER 8   Relabeling and the Typological Classification
of Creoles   223

CHAPTER 9   Conclusion: A Strong Alternative to the Bioprogram
Hypothesis   258

References   273
Index of Subjects   295
Index of Authors   299
Index of Languages   305

PREFACE

This book examines the cognitive process of relabeling in language genesis. Its content is based on two intensive courses that I gave as a guest lecturer, one at the University of Hong Kong in November 2011 ("The Hong Kong Lectures on Relabeling"), and one at the University of Puerto Rico – Rio Piedras in January 2013 ("Relabeling in Language Genesis"). I would like to thank these two universities for giving me, through Umberto Ansaldo and Yolanda Rivera Castillo, respectively, the opportunity to present the latest developments in my research. I would also like to thank the participants in these courses for their most insightful questions, comments, and discussions.

The research reported in this book has been funded by SSHRCC (Social Sciences and Humanities Research Council of Canada) without interruption for the last thirty years. Other agencies, such as FCAC, FCAR, FQRSC, PAFAC, and OLF, have also contributed to funding parts of this research, and I am grateful to all of them. I would also like to thank Anne Rochette, Dean of the Faculty of Humanities at Université du Québec à Montréal; Yves Mauffette, Vice-Principal, Research; Pierre Poirier, Head of the Cognitive Science Institute; Anne-Marie DiSciullo, Head of the Department of Linguistics; Lucie Ménard, Professor in the Department of Linguistics; and France Martineau, head of the "Le français à la mesure d'un continent" project, for their financial help with the last stage of preparation of this manuscript.

Many thanks to Andrée Bélanger for formatting the manuscript, to Renée Lambert-Brétière and Robert Papen for their comments on an earlier version of the manuscript, and to Zofia Laubitz for copyediting it.

LIST OF ABBREVIATIONS

1PL	first-person plural
1SG	first-person singular
2PL	second-person plural
2SG	second-person singular
3PL	third-person plural
3SG	third-person singular
ACC	accusative
A(DJ)	adjective
ADV	adverb
AN	animate
ANT	anterior
AP	plural article
ASP	aspect
AspP	aspect phrase
AUX	auxiliary
CAAE	Central Australian Aboriginal English
CASE	case
CL	classifier
COMP	complementizer
CONT	continuative
COP	copula
CP	complementizer phrase

CV	consonant vowel
DEF	definite determiner
DEF.FUT	definite future
DEIC	deictic
DEM	demonstrative
DET	determiner
DM	discourse marker
EMC	English Maroon Creoles
EMP	emphasis
EX	exclusive
f.	feminine
FinP	finite phrase
FOC	focus
FUT	future
FUT-POSSIB	future-possibility
GEN	genitive
GENP	genitive phrase
G/L	Goal/Location
HCE	Hawai'i Creole English
IM	Inner Mbugu
IMP	imperfective
INAN	inanimate
INDEF	indefinite
INFL	inflection
INS	insistence
INT	interrogative
IP	inflection phrase
IRR	irrealis
LOC	locative
m.	masculine
MC	Mindanao Chabacano
ML	Media Lengua
M(O)	mood
MoodP	mood phrase
N	noun

NC	nominal classifier
NEG	negation
NP	noun phrase
NSWP	New South Wales Pidgin
NUM	number
OBJ	object
OBJB	objective phrase
OBL	oblique
OBV	obviative
OP	operator
PA	past
PART	partitive
PC	pidgin(s) and creole(s)
PERF	perfective
PL	plural
POSS	possessive
P(OST)	postposition
P&P	Principles and Parameters
PP	pre-/postpositional phrase
PR	pronoun
P(REP)	preposition
PROG	progressive
PROX	proximate
PST	past
Q	question marker
RC	relative clause
RCP	reciprocal
RCxG	Radical Construction Grammar
RE-	reduplication
RES	resumptive
S	sentence
SBJ	subject
SG	singular
SIP	Solomon Islands Pijin
SLM	Sri Lankan Malay

SUB	subjunctive
SVC	serial verb construction
T	tense
TC	Ternate Chabacano
TP	tense phrase
TMA	Tense-Mood-Aspect
TNS	tense
TOP	topic marker
TR	transitive
V	verb
VAL	validator
VP	verb phrase
XP	x phrase

Relabeling in Language Genesis

CHAPTER 1 | Introduction

THE SUBJECT OF THIS book is relabeling (a.k.a. relexification), a major cognitive process in language contact and genesis. For example, this process has been shown to play a role in the formation of mixed languages, involving two languages, and in the formation of pidgins and creoles, involving several languages. I will therefore begin this introductory chapter by providing a formal definition of the process.

1. What Is Relabeling?

Relabeling is a process that consists in assigning a lexical entry a new label derived from a phonetic string drawn from another language. It is schematically represented in (1). Given a lexical entry as in (1a), assign this lexical entry a parallel phonological representation derived from another language's phonetic string (a process known as paralabeling), as in (1b), and eventually abandon the original phonological representation. This process yields lexical entries that have the representation in (1c), that is, lexical entries that have the semantic and syntactic properties of the original ones and phonological representations derived from phonetic strings drawn from another language.

(1)   a. $\begin{bmatrix} \text{/phonological representation/}_i \\ \text{[semantic features]}_i \\ \text{[syntactic features]}_i \end{bmatrix}$

b. $\begin{bmatrix} \text{/phonological representation/}_i \text{ /phonological representation/}_{j'} \\ \text{[semantic features]}_i \\ \text{[syntactic features]}_i \end{bmatrix}$

c. $\begin{bmatrix} \text{/phonological representation/}_{j'} \\ \text{[semantic features]}_i \\ \text{[syntactic features]}_i \end{bmatrix}$

In diagram (1), the label assigned to the lexical entry created by relabeling is identified as j'. Since relabeling proceeds on the basis of another language, the new label is identified as j instead of as i, thus relating it to this other language. However, the phonological representation of the new label, the creole label, does not correspond to that of the language from which it is derived. As Brousseau and Nikiema (2006) and Steele and Brousseau (2006) argue at some length, the phonological system of a language created by relabeling, for example a creole, does not correspond to that of the language that has provided its labels. Rather, it represents a principled compromise between the phonological systems of the native languages of a creole's creators, the substrate languages, and of the lexifier language, the superstrate language. For these reasons, the new label in (1) is identified as j' rather than as j.

Relabeling is exemplified in (2), based on Haitian and two of its source languages: Fongbe, a major substrate language (Lefebvre 1998: 52–58; Singler 1996), and French, the superstrate language. The example involves the Fongbe lexical entry /hù/, the French lexical entry /asasine/ and the Haitian lexical entry /ansasinen/. As discussed in Lefebvre (1999), the Haitian verb *ansasinen* conveys the concepts 'to murder' and 'to mutilate' (e.g., *ansasinen janm* 'to mutilate one's leg') (Valdman et al. 1981). The phonological representation of this Haitian verb is derived from the French verb *assassiner*, which is associated with the concept 'to murder' but not with 'to mutilate' (e.g., Furetière 1984). In French, the notion 'to mutilate' is conveyed by a separate verb: *mutiler* (e.g., *se mutiler le pied* 'to mutilate one's foot'). The semantics of the Haitian lexical entry corresponds to that of the corresponding Fongbe verb. Like its Haitian counterpart, the Fongbe verb *hù* is associated with the concepts 'to murder' (Segurola 1963) and 'to mutilate' (e.g., *hù àfɔ* 'to mutilate one's foot') (Lefebvre's informants). Furthermore, in both languages, the verb may take a complement meaning 'tree': *ansasinen pyebwa* and *hù àtín*, respectively, 'to destroy a tree' (lit.: 'to assassinate a tree'). The corresponding French verb cannot be used in this way. Clearly, the substrate lexical entry is the source of the semantics of the Haitian verb *ansasinen*. (For further discussion on the semantics of these verbs, see Lefebvre 1999: 69–70.) This follows from the process of relabeling as depicted in (2), based on the model in (1). In (2), Fongbe *hù* 'to murder, to mutilate' is assigned a parallel phonological representation *ansasinen* 'to murder, to mutilate' derived from the phonetic representation [assasine] of the French verb *assassiner* 'to murder' (2b). When the Fongbe label ceased to be used, the original lexical entry had been relabeled as in (2c). (For a discussion of how the phonetic strings of the superstrate language are assigned a phonological representation in the creole, see Brousseau and Nikiema (2006), Steele and Brousseau (2006), and the references cited therein).

(2)   a.   FONGBE

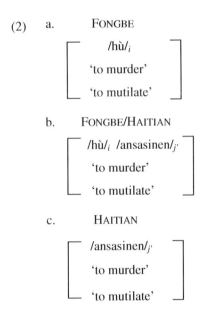

b.   FONGBE/HAITIAN

c.   HAITIAN

Relabeling is semantically driven. The two lexical entries that are associated in the process of relabeling must share some semantics (Muysken 1981a). The data in (2) show, however, that the two entries need not be entirely semantically congruent. While Fongbe *hù* means both 'to murder' and 'to mutilate,' French *assassiner* means only 'to murder.' Muysken (1981a: 62) further states that "other features of the two lexical entries, may, but need not, be associated with each other." For example, the form of the Haitian verb *bezwen* 'to need' is derived from that of the French noun *besoin* 'need,' showing that the categorial features of the two lexical items that are associated in relabeling do not play a role in the process. This is congruent with the fact that the only property that is required for relabeling to take place is partially shared semantics between the two lexical entries involved. According to Lefebvre and Lumsden (1994a), this partially shared semantics is captured on the basis of the occurrence of lexical items in specific linguistic and pragmatic contexts. Several examples of relabeling of different kinds will be presented throughout this book. Since relabeling is semantically driven, lexical items that do not have any semantic content, such as syntactic cases, as opposed to semantic cases, cannot be relabeled. Examples of such cases will be discussed in this book.

Since relabeling proceeds on the basis of superstrate forms, it is constrained by what the superstrate language has available to relabel a substrate lexical entry (e.g., Bao 2005; Lefebvre 1998; Lefebvre & Lumsden 1994a; Siegel 2008; Smith 2001; Terrill 2011). Comparative work on creole languages that have the same substrate languages but different superstrate languages, such as Haitian Creole, Saramaccan, and Papiamentu, provides us with a wealth of data to document this constraint. Several examples of this constraint will be provided in the following chapters.

2. Why This Book

The process of relabeling (a.k.a. relexification) has been shown to play a role in the formation of mixed languages (e.g., Media Lengua, Muysken 1981a; Ma'a, Mous 1994, 1995, 2001; Michif, Bakker 1989, 1992, 1994). Based on subsets of data, it has also been shown to play a role in the formation of creole languages (e.g., for Ndjuka, see, e.g., Huttar 1975; Migge 2003; for Sranan, see, e.g., Bruyn 2003; Voorhoeve 1973; for Kriol, see, e.g., Koch 2000; Munro 2004; for Singapore English, see, e.g., Bao 2005, 2010). On the basis of a detailed and extensive comparative study of Haitian and its source languages, French and Fongbe, Lefebvre and colleagues have documented the fact that relabeling played a central role in the genesis of this creole; the results of this study were published in Lefebvre (1998 and the references cited therein). Why then write another book on this topic?

Several reasons justify at least one more book on the topic. First, relabeling is important because of the contexts and situations in which it may be called upon. As will be seen in Chapter 2, this cognitive process plays a role in the first phase of second-language acquisition and in the formation of mixed languages, pidgin and creole languages, language varieties that are referred to as New Englishes, and so on. Since the process is so important in second-language acquisition, as well as in the formation of new languages, it ought to be extremely well documented and understood.

Second, by its very nature, relabeling takes place in the lexical component of the grammar. The initial study was carried out within the framework of Principles and Parameters (P&P; Chomsky 1989). Within this framework, the syntactic component of the grammar constitutes the main object of study, leaving the lexical component rather unexplored. By contrast, in other frameworks, such as in Construction Grammar frameworks, the lexicon constitutes the main component of the grammar. By hypothesis, a relabeling-based account of creole genesis could benefit from developments in these frameworks. As will be seen in Chapters 4, 5, and 6 of this book, this is indeed the case. For reasons that will be explained in Chapter 4, we chose the Radical Construction Grammar model (RCxG) developed by Croft (2001). The approach to the lexicon in RCxG is quite different from that in Principles and Parameters (Chomsky 1989). In fact, the two models do not divide up the lexicon in the same way and therefore, in some cases, they make different predictions for a relabeling-based account of creole genesis. Some data that were problematic for a relabeling-based account of creole genesis within the Principles and Parameters model find a straightforward explanation within this Cognitive Grammar framework (Chapter 4).

Third, accounts of how word order is established in creole genesis have always been problematic, as the literature on the topic shows. The hypothesis on how word order is established in creole genesis presented in Lefebvre (1998), which was based on Lefebvre and Lumsden (1992), failed to account for data other than those of Haitian. The RCxG model provides us with new tools to address this problem (see Chapter 5).

Fourth, a wealth of new data has become available since 1998 (see Chapter 3). For example, in the last 15 years, we have expanded our database to include other Caribbean creoles such as Saramaccan and Papiamentu. These have the same pool of substrate languages as Haitian (Gbe and other West African languages) but different superstrate languages: English and Portuguese for Saramaccan, and Portuguese and Spanish for Papiamentu. The comparison of three creoles that have evolved from a single substrate but different superstrate languages provides the type of corpus that is needed to deepen our understanding of the contribution made by superstrate languages in creole genesis (see Chapter 7). Data on creoles from different parts of the world, including Asia, Australia, and Africa—thus, creoles with different substrates—have also been made available in publications. These are cited throughout this book. Significant databases on creoles from different substrates make it possible to address new issues such as the typological classification of creoles (see Chapter 8).

Finally, several questions, comments, and critiques have been directed at the relabeling-based theory of creole genesis outlined in Lefebvre (1998 and related work). Additional research conducted since then has given me the opportunity to consider these issues, most of which are addressed in this book (see Chapters 3, 4, 5, and 6).

In short, the aim of this book is to present a coherent picture of the progress that has been made on the topic of relabeling over the last 15 years. This progress brings us closer to understanding the principled contribution of the substrate and superstrate languages to creole genesis. As will become evident to the reader, what is visible or overt tends to be drawn from the superstrate, whereas what is invisible or covert tends to be drawn from the substrate.

3. Overview of Chapters

The book is organized as follows. Chapter 2 covers relabeling as a major process in language contact and language genesis. First, it assesses the role of relabeling in language contact situations, showing that processes referred to in the literature as, for example, relexification, calquing, transfer, and so on, often correspond to what I refer to as relabeling. The use of different terms may suggest that several different processes are available in language contact and language genesis. Provided that it is possible to show, however, that, in some cases, these processes produce the same result, a fair conclusion would be that all of them may reduce to one, namely relabeling. Since we are dealing with cognitive processes, this is a welcome result. In my view, it is preferable to identify the smallest possible number of processes and let the differences between the various cases follow from the social variables that define different language contact situations. Chapter 2 also assesses the extent of relabeling across language contact/genesis situations, highlighting the importance of the process of relabeling in different situations. Finally, this chapter investigates the scope of relabeling across lexicons. It is shown that, in different situations, relabeling may affect different portions of the lexicon, yielding language varieties that do not look the same on the surface. The approach taken in this chapter makes it possible to develop a unified analysis of the contribution that a single process, relabeling, makes to the composition of different language varieties arising in different contact situations, and thus to associate a number of contact phenomena and situations that would otherwise remain separate.

Chapter 3 contains a statement of the relabeling-based theory of creole genesis as it has been updated over the last 15 years. The chapter is meant to introduce the relabeling-based account of creole genesis to readers who are not familiar with it and to introduce the latest developments to readers who are familiar with it. Basically, in this theory, relabeling plays a central role in the genesis of creoles; other processes such as leveling, grammaticalization, and so on, apply to the output of relabeling. The summary of the theory presented in Chapter 3 incorporates the most recent additions and revisions to the theory. It also includes replies to major comments and critiques that have been directed at it over the years. Furthermore, it includes new data from Saramaccan, Papiamentu, and other creoles that allow for a wider and deeper discussion of the issues involved.

By hypothesis, different theories of the lexicon should make different predictions as to the nature of the lexical items to which relabeling can apply. The aim of Chapter 4 is to evaluate the predictions of two different approaches to the lexicon—the Principles and Parameters (P&P) framework (Chomsky 1989) and the Radical Construction Grammar (RCxG) framework (Croft 2001)—for a relabeling-based account of creole genesis. This will be done on the basis of data drawn from a subset of Caribbean creoles and their contributing languages. The analysis shows that, where the P&P model failed to account for some data within a relabeling-based account of creole genesis, the RCxG framework succeeds in accounting for them.

Since creoles' word order does not systematically reflect that of either of their contributing languages, word order in creoles and in creole genesis has long been a puzzle for researchers. This puzzle has stimulated a significant amount of research from different perspectives. On the basis of a sample of creoles, Chapter 5 addresses the question of how word order is established in a relabeling-based account of creole genesis from an RCxG perspective. Our proposal allows for a principled account of how the various word orders are established in creole genesis.

There are differences between creoles that share the same substrate. For example, although Haitian and Saramaccan share a common Gbe substrate, there are differences between them. While Saramaccan has postpositions and morphological reduplication, on the model of its substrate languages, Haitian does not. Chapter 6 shows that, in relabeling, creoles' creators have options; consequently, they may choose different ones, resulting in differences between creoles. The content of this chapter echoes Smith's (2001) article "Voodoo Chile."

Much of the research on relabeling has concentrated on the contribution that the substrate languages make to creoles. Much less work has been done on the contribution of superstrate languages to creole genesis. Chapter 7 explores the role of the superstrate languages in the makeup of creoles. The assumption underlying this chapter is that, like the substrate languages' contribution to creoles, the contribution of superstrate languages must be principled. The methodology developed to accurately identify superstrate languages' contributions to creoles consists in comparing creoles that share the same substrate languages but have different superstrate languages. The superstrate languages' contribution to creoles will be shown to be concentrated in the labels and in word order, thus in what is "visible." Labels and word order together constitute the "form," as opposed to the "meaning" and "function" of an expression. The conclusion of this study is thus that the contributions of both substrate and superstrate to a creole are principled.

The fact that pidgins and creoles draw their properties from two sources (substrate and superstrate languages) raises the question of their typological classification, which has been debated in the literature for quite some time. Chapter 8 addresses this issue. It is based on 25 comparative studies of some 30 creoles and their substrate languages. As the substrate languages of these creoles are typologically different, a detailed investigation of substrate features in the creoles leads to a particular answer to the question of how creoles should be classified typologically. It is shown, however, that the contribution of the substrate languages to the typological features of a creole is not equally important in all components of the grammar. It is argued that the typological features of a creole pair with those of the substrate languages in areas of the grammar where the substrate languages make contributions, but with those of the superstrate language in areas of the grammar where the superstrate languages contribute. This is congruent with the fact that the respective contributions of substrate and superstrate languages to creoles are principled, as argued in Chapter 7. Finally, Chapter 9 concludes the book.

CHAPTER 2 | Relabeling: A Central Process in Language Contact/Genesis

1. Introduction

The problem of language contact may be approached from two opposite angles: the processes at work in language contact situations, or, ignoring the processes, the language varieties resulting from contact. In this chapter, I look at contact phenomena from the former rather than from the latter angle.* I focus on one process: relabeling. Relabeling is a mental operation that consists in assigning a lexical entry of a given language, L_1, a new label taken from another language, L_2 (see Chapter 1).

The importance of relabeling in language contact has been greatly underestimated. One reason for this is the fact that this process is referred to in the literature by a number of terms, which has obscured its unity and prominence in language contact situations. In section 2, I provide an overview of the various terms used in the literature to refer to the process that I refer to as *relabeling*. In section 3, I show that relabeling plays a role in a wide range of language contact situations. However, the language varieties that have involved relabeling do not all look the same on the surface. Section 4 shows that this is due to the uneven extent of relabeling across lexicons, which, in turn, is determined by a number of variables that define the situations in which this process is applied. These variables include the number of languages involved, the amount of access to L_2, whether code

*A preliminary version of this chapter was presented at the Symposium on Language Contact and Dynamics of Language: Theory and Implications, held at the Max Planck Institute for Evolutionary Anthropology, Leipzig, May 10–13, 2007. I would like to thank the participants in the symposium, as well as the reviewers, for their comments and questions, which contributed to shaping the final version of this chapter.

switching is involved, and whether language shift is involved. Section 5 concludes the chapter.

2. The Vocabulary Issue

In the literature on language contact, several different terms are used to refer to the process that I call relabeling. Nevertheless, the results of the process referred to by these terms often correspond to the outcome of re-labeling. This section documents these claims.

2.1. Relexification as Relabeling

Muysken (1981a: 61) defines *relexification* as follows: "Given the concept of lexical entry, relexification can be defined as the process of vocabulary substitution in which the only information adopted from the target language in the lexical entry is the phonological representation."[1] Relexification is represented in (1) from Muysken.

(1)

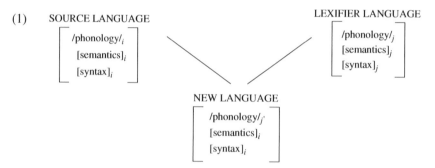

The process is exemplified in (2), on the basis of data discussed in Chapter 1 (see (2) in Chapter 1).

(2)

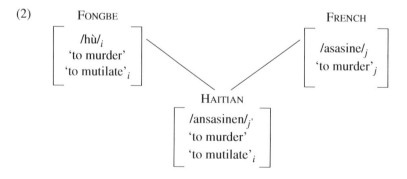

---

[1] In my view, it is not the phonological representation of the target language lexical entry that is involved in relexification, but rather a phonetic string. See Chapter 1 for discussion of this point.

According to this definition, relexification is a mental process that builds a new lexical entry by copying an existing one and replacing its phonological representation with a representation drawn from another language. The process diagrammed in (1) can be restated as relabeling (= (1) in Chapter 1), and indeed, its end result corresponds to that of relabeling (see (2) in Chapter 1). Relexification thus reduces to relabeling. This is a welcome result because it clears up the confusion associated with the term *relexification*. Indeed, at times, relexification has been wrongly interpreted as yielding a language that has the lexicon of one language and the syntax of another, a view that is hardly conceivable in current models of grammar, in which lexical and syntactic features are expected to match. This is what led me to replace the term *relexification* by *relabeling* in the first place.

2.2. Paralexification as Paralabeling

Mous (1995) identifies a cognitive process he refers to as *paralexification*. This process provides a second phonological form for a given lexical entry. "Paralexification is the addition of a word form to a lexical entry. This added form is on a par with the existent word form of the lexical entry in question. That is: two word forms share meaning, metaphorical extensions, and morphological properties such as noun class membership for nouns and predicate frame for verbs" (1995: 1). Mous's definition of paralexification can be schematized as in (3), in which a given lexical entry has two phonological representations—the original one and a second one drawn from another language—but only one set of semantic and syntactic features.

(3)
$$
\begin{bmatrix}
/phonology/_i / \; /phonology/_{j'} \\
[\text{semantic feature}]_i \\
[\text{syntactic feature}]_i
\end{bmatrix}
$$

The process of paralexification in (3) can be viewed as paralabeling (see (1b) in Chapter 1), the first step in relabeling. Both representations describe a process that, in its initial stage, consists in creating a second phonological representation for a given lexical entry. Paralexification can thus be equated with paralabeling.

2.3. Calquing as Relabeling

In his work on Solomon Islands Pidgin, Keesing (1988: 1–2) writes:

> Sitting on a Solomon Islands mountain in 1977, [. . .] I was led to think more
> seriously than I ever had about the history and structure of Solomon Islands

Pidgin. I had earlier been struck, when I had learned Solomon Pidgin in the 1960s through the medium of Kwaio, an indigenous language I already spoke fluently, that this learning task mainly required learning Pidgin equivalents of Kwaio morphemes. The syntax of Solomon Pidgin was essentially the same as the syntax of Kwaio, although somewhat simpler and lacking some of the surface marking; in most constructions, there was a virtual morpheme-by-morpheme correspondence between Kwaio and Pidgin. [. . .] Although most of the Pidgin lexical forms were ultimately derived from English, I found this largely irrelevant to my language-learning task. The semantic categories they labelled corresponded to Kwaio ones, not English ones; grammatical morphemes corresponded to Kwaio ones, not English ones. Thus semantically Pidgin *dae* corresponded directly to Kwaio *mae* 'be dead, die, be comatose, be extinguished,' not to English 'die.' Pidgin *baebae* corresponded to the Kwaio marker of future / nonaccomplished mode, *ta-*, not to English 'by and by.'

Keesing identifies the data he describes as resulting from the process of calquing. In this view, the creators of the Pidgin calqued the properties of their native lexicons (e.g., Kwaio) onto English forms. Keesing uses the term *calquing* to refer to the process that I refer to as relabeling. Furthermore, the results of calquing, as described above, present the division of properties that is expected of lexical entries produced by relabeling (see (1) in Chapter 1). The conclusion I draw from this state of affairs is that cases of calquing, such as those described by Keesing, are in fact cases of relabeling.

2.4. Full Transfer as Relabeling

The notion of transfer (which goes back to Weinreich 1953: 1) refers to the use of features of their first language by people speaking a second language. In Andersen's (1983: 7) view, this process may also manifest itself in second-language acquisition: "*Transfer* from a learner's previously acquired language [. . .] is assumed to interact with the normal acquisitional process by causing the learner to perceive input in terms of certain aspects of the structure of the previously acquired language." Some cases of transfer may involve the entire set of features of a given lexical item. Such cases are in fact instances of relabeling.

For example, in the Full Transfer/Full Access model of second-language acquisition developed by Schwartz and Sprouse (1996: 41) and related work, "the entirety of the L_1 grammar (excluding the phonetic matrices of lexical/morphological items) is the L_2 initial state (hence the term 'Full Transfer')." Sprouse (2006: 170) thus remarks that "[f]ull Transfer can be restated in terms of Relexification"—hence relabeling—and that "[r]elexification is at the core of the second language instinct, accounting both for the L_2 initial state and for the frequent failure of failure-driven revision to effect convergence on the target language."[2]

2.5. Misascription as Relabeling

Allsop (1980: 95) uses the term *misascription* to refer to cases of full transfer of substrate features to an incipient creole's lexical entry: "By this term I mean not only the semantic shifting, but the ascribing of the wrong sense or the wrong usage or the wrong grammatical function to a word or phrase of the target language." What Allsop means by "wrong" corresponds to a speaker's native language features. Misascription yields the same result as relabeling, and is thus the same process.

2.6. Reinterpretation/Restructuring as Relabeling

The process of restructuring, as described by some authors, produces results that are comparable to those produced by relabeling. For example, consider Migge's (2003: 12) general statement concerning the processes involved in the creation of English Maroon Creoles (EMC):

> In relation to the processes and mechanisms of contact involved in creole formation, sociohistorical research suggests that the agents of creole formation acquired structures from the dominant European varieties and structurally reinterpreted them based on the patterns from their native languages.[3] The degree of reinterpretation was constrained by the nature of the contact setting(s). Settings in which the majority of the agents of creole formation had little access to the European varieties (*cf.* Suriname creole) triggered a relatively great amount of reinterpretation while settings involving a relatively great amount of knowledge of the European varieties gave rise to a relatively small degree of restructuring.

---

[2] As is extensively discussed by Lardière (2006), however, with sustained exposure to L_2, L_2 learners do go beyond relexification (relabeling) and actually acquire features of L_2.

[3] In my view, one cannot both "acquire" and "reinterpret" structures. By definition, these two options must be mutually exclusive.

Examples of the output of restructuring provided by Migge (2003: 63) are reproduced in (4):

(4)	EMC	GBE	ENGLISH
	mofu	*nu*	*mouth*
Meaning	animate mouth, opening, edge beginning/end, message, word	animate mouth, opening, edge, beginning/end	animate mouth, opening of a river
Category	N	N	N
	ondo(o)	*gomɛ* (A, G), *gule* (M), *gɔma* (W), *gun* (X)	*under*
Meaning	lower side, under or below some location	lower side, under or below some location	under or below some location, less than, in some condition
Category	N	N	P
	gi	*na*	*give*
Meaning	give, present; marks recipient, benefactor, experiencer, etc., comp.	give, present; marks recipient, benefactor, experiencer, etc., comp.	give, present
Category	V, P, COMP	V, P, COMP	V

(from Migge 2003: 63; A, G, M, W, and X refer to different dialects of Gbe)

Note that the word *nu* in the first example in (4) is also used in the expression 'say a word' in Fongbe: *kɛ nu ɖókpó* ('open mouth one') (Rassinoux 2000). The examples in (4) show that the results of the process referred to by Migge as reinterpretation/restructuring correspond to those of the process that I refer to as relabeling. The use of these terms in these cases thus corresponds to what I refer to as relabeling.

2.7. Reanalysis as Relabeling

Reanalysis is yet another term sometimes used with the same meaning as "relabeling." Siegel (2000a: 1) cites a standard definition of reanalysis: "The historical process by which a well-formed surface string comes to be interpreted as having a different structure from formerly" (Trask 1993: 228). Siegel goes on: "In language learning and in language contact situations, structures from the target language (usually the superstrate language) may be reinterpreted according to the syntactic or semantic properties of the learner's native language (the substrate language). The process of reinterpretation is basically the same, although in the case of language contact, it is influenced by another language and may lead to the creation of a new variety rather than to internal change in the existing variety" (2). He later writes: "In the context of language contact, this process is referred to as 'relexification' by some researchers (Lefebvre 1998; Lumsden 1999) [. . .]" (2), hence relabeling.

An example of reanalysis used in the sense of relabeling is provided by Koch (2000), who seeks to explain the presence of the transitivity marker *-im* on Australian Pidgin verbs, modeled on the substrate languages of this pidgin. Koch establishes that the form of the transitivity marker comes from the reduced forms of English *him* and *them*, phonologically cliticized onto the verb that precedes them. According to his analysis, these forms have been reanalyzed as part of the verb: "This reanalysis of the object enclitics as part of the verb would have been facilitated by certain expectations based on the phonotactics of their first language [Australian Languages]" (Koch 2000: 18). Koch's use of the term *reanalysis* here corresponds to my definition of relabeling. Other authors use the term in the same way as Koch does (e.g., Bruyn 2003; Detges 2003; Kriegel (ed.) 2003, and several chapters therein; as well as several chapters in Siegel (ed.) 2000b).

2.8. Summary

In the literature, several terms are used to refer either to the same process as that referred to by the term *relabeling* or to the same end results as those produced by relabeling. The terms discussed here are the following: *relexification, paralexification, calquing* (in some cases), *transfer* (in some cases), *misascription, reinterpretation, restructuring,* and *reanalysis*. Other terms, such as Bakker's (1994) *language intertwining,* Van Coetsem's (2000) *imposition* (discussed in Winford 2007), and *metatypy,* as used by Ansaldo (2011a) and Ross (2007), could possibly be added to this list. From a conceptual point of view, however, these terms are not necessarily equivalent. For example, relabeling, like relexification and paralexification, consists in associating a label from L_2 with an L_1 lexical entry. In contrast, transfer, reanalysis, or restructuring, as defined by the authors cited above, consists in associating features of an L_1 lexical entry with a label in L_2. I shall leave discussion of the conceptual differences in the directionality of these processes for future research. In spite of the conceptual differences between the processes discussed in this section, all yield the same result, that is, lexical entries that inherit their semantic and syntactic properties from L_1 and their labels from L_2. This suggests that there might be a single process available in these cases. If all the cases discussed above are identified as instances of relabeling, the process appears to be more widespread in terms of tokens of use than might appear at first glance. As will be seen later, relabeling is also important for another reason: it is called upon in a wide variety of language contact and genesis contexts.

3. Relabeling across Language Contact/Genesis Situations

The process of relabeling is used in a variety of language contact situations as well as in language genesis originating in situations of language contact. This section reviews the different types of situations.

3.1. Relabeling in the First Phase of L_2 Acquisition

As we saw in section 2.4, relabeling is an important process in the first phase of L_2 acquisition (Sprouse 2006). Cases of interference that involve the full transfer of features exemplify this case. For example, Lafage (1985) shows that some Gbe speakers who are learning French tend to use the Gbe determiner system when speaking their L_2. This is illustrated in (5). In (5a), we see that the nominal determiner *là* is postnominal, as in Gbe. In (5b), we see that the possessor is realized as a personal pronominal form following the noun, again as in Gbe.[4] In (5c), the form *là* is identified by Lafage as an *article de phrase* or "clausal determiner," which corresponds to the clausal determiner in Gbe languages.

(5) a. *N'y a qu'à pousser auto-là.* L_2 FRENCH, L_1 EWE
         'All you need to do is to push the car.'   (Lafage 1985: 409)

    b. *Père-lui* L_2 FRENCH, L_1 EWE
         father he
         'his father'   (Lafage 1985: 417)

    c. *Son   argent   n'a   pas   suffi   là*
         his   money   AUX   NEG   be.enough   DEF
         'He didn't have enough money'
         [Lit.: His money was not enough]   (Lafage 1985: 407)

The data in (5) follow from relabeling in the first phase of L_2 acquisition.

---

[4] In Gbe, the pronominal form is followed by a genitive case marker. Such a case marker is not overtly manifested in the French of Ewegbe speakers.

3.2. Relabeling in the Genesis of Mixed Languages

Relabeling is also critical in the creation of mixed languages such as Media Lengua, Michif, Ma'a, Romani, and so on. These languages are created by bilingual speakers in bi-ethnic communities in order to mark an ethnic group identity and set this group apart from the neighboring ones (see, e.g., the chapters in Bakker & Mous (eds.) 1994). Such cases of relabeling will be further discussed in section 4 of this chapter.

3.3. Relabeling in Creole Genesis

Relabeling is also a major process in the formation of creole languages (e.g., Bruyn 2003; Koch 2000; Lefebvre 1998, and the references therein; Migge 2003; etc.). Creole languages are created in contexts where several substrate languages and at least one superstrate language come into contact and where a lingua franca is needed to enable speakers who do not have a common language to communicate with one another. In these contexts, speakers of the substrate languages have limited access to the superstrate language, a situation that is favorable to relabeling. The relabeling of several substrate lexicons on the basis of one (or two) superstrate language(s) provides the speakers of an early creole community with a common vocabulary, thus a lingua franca (Lefebvre & Lumsden 1994a). How relabeling applies in the formation of creole languages is addressed in Chapter 3.

3.4. Relabeling in the Formation of New Englishes

New English varieties developing in Asia (e.g., Singapore English) are not referred to as creoles. Nevertheless, they share two major features with creoles. The first one is the contexts or situations in which they develop. As we saw earlier, creoles are created in multilingual situations involving several substrate languages and a superstrate language. Multilingualism, together with absence of a common language, creates the need for a lingua franca. Like creoles, New Englishes arise in multilingual communities that need a lingua franca. For example, Singapore English was created in a community involving several Sinitic languages, as well as Malay and Tamil. The speakers of these languages needed a lingua franca and developed one on the basis of their native languages (the substrate languages) and English (the superstrate language). The second feature that New Englishes share with creoles is the major process by which they are formed. Just as relabeling plays a central role in the genesis of creole languages (see Chapter 3), it appears to play a major role in the formation of New Englishes (e.g., Bao 2005, 2010).

3.5. Relabeling in Language Death

Situations of language death also involve relabeling. Hill and Hill (1977) show that the lexicon of Tlaxcalan Nahuatl, an indigenous language of Mexico, is being relexified—relabeled—by Spanish words, which is contributing to the death of the language.

3.6. Summary

The survey of language contact/genesis situations that involve relabeling reveals that this cognitive process plays a role in the first phase of second-language acquisition: in the creation of mixed languages, creole languages, and New Englishes; and in language death. We can therefore conclude that the process is an important one, given the range of situations in which it applies.

4. The Variable Extent of Relabeling across Lexicons

The language varieties that result from relabeling do not all have the same surface characteristics. I argue that this is primarily due to the variable extent of relabeling across lexicons in different contact situations. To demonstrate my point, I will consider several case studies, each of which shows that the variable extent of relabeling across lexicons yields different language varieties. In addition, the variable extent of relabeling across lexicons correlates with a number of factors that define the situations in which relabeling is used. These factors include the number of languages involved, the amount of access to the "lexifier"/"target"/L_2 language, whether code switching is involved, and whether language shift is involved.

4.1. Relabeling of Major Category Lexical Items: Media Lengua

Media Lengua (ML) is a mixed language created by bilingual Quechua-Spanish speakers in Ecuador (Muysken 1981a, 1988b). The labels of its lexicon are derived from two sources. While the labels of major category lexical entries (i.e., nouns, verbs, adjectives, postpositions) are almost entirely derived from Spanish, the labels of affixes and functional categories come from Quechua. The examples in (6) and (7) illustrate this division.

(In the Media Lengua examples below, the Spanish forms are in roman characters and the Quechua ones in italics.)

(6) a. *No* *sé.*   SPANISH
    not know-1ST
    'I do not know.'

  b. *Mana* *yacha-ni-chu.*   QUECHUA
    No   sabi-*ni-chu.*   MEDIA LENGUA
    not   know-1ST-VAL
    'I do not know.'   (= (3) in Muysken 1981a)

(7) a. *Si llueve demás, no voy a ir.* SPANISH
    if rain-3RD too-much, not go-1ST to go
    'If it rains too much, I will not go.'

  b. *Yalli-da*   *tamia-pi-ga, mana ri-sha-chu.* QUECHUA
    Dimas-*ta*   llubi-*pi-ga,* no i-*sha-chu.* MEDIA LENGUA
    if too-much-ACC rain-LOC-TOP not go-ASP-VAL
    'If it rains too much, I will not go.' (= (1) in Muysken 1981a)

Although the lexical categories of ML derive their labels from Spanish, their semantic content is derived from Quechua. In (8) we see that the meanings associated with the ML form *sinta-ri-* (<Sp. *sentarse*) correspond to those associated with the Quechua *tiya-ri-*. In contrast, there is only one meaning associated with the Spanish verb *sentarse*: 'sit down.' The other meanings that are associated with *sinta-ri-* and *tiya-ri-* in ML and Quechua, respectively, correspond to different verbs in Spanish: *estar sentado* 'sit,' *vivir* 'live,' *estar* 'locative be,' and *hay* 'there is' (Muysken 1981a: 56).

(8) ML	SPANISH	QUECHUA
sinta-ri-	*sentarse* 'sit down'	*tiya-ri-*
'sit'	*estar sentado*	'sit'
'live'	*vivir*	'live'
'locative be'	*estar*	'locative be'
'there is'	*hay*	'there is'

Lexical entries of this type have been created through relexification (Muysken 1981a), that is, through relabeling.

In short, ML represents a case where only major category lexical items have been relabeled.

4.2. Relabeling of Major Category Lexical Items and of Some Affixes: Inner Mbugu or Ma'a

Inner Mbugu (IM) or Ma'a is a mixed language created by Normal Mbugu (NM) (Bantu) speakers in Tanzania (Mous 1994, 1995, 2001). Mous (2001) emphasizes that corresponding lexical entries in IM and NM are complete synonyms, even though their labels are different. A sentence containing the verb 'to break' exemplifies this fact.

(9)   a.   *Áa-pú*   *ndaté*   *kú'u.*   INNER MBUGU
              1:PST-break   stick.9   his
              'He broke his stick.'

        b.   *Áa-baha*   *ndatá*   *y-akwé.*   NORMAL MBUGU
              1:PST-break   stick.9   9-his
              'He broke his stick.'   (= (5a) in Mous 2001)

Another set of examples illustrating semantic parallels between IM and NM is provided in (10), showing that, in both languages, parallel lexical items share metaphorical uses.

(10)   IM   NM

       mxatú   *mtí*   'tree, afterbirth'

       hlúku   *gwisha*   'to drop, give birth'

       hí   *chuma*   'to sew, mold'

       gewa   *jughulwa*   'to be opened, be allowed to get married'

                                                (= (6) in Mous 2001)

An extensive discussion of the various sources of the labels of IM lexical entries may be found in Mous (2001). Suffice it to say here that these labels come from a variety of neighboring languages, including Cushitic ones, and from modifications of the corresponding forms in NM. In this respect, IM or Ma'a differs from other reported cases of mixed languages (e.g., Media Lengua) in which the labels of the relabeled lexical entries are generally derived from only one language (e.g., Spanish, in the case of ML).

Both IM and NM share the same grammar, which is basically that of Pare. They share the same complex verbal inflectional system and the same richness in "tense" (over 40 tenses have been identified so far): "The two varieties share all of these tenses with exactly the same morphological form, including tone patterns" (Mous 2001: 293). Both languages share the same complex system of subject and object concords, realized by the same morphological forms. They have the same verbal suffixes and the same tense, mood, and aspect prefixes and suffixes (Mous 1994, 2001). Based on the above description, IM can be characterized as having major category lexical items with the properties of those of NM but labels derived from various surrounding languages, while functional categories come from NM. IM would appear to be identical in nature to Media Lengua were it not for the fact that noun class morphemes have also been relabeled. Examples of noun class morphemes in IM and NM are provided in (11), along with the hypothesized source of each IM form.

(11)

Class	NM / Pare		Subj.	Obj.	IM	Source of IM
1	*m-nhtu*	'person'	*é / á*	*mù*	*m-hé*	Iraqw (SC): *hee*
2	*va-nhtu*	'people'	*vé / vá*	*vá*	*va-hé*	Iraqw (SC): *hee*
3	*m-kóno*	'arm'	*ú*	*ú*	*m-harégha*	Oromo (EC): *harka*
4	*mi-kóno*	'arms'	*í*	*í*	*mi-harégha*	Oromo (EC): *harka*
14.1	*vu-shó*	'face'	*vú*	*vú*	*vu-basá*	Origin unclear
6	*ma-shó*	'faces'	*é / á*	*á*	*ma-basá*	Origin unclear

(= (14) in Mous 1994: 187)

In short, IM or Ma'a represents a case where, in addition to major category lexical items, some affixes have been relabeled.

4.3. Relabeling of Some Major Category Lexical Items with Code Switching: Michif

Michif is a Cree-French mixed language developed by the Métis buffalo hunters of Canada and the northern United States (Bakker 1989, 1992, 1994; Papen 1988). The labels of its lexicon are derived from two sources: French and Cree.

As in Media Lengua, where all affixes come from Quechua, in Michif all affixes are derived from Cree. These affixes appear on both nouns and verbs regardless of whether they are of French or Cree origin. For example, in (12) the obviative affix occurs on the object noun. (In the Michif examples below, words of Cree origin are in italics; words of French origin are in roman characters.)

(12) La jument l' étalon - *wa*   *otin* - *êw*.   MICHIF
     the mare   the stallion - OBV   take - (s)he / him / her
     'The mare takes the stallion.'   (= (3) in Bakker 1994: 21)

In (13), the Cree affix *-ipan* 'deceased' is suffixed to a noun of French origin.

(13) mũ   vjø   *-ipan*   MICHIF
      my   husband deceased
      'my deceased husband'   (= (49) in Bakker 1992: 169)

Similarly, in (14) the Cree plural suffix appears on a noun of French origin.

(14) John *tahkuht* - *am* li: fiy *anIhI*   *si:*   zarɛj - *Iwa:w*. MICHIF
      John bite   3->4 AP girl DEM-OBV 3.POSS.PL ear - 3.PL
      'John bites the girls' ears.'   (= (56) in Bakker 1992: 171)

Cree affixes also occur on verbs that are of French origin. In (15), the verb meaning 'to bet' is *ga:ž:* from French *gager*.

(15) *gi:*   - *lɪ* - ga:ž- i: - *n* syr lɪ brõ̃   MICHIF
      1.PST   the   bet INFL - 1 on the brown
      'I bet on the brown one.'   (= (74) in Bakker 1992: 174)

The above data illustrate the kind of mix found in Michif. As Bakker (1994: 167) observes: "Michif structure is the result of the combination of Cree grammar with French lexicon. [. . .] The grammatical bound elements are Cree and the lexical-free elements are French." As he points out, however, while 90% of nouns have a French form, a mere handful of verbs have a label derived from French, and the great majority have come from Cree. According to Bakker, the verb generally has a Cree form because it consists of grammatical bound elements. Bakker (1994: 21) attributes this fact to the polysynthetic nature of Cree:

For the mixed language of the Métis, one would expect a Cree grammatical system with French lexicon. But the problem is that here it is impossible to combine the two in the same way as in the other cases, due to its polysynthetic structure and often blurred morpheme boundaries in the verb. There is a continuum between stem-formational, derivational and inflectional morphemes in the verb, which makes it impossible to separate the stems from the affixes. French verb stems cannot be combined with Cree verbal morphology without destroying the whole organization of the Cree structure (only in some marginal cases which look like loanwords this is apparently possible, as discussed above). For that reason, Cree verbs belong as a whole to the grammatical system and therefore have to remain Cree in a combination with other languages.

Michif nouns appear to have been derived by relabeling. While their semantic and syntactic properties are derived from Cree, their labels are derived from French. For example, Michif nouns are identified for the feature [α animate], as Cree nouns are. This is evidenced by the fact that Michif demonstratives, which are Cree in origin, agree in number and animacy with the nouns they modify. The Michif agreement facts are illustrated in (16).

(16)　a.　*anima*　　lɪ　　li:v　　　b.　*ana*　　lɔm　　　　　　　MICHIF
　　　　　that.INAN　the　book　　　　　this.AN　man
　　　　　'that book'　　　　　　　　　　'this man'
　　　　　　　　　　　　　　　　　　　　　(= (38), (39) in Bakker 1992: 17–18)

A second example showing that some Michif lexical entries must have been created through relabeling resides in the semantic properties of the locative preposition *da* / *dã* meaning 'in, on, at.' This preposition derives its label from the French preposition *dans* 'in.' As noted by Bakker (1992: 171), however, the range of meanings covered by the Michif preposition is much broader than that covered by its French source but parallels that of the corresponding Cree lexical entry. Cree has a locative postposition *-ihk* (with an allomorph *-ohk*) meaning 'in, on, at.' These facts are illustrated in (17) and (18).

(17)　a.　ãnarjɛr　dã　lɪ　ša:r　　　　　　　　　　　MICHIF
　　　　　in-back　LOC　the　car
　　　　　'behind the car'　　　　　　　　(= (57) in Bakker 1992: 171)

　　　　b.　*otahk*　　*otãpãnask-ohk*　　　　　　　　CREE
　　　　　behind　car　　　LOC
　　　　　'behind the car'　　　　　　　　(= (59') in Bakker 1992: 171)

(18) a. dã   lı   frıdž   uhoĩ   MICHIF
          LOC   the   fridge   from
          'out of the fridge'   (= (58) in Bakker 1992: 171)

      b. *tahkascikan-ihk*   *ohci*   CREE
          fridge   LOC   from
          'out of the fridge'   (= (58') in Bakker 1992: 171)

Bakker (1989, 1994) provides many more examples of the same type.

So, like Media Lengua, Michif is a mixed language produced by relabeling. The type of mix we find in Michif, however, is different from the mix we find in Media Lengua. While almost all major category lexical items in Media Lengua derive their labels from Spanish, in Michif, only a subset of these, mainly nouns, have been relabeled. Furthermore, words associated with the nominal structure tend to have labels derived from French, whereas words associated with the verbal structure tend to have labels derived from Cree. Although the forms of personal and demonstrative pronouns come from Cree, the forms of possessive pronouns are from French. Labels for numerals and adjectives are always from French. As for adpositions, the labels of prepositions in Michif tend to be derived from French and those of postpositions from Cree. Labels for adverbial particles, negative elements, and conjunctions appear to be drawn from both source languages. Articles' labels are from French and verbal morphology from Cree. In light of this description, it appears that French-derived labels are predominant in noun phrases, while Cree labels predominate in verb phrases. How did this situation arise?

In this case, in addition to relabeling, code switching between French and Cree also appears to have played a role in the makeup of the language (e.g., Muysken 2007; Papen 1988, and the references therein). This led to data such as those in (12) to (15) where the nominal structures, including the article, are from French, and the verbal structures from Cree.

To sum up, Michif represents a case where relabeling has applied to lexical categories other than verbs, and where the French nominal structures and Cree verbal structures reflect an earlier stage of code switching between the two languages by bilingual speakers.

4.4. Relabeling and Language Shift: Angloromani

Angloromani is a mixed language created by bilingual Romani-English speakers shifting to English (Boretzky & Igla 1994). The phonological representations of its lexicon are derived from two sources. While the labels of major category lexical entries are from Romani, the labels of functional categories are from English. Boretzky and Igla demonstrate that almost all bound grammatical morphemes of English occur in Angloromani. This is exemplified in (19) from Leland (1874), cited in Boretzky and Igla (1994: 47).

(19) Plural -*s*:   *chal-s*   'fellows'
      Genitive -*'s*:   *mo kako's chavo*   'my uncle's son'
      3rd-person -*s*:   *pen-s*   'says'
      Past -*ed*:   *chin-ed*   'broken'
      Progressive -*ing*:   *haw-in*   'eating'
      Comparative -*er*:   *kushti-er*   'more beautiful'
      Superlative -*est*   *kushti-est*   'most beautiful'
                                                    (Boretzky & Igla 1994: 47)

Note that this is the opposite of ML, in which the labels of major category lexical entries are from Spanish and the functional categories from Quechua.

Boretzky and Igla (1994: 60) remark that there are two ways of looking at the genesis of Angloromani: "One might speak of Romani having replaced its grammar—regrammaticalization, or of another language having replaced its lexicon—relexification." They argue at length against the former view, and in favor of the latter: "Our claim is that the Romani mixed dialects came into being by the relexification of the contact language, and, furthermore, that this was an intentional process that could only occur at a given stage between bilingualism and language shift, [. . .] when the speakers, as an entire group, are no longer fully bilingual, but have not accomplished language shift either" (60). According to Boretzky and Igla, the speakers who played the most active role in creating Angloromani were those who no longer had Romani as their first language, but English. The latter speakers would have relabeled the major category lexical items of English on the basis of Romani words to which they still had access, while keeping the English functional categories.

Briefly, Angloromani represents a case in which the major category lexical entries of the contact language, in this case English (instead of those of the community's first language), have been relabeled on the basis of that first language.

4.5. Relabeling of Whole Lexicons: Pidgins and Creoles

Radical creoles are those that are farthest from their superstrate languages (e.g., Haitian, Saramaccan). The labels of their lexical entries are derived from one (e.g., Haitian) or possibly two (e.g., Saramaccan) superstrate languages, while the bulk of the semantic and syntactic properties are derived from the substrate languages (West African languages in both these cases).[5] The fact that hardly any forms have been retained from the substrate languages[6] suggests that, in creole genesis, most substrate lexical entries are relabeled. This differs from mixed languages, in which the original lexicons are only partially relabeled. Why do creoles and mixed languages differ with respect to the extent of relabeling across the lexicon?

Situations where creoles emerge differ from those in which mixed languages emerge. First, while the creation of mixed languages generally involves only two languages (e.g., Media Lengua, Michif, Angloromani), the creation of creole languages usually involves several: most often, one superstrate language and several substrate languages (e.g., Haitian, Kriol). Second, while mixed languages are created to identify in-group speakers and set them apart from neighboring groups, creole languages are created to serve as a lingua franca, allowing speakers of different native languages to communicate. Third, while the creators of mixed languages are generally bilingual and speak both languages involved, the creators of creole languages generally have little access to the superstrate language. These differences have a major impact. Since mixed languages involve only two languages, and since the creators of mixed languages are bilingual, the extent of relabeling across the original lexicon may affect only a portion thereof. Relabeling only has to be extensive enough to make the new language incomprehensible to the outsiders. However, since creole languages are derived from several languages, the creators of a creole have only limited access to the superstrate language, and hence are not bilingual, and the purpose of creating a creole is to provide a multilingual community with a lingua franca, the relabeling of the original lexicon must involve the whole thing, including affixes and functional categories. In addition, of course, the development of creoles involves other processes than relabeling (e.g., grammaticalization, reanalysis, lexical diffusion, leveling, etc.;

---

[5] Creoles that are less "radical," that is, those that are closer to their superstrate language(s) represent cases where there has been more exposure to the superstrate language, and thus more acquisition and less relabeling (Lefebvre 1998, 2006).
[6] For a discussion of this fact, see Lefebvre (1998, 2002).

see Chapter 3), which are not necessarily involved in the development of mixed languages (Lefebvre 1998, and the references therein, 2006).

At first glance, the fact that substrate forms are essentially absent from a given creole hides or downplays the contribution of substrate languages. Detailed three-way comparisons between a creole's lexicon and those of its contributing languages (substrate and superstrate) show, however, that although the labels of the creole's lexical entries come from the super-strate, the bulk of their semantic and syntactic properties come from the substrate languages (e.g., Koopman 1986; Lefebvre 1998; Migge 2003). Furthermore, patterns of variation between the substrate languages have been shown to be reproduced in a creole through relabeling. For example, Haitian exhibits patterns of variation in its determiner system, its TMA system, and so on. Lefebvre (1998) demonstrates that these patterns of variation reproduce those that are manifested in Haitian's substrate languages. The relabeling of different languages' lexicons on the basis of a single superstrate language provides the speakers of a creole community with a common vocabulary (Lefebvre & Lumsden 1994a). In relabeling, however, speakers of the different substrate languages reproduce the specificities of their respective lexicons, thereby creating variation in the creole. This situation is schematically represented in (20) for Haitian.

(20)   Haitian:

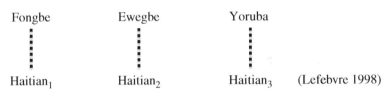

| Fongbe | Ewegbe | Yoruba | |
| Haitian₁ | Haitian₂ | Haitian₃ | (Lefebvre 1998) |

Similar data are documented for other creoles such as Solomon Islands Pidgin, whose substrate languages are both Austronesian and non-Austronesian languages, while its lexifier language is English. While Keesing (1988) documents the fact that the variety of Solomon Islands Pidgin that he studied reproduces the properties of Austronesian languages such as Kwaio, Terrill and Dunn (2006) show that the varieties they studied reproduce the properties of Papuan languages. Furthermore, the latter study involved speakers of two Papuan substrate languages—Lavukaleve and Touo—which are not known to be related to each other. The overall conclusion of Terrill and Dunn's study is that the variety of Solomon Islands Pidgin spoken by the Lavukaleve reproduces the semantic properties of Lavukaleve, whereas the variety spoken by the Touo reproduces the semantic properties of Touo. The relabeling of lexicons from different language families on the basis of a single language, English, provides the speakers of the Solomon Islands with a common vocabulary. In relabeling, however, speakers of each language reproduce the features of their own lexicons, and the result, again, is variation in the pidgin. This situation is schematized in (21).

(21)   Solomon Islands Pidgin:

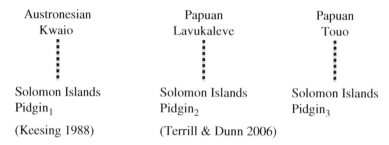

Austronesian	Papuan	Papuan
Kwaio	Lavukaleve	Touo
Solomon Islands Pidgin$_1$	Solomon Islands Pidgin$_2$	Solomon Islands Pidgin$_3$
(Keesing 1988)	(Terrill & Dunn 2006)	

In brief, pidgin and creole languages represent cases in which the whole lexicons of substrate languages have been relabeled on the basis of the superstrate language(s).

4.6. Relabeling of Whole Lexicons: New Englishes

As mentioned in section 3.4, relabeling has been shown to play a role in the creation of New Englishes in Asia, and this role is similar to the one it plays in the formation of creoles. For example, in the formation of Singapore English, relabeling seems to have applied to the entire lexicons of the substrate languages. Bao and Wee (2005) show that "the aspectual system of Singapore English is essentially the Chinese one filtered through the morphosyntax of English. Substrate influence is systemic, and the competing grammatical subsystems do not mix" (Bao & Wee 2005: 237). They point out that substrate transfer is not complete, however, as the stative imperfective and tentative aspects have not been reproduced in Singapore English (250).[7] Furthermore, Bao and Lye (2005: 267) show that Singapore English, like Chinese (the main substrate pool of languages) is topic-prominent and that the structure of the conditional construction "is a direct consequence of this typological status." These points suggest that Singapore English was formed through the relabeling of entire lexicons. A strong argument in favor of this view is the fact that, as Bao and Wee (1999) document, there are three passive constructions in Singapore English: one that

---

[7] In my view, this might be due to the absence of available forms in the lexifier language, a topic that will be addressed in Chapter 3.

corresponds to English (the *by*-phrase construction), one that corresponds to Malay (the *kena* construction), and one that corresponds to Chinese (the *give* construction). The first one corresponds to the grammar of speakers who have mastered English as a second language. The other two correspond to the versions of the passive produced by speakers of Malay and Chinese who have not mastered English, and who have relabeled the lexical items involved in their own passive constructions with English words.

Again, the relabeling of lexicons from different language families on the basis of a single language, English, gives the speakers of Singapore a common vocabulary. However, in relabeling, speakers of each language reproduce the specificities of their own lexicons, yielding variation in the New English variety so created. This situation is schematically represented in (22).

(22)   Singapore English:

In brief, in some languages that are not known as creoles but which were created in similar situations and by the same process, the whole lexicons of the original languages (the substrate) have been relabeled on the basis of the colonial language(s) (or superstrate language(s)).

4.7. Summary

The various case studies summarized in this section show that a single process—in this case, relabeling—may produce different outputs. A main variable in determining the output is the extent of relabeling across lexicons, including whether all major categories have been relabeled (all in Media Lengua, only nouns in Michif) and whether functional categories have been relabeled (none in Media Lengua, some in Ma'a, all in creoles and in New English varieties). This variation is also correlated with a number of other variables, such as the number of languages involved (two in the case of mixed languages, several in the case of pidgin and creole languages and New Englishes), whether speakers are bilingual or not (bilinguals in the case of mixed languages but not in the case of pidgins, creoles, and New Englishes), the amount of access to the "lexifier"/"target"/ L_2 language (e.g., little in the case of radical creoles, more in the case of less radical ones), whether code switching is involved (e.g., Michif), and whether language shift is involved (e.g., Romani). Other variables may also play a role. Those that I have discussed in this section appear to be the prominent ones on the basis of the available documentation.

The cases of relabeling that have been discussed so far involve major category lexical items and some affixes (cf. IM or Ma'a). The sole agglutinative language discussed in this section was Cree, the substrate language of Michif. We saw that, in the formation of Michif, the agglutinative morphology remained Cree. This was attributed to the "polysynthetic structure and often blurred morpheme boundaries in the verb" (Bakker 1994: 21). It does not entail, however, that the semantics encoded in agglutinative morphology cannot be reproduced by relabeling. In Chapter 3 (section 2.2.4), it will be shown that, in the formation of Kriol, the agglutinative morphology of Australian Aboriginal languages was extensively relabeled on the basis of English free forms.

5. Conclusion

In this chapter, I looked at language contact phenomena from the perspective of the processes at work in the creation of new language varieties rather than of the language varieties themselves. I concentrated on one process: relabeling. First, I showed that this process is much more important and widespread than it appears to be at first glance. For one thing, several other terms used in the literature actually refer to this process in some instances. When such cases are identified as cases of relabeling, the importance of the process is revealed. Second, I showed that relabeling applies in a number of language contact situations: during the first phase of second-language acquisition, in the creation of mixed languages and of pidgins and creoles, in the formation of New Englishes, and in language death. The extent of recourse to the process across various language contact situations attests to its importance. Another section of the chapter considered the extent of relabeling across lexicons. The variability of its use across lexicons was shown to correlate with a number of factors defining the situations in which the process is called upon. These factors include the number of languages involved, the amount of access to the "lexifier"/"target"/L_2 language, and whether code switching or language shift is involved. The general approach taken in this chapter shows that it is possible to make a unified analysis of the contribution of a single process to the makeup of various language varieties arising in different language contact situations, and thus to link a number of contact phenomena and situations that would otherwise remain separate.

CHAPTER 3 | The Relabeling-Based Theory of Creole Genesis

1. Introduction

This chapter constitutes a summary of the theory of creole genesis that I have developed over the years, along with my colleagues.[*] The content of this chapter thus builds on Lefebvre (1998) and the references therein. The theory presented here rests on the premise that, because creoles are natural languages, it must be possible to account for their properties and for their emergence and development within the framework of the major processes at work in language creation and language change in general. This approach presupposes that creole languages are no different from other languages. The central process hypothesized to be involved in the creation of a creole is relabeling (a.k.a. relexification), a cognitive process that consists in assigning a new label to an existing lexical entry (see Chapter 1); this process has been shown to play a central role in the creation of mixed languages (e.g., Media Lengua, Muysken 1981a; Michif, Bakker 1989, 1992; Ma'a, Mous 1994, 2001; see Chapter 2). Other major processes that are hypothesized to play a role in the development of a creole include grammaticalization and reanalysis, two processes shown to play a role in language change in general (e.g., Haspelmath 1998; Heine 1997; Lightfoot 1979); diffusion

[*]The content of this chapter was presented at the International Conference on Historical Linguistics in Montreal, August 2007; at Bloomington, Indiana, November 2007; at the University of Hyderabad, India, January 2009; at the National University of Singapore, March 2009; at the Chinese University of Hong Kong and at the University of Hong Kong, April 2009; and at the SPCL conference in Cologne, Germany, August 2009. Thanks to the participants in these events for their insightful questions and comments. Thanks also to Danielle Dumais for her help in deciphering the early Saramaccan data, and to Anne-Marie Brousseau and Claude Dionne for their most insightful comments on an earlier version.

across the lexicon, a process that consists in the spreading of a feature to a wider range of lexical items (e.g., Bybee 2006); and leveling, a process that involves the reduction of variation between dialects or idiolects of the same language in situations where they come into contact (e.g., Trudgill 1986). In creole genesis, relabeling is a key tool for creating new lexicons.[1] This process thus plays a central role in creole genesis. The other processes apply to the output of relabeling.

The relabeling component of creole genesis identifies the proposed account as an extension of the second-language acquisition theory of creole genesis (Lefebvre & Lumsden 1989). For example, Alleyne (1971, 1981), Andersen (1980), Chaudenson (1993), Mufwene (1990), Schumann (1978), Thomason and Kaufman (1991), and Valdman (1980) have proposed that creoles constitute a crystallized incomplete stage of second-language acquisition. In the proposed account, relabeling is considered to be an important tool for acquiring a second language in contexts where exposure to the "target" language may be quite reduced. Without this component, the second-language acquisition theory of creole genesis cannot explain why creole languages have crystallized in the way they have.

The summary of the theory presented here includes the most recent additions, revisions, and developments. Domains in which aspects of the original theory have been modified or new aspects have been added include the representation of relexification as relabeling (Chapter 1), the question of how relabeling proceeds in the case of functional categories (section 2.2), the relabeling versus grammaticalization account of some functional categories in creole genesis (section 2.3), whether relabeling applies to agglutinative languages (section 2.2.4), the distinction between grammaticalization and reanalysis in creole genesis (section 3.2), and the role of diffusion through the lexicon in a creole's development (section 3.3).

This chapter also includes replies to major comments and critiques that have been addressed to this theory in the last few years, presenting potential counterexamples to relabeling and word order issues.

In addition, new data are presented from further research on the same languages (Haitian and Fongbe), as well as from other creoles. The latter include Saramaccan, Martinican Creole, and Papiamentu, for which original data were collected and analyzed by myself and/or members of

---

[1] See, e.g., Brousseau et al. (1989); Lefebvre (1982, 1984, 1986, 1993, 1994a, 1996, 1998); Lefebvre and Kaye (1985–1989 projects); Lefebvre and Lumsden (1989, 1994a); Lumsden (1999).

my teams.[2] These creoles share with Haitian the same substrate languages, mainly Gbe and other Kwa languages. (For Haitian and Martinican, see Singler 1996; for Saramaccan, see Arends 1995; Smith 1987; for Papiamentu, see Parkvall 2000.) They differ in their superstrates: Haitian and Martinican are French-based, Saramaccan is English-, Portuguese-, and Dutch-based (50%, 35% and 10%, respectively), and Papiamentu is Portuguese-/Spanish-based.[3] Data from Kriol—an Australian creole that has evolved from the contact between some hundred Aboriginal languages and English—will also be discussed, mainly on the basis of work by Munro (2000, 2004).

The content of this chapter is intended to introduce the relabeling-based theory of creole genesis to readers who are not familiar with it, while presenting its latest developments to those who are. From a general point of view, this chapter provides the foundations upon which the subsequent chapters of this book are built.

The following introductory sections summarize the properties that any theory of creole genesis must be able to account for, present the scenario of creole genesis that will be assumed in this chapter, and set out the organization of the chapter.

1.1. Properties That Any Theory of Creole Genesis Must Be Able to Account for

The history and structure of creole languages are characterized by the following features.[4] They emerge in multilingual contexts (Whinnom 1971), where there is a need for a lingua franca (e.g., Foley 1988; Hymes 1971a; Singler 1988; Thomason & Kaufman 1991). Crucially, the speakers of the substrate languages have little access to the superstrate language (e.g., Foley 1988; Thomason & Kaufman 1991). In contrast to regular cases of linguistic change, creole languages are created in a relatively short span of time (e.g., Alleyne 1966; Bickerton 1984; Chaudenson 1977; Hall 1958; Hancock 1987; Thomason & Kaufman 1991; van

---

[2] Work on these creole languages, including fieldwork trips, was financed by SSHRCC as part of the project entitled "Constraints on the Cognitive Process of Relexification."

[3] Authors agree that, while the forms of the lexical entries of modern Papiamentu are predominantly derived from Spanish, they were initially derived mainly from Portuguese (e.g., Goodman 1987; Kouwenberg & Murray 1994: 5; Kouwenberg & Muysken 1995: 205; Lenz 1928; Navarro 1953; Van Wijk 1958). In this case, there appear to have been two successive waves of relabeling, the first on the basis of Portuguese, and the second on the basis of Spanish.

[4] An extensive discussion of these features may be found in Lefebvre (1998: 1–5), based on a preliminary outline in Lefebvre and Lumsden (1989).

Name 1869; Voorhoeve 1973).[5] Creole languages tend to be isolating languages (Hagège 1985; Hesseling 1933; Schuchardt 1979), even when they emerge from contact situations involving only agglutinative languages (Mufwene 1986, 1990). Creoles manifest properties of both their superstrate and substrate languages in a principled way: while the forms of the lexical entries of a radical creole[6] tend to be derived from their superstrate language, the syntactic and semantic properties of these lexical entries tend to be derived from the substrate languages, as has been observed in several instances (e.g., Adam 1883; Alleyne 1966; Goodman 1964; Holm 1988; Sylvain 1936). Any theory of creole genesis must be able to account for these properties.

Furthermore, like any theory, a theory of creole genesis must have the properties of a scientific theory. First, it must be stated in terms that are precise enough to be falsifiable. The relabeling account of creole genesis is falsifiable. If the three-way comparison of the lexical properties of a radical creole with those of its source languages were to show that the semantic and syntactic properties of the creole lexical entries are *not* systematically parallel to the syntax and semantics of the substrate languages, then the theory would be falsified (Lefebvre & Lumsden 1989). Second, like any theory, a theory of creole genesis must make predictions, and these must be borne out by the data.

As will be shown in this chapter, the relabeling-based theory of creole genesis presented here accounts for all of these features in a straightforward way. This theory has not been falsified on the basis of Haitian Creole (Lefebvre 1998, 1999, 2004b, and the references therein; Lumsden 1999). As will be shown in the following sections of this chapter, new data provide further support for this theory of creole genesis. Furthermore, as will be demonstrated below, the relabeling-based account of creole genesis makes clear predictions that will be borne out by the data. I therefore submit this theory as a "plausible alternative" to the Bioprogram Hypothesis.[7]

---

[5] Arends (1995) argues that creolization is a gradual process. Quite independently of his approach, though, the changes observed in the creation of creole languages can, without a doubt, be claimed to occur in a relatively short span of time compared to regular cases of linguistic change. For a discussion of this issue, see Lefebvre (2009b).

[6] I take radical creoles to be the farthest from their superstrate languages and closest to their substrate languages.

[7] In a letter to the editor of *Language*, Bickerton (2006: 231) claimed that "[n]o plausible alternative to the bioprogram has yet emerged."

1.2. The Scenario of Creole Genesis

The scenario of creole genesis that will be assumed throughout this chapter is that developed in Lefebvre and Lumsden (1994a) and Lumsden and Lefebvre (1994), with subsequent additions of my own. This scenario has the following main features. Communities where creole languages emerge involve several substrate languages spoken by the majority of the population and one (or two) superstrate language(s) spoken by a relatively small but economically powerful social group. Crucially, the substrate community does not have a common language. This situation creates the need for a lingua franca, not only to permit communication between the speakers of the substrate languages and those of the superstrate language, but also to permit the speakers of the substrate languages to communicate among themselves (e.g., Foley 1988; Singler 1988: 47; Thomason & Kaufman 1991). Speakers of the substrate community have little access to the superstrate language and thus do not have appropriate conditions to learn it. They use relabeling as a primary tool for acquiring the superstrate language, or for simply developing a common vocabulary. They therefore relabel their own lexicons on the basis of phonetic strings in the superstrate language. I assume the relabeling of a lexicon to be a gradual process. Consequently, speakers who are creating a creole are hypothesized to add new labels to the lexical entries of their original lexicons one by one; thus, at some point, they may have two labels for, say, 20% of their lexicon. I also assume that, in the incipient creole community, the speakers who have two labels for a given lexical entry use the original one to talk with people of their initial linguistic group (e.g., a Fongbe speaker will use the Fongbe labels when talking to another Fon), and the other one (i.e., the one drawn from French in the case of the French Caribbean creoles) to communicate with speakers of other linguistic groups. The relabeling of several lexicons on the basis of a single language provided the early creole community with a common vocabulary. The two parallel lexicons may be used alternately over an undetermined period of time within a given community. This is the case, for example, in the Solomon Islands, where local languages and the creole have coexisted since colonization. Alternatively, the two parallel lexicons may be used for a certain period of time and then the original lexicons may cease to be used, leaving a given community with only the relabeled lexicon. This is the case of the Caribbean creoles. For example, in Haiti, African languages were spoken up until the beginning of the nineteenth century (Hilaire 1993). The early Haitian community was thus left with the relabeled lexicons from that time. In the scenario of creole genesis developed here, a creole is born when its creators cease to target the super-strate language and start targeting the relabeled lexicons. At this point, re-labeling ceases. The other processes mentioned earlier can now start applying to the output of the relabeled lexicons.

Relabeling is an individual mental process. Each individual relabels his or her own lexicon, thus reproducing in the creole the idiosyncrasies of that lexicon, with the result that the product of relabeling is not uniform across the early creole community. In this view, the variation found in an early creole community is the product of the relabeling of several non-homogeneous—though not totally disparate—lexicons. The process of leveling may apply to the output of relabeling to reduce this variation. Other processes, such as grammaticalization, reanalysis, and diffusion across the lexicon, fed by the output of relabeling, may also apply.

1.3. Organization of the Chapter

The chapter is organized as follows. Section 2 covers relabeling as the central process in creole genesis. It documents the fact that relabeling applies to all types of syntactic categories, including free or bound functional categories. It shows how the process applies in the case of functional categories, and addresses the controversy concerning the relabeling versus grammaticalization of functional categories. It discusses the predictions made by the relabeling-based account of creole genesis. Finally, it addresses the issue of the variable extent of relabeling across different situations in which creoles emerge. Section 3 summarizes the interplay between relabeling and other processes that play a role in the development of creoles. Section 4 concludes the chapter.

2. Relabeling: The Central Process in Creole Genesis

This section discusses relabeling as the central process in creole genesis. It is shown that relabeling applies to all types of syntactic categories—both free and bound lexical, and free and bound functional, categories (section 2.1). It addresses the question of how the relabeling of functional categories occurs in creole genesis (section 2.2). The debate on whether functional categories acquire their properties by relabeling or by gram-maticalization is taken up in section 2.3. A relabeling-based account of creole genesis makes certain predictions, and these are discussed in section 2.4. The question of the variable extent of relabeling across lexicons is considered in section 2.5.

2.1. Does Relabeling Apply to All Types of Syntactic Categories?

Lexical or major categories are those that are defined by the major features [α N, β V], where α and β take the values + or –. The combinations of these feature values identify the four major lexical categories in (1).

(1)　[+ N, – V]:　Nouns
　　　[+ N, + V]:　Adjectives
　　　[– N, + V]:　Verbs
　　　[– N, – V]:　Adpositions (pre- and postpositions)

Derivational affixes are also identified for major features. For example, in English the suffix *-er* is identified for the features [+ N, – V] since it derives nouns from a verbal base, for example, *driv-er*, an agentive noun, from *drive*, a verb. Below, it is argued that both free and bound major categories may undergo relabeling. Functional or minor categories are defined by minor features such as +/–T(ense), +/– D(efinite). These categories can also be free or bound, and both free and bound functional categories are claimed to undergo relabeling.

2.1.1. The Relabeling of Free Major Category Lexical Entries

The relabeling of free major category lexical entries has been extensively documented in the literature (for Haitian, see Koopman 1986; Lefebvre 1998, 1999; Lumsden 1999; for Ndjuka, see Huttar 1975; Migge 2003; for Solomon Islands Pidgin, see Keesing 1988). I will provide two sets of examples.

A first set of data involves verbs meaning 'to seem.' In Papiamentu, the verb *parse* means both 'to seem' and 'to resemble' (Maurer 1988b: 60). It could be argued that the two meanings associated with *parse* come from Spanish. Indeed, the Papiamentu form *parse* is derived from the Spanish form *parece*; the Spanish verb *parecer* means both 'to seem' and 'to resemble.' A similar analysis does not carry over to Haitian, however. As in Papiamentu, the Haitian verb *sanble* means both 'to seem' and 'to resemble' (Valdman et al. 2007: 650). The French verb *sembler*, from which the form of the Haitian verb is derived, means 'to seem,' but it does not mean 'to resemble,' a concept that is rendered by the verb *ressembler*. Interestingly enough, the Saramaccan verb *djéi*, like the corresponding verbs in Papiamentu and Haitian, also means 'to seem' (McWhorter & Good 2012) and 'to resemble' (Rountree et al. 2000). The double meaning of these verbs in the above-mentioned Atlantic creoles corresponds to that of the corresponding verbs in the substrate languages. For example, in Fongbe, the verb *ɖì* means both 'to seem' and 'to resemble' (Segurola & Rassinoux 2000: 146). The above data follow straightforwardly from the relabeling of the substrate verb on the basis of semantically close verbs in three different superstrate languages. As will be seen in Chapter 6, the semantics of creole verbs has syntactic consequences that further distinguish them from their closest superstrate verbs.

Another example involves strong personal pronouns. In Haitian, the form *nou* refers to both first- and second-person plural, thus meaning 'we/us/you (PL).' The French pronominal form *nous* refers only to first-person plural, thus meaning only 'we, us,' while the form *vous* refers to second-person plural, meaning 'you (PL).' Migge (2003: 49) reports that in Sranan Tongo, as well as in English Maroon creoles, the same form refers to both first- and second-person plural. Again, this follows from relabeling. For example, in Fongbe, the same form is used to refer to first- and second-person plural (Brousseau 1995). As Lefebvre (1998: 142) reports, traditional Fongbe grammars (e.g., Anonymous 1983) sometimes represent the form meaning 'we' as *mǐ* (bearing a complex low-high tone) and the form meaning 'you (PL)' as *mī* (bearing a mid-tone). Mid- and low-high tones are phonetic variants (Capo 1991); the distinction between the two is thus phonemically irrelevant. Furthermore, extensive fieldwork by Brousseau (1995) on the tonological specification of the form *mí* reveals that it always bears a phonological high tone—hence the fact that, in the Caribbean creoles discussed above, the same form refers to both first- and second-person plural must follow from relabeling.

2.1.2. Do Derivational Affixes Undergo Relabeling?

In Lefebvre (2003), drawing on Lefebvre (1998) and Brousseau et al. (1989), it is shown that the inventory of derivational affixes in Haitian is very small compared to that of French, but very similar to that of Fongbe in terms of both size and subsets of affixes.

Indeed, while French has over 80 derivational suffixes (excluding Greek and Latin affixes involved in the vocabulary of the natural sciences, as well as all prefixes) (Dubois 1962), both Haitian and Fongbe have about a dozen derivational affixes. Haitian affixes and their Fongbe equivalents are shown in Table 3.1 (= Table 3 in Lefebvre 2003: 66).

While the properties of the Haitian affixes reproduce those of the substrate languages, the labels of these affixes are derived from French. On the basis of this state of affairs, it is argued that derivational affixes do

TABLE 3.1 The Haitian Affixes and Their Fongbe Corresponding Terms

		HAITIAN	FONGBE
1.	Agentive suffix	-è	-tɔ́
	base	V	V/N
	output	N	N
2.	Attributive suffix	-è	-nɔ̀
	base	N	N/V
	output	N	N
3.	Verbalizing suffix	-e	–
	base	N	
	output	V	
4.	Inversive prefix	de-	mà-
	base	V	V/A
	output	V	V/A
5.	Privative prefix	de-	ɖè
	base	*denominal verb	
	output	V	
6.	Diminutive affix	ti-	-ví
	base	N	N
	output	N	N
7.	Nominalizing suffix	-ay	copy prefix
	base	V	V
	output	N	N
8.	Nominal conversion	ø	copy prefix
	base	V	V
	output	N	N
9.	Adjectival/participial conversion	ø	copy prefix
	base	V	V
	output	A	A
10.	Adverbial suffix	-man	–
	base	A	
	output	ADV	
11.	Place of origin/residence suffixes	-wa/-yen	-tɔ́/-nù
	base	N	N
	output	N	N
12.	Ordinal suffix	-yèm	-gɔ́ɔ́
	base	Q	Q
	output	A	A

SOURCE: Adapted from Lefebvre (1998: 320–321).

undergo relabeling. Since derivational affixes are lexical categories that are listed in the lexicon, they are assumed to undergo relabeling in the same way as other lexical categories do. In Lefebvre (1998: 323–333), it is argued that the creators of Haitian Creole relabeled the affixes of their own lexicons with French phonetic matrices. In this scenario, the creators of Haitian would have identified phonetic matrices of French with appropriate meanings to relabel the derivational affixes of their own lexicons on the basis of pairs of French words such as *faire* 'to do' and *dé-faire* 'to undo,' or *travaill-er* 'to work' and *travaill-eur* 'worker.' Hence, a Fongbe speaker relabeling his or her lexicon on the basis of data from French would have identified French *dé-* as sharing with Fongbe *mà-* the meaning 'inversive' and (s)he would have assigned the Haitian lexical entry corresponding to *mà-* the phonological form *de-*. Similarly, the agentive affix *-tɔ́* would have been relabeled as *-è* on the basis of the French agentive affix *-eur*, and so on. Note that Haitian *de-* is not only inversive; it is also privative, as in *de-gonfle* 'to deflate' ('to remove air'). Brousseau (1994) argues that the substrate privative verb meaning 'to remove,' *ɖè* in Fongbe, was also relabeled on the basis of French *dé-* which, in addition to its inversive meaning, may also have a privative meaning (e.g., *dé-gonfler* 'to deflate'). This shows that two morphemes may be relabeled on the basis of the same superstrate form, provided that the lexical entries involved share some semantic content. Since French *dé-* is both inversive and privative, it could serve as a phonetic string to relabel both the inversive prefix of the substrate languages (*mà-* in Fongbe) and the privative verb of the substrate languages (*ɖè* in Fongbe), yielding Haitian *de-* with both an inversive and a privative interpretation. Note that Fongbe *ɖè* and French *dé-* are also phonetically similar. The relabeling of one by the other is thus identified by Brousseau (1994) as a case of phonological conflation.

DeGraff (2001) challenges our work on the productive morphology of Haitian Creole, claiming that there are eight productive affixes in addition to those we have identified. He claims that the following forms are also productive affixes: *en-*, *-ab*, *-adò*, *-èt*, *-man*, *-syon*, *-es*, and *-te*. However, a detailed analysis of these forms following the methodology established in Lefebvre (2003, and the references therein) does not confirm that most of them are productive. Except for *-syon*, which can be argued to be productive (Denis 2004: 30–54), the forms in DeGraff's list are not productive affixes of Haitian Creole (for *-es* and *-te*, see Denis 2004: 53–88; for *en-*, *-èt*, and *-man*, see Lefebvre 2003: 48–61; for *-adò*, see Lefebvre 2004b: 286–292).

While Dijkhoff (1993) reports a situation similar to Haitian for Papiamentu, Braun and Plag (2003) remark that, in the formation of Sranan, the derivational morphemes of the input languages have been completely lost. The same is true of Saramaccan, whose sole derivational affix, other than morphological reduplication, is *-ma* (from English *man*) "agentive and attributive" (Good 2004: 582). One could consider these facts as a problem for the claim that derivational affixes can undergo relabeling. Braun and Plag present two hypotheses, however, that could explain the discrepancy between Haitian and Papiamentu, on the one hand, and Sranan and Saramaccan, on the other. The first one has to do with the constraint imposed by the superstrate language on the process of relabeling. In both Spanish and French, due to their position in the word, suffixes are generally stressed and thus are salient. As Braun and Plag (100) remark, however, "this does not explain why English auto-stressed suffixes like *-ation* did not make it into the creole and why prefixes, which mostly have secondary stress in English, French and Spanish, did only survive in the said Romance-based creoles." The second hypothesis that Braun and Plag submit for further research is the difference between exposure to the superstrate languages in the two situations. There is a consensus in the literature that the creators of Haitian and those of Papiamentu had more exposure to French and Portuguese/Spanish, respectively, than the creators of Sranan and Saramaccan had to English (for Haitian Creole, see Singler 1996; for Saramaccan, see Arends 1995; Migge 1998; Smith 1987; for Papiamentu, see Parkvall 2000; Potsma 1990). (For further discussion of this issue, see Chapter 6.)

My conclusion is thus that all types of major category lexical entries, including derivational affixes, may undergo relabeling. Differences between creoles can be explained by differences in their substrates/superstrates and/or by the relative amount of access the creole creators had to the superstrate language during the formation period.

2.1.3. Do Functional Categories Undergo Relabeling?

The relabeling-based hypothesis of creole genesis holds that functional categories may undergo relabeling, provided that they have some semantic content (Lefebvre 1998). This position is congruent with the fact that relabeling is semantically driven (see Chapter 1). The claim that functional categories can undergo relabeling is supported by the extreme similarity between the semantic and syntactic properties of radical creoles' functional categories and those of the corresponding items in their substrate languages. This section provides an overview of the determiner, T(ense)-M(ood)-A(spect), complementizer, validator, and conjunction subsystems of the grammars of Haitian, Saramaccan, and their source languages, showing the similarity between the functional categories in the creoles and their substrates. In my view, this similarity argues for a relabeling account of the data. Views challenging the approach advocated here will be discussed in section 2.3. The question of how relabeling proceeds in the case of functional categories will be addressed in section 2.4.

2.1.3.1. The Determiner System

Consider the nominal structure of French, shown in (2), and that of Fongbe and Haitian, shown in (3) and (4), respectively.

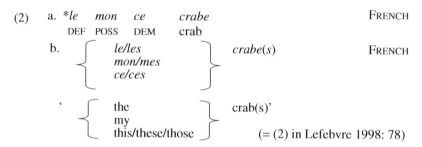

(2) a. **le* *mon* *ce* *crabe* — FRENCH
DEF POSS DEM crab

b. { *le/les* | *mon/mes* | *ce/ces* } *crabe(s)* — FRENCH

'{ the | my | this/these/those } crab(s)'

(= (2) in Lefebvre 1998: 78)

(3) a. Noun-POSS Phrase- DEM-DEF-PL

b. *àsɔ́n* [*nyɛ̀* *tɔ̀n*] *élɔ́* *ɔ́* *lɛ́* — FONGBE
crab me GEN DEM DEF PL
'these/those crabs of mine' (in question/that we know of)

(= (1) in Lefebvre 1998: 78)

(4) a. Noun-POSS Phrase- DEM-DEF-PL

b. *krab* [*mwen* ø] *sa* *a* *yo* — HAITIAN
crab me GEN DEM DEF PL
'these/those crabs of mine' (in question/that we know of)

(= (1) in Lefebvre 1998: 78)

There are two striking facts about these nominal structures. First, in French, the functional categories precede the noun, whereas in both Fongbe and Haitian, they follow it. Second, in French, there can be only one determiner per structure, but in Fongbe and Haitian, the possessor, the demonstrative, the definite determiner, and the plural marker may all co-occur within the same structure. Consider further the nominal structure of English shown in (5) and that of Saramaccan in (6).

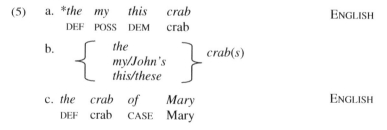

(5) a. **the* *my* *this* *crab* — ENGLISH
DEF POSS DEM crab

b. { *the* | *my/John's* | *this/these* } *crab(s)*

c. *the* *crab* *of* *Mary* — ENGLISH
DEF crab CASE Mary

(6) a. DEF SG/ DEF PL-Noun-DEM-POSS Phrase

b. *déé/di   fisi   akí   u   mí*   SARAMACCAN
PL/DEF   fish   DEM   CASE   me
'this/these fish(es) of mine' (in question, that we know of)

Again, there are two striking facts about these nominal structures. First, in English, the determiner precedes the noun and so does the definite determiner in Saramaccan, unlike those in Haitian Creole and Fongbe. Second, in English, there can be only one determiner per structure, but, in Saramaccan, as in Haitian and Fongbe, the possessor, the demonstrative, the definite determiner, and the plural marker may co-occur within a single structure.

Drawing on the work of Lefebvre (1998, 2012), the following subsections compare the properties of the definite determiners—definite determiners per se, number, and demonstrative terms—of Fongbe, Haitian, and Saramaccan. It will be shown that, except for word order (discussed in Chapter 5), the detailed properties of the definite determiners that participate in the nominal structure of Haitian and Saramaccan are remarkably parallel to those of Fongbe. Early Saramaccan data from Wietz (1805)[8] will also be presented to show that the synchronic properties of the definite determiners of Saramaccan already existed in the early creole.

2.1.3.1.1. DEFINITE ANAPHORIC DETERMINERS

The three definite determiners shown in (3), (4), and (6), that is, *ɔ́* for Fongbe, *a* for Haitian, and *di* for Saramaccan (and their allomorphs) have the property of being anaphoric. They can only be used in contexts where the noun being referred to has previously been mentioned in the discourse or is part of the shared knowledge of the participants in the interaction. This is reflected in the translation of (3), (4), and (6) by the specification 'in question, that we know of.' (For Haitian, see Aboh 2006; Fattier 1998, vol. 2: 836–837; Lefebvre 1998, and the references therein; for Fongbe, see Lefebvre & Brousseau 2002, and the references therein; for Saramaccan, see Aboh 2006; Bally 2007b; Lefebvre 2012). As is shown in (7), the anaphoric property of the Saramaccan determiner is already attested in

---

[8] Wietz (1805) consists in the Saramaccan translation of the Acts of the Apostles. The corpus contains 13 chapters that comprise 14,151 words. There are 574 occurrences of the definite determiner *dissi/di* (186 of *dissi* and 388 of *di*), 817 occurrences of *dem* encoding either third-person plural personal pronouns or plural in the nominal structure, and 162 occurrences of *wan* encoding either the number 'one' or the indefinite determiner 'a.'

Wietz (1805). In (7), the first occurrence of *fotto* is indefinite. The second one refers back to the first one, and it now occurs with the determiner *di*.

(7)   *Philippus kom   na   wan fotto na   Sarmaria kondre*   SARAMACCAN
       Philip   come LOC a   town LOC Samaria country
       [...] *dem bi   habi bigi pren na   di   fotto*
       3PL PA have   big joy LOC DEF town
       'Philip came to a town in the country of Samaria.
       They had a lot of joy in the town.'   (Chapter 8, V 5–8 in Wietz 1805)

The properties of the definite determiners in all three languages are summarized in (8).

(8)   Properties of definite determiners

FONGBE	HAITIAN	SARAMACCAN
– anaphoric	– anaphoric	– anaphoric
– unmarked for gender and number	– unmarked for gender and number	– unmarked for gender and number
– no partitive forms	– no partitive forms	– no partitive forms
– impossible with generic or mass nouns	– impossible with generic or mass nouns	– impossible with generic or mass nouns
– availability of bare nouns	– availability of bare nouns	– availability of bare nouns
– postnominal	– postnominal	– postnominal
(Lefebvre 2004a: 90)	(Lefebvre 2004a: 90)	(Bally 2007b)

The inventories in (8) show that, except for word order, the properties of the three definite determiners are the same.

Furthermore, the definite determiners involved in the nominal structure of the three languages also play a crucial role in the structure of the clause. In all three languages, the determiner occurs in relative and factive clauses, as shown in (9) and (10), respectively. Note that while, in Fongbe and Haitian, the determiner is clause-final, in Saramaccan, it is clause-initial.

(9)   DEF in relative clauses

     a. *àsɔ́n   ɔ́   [ɖé-è   Kɔ̀kú   ɖù ɔ́]...*   FONGBE
         crab   DEF OP-RES Koku   eat DEF
         'the crab that Koku ate...'   (Lefebvre's field notes)

     b. *crab   la   [Ø   Mari   manje   a]...*   HAITIAN
         crab   DEF OP Mary   eat   DEF
         'the crab that Mary ate...'   (Lefebvre's field notes)

c. *Di mujɛ́ɛ* [*dí* Ø *bái* di *ganían*] *pikí.*   Saramaccan
    DEF woman DEF OP buy DEF chicken be.small
    'The woman who bought the chicken is small.' (= (6) in Bally 2007a)

(10)   DEF in factive clauses

    a. *wá* *ɖé-è* *Kɔkú* *wá* *ɔ́,* ....   Fongbe
      arrive OP-RES Koku arrive DEF
      'the fact that Koku has arrived ...'   (Lefebvre's field notes)

    b. *rive* Ø *Jan* *rive* *a,* ...   Haitian
      arrive OP John arrive DEF
      'the fact that John has arrived . . .'   (Lefebvre's field notes)

    c. ***Di*** *dóu* Ø *Carlo dóu, hén mbéi* *Málita wái.*   Saramaccan
      DEF arrive OP Carlo arrive   and.then make Malita be.happy
      'The fact that Carlo has arrived made Malita happy.'
                                    (= (7c) in Bally 2007a)

The determiner *dissi/di* was also involved in relative clauses in early Saramaccan, as all the relative clauses found in the Acts of the Apostles (Wietz 1805)—185 tokens—are introduced by *dissi* or *di*. A few examples are provided in (11).[9]

(11)   a. *Dem putta* *tu* *sombre Joseph,* ***dissi*** *dem* *kali*
       3PL present two man Joseph DEF 3PL call
       Barsabas   Saramaccan
       Barsabas
       'They presented two men, Joseph that they call Barsabas.'
                             (Chapter 1, V 23 in Wietz 1805)

    b. *unu* *tulu **di*** *unu* *tan libi na Jerusalem*   Saramaccan
      you(PL) all DEF you(PL) IMP live in Jerusalem
      'you all who live in Jerusalem'   (Chapter 2, V 14 inWietz 1805)

I did not find any instances of factive clauses in the translation of the Acts of the Apostles.

    The definite determiner may also occur at the end of simple clauses, as is shown in (12). In this case, the determiner determines the event denoted by the clause (Lefebvre 1998, Chapter 8).

---

[9] The literature on Saramaccan often identifies the form *dissi/di* occurring in relative clauses as a relativizer or a relative pronoun (e.g., Rountree 1992: 18). In my analysis, *dissi/di* in relative clauses is the same definite determiner that occurs in nominal structures. This parallels the data found in Haitian and in Fongbe, as the examples in the text show.

(12) *É*   *wá*   *ɔ́.*   FONGBE
      Li   *rive*   *a.*   HAITIAN
      3SG   arrive   DEF
      '(S)he has arrived.' (as we knew (s)he would)   (Lefebvre's field notes)

This use of the anaphoric determiner has not been attested in Saramaccan so far. Does this constitute a problem for the claimed similarity between Fongbe, Haitian, and Saramaccan? No. In Lefebvre (1998), I document the fact that, for all Haitian and Fongbe speakers with whom I worked, the determiner appears in relative and factive clauses, as in (9) and (10). However, speakers of both Haitian and Fongbe manifest variation as to the distribution of the determiner in simple clauses such as (12). In both languages, there are three patterns of variation. In the first two, the determiner is available in simple clauses; in the third, it is not. "A third Haitian grammar shows no use of the determiner in simple clauses. This parallels a third Fongbe grammar found among speakers of Ouidah as well as the grammars of speakers of some other substrate languages" (Lefebvre 1998: 246). The fact that the Saramaccan speakers consulted do not use the determiner in simple clauses is therefore not surprising. The grammar of these speakers simply corresponds to the third grammar identified in Fongbe and other substrate languages.[10]

I therefore conclude that, abstracting away from word order, the detailed properties of the definite determiners in Haitian and Saramaccan are the same as those of the Fongbe determiner. Aboh (2006) draws a similar conclusion on the basis of a comparison of the properties of the Haitian, Sranan, Saramaccan, and Gungbe definite determiners. Lefebvre (1998: 79–84) argues that the detailed properties of the Haitian definite determiner differ from those of the French determiners. Likewise, Aboh (2006) argues that the detailed properties of the Saramaccan definite determiner are distinct from those of the English determiner. Lefebvre (1998, 2012) shows that this situation follows straightforwardly from the process of relabeling. It is demonstrated that the Fongbe definite determiner *ɔ́* was relabeled as *la* on the basis of the French postnominal deictic form *là,* yielding the Haitian postnominal definite determiner *la,* while the same Fongbe determiner was relabeled as *disi* on the basis of the English prenominal deictic form *this,* yielding the Saramaccan prenominal definite determiner

_____

[10.] I do not exclude the possibility that in a larger sample of speakers the definite determiner might be found as an event determiner in Saramaccan.

disi, truncated to *di*. The relabeling account of the properties of the creoles' definite determiners will be examined in section 2.2 in the context of the more general discussion of how relabeling applies to functional categories.[11] Word order issues will be discussed in Chapter 5.

2.1.3.1.2. THE EXPRESSION AND PROPERTIES OF NUMBER

In the three languages examined here, plurality is encoded as a free morpheme, as is shown in (3) to (6). In Fongbe, this morpheme is *lé* (see (3)); in Haitian, it is *yo* (see (4)); in Saramaccan, it is *déé* (see (6)).

A basic fact about number in the three languages under comparison here is that it is expressed as part of the determiner system. Although some Fongbe and some Haitian speakers allow the plural marker to co-occur with the definite determiner, as shown in (3) and (4), respectively, other speakers of the two languages do not allow this. When the plural marker occurs without the definite determiner, however, it is always interpreted as definite. The two patterns are schematized in (13) (where G = grammar).

(13)	HAITIAN	FONGBE
G$_1$	*la* and *yo* can co-occur (d'Ans 1968: 105; Faine 1937: 83; Fattier 1998: 838; Fournier 1977: 43; Goodman 1964: 45; Joseph 1988: 201; Lefebvre & Massam 1988: 215; Ritter 1992: 207–209; Sylvain 1936: 55; Valdman 1978: 1994–1995)	*ɔ́* and *lé* can co-occur (Brousseau & Lumsden 1992: 22; Lefebvre 1998: 85)
G$_2$	*la* and *yo* cannot co-occur (DeGraff 1992a: 107; Fattier 1998: 838; Joseph 1988: 201; Lumsden 1989: 65)	*ɔ́* and *lé* cannot co-occur (Agbidinoukoun 1991: 149)
		(= (76) in Lefebvre 2004a: 91)

According to the available literature on Saramaccan, *di* and *déé* are mutually exclusive. I take this fact to attest to the existence of G$_2$ in Saramaccan, as in Haitian and Fongbe (see (13)). However, as is shown in Lefebvre (2012), *di* and *déé* may co-occur in contexts of noun omission, as is shown in (14) and (15).

---

[11] Note that all these languages have indefinite determiners. They are not discussed here.

(14) *Ambé   déé   dí   —   dé?*   SARAMACCAN
      who   PL   DEF   N   DEM
      'Who are those people?'   (Rountree & Glock 1982: 31)

(15) *Basiá ké   nján déé   dí   —   dé*   SARAMACCAN
      Basia want eat   PL   DEF   DEM
      'Basia wants to eat those ones.'   (= (80) in Bally 2005: 31)

These data would appear to attest to the existence of G_1 in Saramaccan. Thus, both Fongbe patterns in (13) appear to have been reproduced in Saramaccan. (For further discussion, see Lefebvre 2012.)

Both creoles, then, resemble their substrate languages in realizing number as part of the determiner system. Haitian is also like its superstrate language, as French also realizes number on the determiner (e.g., *la/les bague(s)*: 'DEF.SG/DEF.PL ring(s)'). However, Saramaccan differs from its superstrate language since, in English, number is not part of the determiner system (except with the demonstrative determiners *these/those*) but is realized on the noun (e.g., *the rings*).

Because the category number is part of their determiner systems, Fongbe, Haitian, and Saramaccan are able to allow the head noun position to be empty in nominal structures, as illustrated in (16), where the — stands for an empty position. The surface location of the empty positions in (16) follows the respective word order of the nominal structures in the three languages.

(16) a. —   *kíkló éló   ó*   FONGBE
          N   big   DEM   DEF
          'this/that big one'   (= (60) in Lefebvre 1998: 98)

      b. *gwo   —   sa   a*   HAITIAN
          big   N   DEM   DEF
          'this/that big one'   (= (38) in Lefebvre 1998: 91)

      c. *di   —   akí*   SARAMACCAN
          DEF   DEM
          'this one'   (= (17) in Bally 2007a)

The data in (17) show that the possibility of an empty nominal head was available in early Saramaccan.

(17) *di   —   aki   dissi unu   si*   SARAMACCAN
      DEF   N   DEM   DEF   you.PL see
      'this one that you saw'   (Chapter 3, V 16 in Wietz 1805)

According to Bouchard (2002, Chapter 4), noun omission is allowed in nominal structures only in languages in which number is part of the determiner system. In languages where number is realized on the noun, such as English, if the noun were omitted, the category number could not be realized. This explains the impossibility of *the big PL* and the obligatoriness of *one* insertion in the empty noun position, as in *the big ones*. So, with respect to noun omission, both creoles are like their substrate languages. Haitian is also like French, in which number is part of the determiner system, hence the grammaticality of *les grandes* 'DEF.PL tall,' that is, 'the tall ones.' However, Saramaccan differs from English, in which number is not part of the determiner system, as we saw above.

As Lefebvre (2012) discusses at length, a less superficial fact has to do with the conceptual role of the category number in the languages under comparison. In her recent comparative work on number in French and Haitian, Déprez (2005, 2006) shows that number plays a different conceptual role in languages of the French type and languages of the Haitian type. In French, number marking is necessary to express plurality, whereas in Haitian, it is not. Bare count nouns in Haitian are singular or plural without overt morphological differences, depending on their context of use or lexical meaning. This contrast is illustrated in (18) and (19). In (18), constructed on the basis of the analysis in Déprez (2006), the French noun must be marked singular (a) or plural (b).

(18) a. *L'   oiseau fait   son   nid au printemps*   FRENCH
          DEF   bird   make   its   nest at spring
          'The bird makes its nest in the spring.' (specific or generic)
          *'birds make their nests in the spring'

      b. *Les   oiseaux font   leur nid au printemps.*   FRENCH
          DEF-PL birds   make   their nest at spring
          'Birds make their nests in the spring.'

In (19), the Haitian bare count noun can be interpreted as either singular or plural.

(19) *Zwazo fè   nich li/yo   nan   Prentan.*   HAITIAN
      bird   make   nest 3SG/3PL   in   spring
      'Bird(s) make(s) its/their nest(s) in the spring.'   (= (8) in Déprez 2006)

Déprez proposes to account for this difference between the two types of languages as follows. Languages vary as to how they individuate kind terms. In French, individuation is achieved through number, whereas in Haitian, it is spatial, that is, located in the discourse space/time. The role of number is thus different in the two languages: in French, number is used for individuation; in Haitian, it is used for re-identification. This is shown in (20), where the first occurrence of the noun is unmarked for plural, while the second one is marked for plural, identifying the latter as having the same referent as the former.

(20) *Gen* **liv** *ak* **magazin** *sou tab sa   a.*   HAITIAN
      there-is book with magazine on table DEM DEF
      Pran **liv** **yo** */ *liv*
      take book PL book
      'There are books and magazines on the table. Take the books.'

                                                        (= (15b) in Déprez 2006)

Interestingly, Haitian is like Fongbe in this respect. Dumais (2007) shows that Fongbe bare count nouns are singular or plural without overt morphological differences, depending on their contexts of use or lexical meanings, as is exemplified in (21).

(21) *Kɔkú   xɔ   xwé/wémà   nú   Àsíbá.*   FONGBE
      Koku   buy   house/book for   Asiba
      'Koku bought a house/books for Asiba.'   (= (13) in Dumais 2007)

As in Haitian, it thus seems that in Fongbe, number is used for re-identification rather than for individuation. This is shown in (22), where the first occurrence of *àhwàn-nɛ́* is not marked for plural but the two following occurrences are, relating them to the previously mentioned bare noun.

(22) *É   yé   hùn   kávì   ɔ́,   yé   mɔ̀   àhwàn-nɛ́*
      OP 3PL open   calabash DEF 3PL see   pigeon
      àsì   ɖòkpó àsú   ɖòkpó.   FONGBE
      female one   male one
      'When they opened the calabash, they saw pigeons, one female, one male.'
      Énɛ́   ɔ́   gúɖò ɔ́,   yé   jɛ̀   nú   ɖùɖù ná   àhwàn-nɛ́ lɛ́ jí,
      DEM   DEF after DEF 3PL fall thing eating give pigeon   PL on
      'After that, they started giving the pigeons something to eat,

káká	*bɔ*	**àhwàn-né**	*lé*	*jì*	*ví*	*gègé.*
until	COMP	pigeon	PL	give.birth	offspring	a.lot

'until the pigeons reproduced a lot.'

(from Lefebvre & Brousseau 2002: 540)[12]

Haitian is therefore like Fongbe with respect to the role of number.

As Bally (2007b) documents, examples abound in Saramaccan showing that bare nouns can be interpreted as either singular or plural depending on their contexts of use or lexical meanings. In (23), the bare noun is interpreted as plural, whereas the bare noun is interpreted as singular in (23).

(23) a. *Un   kisi   matjáu.*   SARAMACCAN
          2PL take axe
          'You took axes.'   (= (13a) in Bally 2007b)

    b. *Mi   téi   ufángi   fáa   di   pau   túe*   SARAMACCAN
          1SG take machete chop DEF tree throw
          'I took a machete and felled the tree.'

(= (58b) in Veenstra 1996a: 128)

Because of this, Bally suggests that Saramaccan is a language in which individuation is not achieved through number, but number is instead used for re-identification. This is illustrated in (24).

(24) *mí   tata   ku   wanlɔ   wotowot **sɛmbɛ**...*   SARAMACCAN
      my   father with some   other   persons
      *nɔɔ hɛn   **déé** sɛmbɛ...*
      and.then PL   person
      '. . . my father with some other persons...
      and then the persons (that we know of)...'   (Bally 2005: 167–168)

While the two creoles resemble their substrate languages regarding the role of number, they differ from their respective superstrate languages, French and English. In the former languages, number is used for re-identification, whereas in the latter, it is used for individuation.

---

[12] This example is drawn from a Fon story I collected from Josiane Dakpo. This story and its translation are reported in Appendix II of Lefebvre and Brousseau (2002). Examples similar to those in (22) can be found in this text.

Finally, a last interesting fact about number is that, in the two creoles, the morpheme that serves as a plural marker also serves as a third-person plural personal pronoun. This is illustrated in (25) to (27) for Haitian, early Saramaccan, and modern Saramaccan, respectively. Note that, in written modern Saramaccan, the morpheme that realizes PL is spelled *déé* when it determines a noun, and *de* when it is used as a pronoun. *Déé* and *de* could be considered either as allomorphs of the same morpheme or as two distinct morphemes that have evolved from a common origin, such as *dem* in (26). I leave the discussion of this problem for future research.

(25) a. *krab yo*   b. *Yo   pati.*   HAITIAN
          crab PL   3PL   leave
          'the crabs (in question)'   'They left.'

(26) a. *dem Apostel*   b. *Dem takki na dem.* EARLY SARAMACCAN
          PL   apostles   3PL   Say   to 3PL
          'the Apostles (in   'They told them.'
               question)'
          (Chapter 1, V 2 in   (Chapter 1, V 11 in
               Wietz 1805)   Wietz 1805)

(27) a. *déé fisi*   b. *De   kom.*   SARAMACCAN
          PL   fish   3PL   come
          'the fishes (in question)'   'They came.'

The double function of *yo* and *dem* parallels that observed in some of the substrate languages of the creoles, such as Ewegbe, in which the morpheme *wó* encodes both plural in nominal structures and the third-person plural personal pronoun, as shown in (28) (Lefebvre 1998: 84–87; Westerman 1930).[13]

(28) a. *àtí   wó*   b. *Wó   mlɔ́.*   EWEGBE
          tree PL   3PL   lie
          'the trees'   'They lied.'

---

[13] Ritter (1992) provides a theoretically motivated account of this homophony: while first- and second-person personal pronouns belong to the category Det(erminer), third-person personal pronouns are in the category Num(ber).

While the Haitian and Saramaccan data parallel the data from Ewegbe, they differ from those of Fongbe, which has two different morphemes to encode plural in nominal structures and third-person plural personal pronouns, as shown in (29).

(29) a. *àsɔ́n   lɛ́*   b. *Yé   yì.*   Fongbe
          crab   PL   3PL   leave
          'the crabs (in question)'   'They left.'

Martinican Creole, however, parallels Fongbe in having a plural marker that is distinct from the third-person plural personal pronoun, as in (30).

(30) a. *se   liv   la*   b. *Yo   dòmi*   Martinican Creole
          PL   book   DEF   3PL   sleep
          'the books' (in question)   'They slept.'   (Lefebvre's field notes)

Here again, the creoles replicate the patterns of their substrate languages. The discussion of these data will be resumed in section 3.1 on the interplay between relabeling and leveling.

The data reported on in this section show that the properties of the category number in the two creoles are the same as those of their substrate languages. They even reproduce the variation found between the substrate languages (e.g., Ewegbe and Fongbe). The data also show that the properties of number differ significantly from those of number in the superstrate languages of these creoles, namely French and English. In Lefebvre (1998, 2012), it is argued that this situation follows straightforwardly from the process of relabeling. The Ewegbe pronominal form and plural marker *wó* was relabeled on the basis of the French pronominal form *eux,* yielding the Haitian pronoun and plural marker *yo*; the same substrate form was relabeled on the basis of the English pronominal form *them,* yielding the Saramaccan pronominal and plural marker *dem*. The account of these derivations will be taken up in section 2.2 in the context of a more general discussion of how relabeling applies in the case of functional categories.

2.1.3.1.3. DEMONSTRATIVE TERMS AND THEIR INTERPRETATION

As shown in (3), (4), and (6), the nominal structures of all three languages under consideration may also involve demonstrative terms. On the basis of the available data, there appear to be three patterns of variation. In the first pattern, there are two demonstrative terms: *sa* and *sila* in Haitian, and (é)ló and (é)né in Fongbe. The syntactic and distributional properties of the two terms are exactly the same in both languages (Lefebvre 1997, 2004b, Chapter 9). Furthermore, in both languages, there are also three semantic patterns for the two demonstrative terms. These semantic patterns are reproduced in (31) as G_1, G_2, and G_3, where alpha is a variable that may take the value + or −.

(31) a. G_1 *sa* [+ proximate] *sila* [− proximate] HAITIAN
          G_2 *sa* [α proximate] *sila* [− proximate]
          G_3 *sa* [α proximate] *sila* [α proximate]
          Sources: G_1: Goodman (1964: 51), Tinelli (1970: 28). G_2:
          Étienne (1974), Lefebvre (1997), Sylvain (1936). G_3:
          Férère (1974: 103), Joseph (1988), Valdman (1978: 194),
          Valdman et al. (1981), and my own field notes.

      b. G_1 (é)ló [+ proximate] (é)né [− proximate] FONGBE
          G_2 (é)ló [α proximate] (é)né [− proximate]
          G_3 (é)ló [α proximate] (é)né [α proximate]
          Sources: G_1: Anonymous (1983), Segurola (1963), and
          my own field notes. G_2: Lefebvre (1997). G_3: my own
          field notes.

                                          (= (82) in Lefebvre 2004b: 94)

The first pattern involving two demonstrative terms is also found in Saramaccan, where *disi* (<English *this*) corresponds to Fongbe *éló*, and *dé* (<English *there*) corresponds to Fongbe *éné*. Lefebvre (2012, section 4) documents the fact that several patterns of interpretation may be assigned to *disi* and *dé*. I refer the interested reader to this paper for a detailed discussion of these data.

In the second Haitian pattern, there is only one demonstrative term, *sa* (Valdman 1996; Vilsaint 1992), which serves as a general demonstrative expression. This pattern is found in a subset of Kwa languages (Hérault (ed.) 1983). To my knowledge, this pattern has not been attested so far for Saramaccan.

In the third pattern, locative adverbs may serve as demonstrative terms in nominal structures. For Haitian, DeGraff (1999: 362) notes: "In my own idiolect, the locative adjuncts (*bò*) *isit* (Lit.: side here) '(over) here,' and (*bò*) *lòtbò* (Lit.: side there) '(over) there' do encode the [+/− proximate] opposition." This pattern replicates another pattern found in Fongbe. Segurola and Rassinoux's (2000) Fongbe dictionary provides the following

examples: *dě* 'here,' *àkpá dě* (Lit.: side here) 'this side,' *dɔn* 'over there.'
Saramaccan also uses locative adverbs as demonstrative terms. Rountree
(1992: 49) mentions the locative adverbs *akí* 'here' and *alá* 'over there.'
The data in (32) show that these two locative adverbs may also serve as
demonstrative terms in modern Saramaccan nominal structure.

(32) a. *di   batá   akí*   SARAMACCAN
          DEF   bottle DEM
          'this bottle'   (= (14) in Bally 2005)

      b. *di   batá   alá*   SARAMACCAN
          DEF   bottle DEM
          'that bottle'   (= (16) in Bally 2005)

Akí and *alá* were already used in this way in early Saramaccan. Indeed,
Schumann (1778) lists *akí*, Riemer (1779) lists both *alá* and *akí*, and in the
Saramaccan translation of the Acts of the Apostles by Wietz (1805), there
are several occurrences of both these lexical items used as demonstrative
terms in nominal structure, as illustrated in (33).

(33) a. *dem   sombre   akí*   SARAMACCAN
          PL   man   here
          'these men'   (Chapter 2, V 15 in Wietz 1805)

      b. *dem   sombre   alá*   SARAMACCAN
          PL   man   there
          'those men'   (Chapter 8, V 5 in Wietz 1805)

It thus appears that the demonstrative terms in Haitian and Saramaccan
draw their properties from those of their substrate languages. For a detailed comparison of the properties of demonstrative terms in Haitian and
French, see Lefebvre (1997, 1998: 89–101). A detailed comparison of the
properties of the Saramaccan demonstrative terms and those of English/
Portuguese can be found in Lefebvre (2012). In Lefebvre (1998, 2004b,
2012), it is argued that this situation follows straightforwardly from the
process of relabeling.

2.1.3.1.4. SUMMARY

The data reported on in this section show that, abstracting away from
word order, the properties of the definite determiners, the expression and
role of number, and the properties of the demonstrative terms in Haitian

and Saramaccan parallel those of Fongbe and other substrate languages. These properties differ from those of the corresponding terms in the creoles' respective superstrate languages.[14] This situation follows from a relabeling-based account of creole genesis.

2.1.3.2. The TMA System

The same situation obtains when we consider tense, mood, and aspect (TMA) systems. Whereas French encodes tense, mood, and aspect by means of affixes on verbs or auxiliaries (*avoir* 'to have' and *être* 'to be'), both Haitian and Fongbe lack such affixes and auxiliaries. Instead, they have TMA markers that occur between the subject and the verb. The inventories of TMA markers in Haitian and Fongbe are shown in (34).

(34)   Inventories of TMA markers in Haitian and Fongbe

ANTERIOR		IRREALIS		NON-COMPLETE			
Past / Past perfect		Definite future		Habitual		Imperfective	
H	F	H	F	H	F	H	F
te	kò	ap	ná	—	nɔ̀	ap[15]	ɖò...wɛ̀
		Indefinite future					
		H	F				
		a-va	ná-wá				
		Subjunctive					
		H	F				
		pou	ní				

(= (115) in Lefebvre 1996)

[14.] As shown in (3), (4), and (6), the nominal structure of all three languages under comparison in this chapter may also contain a possessive phrase. This phrase is not discussed here; however, for the sake of completeness, a few words may be said about possessives. While both French and English have a paradigm of possessive determiners that are mutually exclusive with the definite determiners, Haitian and Saramaccan lack such determiners, just like their Gbe substrate languages. See Lefebvre (1998: 143–149) for details. Both creoles express possession by means of a possessive phrase that is not in complementary distribution with the determiner of the nominal structure, as shown in (3) to (6). This possessive phrase comprises a personal pronoun and a case marker. This pattern replicates that found in the substrate languages. For example, in Fongbe, the possessive phrase is composed of a personal pronoun and the genitive case (Brousseau & Lumsden 1992; Lefebvre 1998: 101–110). Haitian replicates this pattern in exhibiting a personal pronoun and a null case marker, which Lumsden (1991) argues has the properties of genitive case, as opposed to accusative case. Saramaccan also replicates this pattern in having a personal pronoun preceded by *u*, a morpheme hypothesized to be a case marker in Lefebvre and Loranger (2006) (see Kearns, in progress, for further discussion of this topic). So, even for this category, the two creoles pair with their substrate languages rather than with their superstrates.

[15.] Definite future and imperfective are both rendered as *ap* in Haitian Creole. In Lefebvre (1998: 119–129) it is argued that *ap*, which corresponds to two different substrate morphemes, has two

With the exception of the habitual marker, which is absent in Haitian, the inventories of TMA markers are the same size in both languages. The morphemes involved in both inventories share semantic and distributional properties. The Fongbe and Haitian morphemes in (34) combine in similar ways to form complex tenses. Finally, while in French every sentence must be overtly marked for tense, mood, and aspect, both Haitian and Fongbe allow bare sentences, that is, sentences that have no overt TMA marking. As Lefebvre (1996, and the references therein) discusses at some length, in this case, the temporal-aspectual interpretation of the clause is computed from the various components that participate in establishing its aspectual properties: the aspectual class of the verb, the definiteness of the direct object of the verb, and the definiteness of the subject. In Lefebvre (1996, 1998, and the references therein), the similarity between the Haitian and Fongbe TMA subsystems is argued to follow mainly from the relabeling of the substrate lexical entries on the basis of French periphrastic expressions involved in the expression of tense, mood, and aspect in colloquial French, and less importantly, from grammaticalization, as discussed in section 2.3 (Lefebvre 1996, 1998: 134–137, and the references therein). The derivation of the imperfective aspect will be discussed in Chapter 4.

With respect to its TMA system, Saramaccan is very similar to Haitian and Fongbe. It encodes tense, mood, and aspect by means of TMA markers, the inventory of which comprises the marker of anteriority *bì* (<English *been*), the future marker *ó* (<English *go*), the subjunctive marker *fu* (<English *for*), and the imperfective marker *ta* (<Portuguese *esta*, according to Byrne 1987, <English *stand*, according to Veenstra 1996a) (for *fu*, see Lefebvre & Loranger 2006, and the references therein; for discussions of the TMA system, see Bally 2004, 2011; Rountree 1992; van de Vate 2011). This inventory is represented in Table 3.2, together with that of Fongbe.

As is the case in Haitian and Fongbe, these markers combine to form complex tenses (Bally 2004; Rountree 1992). Furthermore, Saramaccan, like Haitian and Fongbe, but unlike English, allows for bare sentences. Saramaccan bare sentences are assigned a temporal-aspectual interpretation in the same way as Haitian and Fongbe bare sentences (Bally 2004).

---

sources in the superstrate language. The French expression *être après* 'to be in the process of' was the source of the new label for the substrate imperfective marker. The presentential adverb *apré* 'then, later' (<French *après* 'then, later') made its way between the subject and the verb and was grammaticalized as an irrealis mood marker (see section 3.2.1). A synchronic analysis should consider the possibility that there is only one *ap* in contemporary Haitian.

TABLE 3.2 Inventories of TMA Markers in Saramaccan and in Fongbe

ANTERIOR		IRREALIS		NON-COMPLETE			
Past / Past perfect		Definite future		Habitual		Imperfective	
SA	F	SA	F	SA	F	SA	F
bì	kò	ó	ná	—	nɔ̀	tá	ɖò…wɛ̀
		Indefinite future					
		SA	F				
		ó	ná-wá				
		Subjunctive					
		SA	F				
		fu	ní				

Finally, in their comparison of Surinamese creoles and Gbe languages, Winford and Migge (2007) expand the inventory of TMA markers to include aspectual and modal verbs. Their conclusion is that the properties of the TMA markers and of the aspectual and modal verbs in Surinamese creoles are very similar to those in the Gbe languages.[16] Again, this follows from relabeling.

Regarding its TMA system, it has sometimes been claimed that Papiamentu does not present the canonical Tense-Mood-aspect order observed in other Caribbean creoles (e.g., Muysken 1981b). This is mainly because, in this language, the morpheme *lo*, the future marker, occurs before the pronominal subject and the negation marker instead of between the negation marker and the verb, as in the other creoles discussed above. The position of *lo* is exemplified in (35).

(35)   *Lo   mi   no   lubidá.*
       IRR 1SG NEG forget
       'I won't forget.'   (= (78) in Maurer 1988b: 94, from IPEP 1983)

Kouwenberg and Lefebvre (2007), however, proposed a revised account of the TMA system of Papiamentu. Their analysis is conducted within the split CP (Rizzi 1997) and split INFL (Pollock 1989) frameworks. In this account, *lo* heads the functional projection FinP, just above IP. The marker *tabata*, past imperfective, heads the functional projection TP. The mood marker *pa* heads the functional projection MoodP, and the marker *a*, perfective, heads the functional projection AspP. Furthermore, it is shown

---

[16.]Note that Wietz (1805) contains occurrences of *bi* and *go*, but not of *ta* or *fu*.

that, as in Haitian, Saramaccan, and Fongbe, these markers combine to form complex tenses (see also Maurer 1988b). Although the Papiamentu data show some minor differences from Haitian, Saramaccan, and Fongbe, Kouwenberg and Lefebvre's analysis makes it unnecessary to consider Papiamentu as having a TMA system that differs significantly from those of the other Caribbean creoles.

2.1.3.3. The Complementizer System

The discussion of the complementizer system summarizes data and analyses based on the following major sources: for Fongbe, Lefebvre and Brousseau (2002); for Haitian, Koopman and Lefebvre (1981, 1982) and Sterlin (1988, 1989); for Saramaccan, Lefebvre and Loranger (2006, 2008). The complementizer systems in the languages under comparison all make some kind of distinction between indicative and irrealis/subjunctive mood. Two striking facts, however, set Haitian, Saramaccan, and Fongbe apart from French and English/Portuguese. First, in all three languages, the same morpheme serves both as an irrealis mood marker occurring between the subject and the verb as in (36a) to (38a), and as an irrealis subjunctive complementizer, as in (36b) to (38b).[17]

(36) a. *Mí* **ní** *ɗù* *nú.* FONGBE
1PL SUB eat thing
'Let's eat.'
[Lit.: 'We must eat.'] (= (21c) in Lefebvre & Brousseau 2002)

b. *Ùn* *jló* **ní** *à* *ní* *wá.* FONGBE
1SG want COMP 2SG SUB come
'I want you to come.'
[Lit.: 'I want that you come.'] (= (14) in Lefebvre & Brousseau 2002)

(37) a. *Tut* *sòlda* **pou** *vini* *laplas* *kunyè* *a.* HAITIAN
all soldier SUB come square now DET
'All soldiers must come to the square now.' (Sylvain 1936: 90)

b. *Yo* *te* *vle* **pou** *m* *te* *antre nan troup Jakmèl.* HAITIAN
they ANT want COMP me ANT join in troops Jacmel
'They wanted me to join Jacmel's troops.'
[Lit.: 'They wanted that I joined Jacmel's troops.']
(= (10) in Koopman & Lefebvre 1982)

---

[17] As Lefebvre and Therrien (2007a) show in detail, Papiamentu *pa* has the same functions as Haitian *pou* and Saramaccan *fu*.

(38) a. *I   ku   en   fu   go.*   SARAMACCAN
          you   with   him   SUB   go
          'You and he should go.'   (= (5a) in Muysken 1987: 90)

     b. *A   ke   fu   a   bi   sa   baja.*   SARAMACCAN
          she   wish   COMP   she   TNS   MO   dance
          'She wished she could dance.'   (= (4g) in Wijnen & Alleyne 1987: 48)
          'She wanted to be able to dance.'

                                         (= (4g) in Wijnen & Alleyne 1987: 48)

This contrasts with French and English/Portuguese, which do not have a mood marker that is positioned between the subject and the verb and is homophonous with a subjunctive complementizer (see also Aboh 2007 for similar observations based on a comparison between English, Saramaccan, and Gungbe). There is one difference between Fongbe and the two creoles under discussion here. As can be seen in (36), Fongbe *ní* occurs twice within the same clause: once as a complementizer and once as a mood marker. Not only is this co-occurrence permitted, it is obligatory. In contrast, in the two creoles, the corresponding morphemes, *pou* in Haitian and *fu* in Saramaccan, do not occur twice within the same clause. When they occur in the complementizer position, they cannot also occur in the mood position between the subject and the verb in the same clause. This difference between the two creoles and their substrate language calls for an explanation that will have to await future research.

The second set of facts that sets Saramaccan and Fongbe apart from English and Portuguese has to do with the lexical item that serves as a tensed complementizer selected by verbs of the SAY-class. For example, in Saramaccan, the form of the [+T] complementizer selected by utterance, cognition, and perception verbs is *táa* (<English *tell*). Lefebvre and Loranger (2008) argue that Saramaccan *táa* cannot possibly have been phonologically derived from Saramaccan *táki* (<English *talk*) 'to talk, to say,' as is generally assumed in the literature (e.g., Arends 1997; Bakker et al. 1995; Byrne 1987; McWhorter 1992; Veenstra 1996a, 1996b). They provide several arguments showing that, from a phonological point of view, *táa* must have been derived from English *tell*. While English *tell* is only a speech verb, Saramaccan *táa* is a multifunctional lexical item that serves as a verb meaning 'to say, to tell,' as a quotative marker meaning 'saying,' as a [+T] complementizer, and as a marker conveying similarity or manner 'as if, like.' The multifunctionality of *táa* replicates the substrate data, as is shown in (39), on the basis of Fongbe.

(39) *táa*: verb: 'say', 'tell'   SARAMACCAN
          [+T] complementizer: 'that'
          quotative marker: 'saying'
          marker conveying similarity or manner: 'as if, like'
     ɖɔ: verb: 'say', 'tell'   FONGBE
          [+T] complementizer: 'that'
          quotative marker: 'saying'
          marker conveying similarity or manner: 'as if, like'
                                                        (from Lefebvre & Loranger 2008)

As Lefebvre and Loranger show, the properties of Saramaccan *táa* are just like those of the corresponding lexical entries in Fongbe and other languages of the same family (see Güldemann 2001 for a thorough discussion of these phenomena based on a wide range of African languages). Interestingly enough, *táa* seems to have been in use in early Saramaccan, as it is found in letters that were sent to Schuchardt in 1882 (for a discussion of these data, cited from Schuchardt (ed.) (1914), see Lefebvre & Loranger 2008: 497–498). The data in (39) follow from relabeling.

While other English-based Caribbean creoles follow the Saramaccan pattern in having a multifunctional item that serves as a complementizer selected by utterance verbs (e.g., see Winford 1993 for Guyanese), French-based Caribbean creoles such as Haitian and Martinican Creole have a phonologically null complementizer. The reason for this discrepancy between English- and French-based creoles must await future research.

2.1.3.4. The Conjunction System

The properties of Haitian, Saramaccan, and Fongbe conjunctions are quite similar and contrast with those of French and English.

Fongbe has a conjunction *bɔ* that best translates as 'and then.' This conjunction is used only to conjoin tensed clauses (Lefebvre 2004a, and the references therein). Likewise, Haitian has a conjunction *(e)pi* (<French *et puis*) that also translates as 'and then'; according to our informants, it is used only to conjoin tensed clauses (Lefebvre 2004a, and the references therein). Note that some Haitian dictionaries (e.g., Valdman et al. 1981; Valdman et al. 2007) show examples in which *epi* may conjoin two NPs as well as clauses. My understanding is that *epi* is used to conjoin NPs in the lexicon of speakers who have had more exposure to French than my informants, who reject this use of *epi*. Support for this line of analysis comes

from Fattier's (1998: 962) statement on the conjunction *epi* and its variants: "Les conjonctions variées citées sur la carte ne peuvent coordonner, à notre connaissance, que des éléments phrastiques. Elles ont pour la plupart en commun le fait de représenter le même rapport logique de successivité."[18] As for Saramaccan, it has a conjunction *hen* that translates as 'and then'; it is used only to conjoin tensed clauses (Rountree et al. 2000). These facts are illustrated in (40a), (40b), and (40c), respectively, for the three languages.

(40) a. *Kòkú   wá   bò   Àsíbá   yì.*   FONGBE
       Koku   arrive and-then Asiba   leave
       'Koku arrived and then Asiba left.'

                                  (= (1) in Lefebvre & Brousseau 2002: 113)

   b. *Jan   pati   (e)pi   Mari   rive.*   HAITIAN
      John   leave   and-then Mary   arrive
      'John left and then Mary arrived.'   (= (70) in Lefebvre 1993)

   c. *Kofi si   di   mujee   hen   a   go ta   waka a   di*
      Kofi see DEF woman   and-then 3SG   go ASP   walk LOC DEF
      keiki.   SARAMACCAN
      church
      'Kofi saw the woman and then he walked to the church.'

                                          (= (39a) in Byrne 1987: 52)

Interestingly enough, in all three languages, these conjunctions participate in temporal adverbial constructions that involve verb-doubling phenomena (which will be further discussed in Chapter 4, section 5), as is illustrated in (41).

(41) a. TEMPORAL ADVERBIAL
       ***Wá**   Jan   wá   (tróló)   bò   Màrí   yì.*   FONGBE
       ***Rive** Jan   rive   epi   Mari   pati.*   HAITIAN
       arrive   John   arrive as-soon-as and.then Mary   left
       'As soon as John arrived, Mary left.'   (Lefebvre's field notes)

---

[18] Translation: The various conjunctions noted on the map, to our knowledge, can only coordinate clausal elements. Most of them have in common the property of representing the same logical relation of successivity.

b. TEMPORAL ADVERBIAL

Ko *Rohit ko* *a* *wosu pala,* *hen* *Rowe*
arrive Rohit arrive LOC house as-soon-as and.then Rowe

go. SARAMACCAN

leave

'As soon as Rohit arrived at the house, Rowe left.'

(Lefebvre's field notes)

The Haitian conjunction *(e)pi* 'and then' is phonologically derived from French *et puis* 'and then' > *epi* 'and,' but the two forms do not have the same distribution. For example, while French *epi* may conjoin both clauses and NPs, in the basilectal variety of Haitian, *(e)pi* cannot conjoin NPs. The phonetic source of Saramaccan *hen* may be the English form *and*. Like Fongbe *bɔ* and Haitian *(e)pi* (basilectal variety), but unlike English *and*, Saramaccan *hen* does not conjoin NPs.[19]

In Fongbe, Haitian, and Saramaccan, NPs are "conjoined," so to speak, by means of the preposition meaning 'with,' as shown in (42).

(42) a. *Kɔkú* *kpó(ɖó)* *Àsíbá* *kpó/kpá* FONGBE
Koku with Asiba with/with
'Koku and Asiba' (= (9) in Lefebvre 2004b: 127)

b. *Jan* *(kòl)ak* *Mari* HAITIAN
John with Mary
'John and Mary' (= (80) in Lefebvre 2004b: 157)

c. *Sambili* *ku* *Agoutupe* SARAMACCAN
Sambili with Agoutupe
'Sambili and Agoutupe' (Rountree 1992: 64)

The prepositions meaning 'with' above cannot be analyzed as conjunctions, because the phrases they head can be extraposed, as is shown in (43).

(43) a. *Àsíbá kpóɖó Kɔkú* *kpó* *yì* *àxì* *mὲ.* FONGBE
a'. *Àsíbá* *yì* *àxì* *mε* *kpóɖó Kɔkú kpó.*
Asiba go market in with Koku with
'Asiba went to the market with Koku.' (= (53) in Lefebvre 2004a)

---

[19] For an account of why Fongbe *bɔ* and Haitian *(e)pi* (basilectal variety) cannot conjoin NPs, see Lefebvre (2004a). The same analysis carries over to Saramaccan.

b. *Mari ak Jan ale nan mache.*   HAITIAN

b'. *Mari ale nan mache ak Jan.*

   Mary go in market with John

   'Mary went to the market with John.' (= (81), (85) in Lefebvre 2004a)

c. *Basía ku Malítá tá nján.*   SARAMACCAN

c'. *Basía tá nján ku Malítá.*

   'Basia is eating with Malita.'   (Bally 2005: 81)

It is a well-known fact that conjunctions cannot be extraposed with the NP they conjoin, as is illustrated in (44).

(44)   a. *John and Mary went to the market.*   ENGLISH

    a'. **John went to the market and Mary*

    b. *Jean et Marie sont allés au marché.*   FRENCH

    b'. **Jean sont allés au marché et Marie*

To sum up, while Fongbe, Haitian, and Saramaccan use different lexical items to conjoin clauses and NPs, French uses *et* or *epi* 'and' in both contexts, as does English with *and*. Here again, the creoles resemble their substrate languages (Lefebvre 2004a) and contrast with their superstrate languages. This follows from relabeling.

2.1.3.5. Validators

Validators are markers expressing the speaker's point of view of a proposition. While neither French nor English has such markers, Fongbe exhibits a series of them. They include a yes-no question marker and a marker of insistence, illustrated in (45). (For an extensive discussion of these markers, see Lefebvre & Brousseau 2002: 123–133).

(45)   a. *Kɔkú xɔ àsɔ́n lέ à?*   FONGBE

      Koku buy crab PL Q

      'Has Koku bought the crabs?'(= (36) in Lefebvre & Brousseau 2002)

  b. *Mà xɔ àsɔ́n lέ ó!*   FONGBE

      NEG buy crab PL INS

      'Don't buy the crabs!' (with insistence)   (= (27) in da Cruz 1994)

Although the Haitian and Saramaccan data on this topic are incomplete, there is some evidence that both languages have such markers. For example, Joseph (1995) argues that Haitian does have a form equivalent to the

Fongbe marker *ó* in (45). The form of this marker is *non* (<French *non* 'no'), as shown in (46), which parallels the Fongbe sentence in (46).

(46) a. *Pa   ale   non!*   HAITIAN
     b. *Mà   yì   ó!*   FONGBE
        NEG   go   INS
        'Don't go!'   (= (36a) in Joseph 1995)

A more elaborate discussion of these facts may be found in Lefebvre (1998: 213–17).

As for Saramaccan, Rountree (1992) reports that it has a question marker and a marker of emphasis, illustrated in (47). These correspond to the Fongbe markers in (45a) and (45b), respectively.

(47) a. *A   sa   kë   fufuuma   nö?*   SARAMACCAN
        3SG   can   want   thief   INT
        'Could it be a thief?'   (= (132) in Rountree 1992: 28)

     b. *Mi   lobi   di   soni   aki   e!*   SARAMACCAN
        1SG   like   DEF   thing   here   EMP
        'I really like this!'   (= (134) in Rountree 1992: 29)

The presence of validational markers in Haitian and Saramaccan follows the grammatical pattern of the Gbe lexicons. Though more research is required on this topic, the creole data presented above can be accounted for by means of relabeling.

2.1.3.6. Summary

The properties of the functional categories involved in the determiner, TMA, complementizer, conjunction, and validator subsystems of the grammars of Haitian, Saramaccan, and Fongbe are extremely similar, and those of the two creoles differ from of the equivalent systems in their respective superstrate languages. This argues for a relabeling account of the lexical items involved. In section 2.2.4, it will further be shown that functional morphology in agglutinative languages can also undergo relabeling. I therefore conclude that functional categories can in fact undergo relabeling. Other views will be discussed in section 2.3. But before examining them, I turn to the question of how relabeling applies to functional categories.

2.2. How Are Functional Categories Relabeled in Creole Genesis?

This section discusses the various components of the relabeling of functional categories in creole genesis. It suggests a hypothesis about the properties of superstrate forms that are suitable for relabeling a substrate functional item. It demonstrates that relabeling is constrained by what the superstrate language has available to relabel a substrate functional item, and shows how relabeling proceeds in the case of agglutinative languages. I begin by presenting the initial hypothesis (Lefebvre & Lumsden 1994a) regarding this issue. (The problem of word order will be addressed in Chapter 5.)

2.2.1. The Initial Hypothesis

Like major category lexical items, minor or functional categories may undergo relabeling provided that they have some semantic content. Thus, functional categories that have semantic content, such as determiners, pronouns, TMA markers, and the like,[20] can be relabeled. As discussed in Lefebvre (1998), however, they are not relabeled on the basis of the corresponding superstrate functional categories. Indeed, since the creators of a creole do not have much exposure to the superstrate language, as we saw in the introduction to this chapter, they are unable to identify the functional categories of the superstrate language as such. For example, the creators of Haitian did not identify the French determiner as a determiner, for the latter constitutes part of several Haitian words, as is illustrated in (48a) involving the French definite determiner and (48b) involving the French partitive determiner.

(48)   Haitian nouns   Corresponding French DPs
   a. *larivyè*   'river' < *la rivière*   'the river'
   b. *dlo*   'water' < *de l'eau*   'water'
                                                 (from Valdman et al. 1981)

Lefebvre and Lumsden (1994a) hypothesize that the creators of a creole relabel a functional category on the basis of a superstrate form that has the following characteristics: (1) it is a salient, and hence a free, form; (2) it shares some semantics with the original lexical entry; (3) it may also share some phonological/phonetic properties (Kihm 1989, 1994) with the original lexical entry; and (4) it also shares a similar surface position with the

---

[20] Chomsky (1995: 240) writes: "T, D, and C have semantic properties."

original lexical entry (see also Kihm 2011). The relative importance of these characteristics is evaluated in the following text on the basis of the derivation of several functional categories.

2.2.2. The Haitian Definite Determiner

As we saw in 2.1.3.1.1, the semantic, syntactic, and distributional properties of the Haitian and Fongbe definite determiners are extremely similar. By hypothesis, this similarity follows from the relabeling of the substrate definite determiner on the basis of a French form. The following paragraph summarizes the historical derivation presented in Lefebvre (1998: 79–84).

Authors agree that the French form *là* 'there' occurring at the end of constituents is the source of the label of the Haitian determiner (e.g., Faine 1937; Fournier 1977; Goodman 1964; Lefebvre 1993, 1998; Valdman 1978). In addition to its use as a locative adverb meaning 'there,' French *là* may appear following the noun as an emphatic deictic marker, as in (49a), or as a discourse marker (DM) (Vincent 1984) after a noun phrase or a clause, as in (49b).

(49) a. *Cet   homme-là   vient   d'arriver.*   FRENCH
          DEM   man [+DEIC] come   arrive
          'This / that man just arrived.'

      b.' *L'   homme là   vient   d'arriver.*   VERNACULAR FRENCH
          DEF man   DM come arrive
          'The man [there] just arrived.'

      b." *Un   homme   là   vient   d'arriver.*   VERNACULAR FRENCH
          DEF man   DM come arrive
          'A man [there] just arrived.'

      b.''' *Un/l' homme là, qui   vient d'arriver là...* VERNACULAR FRENCH
          DEF   man   DM who come arrive   DM
          'A / the man [there] who just arrived [there]...'

                                            (= (30) in Lefebvre 1994a)

The substrate definite determiners and French *là* share some semantics, as both have anaphoric properties. They also share distributional properties: both occur at the end of constituents, either nominal or clausal (compare the data in (9) and (10) and (49)). For some substrate speakers, the forms involved are also phonetically similar. For example, while in Fongbe the form of the definite determiner is *ɔ̃* [ɔ], in Ewegbe, the definite determiner is *la* [la]. The French form *là* was pronounced [lɔ] or [lɒ] in vernacular French. So it appears that French *là* had suitable characteristics to relabel the Gbe definite determiner. As Lefebvre (1998: 78–79) points out, however, the properties of the substrate definite determiners and French *là* differ in many ways, and so French *là* cannot be argued to be the source of the semantic properties of the Haitian definite determiner. Thus, the relabeling of the substrate definite determiners on the basis of French *là* yielded a Haitian determiner that has the properties of the substrate determiners (see section 2.1.3.1.1).

In the relabeling account of the substrate definite determiner outlined above, the superstrate form has all four characteristics that make it suitable to relabel a substrate lexical entry. This is not always the case, however, as will be seen in the next section.

2.2.3. Relabeling Is Constrained by the Superstrate Language: The Case of the Saramaccan Definite Determiner

As was mentioned in Chapter 1, since relabeling proceeds on the basis of superstrate forms, it is constrained by what the superstrate language has to offer to relabel a substrate lexical entry. I assume that, in processing the superstrate data, the creators of a creole look for a label that has the four characteristics listed above. If they find one, they use it. This is what happened in the case of Haitian, whose creators found in French the adverbial form *là* occurring at the end of constituents to relabel their postnominal determiner. But what happened in the case of English-based creoles created from the same pool of substrate languages?

For example, as we saw in 2.1.3.1.1, except for word order, the properties of the Saramaccan definite determiner are the same as those of the corresponding Fongbe lexical entry. By hypothesis, this lexical entry was created by relabeling. Presumably, the creators of Saramaccan did not encounter in English a form that had the properties and distribution of French *là*.[21] They found the prenominal form *this*, which they incorporated in Saramaccan as *disi* (and reduced to *di*) and used as a prenominal determiner with the properties of their postnominal determiner. Here, I am exploring the view that, if

---

[21] Aboh (2006) claims that English *there* is comparable to French *là* in (49). He does not provide any data supporting his claim, however, and to the best of my knowledge, no data comparable to those for French *là* have been reported in the literature. It appears that English *there* does not have the same distribution as French *là*; therefore, in contrast to French, English did not have a constituent-final form that could be used to relabel the constituent-final determiner in the substrate languages. For further discussion of this issue, see Lefebvre (2012).

the creators of a creole did not find, in the superstrate language, a form with all four characteristics enumerated above to relabel a given lexical entry, they might have looked for one that had only a subset of these characteristics. In the case of *this*, the first (salient and free form) and the second characteristic (shared semantics) are certainly met as English *this* is a salient, free form that shares some semantics with the substrate form, given that both are anaphoric. In this case, however, the lexical entries that are associated in relabeling share no phonological or phonetic properties, nor do they share a similar surface position. This suggests that characteristics 3 and 4 of the superstrate forms used in relabeling are less constraining than the first two. The data discussed in the following section appear to support this view.

2.2.4. The Relabeling of Functional Morphology in Agglutinative Languages: The Case of Kriol

I will address this topic on the basis of Kriol, a creole language that emerged from the contact between about a hundred agglutinative Aboriginal languages and English, in Roper River, Australia, around 1908. According to Munro (2000), Kriol was created to provide the Aboriginal people with a lingua franca. Thus, it is like the other creole languages discussed so far in having several substrate languages and one superstrate language.

The literature on Kriol reveals two relabeling options: some affixes in the substrate languages were relabeled as affixes, while others were relabeled as free morphemes. In both cases, however, the English labels consisted of free forms. Examples of affixes that were relabeled as affixes are discussed in Koch (2000). For example, verbs in Aboriginal languages have a transitivity marker. This morpheme was relabeled in Kriol as *im/it*, on the basis of English *him/it* following the verb (e.g., *see him/it*). For example, consider the Kriol data in (50), where the verb *kill* 'to kill' is followed by the transitivity marker *it*, itself followed by the direct object.

(50) a. *Bel boodgeree kill it pickaninny.*   KRIOL
          Not   good   kill TR babies
          'It is not good to kill babies.'   (= (2) in Koch 2000)

      b. *My gin eatit too much white bread.*   KRIOL
          My wife eat.it too much white bread
          'My wife eats too much white bread.'   (= (3) in Koch 2000)

Similarly, the substrate nominal classifier that appears on pronouns, demonstratives, adjectives, and so on (Baker 1996), was relabeled on the basis of the English word *fellow,* yielding *-fellow/-fela/-pela/-bela/-pala* in Kriol. In (51a), *-pela* is affixed to a personal pronoun; in (51b) *-fellow* is affixed to a demonstrative; and in (51c), it is attached to an adjective.

(51) a. *yu*   / *yupela*
          2SG   2.PL
          'you'   'you PL'   (Koch 2000: 29)

      b. *thatfellow wheel*   (= (64) in Koch 2000: 34 not translated)

      c. *another one blackfellow*
          'another aboriginal'   (= (66) in Koch 2000: 34)

Munro (2004) shows in great detail, however, that the bulk of the agglutinative morphology of Kriol's substrate languages was relabeled as free morphemes. For example, in Aboriginal languages, tense, mood, and aspect are realized as suffixes on the verb, as in (52). In Kriol, tense, mood and aspect are realized as preverbal periphrastic markers, as in (53).

(52) a. *Gu-jandah   Ø-marninyh-mi-ti-tji-**ny**.*   NGALAKGAN
          NC-stick   3SG-make- AUX -RCP-PP
          'He made himself into a stick.'   (Merlan 1983: 104–105)

      b. *Ngu-mu-gol-ye-**nga**   weh-gah.*   NGALAKGAN
          1SG-NC-put-CV-FUT   water LOC
          'I will put it in water.'   (Merlan 1983: 100)

(53) *Main mamai **bin oldei** gemp   langa gemp.*   KRIOL
       POSS mother PST CONT live/stay G/L   camp
       'My mum stayed (slept) at camp.'   (AO58 cited in Munro 2004)

According to Munro, the free forms in Kriol have the same properties as the bound ones in the substrate languages. Sharpe (1972: 9) notes that "In Alawa [a substrate language of Kriol] tense-aspect-mood . . . are indicated by suffixation of auxiliary stems . . . ; in PE [Pidgin English, or Kriol] they are indicated by preposed words. However, the contrasts distinguished are found to be in nearly all respects identical. In surface structure the languages are very different; in deep structure and semantically they are almost identical."

Another example involves negation. In Aboriginal languages, negation is realized by different morphemes, depending on whether the mood is realis or irrealis. This distinction has been preserved in Kriol, which has *neba* and *nomo* in realis mood, and *gan* in irrealis mood. These appear as free morphemes (Munro 2004: 130–136).

Person marking constitutes yet another example. In the substrate languages of Kriol, person is encoded by means of prefixes, as in (54).

(54) *Barda **niw**-anj-anji   gayarra.*   MARRA
      later   1PL.EX.-RCP sat   there
      'Then later, we stayed there.'   (Heath 1981: 332)

The person-marking system of the substrate languages of Kriol distinguishes between singular, dual, and plural, and also between first-person inclusive and exclusive. (Some languages even distinguish between masculine and feminine forms.) These distinctions are exemplified on the basis of Alawa in (55).

(55) The pronominal system of Alawa

	SINGULAR	DUAL	PLURAL
1	*ngina*		
2	*nyagana*	*wurru*	*wulu*
3	*nurla* (m.) *nga durla* (f.)	*yirrurla*	*yilurla*
1 inclusive 1 exclusive		*nyanu* *ngarru*	*nyalu* *ngalu*

(Munro 2004: 122)

These distinctions are summarized in (56) for all the Kriol substrate languages that have been documented.

(56) Person-marking system of Kriol substrate languages

	SINGULAR	DUAL	PLURAL
1	√		
2	√	√	√
3	√	√	√
1 inclusive 1 exclusive		√ √	√ √

(adapted from Munro 2004: 121)

They have been reproduced in Kriol, on the basis of English forms (e.g., *yunmi < you and me*) as shown in (57).

(57) Person-marking system of Kriol

	SINGULAR	DUAL	PLURAL
1	*ai/mi*		
2	*yu*	*yundubala*	*yumop*
3	*im*	*dubala*	*olabat*
1 inclusive 1 exclusive		*yunmi* *mindubala/* *minbala*	*wi* *melabat/mela*

(adapted from Munro 2004: 123)

While in the substrate languages of Kriol, independent pronouns are used exclusively for emphasis or contrastive purposes (Munro 2004: 120), in Kriol independent pronouns are used to encode person and number, though they may also be used for emphasis or contrast. (See Keesing 1988 for similar data from Solomon Islands Pijin.)

The above examples show that, even when the substrate languages are agglutinating, the morphemes of these languages can be relabeled. In all cases, the substrate morphemes have been relabeled on the basis of a free form in the superstrate (e.g., *him/it, fellow, been*, strong pronominal forms, etc.) (the first characteristic in section 2.2.1) with which the substrate lexical entry shares some semantics (the second characteristic). The other two characteristics of the superstrate forms are absent (phonetic/phonological similarity of the forms associated in the process, as well as similar surface word order), thus supporting the suggestion made at the end of the previous section that in relabeling the first two characteristics are more constraining and important than the last two. This is further evidenced by the relabeling of number, to which I now turn.

2.2.5. A Relabeling Account of Number

As we saw in section 2.1.3.1.2, the properties of the plural marker and the conceptual role of number in Haitian are very similar to those of its substrate languages. In Lefebvre (1998: 84–87), relabeling was argued to account for the parallels between the Haitian and substrate language data. Two patterns of variation in the substrate languages were reported, however: languages in which the same morpheme serves as both a plural marker and a third-person plural personal pronoun, such as Ewegbe (Westerman 1930: 45, 57), Yoruba and Mandingo (Goodman 1964: 46–47), and Vai (Mufwene 1986: 138), and languages in which these two categories are encoded by separate morphemes, such as Fongbe. These two patterns are schematized in (58).

(58)

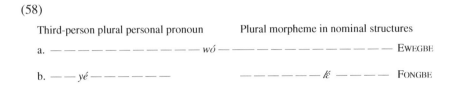

The Haitian and Saramaccan data reproduce the first pattern. The relabeling account for Haitian in Lefebvre (1998) can be summarized as follows. The third-person plural personal pronouns of the substrate languages were relabeled as *yo* on the basis of the French strong third-person personal pronoun *eux* (the second characteristic) (Goodman 1964; Sylvain 1936). According to Brousseau (in preparation), the phonological derivation of *eux* as *yo* is predictable (the third characteristic). The French pronoun *eux* is salient because it is used as an emphatic form, as in (59) (the first characteristic).

(59) *Eux, ils   mangent du   riz   chaque jour.*   FRENCH
      them, they eat   PART rice every   day
      'Them, they eat rice every day.'   (= (40) in Lefebvre 1994a)

In vernacular French, *eux* may also occur as an emphatic pronoun at the end of a nominal constituent, as shown in (60). Note the gender neutralization shown in (60b), also noted by Gougenheim (1973).

(60) a. *Les   gars,   eux,   ils...*   FRENCH
          DEF-PL guys   them, they...
          'The guys, them, they...'

      b. *Les   filles, eux,   ils...*   VERNACULAR FRENCH
          DEF-PL girl   them   they...
          'The girls, them, they...'   (= (41) in Lefebvre 1994a)

From the above examples, we can see that the French pronoun *eux* has a surface distribution similar to the Ewegbe form *wó,* which occurs either as a free pronominal form or as a plural marker occurring postnominally (the fourth characteristic). The form *eux* thus appears to have been suitable to relabel the substrate pronominal lexical entry. Since this lexical entry was also used as a plural marker in the substrate lexicon, it acquired that function in the creole as well.

A similar account is proposed for Saramaccan in Lefebvre (2012). A lexical entry of the type of Ewegbe *wó* would have been relabeled as *dem* on the basis of the free and salient English pronominal form *them* (the first and second characteristics). Through relabeling, *dem* inherited the double function of *wó,* serving as both a third-person plural personal pronoun and a plural marker in nominal structures. Note, however, that, in this case, the third characteristic is not met (phonetic/phonological similarity), nor is the fourth one, as English *them* does not have the same distribution as French *eux* (e.g., *them* does not occur postnominally as an emphatic pronoun).

As noted in section 2.1.3.1.2, Martinican Creole reproduces the Fongbe pattern in which two different forms encode third-person plural personal pronoun and plural in nominal structures. A relabeling account of these facts involves the following features. The third-person plural personal pronoun of Fongbe *yé* was relabeled on the basis of French *eux,* yielding *yo.* The Fongbe plural form *lé* was relabeled as *se* on the basis of French *ces* 'these/those,' a plural demonstrative determiner. *Ces* is a salient form (the first characteristic). Fongbe *lé* and French *ces* share some semantics in that both are plural (the second characteristic). French [sɛ]/[se] and Fongbe [lé] share some phonetic/phonological similarities (the third characteristic). Because French *ces* is prenominal (e.g., *ces pierres* 'these/those stones'), Martinican *se* ended up being prenominal as well, as is illustrated in (30a). Word order will be further discussed in following text and in Chapter 5.

2.2.6. The Initial Hypothesis Revisited

Recall from section 2.2.1 that, according to the initial hypothesis, the creators of a creole relabel a functional category on the basis of a superstrate form that has the following four characteristics: (1) it is a salient thus free form; (2) it shares some semantics with the original lexical entry; (3) it may share some phonological/phonetic properties with the original lexical entry; and (4) it shares a similar surface position with the original lexical entry. The relabeling accounts of the functional categories discussed in sections 2.2.2 to 2.2.5 are summarized in Table 3.3, based on these four characteristics.

TABLE 3.3 Characteristics of Superstrate Forms Used to Relabel Substrate Lexical
Entries

CHARACTERISTIC OF SUPERSTRATE FORM→ RELABELED SUBSTRATE FORM↓	SALIENT/ FREE	SHARES SOME SEMANTICS	SHARES SOME PHONO FEATURES	SHARES SURFACE ORDER (AT LEAST IN SOME CASES)
Haitian substrate definite determiner	√	√	√	√
Saramaccan substrate definite determiner	√	√	–	–
Kriol substrate bound morphology:				
transitive marker	√	√	–	–
nominal classifier	√	√	–	–
Haitian number	√	√	√	√
Saramaccan number	√	√	–	–
Martinican third-person plural pronoun	√	√	√	√
Martinican number	√	√	√	–

The above summary reveals that a superstrate form used to relabel a substrate lexical entry must be a free form that shares some semantics with the substrate lexical entry. It also shows that this form need not share phonetic/ phonological properties with the substrate lexical entry, and that it need not be in a surface position that is similar to that of the lexical entry to be relabeled. This raises the question of how the word order of functional categories is established in relabeling.

Chapter 5 contains an extensive discussion of word order. Suffice it to say for now that, to some extent, the word order of functional categories is determined by the surface position of the phonetic strings from which the new labels are derived. For example, in Saramaccan, the source of the definite determiner *di* is the English prenominal form *this*; consequently, the Saramaccan definite determiner is prenominal. In Kriol, the source of the past tense morpheme is the English form *been,* which occurs between the subject and the verb; consequently, the Kriol past tense marker is placed between the subject and the verb. As we saw in section 2.2.5, the Haitian plural marker *yo*, which also serves as a third-person plural personal pronoun, is postnominal. This is because it is derived from the French pronominal form *eux* 'they,' which, among other positions, occurs postnominally as an emphatic pronoun (Lefebvre 1998: 84–87, and the references therein). In contrast, in Martinican Creole, the plural marker is *se*, derived from French *ces* 'these/those.' French *ces* is prenominal, so Martinican *se* is prenominal as well. Like Haitian *yo*, the Saramaccan plural marker *dem* also serves as a third-person plural pronoun; in contrast to Haitian, however, Saramaccan *dem* is prenominal. Bally (2007b) relates this situation to the saliency of the prenominal position in English for determiners, including articles and demonstratives. Thus, in all these cases, the position of the creole's functional categories appears to be determined by the surface position of the phonetic strings from which the new labels are derived. Therefore, contrary to the initial hypothesis, the Haitian definite determiner is postnominal not because the substrates' definite determiners are postnominal but because its label is derived from a superstrate form that is itself postnominal. It therefore appears that the word order of functional categories in creole genesis is established primarily on the basis of the position of the superstrate form selected to relabel a substrate lexical entry. As will be further discussed in Chapter 5, a direct consequence of the situation discussed above is that word order is not registered among the properties of individual lexical entries.

2.2.7. What Happens When a Functional Category Item of the Substrate Languages Cannot Be Relabeled?

This question relates to two possible situations. First, since relabeling is constrained by what the superstrate language has available to relabel a substrate lexical entry, there may be cases where there is no appropriate superstrate form to relabel a substrate lexical entry. As Lefebvre (1998: 123–129) shows, this happened with the definite future marker of the substrate languages of Haitian, *ná* in Fongbe (see (34)), for which no corresponding superstrate form was available at the time relabeling was taking place. Second, since relabeling is semantically driven, functional categories that do not have semantic content (such as the expression of structural case and operators) cannot be relabeled. In either of these situations, it is hypothesized that the functional category is assigned a null form at relabeling (Lefebvre & Lumsden 1994a). Practically speaking, this means that, when this lexical entry is used, it is not pronounced. A case in point is the covert case marker in (4). As Lumsden (1991) argues, this phonologically null case has the properties of the genitive, rather than objective, case. A similar example involves the Wh-operator. While Gbe languages have an overt Wh-operator in relative and factive clauses (see (9a) and (10a)) (Lefebvre & Brousseau 2002: 118–120), Haitian has a covert Wh-operator (see (9b) and (10b)). In Lefebvre

(1998: 203–205), it is argued that the covert operator in Haitian has the same properties as the overt operator in the Gbe languages. Crucially, it is nominal. Following Lefebvre and Lumsden (1994a), it is further hypothesized that covert lexical entries may be assigned labels by means of grammaticalization in the development of the creole, a topic that is examined in section 3.2.

2.2.8. Summary

Functional categories are not relabeled with superstrate functional categories. Instead, they are relabeled with salient, hence free, forms that share some semantics with the original lexical entries. The selected label may also share phonetic or phonological properties and word order with the original lexical entry, but the latter two features are less important than the former. If a functional category cannot be assigned a label at relabeling, its phonological representation remains null.

2.3. Relabeling or Grammaticalization?

Some scholars have challenged the view that functional categories may undergo relabeling and have proposed that creole functional categories are created by means of grammaticalization. This section begins with a review of this position. In the literature on creole genesis and development, several functional categories have been claimed to have been created through grammaticalization. In section 2.3.2, I review two of these proposals—the creation of the Saramaccan definite determiner *di* and that of the complementizer *táa*—and argue against a grammaticalization account of the data. I then address the question of whether all the functional categories in a given creole are created by relabeling. My conclusion is that some are and some are not. When they are not, grammaticalization may be the process at work. Some criteria are proposed to help distinguish between cases of relabeling and cases of grammaticalization.

2.3.1. Are There Arguments Against the Possibility of Functional Categories Undergoing Relabeling?

The possibility that functional categories can undergo relabeling has been challenged. For example, Muysken (1988c: 15) claims that functional lexical entries do not undergo relabeling because they "do not have a meaning outside the linguistic system that they are part of, since their meanings are paradigmatically defined within that linguistic system." While it may very well be the case that the meanings of functional categories are paradigmatically defined, given that functional categories most often present themselves in paradigms (e.g., number, definiteness, etc.), semanticists (e.g., Larson & Segal 1995, and the references therein) defend the view that most functional categories do have semantic content. For example, the distinctions between definite and indefinite, singular and plural, and so on, are considered to be semantic even though they are not denotational. Furthermore, Chomsky (1995: 240) writes: "T(ense), D(eterminer), and C(omplementizer) have semantic properties." This is congruent with the position I took in section 2.1.3: that functional categories that have some semantic content may undergo relabeling. Muysken (1988c: 15) goes on to say that "when you relexify a system of function words, automatically the semantic organization of the target language comes in, and the result is at best a compromise between source and target language systems." It may be the case that the properties of some function words in a particular contact situation constitute a compromise between source and target language systems. For example, Muysken (1988c) documents this state of affairs in his study of the properties of the deictic terms in Media Lengua. But recall from Chapter 2 that Media Lengua is a mixed language involving two languages that have been mastered, though to varying degrees, by its creators. So, in this case, interference between the two systems of demonstrative terms is not surprising. But, in my view, this state of affairs does not constitute an argument against the possibility of functional categories undergoing relabeling. Independent evidence that demonstrative terms may undergo relabeling in the formation of a mixed language may be found in Bakker's (1992) work on Michif. Evidence that demonstrative terms may undergo relabeling in creole formation was provided in section 2.1.3.1.3. Furthermore, as is shown at some length in this chapter and elsewhere (e.g., Lefebvre 1998, 2001, and the references therein), the bulk of the Haitian and Saramaccan functional categories systematically replicate the substrate data. This follows straightforwardly from relabeling.

Lumsden (1999) claims that functional category lexical entries do not undergo relabeling based on the fact that the functional categories of Quechua were not relabeled in the formation of Media Lengua. He therefore holds that the functional categories of a creole must be created by grammaticalization. In my view, the fact that the functional categories of Quechua were not relabeled in Media Lengua does not in itself constitute an argument against the possibility that functional categories may undergo relabeling. Indeed, in Chapter 2, it was shown that the extent of relabeling across lexicons varies between situations. In some cases, it involves functional categories; in others, it does not.

In her paper on nominal structure in French-based creoles, Déprez (2007) simply assumes that the functional categories of this subsystem of the grammar emerged as a result of grammaticalization. She does not demonstrate that the forms she analyzes entered the creoles as lexical categories and were then grammaticalized as functional categories (possibly with the exception of *baun* in Seychelles Creole). From a general point of view, Déprez's position provides no means of accounting for the striking semantic and syntactic similarity that exists between the functional categories of a creole and those of its substrate languages, as I showed in section 2.1.3. From a more specific point of view, it is not possible to argue against Déprez's grammaticalization account since, as mentioned above, it is taken for granted rather than demonstrated.

In light of this discussion, I will now review the grammaticalization accounts of some functional categories. Two cases will be discussed: the grammaticalization account of the Saramaccan definite determiner (section 2.3.2) and the grammaticalization account of Saramaccan *táa* (section 2.3.3).

2.3.2. Arguments Against a Grammaticalization Account of the Saramaccan Definite Determiner

In section 2.1.3.1.1, I showed that, except for word order, the properties of the Saramaccan definite determiner *di* are the same as those of the corresponding lexical item in the substrate languages. In 2.2.3, I stated that the English form *this,* which occurs prenominally (e.g., *this* N), was used to relabel the definite determiner of the substrate languages of Saramaccan. One might wonder, however, whether *this > disi/di* was actually incorporated into Saramaccan as a demonstrative determiner and later became a definite determiner through grammaticalization. Bruyn (1995) makes a proposal along these lines for Sranan, and she extends it to Saramaccan. Bruyn writes (116–117): "In present day Saramaccan, *di* is the DEF-SG, and deixis is expressed by *alá* 'there,' *akí* 'here' and *dé* 'there' in post-N position (De Groot 1977; Rountree 1992). In the 18th century, *di* as well as *disi* could convey deixis."

For several reasons, I disagree with Bruyn's reading of the historical facts. First, *alá* and *akí* were already used as demonstratives in early Saramaccan, as we saw in 2.1.3.1.3. Second, Bruyn (1995) provides no evidence in support of her claim that prenominal *disi* (spelled *dissi* in early texts) could convey deixis. Both Riemer's (1779) and Schumann's (1778) dictionaries, however, gloss the single lexical entry *dissi/di* as *der, die, das*

'DEF SG, masculine, feminine, neuter' and *dieser, diese, dieses* or 'DEM SG, masculine, feminine, neuter.' This might support Bruyn's claim. However, both Riemer and Schumann have a single lexical entry represented as *dissi/di*. Lefebvre (2012) argues that there must have been two lexical entries labeled as *dissi* in early Saramaccan. One was *dissi/di*, the prenominal definite anaphoric determiner in Saramaccan, corresponding to Fongbe *ɔ́*. In this case, *ɔ́* was relabeled as *dissi* on the basis of the English prenominal demonstrative term *this* (e.g., *this* N), yielding *dissi,* which was later reduced to *di* by syllable truncation (see following text). The other was *dissi*, a demonstrative term of Saramaccan corresponding to Fongbe *élɔ́* 'this.' In this case, *élɔ́* was relabeled as *dissi* on the basis of the English demonstrative term *this* occurring in isolation (e.g., 'I want *this,*' etc.). In Saramaccan, this demonstrative term does not reduce to *di*. Thus, in Lefebvre's (2012) account, *dissi/di* and *dissi* constitute two different lexical entries, each of which corresponds to two different substrate lexical entries that were relabeled on the basis of the same English form occurring in different contexts.

As well, reduction of *disi* to *di* may support a grammaticalization account of the data. This argument is weakened, however, in view of the following facts. The reduction of *disi* to *di* is in fact a case of syllable truncation. This process is productive in Saramaccan and in other Surinamese creoles. As shown in the examples in (61), it can apply to various lexical categories without involving grammaticalization.

(61) *fási* 'manner'   → *fá* 'manner'   SARAMACCAN
     sábi 'to know'   → *sá* 'to know'
     lóbi 'to like/love' → *ló* 'to like/love'
     ábi 'to have (to)'   → *a*   'to have (to)'   (Rountree et al. 2000)

Moreover, syllable truncation already existed in early Saramaccan, as is attested in Schumann (1778). The following examples further show that the process need not involve grammaticalization.

(62) *falá*   'to chatter, → *fa₁* 'to chatter, SARAMACCAN
     (<Port. *falar*) to chat'   to chat'
     fasi   'manner'   → *fa₂* 'manner'   (Schumann 1778)

Moreover, the grammaticalization account in Bruyn (1995) does not explain the fact that the properties of *disi/di*, including its anaphoric properties, are so similar to those of the corresponding lexical entries in the substrate languages, as we saw in 2.1.3.1.1. Finally, the synchronic properties of the nominal structure of Saramaccan appear to have been established quite early in the short history of the language, as we saw in section 2.1.3. This does not support a grammaticalization account of the Saramaccan determiner.

My conclusion is thus that there is little evidence supporting an analysis in which *disi* entered Saramaccan as a demonstrative term. The relabeling analysis proposed in section 2.2.2, however, accounts straightforwardly for the fact that the bulk of the properties of Saramaccan *di* reproduce those of the substrate definite determiner. These properties include its anaphoric nature, as well as its distribution in nominal and clausal structures.

2.3.3. Arguments Against a Grammaticalization Account of Saramaccan *Táa*

Several authors have proposed a grammaticalization account of Saramaccan *táa,* which was discussed in section 2.1.3.3 (e.g., Arends 1997; Bakker et al. 1995; Byrne 1987; McWhorter 1992; Veenstra 1996a, 1996b; see also Heine & Kuteva 2005). According to this account, the verb *táki* was grammaticalized as a *that*-type complementizer. In the process, *táki* was reduced to *táa.* Lefebvre and Loranger (2008) argue against this proposal on the following grounds.

First, the aforementioned proposals assume that *táa* was phonologically derived from *táki.* As Lefebvre and Loranger (2008) argue in some detail, however, there does not seem to be any well-motivated phonological derivation of *táa* from *táki.* Second, methodologically speaking, the proposal suffers from a lack of data-based evidence of the process. The grammaticalization of *táa* from verb to complementizer thus appears to have been assumed rather than demonstrated. In addition, a reliable way to argue for grammaticalization is to show that, at some point, the hypothesized grammaticalized form was not attested, and that, at some other point, it was. This is the methodology adopted by Arends (1997). On the basis of two early Saramaccan texts written between 1790 and 1818—the Saramaka Maroon Letters, and chapters 1 through 14 of the Acts of the Apostles, written by Wietz, a Moravian missionary (Arends & Perl (eds.) 1995)—Arends concludes that the only complementizer in use in early Saramaccan was *fa*, and that it is only in modern Saramaccan that *táa* has become a *that*-type complementizer. In this analysis, a grammaticalization account of the relationship between *táki* and *táa* is necessary. Indeed, as Arends (1997) claims, since there is no contact between modern Saramaccan and

English, the sole possible derivation for *táa* involves grammaticalization from *táki*. While the sources cited by Arends may contain no instance of *táa* used as a complementizer, the data presented in Lefebvre and Loranger (2008: 1197) from letters written in 1882 and cited in Schuchardt (1914: 39, 41) show that, at that time, *táa* was already used as a verb meaning 'to tell,' as an introducer of quotations, and possibly as a complementizer. This suggests that, in early Saramaccan, there may have been two forms, *fa* (from Portuguese) and *táa* (from English), both of which had more or less the same functions as the corresponding lexical items in the substrate languages of Saramaccan.

Furthermore, from a general point of view, the grammaticalization scenario of the relationship between *táki* and *táa* is doubtful because the two items do not have the same properties and because their respective matches are different substrate lexical entries: Saramaccan *táki* matches verbal lexical entries meaning 'to say' and having all the properties of verbs in the African substrate languages, whereas *táa* matches more versatile lexical items that do not have all the properties of verbs in those languages. Finally, the multifunctionality of the relevant substrate lexical entries constitutes an areal feature of African languages that existed at the time the creole was formed (Güldemann 2001, 2002). Thus, it is reasonable to hypothesize that the creole lexical entries involved started out just like the corresponding substrate ones and that they were both created by relabeling.

Consequently, Lefebvre and Loranger (2008) propose that substrate verbs meaning 'to say' and having all the properties of verbs were relabeled on the basis of English *talk*, yielding Saramaccan *táki*, which has all the properties of a verb. The more versatile substrate lexical entries that fulfilled the functions of verb, complementizer, quotation introducer, and conjunction of similarity or manner, but did not necessarily manifest all the properties of verbs, were relabeled as *táa* on the basis of English *tell*. *Táki* is derived from *talk* to which an epenthetic vowel has been added. Insertion of epenthetic vowels was a productive process in the interpretation of English phonetic strings by the creators of Saramaccan; it was applied to make open syllables out of closed ones (Smith 1987). *Táa* is derived from *tell,* just as English *fell* or *fall* was realized as *fáa* in Saramaccan. According to Lefebvre and Loranger (2008), this derivation entailed the following steps: lowering of [ɛ] to [a], insertion of an epenthetic vowel, and /l/ deletion between two /a/s, as illustrated in (63).

(63) *fell* > *fál* > *fála* > *fáa*
     tell > *tál* > *tála* > *táa*

This derivation is fully argued for in Lefebvre and Loranger (2008).[22] It constitutes a straightforward account of all the properties of Saramaccan *táa* shown in (39). It thus appears that the relabeling account of the historical derivation of Saramaccan *táa* is more accurate than the grammaticalization account.[23]

This discussion of the origin of the Saramaccan definite determiner *dissi/di* and of the complementizer *táa* raises the question of whether *all* the functional categories of creoles result from relabeling. This is the question to which I now turn.

2.3.4. Do All the Functional Categories of Creoles Result from Relabeling?

Do all the functional categories of a given creole result from relabeling? I believe that the answer to this question is no, and that each case should be argued on its own merits. For example, Haitian has an indefinite determiner *yon* 'a.' Several authors claim that *yon* is derived from French *un* 'a.' Although some comparative work remains to be done on this lexical item, researchers who have worked on Haitian, French, and Fongbe agree that the properties of *yon* are closer to those of the Fongbe postnominal indefinite determiner *ɖé* 'a' (< *ɔ́ɖé* 'one') than to those of the French prenominal indefinite determiner *un* 'a' (Lefebvre 1998: 87–89). Given this situation, one could conclude that Haitian *yon* is the result of the relabeling of the postnominal indefinite determiner of the substrate languages on the basis of the French prenominal form *un*. This would not constitute an optimal account of the historical derivation of *yon*, however, for the following reasons. As stated in section 2.2.1, the superstrate form that provides the new label for the substrate lexical entry must be salient. The French indefinite determiner *un* is unaccented; it is therefore not salient. Like the French definite determiners (see (48)), it was not identified as such by the creators of Haitian. This is evidenced by the following data: *nanm* 'soul, spirit,' where the initial *n* comes from the *liaison* between the indefinite determiner *une* and *âme* in French ([yna:m]); *nonm* 'man, guy,' where the initial *n* comes from the *liaison* between the indefinite determiner *un* and *homme* in French ([(œ̃nɔm]), and so on. Furthermore, Haitian *yon* cannot possibly have been phonologically derived from *un* [œ̃]. According to Brousseau and Nikiema (2006), the French phoneme /œ̃/ is realized as /ɛ̃/ in Haitian

---

[22.] I am indebted to Juliette Blevins for her help in formulating the phonological arguments challenging a grammaticalization account of Saramaccan *táa*.
[23.] Bruyn (2009) refers to such cases as "apparent" cases of grammaticalization, and Heine and Kuteva (2005) call them cases of polysemy copying.

(e.g., Fr. *brun* [brœ̃] 'brown' > H. *bren* [brɛ̃] 'brown'). If *yon* had been derived from [œ̃], it would be the only case of this phonetic correspondence in the language.

In view of this evidence, I maintain the analysis in Lefebvre (1998: 87–89), which has the following features. The Fongbe numeral *ɖé* 'one' was relexified as *younn* 'one,' on the basis of the French feminine accented form of the numeral 'one' *úne* (where the acute accent represents stress, as in *J'en veux úne* 'I want one'). Brousseau and Nikiema (2006) argue that the phonological interpretation of *úne* as *younn* by the creators of Haitian is similar to the interpretation of *eux* as *yo*. The form *younn* was then grammaticalized as *yon* 'a,' an indefinite determiner, through resyllabification. In this view, *yon* occurs prenominally because it evolved from the numeral *younn* and numerals are prenominal in Haitian (e.g., *de ti-moun* 'two children'), following the French word order (see Chapter 5). Since *yon* 'a' must be derived from Haitian *younn* 'one,' which must be derived from French *úne* 'one,' Haitian *yon* cannot have been created by relabeling. It must have been created through grammaticalization. The Saramaccan indefinite determiner may have been created in a similar way, through the grammaticalization of *wan* 'one' as an indefinite determiner (see Bruyn 1995, 1996, for an analysis of the grammaticalization of *wan* 'one' > 'a' in Sranan).

In conclusion, unlike scholars who claim that, in creole genesis, all functional categories are created through grammaticalization, I prefer to consider each case on its own merits. In this view, Saramaccan *disi/di*, like Haitian *la* (and allomorphs), can be argued to have been created through relabeling. In contrast, Haitian *yon* 'a,' like Saramaccan *wan* 'a,' can be argued to have been created through grammaticalization. In my view, claims about grammaticalization in creole genesis should be restricted to cases based on clear evidence, such as those discussed above or in section 3.2.1, where one can actually see the content word making its way through a subsystem of functional categories.

2.3.5. Summary

This section reviewed the positions of scholars who hold that functional categories can only acquire a label through grammaticalization. Grammaticalization accounts of two functional categories were reviewed and argued against, in favor of relabeling accounts. It was shown that some functional categories acquire their label by means of relabeling and some by means of grammaticalization. Criteria were proposed to help distinguish between the two processes.

2.4. Predictions of a Relabeling-Based Account of Creole Genesis

The relabeling-based account of creole genesis makes several predictions. First, the nature of relabeling predicts a principled division of the properties of a creole's lexical entries between its source languages. Lexical entries produced by this process are predicted to have the semantic and syntactic properties of the original substrate lexical entries and phonological representations derived from a phonetic string in the superstrate language. This prediction is borne out: for Haitian, see Koopman (1986), Lefebvre (1998, and the references therein, 2003, 2004a, 2004b), and Lumsden (1999);[24] for Ndjuka, see Huttar (1975) and Migge (1998); for Sranan, see Voorhoeve (1973); for Saramaccan, see Smith (1987) and Lefebvre and Loranger (2006, 2008); for Solomon Islands Pijin, see Keesing (1988) and Terrill and Dunn (2006). An overall picture of the principled contributions of the substrate and superstrate languages will be provided in the following chapters of this book.

Since relabeling starts with the substrate lexicon, our account predicts that the composition of the substrate lexicon will be determinative in the makeup of creoles' lexicons. If relabeling is indeed a central process in creole genesis, superstrate lexical entries that have no corresponding entries in the substrate languages are predicted not to enter the creole. This prediction, too, is borne out. For example, the French simplexes referring to body parts in (64) do not exist in Haitian. This is because, as shown in (64), the substrate languages did not have corresponding simplexes to relabel. Not surprisingly, Haitian, like Fongbe, encodes body parts by means of compounds.

(64)	FRENCH	HAITIAN	FONGBE	
	lèvre	po-bouch	nù-fló	'lip'
		'skin-mouth'	'mouth-skin'	
	narine	twou-ne	àɔntín-dó	'nostril'
		'hole-nose'	'nose-hole'	
	cil	plim-je	wùn-ɖà	'eyelash'
		'hair-eye'	'eye-hair'	
	nuque	dèyè-kou	kɔ̀-gùdó	'nape'
		'back-neck'	'neck-back'	
	crâne	kalbas-tèt	tà-ká	'skull'
		'calabash-head'	'head-calabash'	
		or tèt-kalbas		(from Brousseau 1989)

---

[24] It is therefore not the case that, as DeGraff (2003: 392) claims, the Haitian lexicon "is mostly derived from French."

Furthermore, the data in (64) show that the creators of the creole used the principles of their own grammar in concatenating words into compounds. However, as the examples in (64) show, the word order in Haitian compounds is opposite to that in Fongbe compounds. According to the analysis in Brousseau (1989), word order in a creole's compounds is established on the basis of word order in syntactic phrases in a given language. So, the word order in *po-bouch* 'lip' replicates that of the corresponding Haitian syntactic phrase *po bouch* 'skin of the mouth,' which, in turn, replicates that of French, the superstrate language, *peau de la bouche*.

Another example involves the paradigm of Wh-words. As shown in (65), French has 12 Wh-words. In contrast, Haitian has only four. (The morpheme in parentheses is optionally pronounced.)

(65) FRENCH   HAITIAN

lequel/laquelle/
lesquels/lesquelles 'which one(s)'   *ki-lès*   'which one'
qui   'who'
que/quoi   'what'   *(ki-)sa*   'what'
où   'where'
quand   'when'
comment   'how'   *kouman*   'how'
combien   'how much,   *konbyen*   'how much,
                   how many'   how many'
pourquoi   'why'

                                          (= (5) in Brousseau 1995)

This situation raises three questions. First, why did the other French Wh-simplexes not make their way into Haitian? Second, why did Haitian end up with exactly four Wh-words? Third, why did it end up with these particular four Wh-words rather than a different subset? Consider the inventories of Wh-words and Wh-phrases in Haitian and Fongbe shown in (66). Tests distinguishing Wh-words from Wh-phrases are discussed at length in Lefebvre (1998: 171–181), based on Brousseau (1995). Lefebvre (1998: 177–178) also discusses the fact that *nĕgbɔn* 'how' in Fongbe is lexicalized. (Morphemes in parentheses are optionally pronounced.)

(66)   HAITIAN   FONGBE
     a. Wh-words: *ki-lès*   *ɖè-té*   'which one'
                  (ki-)sa   *(é-) té/àní*   'what'
                  kouman   *nĕgbɔn*   'how'
                  konbyen   *nàbí*   'how many/much'

b.	Wh-phrases:	*ki moun*	*mè té*	'which person/who'

b. Wh-phrases:
ki moun	*mè té*	'which person/who'
ki bagay	*nú té*	'which thing/what'
(ki) kote/ki bò	*fí (té)*	'which place/where'
ki jan	*àlɔ té*	'which manner/how'
ki kalite	*àlɔkpà té*	'which kind/how'
ki lè	*hwènù té*	'which moment/time/ when'
pu ki(-sa)	*(é) té (w)ú(tú)/ àní (w)ú(tú)*	'what, cause/why'

(= (93) in Lefebvre 1998: 178)

As the data in (66) show, Fongbe also has only four Wh-simplexes and uses Wh-phrases in other cases. The reason that eight of the French Wh-simplexes did not become part of the creole is that the lexicon of the substrate speakers did not have corresponding simplexes to be relabeled. The four Wh-simplexes in Haitian correspond to the four Wh-simplexes in Fongbe. For the rest, Haitian uses Wh-phrases, similarly to Fongbe. Again, the difference in word order between Haitian and Fongbe Wh-phrases is consistent with the generalization that word order in creoles primarily follows that of the superstrate language, as will be discussed at length in Chapter 5. The Haitian quantifier-noun word order follows the French quantifier-noun order rather than the Fongbe noun-quantifier order.

The third prediction made by the relabeling-based account of creole genesis is that, since relabeling is constrained by what the superstrate has available to relabel a substrate lexical entry, in some cases, the superstrate language will not present enough different forms to relabel the semantic distinctions manifested in the substrate lexical entries. Data involving verbs of cutting in Fongbe and Haitian exemplify this situation. They are discussed in Chapter 7, section 4.2.

A fourth prediction is that the substrate languages will determine the parametric options of a creole. In a framework in which parametric options are formulated in terms of correlations between the availability of x (a parametric option) and that of y (a functional category) in a given grammar and lexicon, and given that functional categories do undergo relabeling, it follows that the substrate languages will determine a creole's parametric options. This prediction is borne out by the Haitian data discussed in Koopman (1986) and Lefebvre (1998: 349–375).[25]

---

[25] The one apparent exception to this general pattern, raised by DeGraff (1992a), concerns the null subject parameter. Assuming that the availability of syntactic clitics defines a language as a null

In conclusion, the predictions made by the relabeling account of creole genesis are borne out overall.

2.5. The Extent of Relabeling Is a Function of the Relative Exposure to L_2

As stated in the Introduction to this chapter, the account of creole genesis proposed here is a further development of the second-language acquisition theory of creole genesis in which relabeling is used by speakers of the substrate languages as the main tool for acquiring the superstrate language. In this view, the amount of relabeling in particular situations is a function of the relative exposure of the substrate community to the superstrate language. Creoles that most closely resemble their superstrate languages were created in communities where the speakers of the substrate languages had more access to the superstrate community (Lefebvre & Lumsden 1994a). Creoles that are more radical (i.e., less like the superstrate language) come from communities where language learners had less access to the superstrate community. For example, as Valdman (1993) argues, Louisiana Creole is closer to French than Haitian is because the African population had more access to French in Louisiana than in Haiti. Baker and Corne (1982) also discuss this issue on the basis of data from Mauritius and Reunion creoles. On Reunion, French native speakers outnumbered substrate speakers during the formative period of the creole and Reunion creole grammar displays a significant number of French grammatical categories. By contrast, during the formative period of Mauritius creole, the proportion of native French speakers was much lower and thus the African speakers had much more input into the creole. The extent of relabeling in the formation of a given creole is thus directly correlated with the degree of exposure to the superstrate language: the less access to the superstrate

---

subject language (Hulk 1986; Jaeggli 1984; Roberge 1990), both French and Fongbe are such languages because they have syntactic clitics. (Arguments supporting the analysis of French and Fongbe pronominal clitics as syntactic clitics may be found in Lefebvre 1998: 148–157, and the references cited therein.) Unlike both its source languages, Haitian is not a null subject language because it does not have syntactic clitics (e.g., Cadely 1994; Déprez 1992a; Law 1992; contra DeGraff 1992a). (The debate concerning the syntactic, as opposed to phonological, status of Haitian clitics is reported in detail in Lefebvre 1998: 148–157.) According to the analysis in Brousseau (1995), however, the fact that Haitian does not have syntactic clitics is not a counterexample to the relabeling-based account of creole genesis. Rather, it follows from how functional categories were relabeled. Brousseau's account is summarized in section 3.2.2.

language, the more relabeling takes place; the more access to the superstrate language, the more acquisition takes place.[26]

2.6. Summary

In this section, it was shown that lexical entries of all syntactic categories, free or bound, may undergo relabeling, provided that they have some semantic content and that the superstrate language has an appropriate form to relabel the substrate lexical entry. Lexical entries that do not have any semantic content or for which there is no appropriate form in the superstrate are assigned a null form at relabeling. Such lexical entries may eventually acquire a phonological representation through grammaticalization (see following discussion). It was argued that, in creole genesis, functional categories can be created either by relabeling or by grammaticalization. Substrate lexical entries, free or bound, were shown to be relabeled on the basis of salient free forms in the superstrate language. The claim that relabeling is a central process in creole genesis makes a number of predictions that were shown to be borne out by the data. Finally, the amount of relabeling in the formation of a particular creole was shown to be a function of the relative exposure to L_2 (the superstrate language).

3. The Interplay of Relabeling and Other Processes

As was mentioned in the creole genesis scenario in section 1, other processes that play a role in situations of language change in general are also involved in the further development of a creole. In the case of incipient creoles, however, these processes are hypothesized to apply to the output of relabeling, that is, on the relabeled lexicons. I will discuss the following processes and their relationship with relabeling: leveling, grammaticalization, reanalysis, and diffusion across the lexicon.

3.1. Relabeling and Leveling

Recall from the scenario of creole genesis in section 1 that relabeling is a mental process; as such, it is an individual process. Typically, situations in which pidgins and creoles emerge involve several substrate languages. Each individual speaker of one of the substrate languages relabels his or

---

[26.]Note that complete acquisition of L_2 is a rather rare phenomenon, in spite of full exposure to that language. See Lardière (2006) for an extensive discussion of this issue.

her own lexicon. The relabeling of several lexicons on the basis of a single superstrate language provides the early creole community with a common vocabulary. However, in relabeling, speakers of different substrate languages reproduce the idiosyncratic semantic and syntactic properties of their own lexicons; thus, the product of relabeling is not uniform across the early creole community. In this view, the variation found in an early creole community is the product of the relabeling of various substrate lexicons (Lumsden & Lefebvre 1994). For example, the relabeling of the lexicons of languages X, Y, and Z on the basis of a single superstrate language may yield slightly different lexicons in an incipient creole. This is schematically represented in (67).

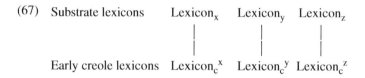

(67)   Substrate lexicons $Lexicon_x$ $Lexicon_y$ $Lexicon_z$

       Early creole lexicons $Lexicon_c^x$ $Lexicon_c^y$ $Lexicon_c^z$

Leveling may apply to the output of relabeling to level out the variation found in the early creole. In the process, different communities may choose different options, as will be illustrated in the following discussion.

For example, with respect to plural marking in Caribbean creoles (sections 2.1.3.1.2 and 2.2.5), the substrate languages offered two options: the Ewegbe type, in which the same morpheme encodes both the third-person plural personal pronoun and the plural in nominal structures (see (28)), and the Fongbe type, in which the third-person plural personal pronoun and the plural in nominal structures are encoded by two separate morphemes (see (29)). By hypothesis, both options (see (58)) were available in the early Caribbean creole communities since they all have essentially the same pool of substrate languages. So, on the one hand, West African speakers who were relabeling Ewegbe-type lexicons ended up with one morpheme encoding both third-person plural personal pronoun and plural in nominal structures. On the other hand, West African speakers who were relabeling Fongbe-type lexicons ended up with two morphemes: one encoding the third-person plural personal pronoun and one encoding plural in nominal structures. Presumably, these two types competed in early creole communities. Based on synchronic data, it appears that the Haitian and Saramaccan speakers settled on the Ewegbe type (see (25), (26)), whereas the Martinican speakers settled on the Fongbe type (see (30)).

This shows that leveling operates on the output of relabeling and that, in the process, different communities may make different choices. Other cases of leveling are discussed in Lefebvre (1998: 110, 137–139). They involve possessive constructions and tense, mood, and aspect markers in Haitian Creole. Lefebvre (2001) analyzes cases of leveling involving demonstrative terms, discussed in section 2.2.3.1.3, and ways of encoding reflexivity in Caribbean creoles. Lefebvre and Therrien (2007b) discuss cases of leveling involving prepositions and conjunctions. It is important to note that, although leveling *can* apply, it *need not* do so. Indeed, several cases of variation in modern Haitian can be argued to reproduce the variation observed between its substrate languages (e.g., Lefebvre 1998, Chapter 4), and even the variation between speakers of the same language (e.g., Lefebvre 1998, Chapter 8).

3.2. Relabeling, Grammaticalization, and Reanalysis

In Lefebvre (1998), grammaticalization is not distinguished from reanalysis, and cases of grammaticalization are treated as cases of reanalysis. Following Lefebvre (2009a), in this section, I will treat the two processes as separate. I will situate the discussion on grammaticalization and reanalysis within Haspelmath's (1998) paradigm, in which the two processes are considered to be distinct. According to Haspelmath (1998: 318), grammaticalization "is the gradual drift in all parts of the grammar towards tighter structures, towards less freedom in the use of linguistic expressions at all levels. Specifically, lexical items develop into grammatical items in particular constructions, which often means that independent words turn into clitics and affixes." The process is gradual; it is unidirectional; it is not necessarily initiated by children, and thus, it takes place in the course not of language acquisition but of language use. In contrast—still according to Haspelmath—reanalysis involves structural ambiguity, that is, a surface string that could be produced by two different grammars. The agents of reanalysis are children; the locus of the process is thus language acquisition. The process is reversible since it consists in assigning a surface string one of two possible analyses. It is abrupt since it results in identifying one of two possible grammars for a given surface string. In Haspelmath's view, reanalysis and grammaticalization are distinguished because grammaticalization is associated with either adults or children, while reanalysis is associated only with children. Keeping the two processes separate may thus possibly help to distinguish the contributions of children from those of adults to the makeup of a creole.

3.2.1. Relabeling and Grammaticalization

I take grammaticalization to be a process whereby a form that is the phonological representation of a lexical category becomes the phonological representation of a functional category (e.g., Heine 1997). I assume that the process is syntactically local. Within the framework developed in this chapter, what is special about it in the development of a creole is the fact that grammaticalization can provide a label for a functional category that was not able to be relabeled. In this view, a covert lexical entry in the creole may surface as the result of grammaticalization. The now overt lexical entry is expected to manifest the properties of the corresponding substrate lexical entry (Lefebvre & Lumsden 1994a).

A classic example of grammaticalization in a developing creole involves the Tok Pisin adverb *baimbai*, grammaticalized as an aspectual marker. According to the analysis by Sankoff and Laberge (1973), this lexical item started out as a sentence-initial adverb meaning 'later,' marking the clause it is part of as irrealis. Sankoff and Laberge (1973) analyze the grammaticalization of *baimbai* as involving the four steps listed in (68).

(68) a. Reduction from *baimbai* to *bai*.
      b. Progressive loss of stress of the monosyllabic form: *bai* to *b'*.
      c. Co-occurrence with adverbs having future meaning.
      d. Word order change from sentence-initial position to preverbal position.

As this presentential adverb was reduced to *bai*, it moved to a position between the subject and the verb. The two positions of this adverb are illustrated in (69a) and (69b), respectively.

(69) a. *Baimbai*   *ologeta*   *wok*   *bilong*   *yumi,*   *i*   *ken*
          later   all   work   of   us   PR   FUT-POSSIB
          kamap.   TOK PISIN
          grow
          'Later, all our work will (be able to) flourish.' (= (2) in Sankoff 1991)

      b. *Mi*   *bai*   *kisim*.   TOK PISIN
          I   FUT   get-TR
          'I'll get it.'   (= (9) in Sankoff 1991)

From this latter position, *bai/b'* eventually became the phonological representation of a functional category that Sankoff identifies as aspect. As Sankoff (1991: 73) puts it, the Tok Pisin category made visible by grammaticalization has the same properties as the corresponding categories in the creole's substrate languages: "The changes ongoing in the Tok Pisin tense and aspect system are making it more like many of the substrate languages, in which tense is quite subsidiary to aspect. But this change is being led by young speakers who do not command substrate grammars, as their parents did and do." This situation creates a paradox that Sankoff (73) proposes to resolve as follows. She suggests that, when using *bai* between the subject and the verb, what the adult non-native speakers of Tok Pisin "did mark was aspect, a category more important than tense in the grammars of the languages they spoke natively. There always has been a stronger relationship between the use of these markers for aspect than for tense in the speech of adults, and this is, I propose, what the native speakers are building on in carrying forth more sweeping changes than their parents were able to do." Assuming this analysis to be correct, this strongly suggests that the properties of the newly emerging category in the creole are due neither to chance nor to universals.

Within the framework presented here, this situation results from the interaction between relabeling and grammaticalization, whereby the latter provides a label for a functional category that could not have been relabeled at the time when relabeling was taking place (Lefebvre & Lumsden 1994a). In this view, the aspectual marker of the substrate languages of Tok Pisin could not be relabeled, and thus it remained covert in the incipient creole. This functional category was nonetheless signaled by the adult, non-native speakers of Tok Pisin in their use of *bai*. Through grammaticalization, *bai* revealed the properties of the hitherto covert functional category in Tok Pisin. As predicted by the relabeling-based account of creole genesis, these properties turned out to be the same as those of the corresponding items in Tok Pisin's substrate languages, that is, aspectual.

The Haitian definite-future marker *ap*, discussed in section 2.1.3.2, has been assigned a similar analysis. Lefebvre (1996) hypothesizes that this morpheme started out as a presentential temporal adverb, *aprè* < French *après* 'after.' After moving to a position between the subject and the verb and being morphophonemically reduced to *ap*, it became a definite-future marker. So, whereas the grammaticalization of *baimbai* as *bai/b'* in Tok Pisin reproduces the properties of the corresponding lexical item in the Austronesian substrate languages, namely aspect, the grammaticalization of *aprè* as *ap* in Haitian reproduces the properties of the corresponding item in the West African substrate languages, namely irrealis mood.

3.2.2. Relabeling and Reanalysis

Recall that, according to Haspelmath (1998), reanalysis involves structural ambiguity, that is, a surface string that may be produced by two different grammars. The agents of reanalysis are children. Thus, the locus of reanalysis is language acquisition. In the data that I have come across over the years, one set clearly fits this definition. These data involve pronouns and pronominal clitics. The relevant facts and analyses in the following discussion are summarized from Lefebvre (1998), based on Brousseau (1995).

Both the substrate and superstrate languages of Haitian have paradigms of personal pronouns and of pronominal clitics, subject and object, that are syntactic as opposed to phonological (Lefebvre 1998: 148–157). Haitian has its own paradigm of personal pronouns. These can appear in full and reduced forms. The reduced pronominal forms cliticize onto a major category lexical item (noun, verb, or preposition). Many researchers have argued that these clitic forms are phonological rather than syntactic clitics (e.g., Cadely 1994; Déprez 1992a; contra DeGraff 1992a, 1992b, 1992c); in their view, Haitian does not have syntactic clitics, in contrast to both of its source languages. Assuming that syntactic clitics should be able to undergo relabeling, since they have some semantic content, how can one account for the fact that Haitian Creole has no syntactic clitics?

In agreement with the general proposal that functional items are relabeled on the basis of salient, free forms in the superstrate, Brousseau (1995) proposes that the creators of Haitian relabeled the clitics of their own lexicon using French strong personal pronouns. For example, in this view, all three Fongbe first-person singular pronominal forms (i.e., the first-person singular strong pronominal form, the first-person singular subject clitic, and the first-person singular object clitic) were relabeled on the basis of French *moi* 'me,' yielding *mwen* in Haitian, as shown in (70) (where [+/– argument] stands for strong and weak forms, respectively).

(70)		Fongbe	Haitian
a.	[1st], [–plural], [+argument]	*nyè*	*mwen*
b.	[1st], [–plural], [–argument], [+nominative]	*un*	*mwen*
c.	[1st], [–plural], [–argument], [–nominative]	*mì*	*mwen*

Consequently, in the incipient creole, there would have been three homophonous forms for the first-person singular pronominal lexical entries. The availability, in the incipient creole, of the lexical entries in (70) would enable the creators of Haitian, who had both strong and weak pronominal forms in their original lexicons, to reproduce these forms in the creole. However, the use of the same superstrate form to relabel several lexical entries in the substrate language(s) resulted in redundancy in the newly created lexicon. Brousseau (1995) proposes that the three homophonous Haitian lexical entries in (70) were reduced to one, yielding a single Haitian lexical entry unspecified for the features [α argument] and [α nominative], as shown in (71).

(71)   /mwen/: [1st], [–plural]   HAITIAN

The fact that the lexical entry in (71) is not specified for the feature [α argument] enabled the creators of Haitian, who had both strong and weak pronominal forms in their original lexicons, to produce these forms while speaking the creole. However, whether the first generation of Haitian native speakers were exposed to the data in (70) or in (71), they had no way of distinguishing between strong and weak forms on the basis of these data. Brousseau also proposes that the first generation of Haitian native speakers could not deduce the availability of syntactic clitics based on the data that they were exposed to. Presumably, they interpreted these data as in (72).

(72)   /mwen/: [1st], [–plural], [+argument]   HAITIAN

The reanalysis of (71) as (72) by children would explain why Haitian Creole differs from both of its source languages in not having syntactic clitics.

The reanalysis of (71) as (72) could not be attributed to the adults who relabeled their native lexicons on the basis of French. As we saw above, these speakers would have used the same form for both the strong and weak pronominal forms when speaking the creole. Only children would have had the possibility of interpreting the data they encountered as either strong or weak forms. The reanalysis of (71) as (72) thus constitutes a case that must be attributed to children.

3.3. Relabeling and Diffusion Through the Lexicon

Another process that plays a role in the further development of creoles is diffusion across the lexicon. Diffusion is a process that consists in the spreading of a feature to a wider range of lexical items, on the basis of a small set of examples (e.g., Bybee 2006, and the references therein). I will illustrate this process on the basis of data involving the double-object construction. I take double-object verbs to be involved in the Recipient-Theme construction (NP NP), as in *John sent Mary a letter*, as opposed to the Theme-Locative construction (NP PP), as in *John sent a letter to Mary*. The content of this section draws on Lefebvre (1994c, 1998, 2009a) and on Lefebvre and Lambert-Brétière (2014).

In Fongbe, only six or seven verbs (depending on the speaker) participate in the Recipient-Theme construction (Lefebvre & Lambert-Brétière 2014). These verbs are listed in (73).

(73) | *ná* | 'to give' | *xwlé* | 'to offer' | FONGBE |
xélé	'to show'	*byɔ́*	'to ask'
kplɔ́n	'to teach'	*tɛ̀*	'to refuse'
sú	'to pay' (for some speakers but not all)

(from Lefebvre & Lambert-Brétière 2014)

According to the relabeling-based account of creole genesis, we would expect to find the same range and inventory of double-object verbs in a creole as in its substrate languages. In the case of Saramaccan, this expectation is borne out, as only a few verbs in this language participate in the double-object construction. Compare the Saramaccan data in (74), from two sources,[27] with the Fongbe data in (73).

(74) | *da* | 'to give' | *da* | 'to give' | SARAMACCAN |
lei	'to show, to teach'	*lei*	'to show'
paka	'to pay'	*paka*	'to pay'
sei	'to sell'	*leni*	'to lend'
(from Bally et al. 2006)		(from McWhorter & Good 2012)

In Haitian Creole, however, there is a much wider range of verbs that can participate in the double-object construction. On the basis of Valdman et al. (1981), Védrine (1992), and a few additions from my field notes, 22 double-object verbs were identified (Lefebvre 1998: 298). Papiamentu has even more double-object verbs than Haitian does. Olguín (2006) provides a list of some 45 double-object verbs for this language. A few examples are presented in (75).

---

[27] Note that the two lists are not exactly the same. In my view, this reflects variation among speakers.

(75)	PAPIAMENTU	SPANISH	ENGLISH
	anunsiá	*<anunciar*	'to announce'
	bisa	*<avisar*	'to say, to tell, to notify'
	dal	*<dar*	'to deliver (a blow)'
	debe	*<deber*	'to owe'
	debolbé	*<devolver*	'to give back'
	dediká	*<dedicar*	'to dedicate'

(from Olguín 2006)

Can the discrepancy between the range of double-object verbs in Haitian and Papiamentu versus their substrate languages be attributed to the superstrate languages? The answer to this question is clearly negative. French and Portuguese/Spanish, which participated in the formation of Haitian, Papiamentu, and Saramaccan, do not have double-object verbs. While English, which also participated in the formation of Saramaccan, has a wide range of double-object verbs, Saramaccan has only a few, as we saw in (74).

Do these data constitute counterexamples to the relabeling-based account of creole genesis? By hypothesis, after relabeling, the incipient creoles (e.g., Haitian or Papiamentu) would have had the same inventory of double-object verbs as, say, Fongbe, Ewegbe, and so on. Also by hypothesis, in the incipient creole of the Gbe speakers, other verbs that are Recipient-Theme verbs in the modern creole would have had the same argument structure as the corresponding verbs in the substrate languages. As Lefebvre and Lambert-Brétière (2014) document, in modern Haitian, double-object verbs that do not have a Fongbe double-object verb counterpart also manifest the properties of the corresponding Fongbe verbs. For example, the Haitian verb *voye* 'to send' is a double-object verb (Valdman et al. 1981); the corresponding Fongbe verb *sè* 'to send' is not. In Fongbe, the concept 'to send' is conveyed with a serial verb construction: *sè* . . . *dó* 'send (something) . . . put (somewhere)' (Segurola & Rassinoux 2000). Haitian has a similar construction: *voye* . . . *mèt* 'send (something) . . . put (somewhere)' (Hall 1953: 79). Lefebvre and Lambert-Brétière hypothesize that the latter verbal properties were transferred into the creole by means of relabeling. In Lefebvre (2009a), it is hypothesized that these verbs were later associated with the double-object construction by means of diffusion across the lexicon: the properties of a small set of verbs were diffused (presumably by analogy) to a larger set of verbs. In this view, the fact that modern Haitian and Papiamentu have more double-object verbs than Fongbe does not constitute a counterexample to the relabeling-based account of creole genesis. Rather, it illustrates how diffusion across the lexicon applies in the further development of creoles.

Diffusion across the lexicon applies in the development of creoles in the same way as in other languages. In this case, however, it is hypothesized to apply to the output of relabeling, that is, after the original lexicons have been relabeled on the basis of the superstrate language. Recourse to this process accounts for some of the discrepancies between certain lexical entries in modern creoles and the corresponding ones in the substrate languages.[28] In light of this situation, I suggest that systematic discrepancies of the type discussed above between the properties of substrate and superstrate subsets of lexical items may be used as a diagnostic tool for identifying cases of diffusion across the lexicon in a creole.

3.4. Summary

Processes that play a role in situations of language change in general, such as leveling, grammaticalization, reanalysis, and diffusion across the lexicon, were shown to play a role in the further development of a creole, indicating that relabeling is not the only process involved in the formation of a creole. In the scenario of creole genesis adopted in this study, these processes apply to the relabeled lexicons, thus attesting to the interaction that exists between these processes and relabeling. Mc-Whorter (2008) refers to these other processes as "patches" to our theory. Should leveling, grammaticalization, reanalysis, and so on, be considered as "patches" in other cases of linguistic change? Certainly not. Why then should they be considered as such in the case of creole development? A theory of creole genesis that excluded these processes would be incomplete, because, as we have seen throughout this section, they interact with relabeling in the formation of a creole. Other processes that play a role in language change in general undoubtedly also play a role in the further development of creole languages. These have yet to be documented within the general framework advocated in this chapter. Innovations are also certainly possible, just as they are in the evolution of all natural languages.

---

[28] Lefebvre (2009a) also discusses the possible contribution of the Bantu languages to the range of double-object verbs in Atlantic creoles.

4. Conclusion

4.1. Summary of the Theory

In this chapter, I have presented an overview of the relabeling-based theory of creole genesis, as it has been updated over the last 15 years. This theory is cast within the framework of the major processes at work in language creation and language change in general. In this account, relabeling (a.k.a. relexification) plays an initial and central role in the genesis of creole languages, as it is the mechanism by which a new lexicon is created. The other processes observed in language change, such as leveling, grammaticalization, reanalysis, diffusion across the lexicon, and innovations, apply to the output of relabeling in the further development of a creole, when the members of a creole community are targeting the relabeled lexicons.

Given a theory of the lexicon in which all major category lexical entries, including derivational affixes, and functional categories are listed, as was assumed in the course of this research, words in all syntactic categories, free or bound, are expected to be able to undergo relabeling. This expectation was shown to be borne out by the data. Since relabeling is semantically driven, however, only categories that have some semantic content may undergo this process. Saliency and (partially) shared semantics were shown to be the two essential characteristics required of a suitable item for the relabeling of functional categories. Furthermore, the relabeling of functional categories, whether free or bound, was shown to proceed on the basis of free forms. A substrate lexical entry that cannot be assigned a label at relabeling is assigned a null form. Such lexical entries may acquire labels later through grammaticalization. The relabeling-based account of creole genesis makes several predictions that were shown to be borne out by the data. In my view, a minimalist account of radical creole genesis could be formulated as follows: relabel what you can and let the language evolve as in other cases of linguistic change.

4.2. The Relabeling-Based Theory of Creole Genesis Accounts for All Necessary Properties

The relabeling-based account of creole genesis provides a straightforward and optimal account of all the properties of creole languages listed in section 1.1.[29] It accounts for the facts that creole languages emerge in

---

[29.] This discussion builds on ideas originally set out in Lefebvre and Lumsden (1989, 1994a), and updated in Lefebvre (1998).

multilingual societies where a lingua franca is needed, that the creators of a creole have relatively little access to the superstrate language, and that creole languages are created in a relatively short period of time. Indeed, only one generation of speakers is required to create a new language by means of relabeling. The fact that creoles are generally isolating languages also follows from the above proposal. Indeed, since the functional categories of creole languages derive their labels from major category lexemes in the superstrate language or from grammaticalization, and since these are typically free morphemes, it follows that creoles will tend to be isolating languages, even when they have evolved from agglutinative languages, as in the case of Kriol, discussed in section 2.2.4 (see also Chapter 8 on this issue). By virtue of the nature of relabeling, creole lexical entries are predicted to have the same semantic and syntactic properties as the corresponding lexical entries in the substrate languages, but phonological representations derived from the phonetic strings found in the superstrate language. The relabeling-based account of creole genesis therefore accounts for the fact that creoles reflect the properties of both their superstrate and their substrate source languages in the way they do. Finally, the claim that the bulk of a creole's lexical entries are formed by relabeling is borne out by the extensive study of Haitian and its source languages (Lefebvre 1998, 1999; Lumsden 1999) and several other languages referred to in this chapter. In my view, the data support the relabeling-based theory of creole genesis in a way that surpasses all expectations. To sum up, the relabeling-based account of creole genesis is able to explain all the properties that define an optimal theory of creole genesis. I therefore conclude that it is a strong "plausible alternative" to the Bioprogram Hypothesis.

4.3. Consequences

The fact that relabeling can be demonstrated to play a role in the formation of new languages (e.g., mixed languages, pidgins, and creoles) and in second-language acquisition (Sprouse 2006) argues that this process is available to human cognition. To my knowledge, no one questions this fact. Rather, the debate appears to concern the relative importance of this cognitive process. On the basis of the information provided in Chapter 2 and of the data and analyses presented in this chapter, I believe that relabeling is a very important process. Since it is available to human cognition, it is most likely that, in the course of history, other languages not known to be creoles or mixed languages may have been formed by this process in situations similar to those we know in which mixed and creole languages emerged.[30]

The nature of relabeling provides a means of creating new languages in a relatively short time. Thus, while language change generally proceeds slowly, the process of relabeling produces cases of accelerated linguistic change. Authors disagree as to the length of time it takes to create a creole. Some say one generation suffices (Hancock 1987; Lefebvre 1998; Thomason & Kaufman 1991). Arends (1986, 1993, 1995) claims that it takes between 100 and 200 years to create a creole. Between these two extremes, we find several intermediary positions. The positions taken by the various authors are not so disparate as they may look at first glance, however, when each author's definition of the endpoint is taken into account. (For further discussion of this issue, see Lefebvre 2009a, section 4.)

The nature of the process requires that those who apply it must be speakers in possession of a mature lexicon. The type of change resulting from relabeling is thus initiated by adults, not children. In other words, adults are the principal agents of creole genesis. This calls into question Bickerton's (e.g., 1981, 1984) claim that children are the principal agents of creolization, as well as the claim that linguistic change in general is attributable primarily to children (see also Hopper & Traugott 1993: 211; Labov 2007: 346, note 4). Rather, it appears that adults may initiate important linguistic changes. This conclusion is in line with that of Sankoff (1991) based on Tok Pisin. However, this conclusion does not mean that I think "that nativisation is unimportant," as DeGraff (2002: 383) claims I do. Nor have I ever claimed that children have no role to play in the creation of creole languages. As was shown by Sankoff (1991, and the references therein), discussed in section 3.2.1, the first generation of native speakers of a creole may continue changes that were initiated by their parents, who are not native speakers of the creole. Children are also the agents of reanalysis (see section 3.2.2). Furthermore, Hudson and Newport (1999, 2005) argue that children play an important role in regularizing unpredictable variation. This is undeniably a role that children may also play in the development of a creole, although it has yet to be documented. Furthermore, as I point out in the conclusion to Lefebvre (1998), children

---

[30] Some scholars claim that transfer, rather than relabeling, is the process at work in the formation of creole languages (e.g., Siegel 1997, 2008). In my view, relabeling predicts the properties of radical creole lexical entries more precisely than transfer. For further discussion of this point, see Lefebvre (2009b, section 2.4).

must play an important role in the development of a creole's morphophonemics. My general assumption regarding children's contribution to the development of a creole is that it is similar to children's contribution to language change in general.

The relabeling-based theory of creole genesis presented here calls into question the assumption that all creole languages are alike, as has been advocated by Bickerton (1981, 1984) and more recently by McWhorter (e.g., 2001). To the best of my knowledge, this assumption was first challenged by Muysken (1988a) on the basis of a comparison of subsets of data drawn from various creole languages. The theory of creole genesis advocated here predicts that different substrate languages will produce different creoles that will reflect the typological differences that exist between their substrates. As will be discussed in depth in Chapter 8, this prediction is borne out.

CHAPTER 4 | Relabeling in Two Different Theories of the Lexicon

RENÉE LAMBERT-BRÉTIÈRE AND CLAIRE LEFEBVRE

1. Introduction

By its very nature, the process of relabeling takes place in the lexical component of the grammar.[*] By hypothesis, different theories of the lexicon should make different predictions as to the nature of the items that are pertinent for relabeling. In this chapter, we test this hypothesis by comparing the predictions of two different approaches to the lexicon, the Principles and Parameters (P&P) and Radical Construction Grammar (RCxG) frameworks, using data drawn from a subset of Caribbean creoles and their source languages. In so doing, we will assume the definition of relabeling provided in Chapter 1. Section 1.1 provides an overview of the two approaches to the lexicon that are compared in this chapter. Section 1.2 sets out the major features of a relabeling-based account of creole genesis within each of these models. Section 1.3 identifies the subset of constructions that will be discussed in this chapter, and section 1.4 provides information on the database.

---

[*]The research reported on in this chapter owes its existence to a question addressed to Claire Lefebvre by Gerrit Dimmendaal at the SPCL conference held in Cologne in August 2009. The question concerned the use of Construction Grammar as a tool for studying creole genesis. The content of this chapter represents what the two authors came up with in response to Dimmendaal's question. We would like to thank Gerrit Dimmendaal for asking the question, and Paul Kay for his most useful comments on an earlier version of this chapter. We would also like to thank the participants in the 2011 SPCL meeting in Portland, Oregon, for their insightful questions and comments on our presentation of the content of this chapter.

1.1. Different Approaches to the Lexicon

Two different approaches to the lexicon are contrasted in this chapter: Principles and Parameters (P&P) (section 1.1.1), and Radical Construction Grammar (RCxG) (section 1.1.2). The choice of the P&P framework is motivated by the fact that the original study conducted to test the role of relabeling in creole genesis was cast within this framework (Lefebvre 1998, and the references cited therein). The motivation for the choice of the RCxG model (Croft 2001), a Construction Grammar model,[1] is two-fold. First, since relabeling is semantically driven, as stated in Chapter 1, we needed a model of grammar for which meaning is the main focus of attention. RCxG is such a model. Second, since creoles do not reproduce the word order of their substrate languages, as will be seen in Chapter 5, we needed a model of grammar in which directionality properties are not specified as part of atomic constructions. Again, RCxG is such a model. The P&P and the RCxG models propose different views of the lexicon. We now turn to the composition of the lexicon in each of them.

1.1.1. The Lexicon in Principles and Parameters (P&P)

The P&P framework is modular, such that each component of the grammar is autonomous. Hence, the lexical and syntactic components function independently of each another (e.g., Chomsky 1989, and subsequent work). The items that are listed in the lexicon in the P&P framework are identified in (1).

(1)   Items listed in the lexicon in the P&P framework:
- simplexes
- affixes
- compounds
- idiosyncrasies of all kinds (e.g., idioms)

---

[1] Construction Grammar was originally developed by Fillmore et al. (1988), Fillmore and Kay (1993) and Kay and Fillmore (1999). Their model is now referred to as *Sign-based Construction Grammar* (SBCxG). This model has evolved in various directions. For example, Goldberg (1995, 2006) developed a model referred to as *Cognitive Construction Grammar* (CCxG), and Croft (2001), a model called *Radical Construction Grammar* (RCxG). The central idea behind all Construction Grammar models is that there is no strict separation between the lexicon and the syntax. Construction Grammar is thus a cognitive model of grammatical representations and, as such, it shares some features with Cognitive Grammar (e.g., Langacker 1987, 1991, 2005). Construction Grammar models differ as to whether their main focus is semantics or syntax, whether word order is specified as part of atomic constructions or not, and so on. We chose the RCxG model for reasons that are made explicit in the text.

Within this model, lexical redundancy rules link lexical items that are derivationally related. Constructions that have been referred to as "discontinuous morphemes" in other models, such as the French negation *ne . . . pas*, do not constitute lexical entries in this model. Rather, each morpheme participating in these constructions is listed independently (e.g., Pollock 1989). The type of information contained in each lexical entry is listed in (2).

(2)   Information contained in a lexical entry in the P&P framework:
- phonological representation
- syntactic category
- semantic representation
- syntactic properties (e.g., gender, number, etc.)
- subcategorization properties
- selectional properties
- directionality properties

Within this framework, the availability of syntactic constructions, such as the double-object construction, is accounted for by means of parameters of variation, which constitute options of Universal Grammar. They are formulated in terms of correlations: property (x), a syntactic construction, is available in a given grammar if property (y), a functional category, is also available in this grammar. For example, the double-object construction (V NP NP) is available in a grammar if Genitive case (e.g., = *'s* in English) is also available in this grammar (Johnson 1991). In this model, parameters of variation are extraneous to the lexicon, and so are syntactic constructions.

1.1.2. The lexicon in Radical Construction Grammar (RCxG)

The RCxG (Croft 2001) model is non-modular, such that components of the grammar are not autonomous. Thus, there is no clear separation between the lexicon and the syntax. The grammar is composed of a continuum of lexical elements going from the simplest bound forms to the most complex structures, referred to as the lexicon-syntax continuum. All types of linguistic units (morphemes, words, phrases, clauses, sentences, texts) have constructional properties and are represented as constructions. Examples of such constructions are represented in Table 4.1.

The lexicon-syntax continuum also includes more complex constructions such as double-object constructions (v NP NP), serial verb constructions (v NP v NP), verb-doubling constructions (see section 5), and so on.

TABLE 4.1 Sample Constructions in RCxG

CONSTRUCTION TYPES	TRADITIONAL NAMES	EXAMPLES
Complex and (mostly) schematic	**syntax**	[SBJ *be*-TNS VERB-*en by* OBL]
Complex and (mostly) specific	**idiom**	[*pull*-TNS NP-*'s leg*]
Complex but bound	**morphology**	[NOUN-*s*], [VERB-TNS]
Atomic and schematic	**syntactic category**	[DEM], [ADJ]
Atomic and specific	**word/lexicon**	[*this*], [*green*]

SOURCE: Table 1.1, Croft (2001: 17).

In Croft's (2001) formalism, a construction consists in the pairing of *form*—comprising syntactic, morphological, and phonological properties—and *meaning*—consisting of semantic, pragmatic, and discourse-functional features, as is schematically illustrated in (3).

(3)

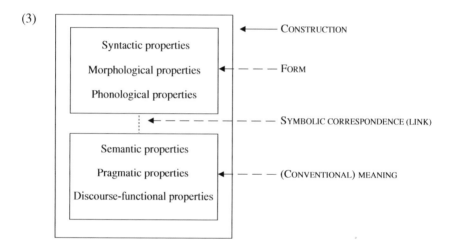

The symbolic link between a construction's form and meaning is internal to that construction. This represents a crucial difference from the modular approach of the P&P model, in which the link between the syntactic and semantic components is achieved by means of interfaces.

Constructions are organized into networks of information: "any construction with unique, idiosyncratic morphological, syntactic, lexical, semantic, pragmatic, or discourse-functional properties must be represented as an independent node in the constructional network [. . .]" (Croft 2001: 25). Generalizations across constructions are represented as inheritance links between constructions. This means that an idiomatic expression like [SBJ *bite the bullet*] must be represented as an independent node in the network, because its semantics is unpredictable; it is an

TABLE 4.2 Processing Procedures for English

STAGE	PROCESSING PROCEDURE	L$_2$ PROCESSING
1	word / lemma	Words
2	category procedure	lexical morphemes
3	phrasal procedure	intraphrasal information exchange
4	S-procedure / word order rules	interphrasal information exchange
5	S-procedure / word order rules	interphrasal information exchange (SV agreement)
6	subordinate clause procedure	main and subordinate clause

SOURCE: Adapted from Plag (2008: 124), citing Pienemann (2000).

instance of the transitive construction [SBJ VERB OBJ] that also has to be encoded separately to represent the argument structure of this construction, in parallel with the regular pattern of the verb [SBJ *bite* OBJ] and the verb [*to bite*] by itself. Atomic constructions do not themselves specify the order of elements with which they may combine. Instead, word order (see Chapter 5) is given as part of the complex constructions in which words appear (e.g., [SBJ *bite* OBJ]).

Within the RCxG model, the existence of complex constructions entails that of their parts. Generalizations about abstract constructions are thus only possible when enough item-based patterns are acquired. For example, the abstract construction [SBJ VERB OBJ] can be generalized from the construction [John$_{sbj}$ eat$_v$ an apple$_{obj}$], but not the other way around. Likewise, the construction [John$_{sbj}$ eat$_v$ an apple$_{obj}$] can only be interpreted after the individual words that are part of it have been acquired. This can be further illustrated on the basis of research on second language acquisition, which shows that constructions are acquired in different stages, starting with the simplest, words, and ending with the most complex, subordinate clauses, as illustrated in Table 4.2.

1.2. A Relabeling-Based Account of Creole Genesis Within These Two Frameworks

The two models of the lexicon described above have in common that they list simplexes, affixes, compounds, and idioms. So, with respect to these items, there is no difference between them as regards relabeling. There are, however, some areas of the lexicon where the two models make different predictions about relabeling. First, in the P&P model, complex constructions (e.g., involving a pre- and a postposition) are not listed in the lexicon, and thus cannot be relabeled as such. In the RCxG framework, complex constructions are listed in the lexicon, and thus they can be relabeled. As will be seen in this chapter, there are complex constructions that appear to have been relabeled as units, and hence RCxG presents an advantage over the P&P model in these cases.

A second difference between the two models has to do with word order. In the P&P model, word order is registered as part of individual lexical entries, but in the RCxG model it is not. As mentioned earlier, since the word order of creoles does not systematically correspond to that of the superstrate lexical items, the RCxG approach presents an advantage over the P&P model in this respect (see Chapter 5). Third, in the P&P model, there is no means of representing subsystems of the grammar. Nevertheless, some subsystems appear to have been adopted wholesale from the substrate languages in the creoles (e.g., the Haitian nominal structure, the Tense-Mood-Aspect subsystem). Here again, RCxG appears to be the most useful framework in that it allows for whole subsystems of the grammar to be represented in the lexicon and hence to be available for relabeling. Finally, the format of the grammar in RCxG allows for two general predictions with respect to relabeling:

1. Relabeling is predicted to be incremental, from simple lexical items, to associations between them, and then to more complex constructions.
2. Relabeling is predicted to account in an integrated fashion for phenomena related to syntax, as well as for phenomena related to the lexicon.

Because the P&P model is modular, it makes no such predictions. We assume that substrate atomic structures—that is, the lexical entries per se—are relabeled on the basis of superstrate forms as discussed in Chapter 1. We also assume that non-atomic constructions, such as the v NP NP construction, of the substrate lexicon-syntax continuum are all available to the creators of a creole. Information related to word order will be discussed in Chapter 5.

1.3. Constructions under Analysis in This Chapter

The subset of constructions that will be discussed in this chapter are the following: Tense-Mood-Aspect (henceforth TMA) systems (section 2), imperfective constructions (section 3), locative constructions (section 4), and constructions involving verb-doubling phenomena (section 5). These subsystems of the grammar, or constructions, were selected for discussion because they all present some kind of problem for the relabeling-based account of creole genesis within the P&P model of the lexicon (Lefebvre 1998, and the references cited therein). Each of these problems is resolved within the RCxG framework.

1.4. The Database

The Caribbean creoles used as databases in this chapter are Haitian (Haiti), Saramaccan (Surinam, French Guyana), and, to a lesser extent, Papiamentu (Aruba, Bonaire, Curaçao). These creoles share the same pool of West African substrate languages, including the Gbe cluster of the Kwa family (e.g., Migge 2003 and Smithh 1987 for Saramaccan; Singler 1996 for Haitian; Smith 2001: 56–57 for Haitian and Saramaccan; Rawley 1981 for Papiamentu), which in turn is part of the larger Niger-Congo group of languages (e.g., Lefebvre 1998: 52–62, and the references cited therein). These creoles have different superstrate languages: French for Haitian, English and Portuguese for Saramaccan, Portuguese and Spanish for Papiamentu.

The Gbe languages and Saramaccan are tone languages. The representation of tones for Fongbe is phonemic and follows the notation adopted in Lefebvre and Brousseau (2002, Chapter 2). Given the variation in the notation of Saramaccan tones in the literature, the tones have been standardized for all the Saramaccan examples following Rountree et al.'s Word List (2000).

2. Tense, Mood, and Aspect Systems of the Grammar

This section considers the TMA systems of the grammar as a whole. The Haitian and Saramaccan data will be discussed in turn, together with data from their respective contributing languages.

Whereas French encodes tense, mood, and aspect by means of affixes on verbs or auxiliaries (*avoir* 'to have' and *être* 'to be'), or by periphrastic expressions (see following text), both Haitian and Fongbe lack such affixes and auxiliaries. Instead, as we saw in Chapter 3, they feature TMA markers that occur between the subject and the verb. The inventories of TMA markers for Haitian and Fongbe are shown again in (4).

(4) Inventories of TMA markers in Haitian and Fongbe

ANTERIOR		IRREALIS		NON-COMPLETE			
Past / Past perfect		Definite future		Habitual		Imperfective	
H	F	H	F	H	F	H	F
m	*kò*	*ap*[2]	*ná*	—	*nɔ̀*	*ap*	*ɖò...wɛ̀*

Indefinite future	
H	F
a-va	*ná-wá*

Subjunctive	
H	F
pou	*ní*

(= (115) in Lefebvre 1996)

With the exception of the habitual marker, which is lacking in Haitian, the size of the inventories of TMA markers is the same in both languages. The morphemes involved in both inventories share semantic and distributional properties. The Fongbe and Haitian morphemes in (4) combine in similar ways to form complex tenses (Lefebvre 1996, and the references cited therein). Finally, in contrast to French, where every sentence must be overtly marked for tense, mood, and aspect, in both Haitian and Fongbe, bare sentences, that is, sentences without any TMA marking, are allowed. In this case, the temporal-aspectual interpretation of a clause is computed from the various components that participate in establishing its aspectual properties: the aspectual class of the verb, the definiteness of the direct object of the verb, and the definiteness of the subject (Lambert-Brétière 2010: 48–53; Lefebvre 1996, 1998: 111–140).

Saramaccan offers parallel data. Recall from 1.4 that Saramaccan has the same pool of substrate languages as Haitian Creole, but English and Portuguese as its superstrate languages. The creators of Saramaccan thus started with the same lexicons as the creators of Haitian. While English and Portuguese encode tense, mood, and aspect by means of affixes on verbs or auxiliaries, similarly to French, Saramaccan lacks such affixes and auxiliaries. Rather, it has TMA markers occurring between the subject

---

[2] Definite future and imperfective are both rendered as *ap* in Haitian Creole. In Lefebvre (1998: 119–129) it is argued that the form *ap*, which corresponds to two different substrate morphemes, has two sources in the superstrate language as well: the presentential adverb *apré* 'then, later'>*ap* (<French *après* 'then, later') is the source of the irrealis mood marker, and the French expression *être après* 'to be in the process of,' in colloquial French progressive constructions, is the source of the imperfective marker.

and the verb. The data in (5) show that the overall TMA system in Saramaccan is quite similar to that in Fongbe (and Haitian), except that it does not distinguish between definite and indefinite future and lacks a habitual marker (Bally 2004; Rountree 1992).

(5) Inventories of TMA markers in Saramaccan and Fongbe

ANTERIOR		IRREALIS		NON-COMPLETE			
Past / Past perfect		Definite future		Habitual		Imperfective	
SA	F	SA	F	SA	F	SA	F
bì	kò	ó	ná	—	nɔ̀	tá	ɖò…wὲ

Indefinite future

SA	F
ó	ná-wá

Subjunctive

SA	F
fu	ní

Based on the work of Bally (2004, 2011), Rountree (1992), and van de Vate (2011) for Saramaccan, and on Lefebvre (1996) and Lefebvre and Brousseau (2002) for Fongbe, the morphemes involved in both inventories share a core of semantic and distributional properties. The Saramaccan and Fongbe morphemes combine in similar ways to form complex tenses. Both languages allow for bare sentences, in which case the temporal-aspectual interpretation of the clause is computed from the various components that participate in establishing its aspectual properties of a clause, as was specified for Haitian and Fongbe earlier. Thus, it appears that the Saramaccan TMA system, like that of Haitian, is quite similar to that of its substrate languages (see also Winford & Migge 2007, for a similar conclusion).[3]

The difference between the TMA systems of the two creoles and those of their superstrate languages is quite remarkable. The similarity between the TMA systems of the two creoles and those of their substrate languages is equally remarkable. Within the P&P model, it is not possible to account for the overall parallels between the two creoles' systems and those of their substrate languages, namely the size of the inventories, the possible combinations of morphemes, their co-occurrence restrictions, and so on. This is because, in this model, there is no means of representing the overall

---

[3] Note that Smith (2001: 62) does not include *fu* as an irrealis mood marker in the Saramaccan TMA system. However, he does include *sa* 'can,' which, on other authors' analysis, is a modal verb rather than a mood marker.

properties of subsystems of the grammar. Within the RCxG framework, however, this information can be encoded because constructions, as well as lexical items and their co-occurrence restrictions, are listed in the lexicon. Hence, in this framework, the constructions represented in (4) and (5) are part of the lexicon-syntax continuum. The combinations of morphemes to form complex tenses would also be specified, and so on.

Bao (2005, 2010) makes a similar proposal based on a different set of languages. Indeed, he accounts for the systemic similarity between the TMA system of Singapore English and that of its substrate languages in terms of "System Transfer." While we agree with his basic idea, we disagree with his characterization of the phenomenon, which he sees as a case of transfer. We prefer to see it as a case of use of the substrate subsystems of the grammar (or constructions) in the rapid formation of new languages, including creoles and new English varieties. In our view, the lexical items involved in these subsystems need only be relabeled on the basis of forms found in the superstrate languages for the creole subsystems in (4) and (5) to emerge. For example, the similarity between the properties of pairs of lexical items involved in the Fongbe and Haitian TMA systems has been argued to follow from the relabeling of the Fongbe lexical entries on the basis of French periphrastic expressions involved in the expression of tense, mood, and aspect in (colloquial) French, yielding the Haitian system (Lefebvre 1996, 1998: 134–137, and the references therein). Hence, the Fongbe lexical entries would have been relabeled as *te* (< past auxiliary *été*), *ap* (< adverb *après* 'then'),[4] *a-va*, a combination of the definite future and of *va*, a defective form of the verb *aller* 'to go,' that replicates the Fongbe combination *ná-wá* involving the definite future marker *ná* and *wá* 'to come,' and *pou* (< *pour* in *être pour* 'to be about to').

Likewise, the Fongbe lexical items were relabeled on the basis of English and Portuguese forms involved in the expression of tense, mood, and aspect, yielding the Saramaccan TMA system.[5] Hence, the Fongbe lexical items would have been relabeled as *bì* (< English *been*; Portuguese *vir* 'to come' (Smith 2001: 64)), *ó* (< English *go*), *fu* (< English *for*) (for *fu*, see Lefebvre & Loranger 2006, and the references therein; for the other markers, see Bally 2004; Rountree 1992; for a historical perspective on these markers, see Smith 2001: 62–63).

---

[4]As is discussed in Lefebvre (1998: 123–129), the history of this Haitian lexical entry also involved reanalysis.

[5]The relabeling account of the Saramaccan data presented here abstracts away from the complex situation that prevailed in Surinam at the time Saramaccan was created, including the multiple successive relabelings on the basis of English and then of Portuguese (e.g., Smith 2001: 64).

To sum up, retention of the TMA subsystem of the grammar from the substrate languages and relabeling of the lexical items involved in this subsystem account for the remarkable parallels between the TMA systems of the two creoles examined and of their substrate languages. The TMA subsystem of the grammar is represented in the lexicon-syntax continuum in the RCxG model, but it is not represented in the P&P model. We now turn to the account of the imperfective construction, which requires further discussion.

3. Imperfective Constructions

The Fongbe imperfective construction involves two lexical items: *ɖò* and *wὲ*, shown in (6). In the literature on Fongbe, *ɖò* is glossed either as 'at' or as 'to be at.' This suggests that *ɖò* has two functions: that of a locative preposition in some contexts and that of a locative copula in others. Lefebvre (1990) argues that, regardless of the context in which it occurs, *ɖò* manifests the same properties. For example, in all contexts, the extraction of its complement triggers the appearance of a resumptive pronoun in the extraction site. Given this situation, we adopt the monosemic analysis presented in Lefebvre (1990) and in Lefebvre and Brousseau (2002: 318–319). In the examples below, the form *ɖò* will be glossed as 'at' or 'be at,' depending on its context of occurrence. (For further discussion, see section 4.) The Fongbe imperfective construction, depicted in (6), also involves the morpheme *wὲ*.[6] The meaning of *wὲ* in this construction is difficult to pinpoint. We therefore simply gloss it as POST (for postposition).

(6) a. *É   ɖò   bì-bí   wὲ.*   FONGBE
         3SG   be.at   RE-cook   POST
         'It is cooking.'   (Segurola & Rassinoux 2000: 99)

     b. *É   ɖò   mì   kpɔ́n   wὲ.*   FONGBE
         3SG   be.at   me   RE-look.at   POST
         'He is looking at me.'   (Segurola & Rassinoux 2000: 153)

---

[6] In Fongbe, the form *wὲ* is also the focus marker. The question of whether there are two *wὲ*s in Fongbe is not addressed here. Note that in other Gbe languages (e.g., Ewegbe) the imperfective construction involves a lexical postposition meaning 'in' instead of a form corresponding to the focus marker. What is important to note here is the fact that in Gbe languages, the imperfective construction involves two morphemes: one meaning 'to be at' and another whose specific meaning may vary (Hazoumê 1990).

As can be seen in (6), the VP of the construction is nominalized. The details of nominalizations in Fongbe can be found in Lefebvre and Brousseau (2002: 195–215). For the purpose of this chapter, suffice it to say that the nominalization of verbs involves reduplication of the stem (e.g., *bí* 'to cook,' *bìbí* 'cooking'). In the examples, this reduplication is glossed as RE- (see Chapter 6 for an extensive discussion of this morpheme). In a nominalization involving an intransitive verb, RE- is manifested overtly, as shown in (6a). In a nominalization involving a transitive verb, RE- is not overtly manifested. Furthermore, as is shown in (6b), in this case, the object precedes the verb instead of following it, as in tensed clauses. The Fongbe imperfective aspect is thus encoded by a construction that involves two lexical items: locative *ɖò* 'be at' and the postposition *wὲ*. For the imperfective aspect interpretation to obtain, both *ɖò* and *wὲ* must co-occur. In (7a), *ɖò* and *wὲ* co-occur, triggering an imperfective interpretation of the sentence. In (7b), however, *ɖò* occurs without *wὲ*, yielding a resultative interpretation.

(7) a. *Sìn   ɔ́   ɖò   fí-fá   wὲ.*   Fongbe
        water   DEF be.at RE-be.cold   POST
        'The water is becoming cold.'   (= (72a) in Brousseau 1993: 87)

      b. *Sìn   ɔ́   ɖò   fí-fá.*   Fongbe
        water   DEF be.at RE-be.cold
        'The water has become cold.'
        [Lit.: 'The water is at cold.']
        *'The water is becoming cold.'   (Lambert-Brétière's field notes)

Within the P&P model, *ɖò* and *wὲ* constitute two distinct lexical entries, schematically represented in (8). In this model, *ɖò* selects *wὲ,* which, in turn, selects a nominalized VP.

(8) a. *ɖò* • phonological representation: *ɖò*
            • syntactic category: Locative preposition/copula
            • semantics: BE AT location/state
            • selectional properties: PostP (e.g., *wὲ*/…)
                                         Place name
                                         Adjective
          • directionality property: *ɖò* ___

b. *wè* • phonological representation: *wè*
       • syntactic category: Postposition
       • semantics: Focus marker
       • subcategorization: nominalized VP / NP
       • directionality property: ___ *wè*

As is specified in (8a), in addition to selecting *wè* in the imperfective construction, *ɖò* may select locative postpositions, as illustrated in (9) (see section 4 of this chapter for a detailed discussion of the locative constructions).

(9) a. *Àwîî ɔ́ ɖò xàsù mè.*   FONGBE
    cat DEF be.at basket in
    'The cat is in the basket.'   (Lefebvre's field notes)

  b. *Àwîî ɔ́ ɖò távò jí.*   FONGBE
    cat DEF be.at table on
    'The cat is on the table.'   (Lefebvre's field notes)

It may also select a place name without a postposition, as in (10).

(10) *É wá-àzɔ́ ɖò Xɔ̀gbónú.*   FONGBE
    3SG work at Porto.Novo
    '(S)he worked in Porto-Novo.'   (Lambert-Brétière's field notes)

Finally, as shown in (7b), *ɖò* may occur in resultative constructions, in which case it selects a resultative adjective. In the P&P model, since *ɖò* and *wè* constitute different lexical entries, they are independently subject to relabeling. Since the complex construction *ɖò . . . wè* is not a lexical entry, it cannot be relabeled as such. In light of the above discussion, we now turn to the Haitian imperfective construction.

In Haitian Creole, the imperfective construction involves only one lexical item: *ap*, illustrated in (11).

(11) a. *L' ap kuit*   HAITIAN
    3SG IMP cook
    'It is cooking.'   (Lambert-Brétière's field notes)

  b. *L' ap gade mwen*   HAITIAN
    3SG IMP look me
    'He is looking at me.'   (Lambert-Brétière's field notes)

The semantically closest lexical item to Fongbe *wè* is *se* 'it is.' This lexical item does not participate in the Haitian imperfective construction. Moreover, nominalization of VPs is not a feature of the Haitian grammar. Syntactic nominalizations appear to have been abandoned in the course of the language's formation (see Chapter 5). Furthermore, Haitian *ap* does not have as wide a distribution as Fongbe *ɖò*. As is shown by the ungrammaticality of the sentences in (12), it does not occur in combination with adpositions in locative constructions (compare with Fongbe (9)).

(12) a. * *Chat la ap nan panyen*   HAITIAN
                cat   DEF   in   basket

      b. * *Chat la ap sou tab*   HAITIAN
                cat   DEF   on   table

In addition, as the ungrammaticality of the sentence in (13) shows, *ap* does not occur with a place name (compare with Fongbe (10)).

(13) * *Li   travaj ap   Pòtoprens*   HAITIAN
           3SG   work   Port-au-Prince

And, as shown in (14), the imperfective marker *ap* followed by an adjective is not assigned a resultative interpretation (compare with Fongbe (7b)). A sentence containing *ap* and an adjective can only be interpreted as future, given that the label of the definite future marker is also *ap* (see note 3).

(14) *Dlo   a   ap   frèt*   HAITIAN
       Water DEF DEF.FUT cold
       *'The water has become cold.' [lit.: The water is at cold.]
       'The water will be cold.'   (Lambert-Brétière's field notes)

So, imperfective *ap* only partially reproduces the properties of Fongbe *ɖò*.

Given the mismatches between Haitian *ap* and Fongbe *ɖò*, and the lack of a Haitian morpheme corresponding to Fongbe *wè* in the imperfective construction, within the P&P model, we must conclude that the process of relabeling fails to account for the properties of *ap*. Still, the details of the imperfective constructions in the two languages are quite similar. For example, as Lefebvre (1998: 119–123) discusses at some length, like Fongbe *ɖò . . . wè*, Haitian *ap* is best characterized as an imperfective aspect. Indeed, it is interpreted as progressive in the context of nonstative verbs, as we saw in (6) and (11). With stative verbs, however, both Haitian *ap* and Fongbe *ɖò . . . wὲ* are interpreted as habitual, as is shown in (15) and (16), respectively.

(15) *Jina   te   kontinye ap   malad   toutan.*   HAITIAN
      Jina   ANT   keep   IMP   sick   all-the-time
      'Jina was sick all the time.'   (Heurtelou & Vilsaint 2004: 132)

(16) *Sìká   ɖò   àzɔ̀n-jὲ   wὲ.*   FONGBE
      Cica   be.at   RE-be.sick   POST
      'Cica is habitually sick.'   (= (75) in Lefebvre 1996)

Furthermore, in both languages, the imperfective construction is used in contexts where we find a gerund in English. This is shown in (17) and (18), respectively.

(17) *Nou ap   jwὲnn Mari ap   prepare pat   la.*   HAITIAN
      we   DEF.FUT find   Mary IMP   prepare dough   DEF
      'We will find Mary preparing the dough.'   (= (21) in Lefebvre 1996)

(18) *N   mɔ̀n Sìká ɖò   wɔ̃   ɖà   wὲ.*   FONGBE
      I   see Cica   be.at   dough RE-prepare   POST
      'I saw Cica preparing dough.'   (= (77) in Lefebvre 1996)

Finally, as was mentioned earlier, in both languages, the aspectual markers combine with other markers in similar ways to form complex tenses. It therefore appears that the properties of Haitian *ap* correspond to those of Fongbe *ɖò . . . wὲ*. Within the P&P model, this situation could not result from the relabeling of *ɖò . . . wὲ* by *ap* since *ɖò . . . wὲ* is not a lexical entry.

The RCxG model provides us with a tool to represent the similarity between the two imperfective constructions. Recall from section 1.1.2 that, within this model, complex constructions, as well as simple ones, are listed in the lexicon. Thus, in this model, in addition to *ɖò* '(to be) at' and *wὲ*, *ɖò . . . wὲ* would be listed in the lexicon as the aspectual imperfective construction. Consequently, it could have been relabeled as a unit. Given that the details of *ap* correspond to those of Fongbe *ɖò . . . wὲ*, as we saw above, we assume that *ɖò . . . wὲ* has been relabeled as *ap*, on the basis of *être après* in the colloquial French progressive construction (Lefebvre 1998: 119–123). This is represented in (19).

(19)

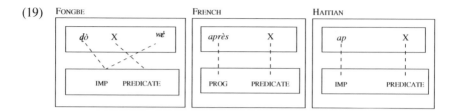

According to this proposal, *ap* relabeled the imperfective construction *ɖò . . . wɛ̀*. This explains both why Haitian *ap* does not have the same properties as Fongbe *ɖò* alone, or as Fongbe *wɛ̀* alone, and why it reproduces the details of the Fongbe aspectual imperfective construction *ɖò . . . wɛ̀* (see (6), (11), (15)–(18)).

As in Haitian, the Saramaccan imperfective construction involves only one lexical item, *tá*, illustrated in (20).

(20) *Dí   ganía   tá   fá.*   SARAMACCAN
     DEF   chicken   IMP   fat
     'The chicken is getting fat.'   (= (5a) in Kramer 2002: 52)

In Saramaccan, the morpheme *wɛ̀* has been retained from Fongbe as a focus marker (Smith 1996), as shown in (21).

(21) *Andí   wɛ̀   i   bói.*   SARAMACCAN
     what   FOC   you   cook
     'What did you cook?'   (= (11b) in Smith 1996: 117)

However, *wɛ̀* does not participate in the Saramaccan imperfective construction (see (20)). Just like Haitian *ap*, Saramaccan *tá* corresponds to Fongbe *ɖò . . . wɛ̀*. Like *ɖò . . . wɛ̀*, *tá* is interpreted as progressive in the context of nonstative verbs, as in (20) (= F (6), H (11)). And like *ɖò . . . wɛ̀*, *tá* is interpreted as habitual when it occurs with stative verbs, as in (22) (= F (16), H (15)).

(22) *Nómo   a   tá   toóbi   mi.*   SARAMACCAN
     always   3SG   IMP   annoy   1SG
     'He is always annoying me.'   (= (25a) in Byrne 1987: 47)

Like *ɖò . . . wè*, *tá* can be used in contexts where we find a gerund in English, as in (23) (= F (18), H (17)).

(23) *Mi   tá   lúku   dí   sódáti   tá   wáka a   dí   wósu.*   Saramaccan
      1SG IMP look   DEF soldier IMP walk   LOC DEF house
      'I am looking at the soldier walking to the house.'

(= (27) in Byrne 1987: 48)

Since the properties of Saramaccan *tá* correspond to those of Fongbe *ɖò . . . wè*, we propose that, in the formation of Saramaccan, Fongbe *ɖò . . . wè* was relabeled as *tá*, on the basis of Portuguese *esta*, according to Byrne (1987), or English *stand*, according to Veenstra (1996a), just as it was relabeled as *ap* in the formation of Haitian (see (19)).

To summarize, in this section, we have shown that the Fongbe, Haitian, and Saramaccan imperfective constructions are semantically equivalent. These constructions differ in that, the Fongbe construction involves two morphemes, *ɖò . . . wè*, whereas in Haitian and Saramaccan, it involves only one morpheme, *ap* and *tá*, respectively. Within the P&P model, the similarity between *ɖò . . . wè* and *ap* or *ɖò . . . wè* and *tá* cannot be accounted for by means of relabeling because, in this model, *ɖò . . . wè* is not a lexical entry. Within the RCxG framework, however, the association of two words forming a complex construction can constitute a lexical entry that can be relabeled, thus accounting for the similarity between the imperfective constructions in the three languages. This line of analysis appears to be along the right lines. As will be seen in the next section, the data on locative constructions are similar.

4. Locative Constructions

In this section, we discuss the locative constructions that involve the Fongbe postpositions *mè* 'in' and *jí* 'on' (Lefebvre & Brousseau 2002, Chapter 11.2) and the corresponding Haitian locative constructions, essentially those involving *nan* with the core meaning 'in' and *sou* with the core meaning 'on' (e.g., Fattier 1998: 896, 904, 929, 931; Gilles 1988; Joseph 1994; Sylvain 1936. For a discussion of dialectal differences involving *nan* and *sou*, see Fattier 1998: 61).[7] The data show that relabeling may apply to

---

[7] We thank Nathan Ménard for very fruitful discussions on the Haitian data presented in this section, and Sasha Gourdet for his help with the data collection.

complex constructions, as well as single morphemes, thus arguing in favor of the RCxG view of the lexicon over the P&P model. They also show that more than one substrate lexical entry may be relabeled on the basis of a single superstrate form. Finally, these constructions reveal a new process that seems to be at work in the formation of creole lexicons.

4.1. In-type Locative Constructions

In Fongbe, some locative constructions involve the postposition *mɛ̀* 'in.' In this case, the postpositional phrase headed by *mɛ̀* follows a verb of change of location such as *byɔ́* 'to enter,' as is shown in (24a). Haitian has prepositions instead of postpositions (see Chapter 5), and the Haitian preposition corresponding to the Fongbe postposition *mɛ̀* in (24a) is *nan*. As in (24a), the prepositional phrase headed by *nan* follows a verb of change of location such as *antre* 'to enter,' as shown in (24b).

(24) a. É   byɔ́   xɔ̀   ɔ́   mɛ̀.   FONGBE
       3SG enter house DEF in
       'He entered in the house.'   (Lefebvre's field notes)

     b. Li   antre   nan   kay   la   HAITIAN
        3SG enter   in   house DEF
        'He entered in the house.'   (= (33b) in Joseph 1994: 35)

Both *mɛ̀* and *nan* may also head a post-/prepositional phrase occurring as the object of a verb meaning 'to go,' as is exemplified in (25).

(25) a. É   ɖì.zɔ̀nlìn yì   jìkpà   mɛ̀.   FONGBE
       3SG walk   go   garden in
       'He walked to the garden.'   (= (445a) in Lambert-Brétière 2010)

     b. Li   mache ale nan jaden   an   HAITIAN
        3SG walk   go   in   garden DEF
        'He walked to the garden.'   (Lefebvre's field notes)

Abstracting away from word order, these examples suggest that the properties of Haitian *nan* replicate those of Fongbe *mɛ̀*. This is accounted for if *mɛ̀* was relabeled as *nan* on the basis of French *dans* 'in,' yielding the Haitian preposition *nan* 'in.' Within the P&P model, the fact that Fongbe *mɛ̀* and Haitian *nan* do not have the same directionality properties poses a problem for a relabeling-based account of creole genesis since directionality properties are part of individual lexical entries. Within the RCxG model, however, the difference in directionality properties does not constitute a problem, since word order is not part of atomic constructions. Although there is some semantic overlap between French *dans* and Haitian *nan*, there are important differences between them (Gilles 1988; Joseph 1994). For example, as will be shown below, Haitian *nan* may also have the meaning conveyed by French *de* 'of, from.' The formalism in (26) indicates that the semantics of the Haitian construction is the same as that of Fongbe.

(26)   FONGBE   FRENCH   HAITIAN

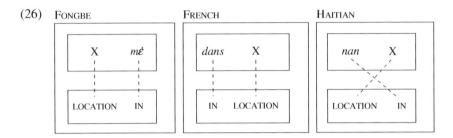

In Fongbe, locative postpositions may combine with the preposition *ɖò* 'at' to form a complex locative expression. Hence, *ɖò . . . mὲ* means 'at . . . in.' Some uses of Haitian *nan* correspond to Fongbe *ɖò . . . mὲ*. This is exemplified in (27).

(27)   a.   É   ɖì.zɔnlìn ɖò jìkpà   mὲ.   FONGBE
            3SG walk   at garden in
            'He walked in the garden.'   (= (445b) in Lambert-Brétière 2010)

       b.   *Li   mache nan jaden   an*   HAITIAN
            3SG walk   at.in garden DEF
            'He walked in the garden.'   (Lefebvre's field notes)

Furthermore, in both Fongbe and Haitian, these locative constructions may have the meaning 'among,' as shown in (28).

(28)   a.   *ɖò   ví   lé   bí   mὲ*   FONGBE
            at   child   PL   all   in
            'among all the children'   (Lambert-Brétière's field notes)

       b.   *nan   tout tablo   sa   yo*   HAITIAN
            at.in   all painting DEM   PL
            'among all these/those paintings'   (= (33f) in Joseph 1994)

In (24) and (25), the pre-/postpositional phrases are in argument positions, whereas in (27) and (28), they are in adjunct positions.

In addition to being a locative preposition meaning 'at,' Fongbe *ɖò* is also a locative predicate meaning 'to be at.' As such, it may combine with a locative postposition, as is illustrated in (29a). Again, the corresponding Haitian locative construction involves only *nan*, as illustrated in (29b).

(29) a. *Àwû ɔ́   ɖò   xàsù   mè.*   FONGBE
       cat DEF be.at basket in
       'The cat is in the basket.'   (Lambert-Brétière's field notes)

    b. *Chat la   nan   panyen an.*   HAITIAN
       cat   DEF be.at.in basket DEF
       'The cat is in the basket.'   (Lambert-Brétière's field notes)

In (29b), *nan* arguably corresponds to the Fongbe complex construction *ɖò . . . mè* 'be at . . . in.' As in Fongbe (29a), the Haitian locative phrase in (29b) is a predicate that requires the semantic component BE.AT.

The analysis in which Fongbe *ɖò* has two functions, as a preposition and as a locative predicate, is supported by extraction facts, which differ depending on the function of *ɖò*. When *ɖò* is a preposition, the constituent it is part of can be fronted and the extraction site remains empty. This is shown in (30).

(30) *Ðò jìkpà   mè   wè,   é   ɖì.zɔ̀nlìn.*   FONGBE
     at   garden   in   FOC   3SG   walk
     'It is in the garden that he walked.'   (Lambert-Brétière's field notes)

Since the constituent headed by *ɖò* is an adjunct, its complement cannot be extracted, as is shown by the ungrammaticality of (31).

(31) **jìkpà mè   wè,   é   ɖì.zɔ̀nlìn ɖò*   FONGBE
     garden in   FOC   3SG   walk   at
     'It is in the garden that he walked.'   (Lambert-Brétière's field notes)

By contrast, when *ɖò* is a locative predicate, the constituent it is part of cannot be extracted, as shown by the ungrammaticality of (32).

(32) **ɖò xàsù   mè   wè,   àwû   ɔ́*   FONGBE
     be.at basket in   FOC   cat   DEF
     'It is in the basket that the cat is.'   (Lambert-Brétière's field notes)

In this case, however, the complement of *ɖò* can be extracted, leaving a resumptive pronoun in the extraction site. This is illustrated in (33).

(33) *Xàsù   mè   wɛ̀,   àwû   ɔ́   ɖò   è.*   Fongbe
      basket in   FOC   cat   DEF be.at RES
      'It is in the basket that the cat is.'   (Lambert-Brétière's field notes)

These extraction facts suggest that Fongbe *ɖò* has two different functions.

Similar facts argue for a double function for Haitian *nan*. When *nan* is a preposition, the constituent it is part of can be fronted and the extraction site remains empty, as shown in (34), which parallels Fongbe (30).

(34) *Se   nan jaden an, li   mache*   Haitian
      FOC at.in garden DEF 3SG walk
      'It is in the garden that he walked.'   (Lambert-Brétière's field notes)

Since the constituent headed by *nan* is an adjunct, its complement cannot be fronted, as is shown be the ungrammaticality of (35), which parallels Fongbe (31).

(35) **Se jaden an,   li   mache nan*   Haitian
      FOC garden DEF   3SG walk   at.in
      'It is in the garden that he walked.'   (Lambert-Brétière's field notes)

When *nan* is a locative predicate, the constituent it is part of can be fronted. In this case, however, the extraction site cannot remain empty, as is shown by the ungrammaticality of (36a); instead, it must contain the morpheme *yé*, as is shown in (36b).

(36) a. **se   nan   panyen an   chat la*   Haitian
          FOC be.at.in basket DEF cat   DEF

      b. *Se   nan   panyen an   chat la   yé.*   Haitian
          FOC be.at.in basket DEF cat   DEF RES
          'It is in the basket that the cat is.'   (Lambert-Brétière's field notes)

According to DeGraff (1992b: 175), *yé* is a pro-predicate, which spells out the trace left by fronting of a nonverbal predicate. The extraction facts above argue that Haitian *nan* has two functions, as a preposition and as a locative predicate.

The extraction facts involving Fongbe *ɖò* and Haitian *nan* with the function of preposition are similar. In both cases, the adjunct phrase headed by a preposition can be fronted (see (30) and (34)). And in both cases, the complement of *ɖò* and *nan*, respectively, cannot be fronted (see (31) and (35)). The extraction facts involving Fongbe *ɖò* and Haitian *nan* as locative predicates are not entirely parallel (see (33) and (36)). In our view, this results from the fact that, while Fongbe has a complex construction involving two lexical items, *ɖò . . . mὲ*, the Haitian construction involves only one lexical item, *nan*. However, the two constructions parallel one another in that both require a resumptive morpheme in the extraction site.

As stated in section 3 above, we adopt the monosemic analysis presented in Lefebvre (1990) and Lefebvre and Brousseau (2002: 318–319). In this view, the semantics of the single lexical entry *ɖò* could be represented as (BE) AT; the realization BE AT would correspond to its function as a predicate, and the realization AT to its function as a preposition. With this assumption in mind, the parallel between the Fongbe and Haitian data in (27) to (36) can be accounted for by relabeling as represented in (37). Hence, *ɖò . . . mὲ* would have been relabeled as *nan* on the basis of French *dans*. This is a plausible account since French *dans* may occur in contexts where we find *nan* in (27) to (36). For example, *Il a marché dans le jardin* (see (27b)), *dans tous ces tableaux* (see (28b)), *Le chat est dans le panier* (see (29b)).

(37)

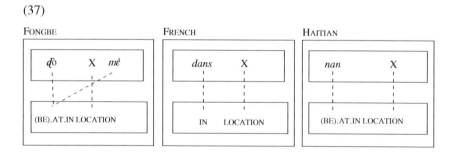

On the above analysis, both *mὲ* in (26) and *ɖò . . . mὲ* in (37) would have been relabeled as *nan* on the basis of French *dans* 'in.' This immediately raises the question of whether a single superstrate form can be used to relabel more than one substrate lexical entry. This is quite possible, as is documented in Lefebvre (1998). An example is provided in (38) showing that Fongbe *gàn* and *hwὲnù* were both relabeled on the basis of French *l'heure,* yielding Haitian *lè*.

(38)

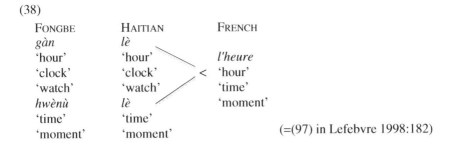

FONGBE	HAITIAN	FRENCH
gàn	*lè*	
'hour'	'hour'	*l'heure*
'clock'	'clock'	'hour'
'watch'	'watch'	'time'
hwènù	*lè*	'moment'
'time'	'time'	
'moment'	'moment'	(=(97) in Lefebvre 1998:182)

There is a use of Haitian *nan* that cannot be analyzed as meaning 'in' (=Fongbe *mè*) nor as 'be at/in' (=Fongbe *ɖò . . . mè*). In this case, *nan* instead means 'of, from.' This is exemplified in (39), where the main verb is *sòti* 'to come out.'

(39) a. *Li   sòti   nan   dlo.*   HAITIAN
       3SG   come.out   NAN   river
       'He came out of the river.'   (= (10) in Gilles 1988: 17)

    b. *Yo   sòti   nan   kay.*   HAITIAN
       3PL   come.out   NAN   house
       'They came out of the house.'   (= (9) in Joseph 1994: 11)

    c. *Li   sòti   nan   peyi   Lafrik.*   HAITIAN
       3SG   come.out   NAN   country Africa
       '(S)he comes from Africa.'   (Valdman et al. 2007: 677)

The use of *nan* with the meaning 'of, from' is also found with verbs such as *retire* and *wete* 'to remove,' as is shown in (40).

(40) a. *Ou mèt retire lèt   h la nan non m . . .*   HAITIAN
       2SG MO delete letter h DEF NAN name 1SG
       'You should delete the letter h from my name . . .'
                                            (Valdman et al. 2007: 637)

    b. *Li   wete.pou.li   nan   reyinyon an lè*   HAITIAN
       3SG   remove.himself NAN   meeting   DEF when
       vòt   la   rive.
       vote DEF arrive
       'He slipped away from the meeting when the time for voting arrived.'
       [Lit.: 'He removed himself from the meeting . . .']
                                            (Valdman et al. 2007: 762)

This use of *nan* is also found with verbs such as *pran* 'to take,' as shown in (41).

(41) a. *Pa   pran l   nan   men m*   HAITIAN
          NEG   take 3SG NAN   hand 1SG
          'Don't grab it from my hands.'   (Valdman et al. 2007: 585)

      b. *M   pran li   nan   men li*   HAITIAN
          1SG take 3SG NAN   hand 3SG
          'I took it from his hand.'   (Valdman et al. 2007: 585)

The French preposition *dans* 'in' cannot be used in these contexts. The French preposition corresponding to the uses of *nan* in (39) to (41) is *de* 'of, from,' which is shown in (42).

(42) a. *Il   est   sorti   de   l'   eau.*   FRENCH
          3SG   be.3SG come.out DE   DEF   water
          'He came out of the river.'

      b. *Ils   sont   sortis   de   la   maison.*   FRENCH
          3PL   be.3PL come.out DE   DEF   house
          'They came out of the house.'

      c. *Il   vient   d'   Afrique.*   FRENCH
          3SG   come   DE   Africa
          'He comes from Africa.'

      d. *Tu   dois   retirer   la   lettre h de   mon nom.* FRENCH
          2SG   have.to remove   DEF letter h DE   my   name
          'You should remove the letter h from my name.'

      e. *Il   est   parti de la   réunion au moment du vote.* FRENCH
          3SG   be.3SG leave DE DEF meeting at time   of vote
          'He left the meeting at the time of voting'

      f. *Il   a   pris le   foulard du   sac.*   FRENCH
          3SG   have.3SG take DEF scarf   DE.DEF bag
          'He took the scarf from the bag.'

The semantic discrepancy between Haitian *nan* and French *dans* in (39) to (41) might be considered as a counterexample to a relabeling-based account of creole genesis. We show below that the data in (39) to (41) do in fact follow from a relabeling-based account of creole genesis.

In Fongbe, the locative construction corresponding to the uses of Haitian *nan* in (39) to (41) involves the postposition *mὲ* 'in,' as in (43).

(43) a. *Kòkú wá sín àxì mὲ.*   FONGBE
          Koku come from market in
          'Koku came from the market.'
                                      (= (11) in Lefebvre & Brousseau 2002: 302)

      b. *Gbèjá ḍòkpó tɔ́n sín dò ɔ́ mὲ.*   FONGBE
          rat   one   come.out from hole DEF in
          'One rat came out of the hole.'   (= (146) in Lambert-Brétière 2009)

      c. *É gó sín tò ɔ́ mὲ.*   FONGBE
          3SG come.out from country DEF in
          '(S)he left the country.'   (Rassinoux 2000: 299)

      d. *lù sín mὲ*   FONGBE
          remove from in
          'remove from within'   (Rassinoux 2000: 319)

Considering the data in (43), we suggest the following account. Having relabeled *mὲ* 'in' and *ḍò . . . mὲ* '(be) at . . . in' as *nan* in the contexts of (24), (25), (27), (28), and (29), the creators of the Haitian lexicon used *nan* in all the contexts where Fongbe *mὲ* occurred, including those in (43).[8] This follows from the nature of relabeling.

The above analysis accounts for the following facts. First, it explains why the properties of Haitian *nan* sometimes correspond to those of Fongbe *mὲ*, and sometimes to the construction involving both *ḍò* '(be) at' and *mὲ* 'in.' Second, it accounts for why Haitian *nan* has a larger semantic range than the French form *dans* 'in' from which it is phonetically derived.

---

[8] The Fongbe preposition *sín* 'from' in the examples in (43) appears to have been relabeled as *sòt(i)* 'from.' In Valdman et al.'s (2007: 678) Haitian dictionary, *sòti,* in one of its uses, is listed as a preposition meaning 'from.' This use is illustrated in (i).

(i) *Avyon ki rive sòti LaFrans lan ap ateri.*   HAITIAN
     plane RES arrive from France DEF IMP land
     'The plane from France is landing.'
     [Lit.: 'The plane that arrives from France is landing.']   (Valdman et al. 2007: 678)

However, unlike the preposition *sín* that co-occurs with *mὲ* 'in' in the Fongbe examples, *sòti* does not co-occur with *nan* 'in' in the Haitian examples presented in this section. Whenever *sòti* is found with *nan*, it is always a (serial) verb meaning 'to come out.' Several examples can be found in Valdman et al. (2007). We leave further discussion of this issue for future research.

Third, it accounts for the fact that Haitian *nan* is sort of a mega-locative lexical item in the language, as Joseph (1994) observed.

4.2. On-type Locative Constructions

The locative constructions with the core meaning 'on' present similar patterns. In Fongbe, the postposition meaning 'on' is *jí*. The phrase headed by *jí* may occur as the complement of a verb of change of location such as *ɖó* 'to put,' as in (44a). The Haitian counterpart of Fongbe *jí* is the preposition *sou* 'on.' The phrase headed by *sou* may appear as the object of the verb *mete* 'to put,' as shown in (44b).

(44) a. *Kɔkú sɔ́ àsɔ́n ɖó távò jí.*   Fongbe
          Koku take crab put table on
          'Koku put the crab on the table.'   (= (1b) in Lefebvre 1991)

      b. *Jan pran sak la mete sou tab la.*   Haitian
          John take bag DEF put on table DEF
          'John put the bag on the table'   (= (12a) in Déchaine 1988: 21)

Again, abstracting away from word order (discussed in Chapter 5), the data in (44) suggest that the properties of Haitian *sou* replicate those of Fongbe *jí*. According to our hypothesis, *jí* 'on' was relabeled as *sou* 'on' on the basis of the French preposition *sur* 'on,' as is represented in (45) within the RCxG model.

(45)

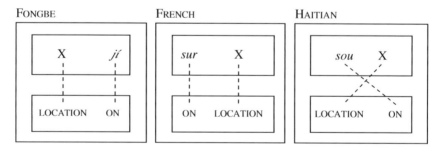

In Fongbe, locative postpositions may combine with the preposition *ɖò* 'at' to form a complex locative expression. Hence, *ɖò . . . jí* means 'at . . . on.' Some uses of Haitian *sou* correspond to *ɖò . . . jí*, as shown in (47).

(46) a. *Kɔkú wlán wémà ɔ́   ɖò távò ɔ́   jí*
Koku write letter DEF at table DEF on
'Koku wrote a letter on the table.'   (Lefebvre's field notes)

b. *Jan   ekri   lèt   la   sou tab   la*
John write letter DEF on   table DEF
'John wrote the letter on the table.'   (Lefebvre's field notes)

In (44) the post-/prepositional phrases are in argument positions, while in (46) they are in adjunct position.

As we saw in the preceding section, Fongbe *ɖò* is not only a locative preposition meaning 'at' but also a locative predicate meaning 'be at.' As such, it may combine with the postposition *jí,* as shown in (47a). The corresponding Haitian locative expression involves only *sou* as is illustrated in (47b).

(47) a. *Àwǐ ɔ́   ɖò   távò jí.*
cat   DEF be.at table on
'The cat is on the table.'   (Lambert-Brétière's field notes)

b. *Chat la   sou   tab   la.*
cat   DEF be.at.on table DEF
'The cat is on the table.'   (Lambert-Brétière's field notes)

As in Fongbe example (47a), the Haitian locative phrase in (47b) is a predicate that requires the semantic component BE.AT.

In section 4.1, we saw that the double function of *ɖò* as a preposition and a locative predicate is supported by extraction facts (see (30)–(33)). Extraction facts also support the double function of *sou* as a preposition and a locative predicate. When *sou* is a preposition, as in (46b), the constituent it heads can be fronted, just like its Fongbe counterpart. This is shown in (48).

(48) a. *Ðò távò ɔ́   jí wè, Kɔkú wlán wémà ɔ́*
at   table DEF on FOC Koku write letter DEF
'It is on the table that Koku wrote the letter.'   (Lefebvre's field notes)

b. *Se   sou tab   la   Jan ekri   lèt   la*
FOC on   table DEF Jan write letter DEF
'It is on the table that Jan wrote the letter.'   (Lefebvre's field notes)

When *sou* is a locative predicate, the phrase it heads can be fronted, provided that the extraction site contains the resumptive form *yé*, as is shown in (49). Recall from section 4.1 that, according to DeGraff (1992b: 175), *yé* is a pro-predicate that spells out the trace left by fronting of a nonverbal predicate.

(49) a. *se sou   tab   la   chat la   HAITIAN
          FOC be.at.on table DEF   cat   DEF

      b. Se sou   tab   la   chat la   yé.   HAITIAN
          FOC be.at.on table DEF   cat   DEF RES
          'It is on the table that the cat is.'   (Lambert-Brétière's field notes)

The extraction facts above argue for the two functions of Haitian *sou*, as a preposition and as a locative predicate.

The parallel between the Fongbe and Haitian data can be accounted for by relabeling as represented in (50), where *ɖò . . . jí* '(be) at . . . on' has been relabeled as *sou* '(be) at on' on the basis of French *sur* 'on.'

(50)

This is a plausible representation since French *sur* does occur in contexts where we find *sou* in Haitian. For example, *Jean a mis le sac sur la table* (see (44b)), *Jean a écrit la lettre sur la table* (see (46b)), *Le chat est sur la table* (see (47b)).

In section 4.1, we saw that some uses of Haitian *nan* correspond to French *de* 'of, from,' rather than to French *dans* 'in.' Similar data involve Haitian *sou*. Some examples are provided in (51).

(51) a. *Ou pa   bezwen leve   li   sou chèz la.*   HAITIAN
          2SG NEG   need   get.up 3SG   SOU chair DEF
          'You do not need to make him get up from the chair.'

                                                      (Valdman et al. 2007: 426)

b. *Retire asyèt sal yo sou tab la.*   HAITIAN
remove plates dirty PL SOU table DEF
'Remove the dirty dishes from the table.'   (Valdman et al. 2007: 637)

c. *Pèp la mande general la wete kò*   HAITIAN
people DEF ask   general DEF remove body
l sou pouvwa a.
3SG SOU power DEF
'The people asked the general to give up power.'
[Lit.: 'The people asked the general to remove himself from power.'
(Valdman et al. 2007: 761)

d. *X pran 500 goud sou chèk tout anplwaye.*   HAITIAN
take   gourds SOU check each employee
'X takes 500 gourds from each employee's check.'
(Valdman et al. 2007: 585)

The corresponding French data involve the preposition *de* 'of, from,' as in *Tu n'as pas besoin de le faire lever **de** sa chaise* (see (51a)), *Enlève les assiettes sales **de** la table* (see (51b)), *Le peuple a demandé au général de se retirer **du** (= de+le) pouvoir* (see (51c)), and *X prend 500 gourdes **du** cheque de chaque employé* (see (51d)).[9] Again, the semantic discrepancy between Haitian *sou* and French *sur* follows from a relabeling-based account of creole genesis. In Fongbe, the locative constructions corresponding to the uses of Haitian *sou* in (51) all involve the postposition *jí*, as is illustrated in (52).

(52) a. *À ná cí.tè sín zìnkpò tòwè jí*   FONGBE
2SG FUT get.up from chair your on
'You will get up from your chair.'   (Maxime da Cruz p.c.)

b. *É fɔ gànnú kwíjíkwíjí lé sín távò ɔ́ jí.*   FONGBE
3SG remove plate dirty   PL from table DEF on
'He removed the dirty plates from the table.
(Maxime da Cruz p.c.)

---

[9] In colloquial French, the preposition *sur* is possible in *X prend 500 dollars sur le cheque de chaque employé*, but must be used in conjunction with the preposition *de* to explicitly mean 'from on,' as in *Tu n'as pas besoin de le faire lever **de sur** sa chaise, Enlève les assiettes sales **de sur** la table*. However, this usage is not always possible, as is shown by the ungrammaticality of **le peuple a demandé au général de se retirer **de sur** le pouvoir*.

c. *Gánsùnvínɔ́ ɔ́   jè.tè   sín   gán   jí.*   FONGBE
   general   DEF retire from power on.
   'The General retired from power.'   (Maxime da Cruz, p.c.)

d. *Ùn   ɖè   élɔ́   sín   sùnzánfúfó   àkwé   tòwè   jí.*   FONGBE
   1SG retire DEM from month.work money your   on
   'I retained this from your salary.'   (Maxime da Cruz, p.c.)

On the basis of data such as those in (52), we suggest that, having relabeled *jí* 'on' and *ɖò . . . jí* '(be) at . . . on' as *sou* in contexts such as (44),
(46), and (47), the creators of the Haitian lexicon used *sou* in all the contexts where Fongbe *jí* occurred, including those in (52). This follows from
the nature of relabeling.

The above analysis accounts for the fact that the properties of Haitian
sou sometimes correspond to those of Fongbe *jí*, and sometimes to the
constructions involving the combination *ɖò . . . jí* '(be) at . . . on.' It also
explains why Haitian *sou* has a larger semantic range than the French form
sur from which it is phonetically derived. Finally, it accounts for the fact
that, like *nan*, *sou* is a mega-locative morpheme in Haitian.

4.3. Summary

The semantic properties of the Haitian prepositions *nan* and *sou* often
correspond to a construction involving two words in the substrate language. They cannot be accounted for within a relabeling account formulated within the P&P model, since, in this model, *ɖò . . . mὲ* and
ɖò . . . jí do not constitute lexical entries. They can, however, be accounted for within a relabeling account in the RCxG framework, in
which associations of two words forming a construction are listed in
the lexicon, thereby allowing for the construction to be relabeled. The
data discussed in this section also show that several lexical entries may
be relabeled on the same superstrate form, yielding "mega" lexical entries in the creole.

5. Verb-Doubling Constructions

Verb-doubling constructions are rather rare among the languages of the
world. They comprise four constructions: temporal and causal adverbials,

factive clauses, and the predicate cleft construction. These four constructions are illustrated in Fongbe in (53). Note that the cluster of these four constructions is a typological feature of West African languages (Koopman 1986) and of the creole languages that have evolved from them (Lefebvre 2011a).

(53)   a.   TEMPORAL ADVERBIAL

         Wá   *Jan*   *wá*   *(tróló)*   *bɔ̀*   *Màrí*   *yì.*   FONGBE

         arrive John arrive as-soon-as and-then Mary leave

         'As soon as John arrived, Mary left.'   (= (1) in Lefebvre 1994a)

     b.   CAUSAL ADVERBIAL

         Wá   *Jan*   *wá*   *útú*   *Màrí*   *yì.*   FONGBE

         arrive John arrive cause Mary leave

         'Because John arrived, Mary left.'   (= (2) in Lefebvre 1994a)

     c.   FACTIVE

         Wá   *ɖěè Jan wá*   *ɔ́*   *víví*   *nú nɔ̀*   *tɔ̀n.*   FONGBE

         arrive OP   John arrive DEF make.happy for mother GEN

         'The fact that John arrived made his mother happy.'

                                        (= (3) in Lefebvre 1994a)

     d.   PREDICATE CLEFT

         Wá   *wὲ*   *Jan*   *wá.*   FONGBE

         arrive it-is John arrive

         'It is arrive that John did (not, e.g., leave).'

                                        (= (4) in Lefebvre 1994a)

Abstracting away from the labels of specific lexical items, the four constructions can be schematized as in (54).

(54)   a.   TEMPORAL ADVERBIAL

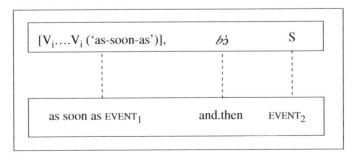

b. CAUSAL ADVERBIAL

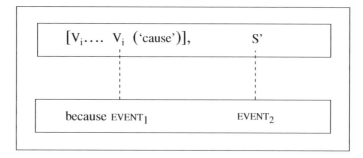

c. FACTIVE

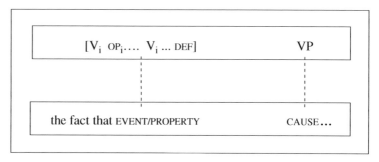

d. PREDICATE CLEFT

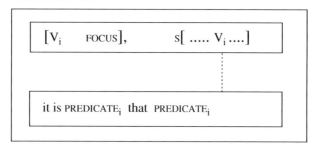

Given the semantics of these constructions, not all verbs may participate in all of them. Restrictions on the verb classes that may participate in these constructions are discussed in Larson and Lefebvre (1991) and Lefebvre and Ritter (1993).

Regardless of their superstrate language—French, English, Portuguese, or Spanish—Caribbean creoles exhibit these four constructions. In (55), the Haitian Creole data are presented. They parallel the Fongbe data in (53), reproduced below.

(55) a. TEMPORAL ADVERBIAL

  Wá *Jan* *wá* *(tróló),* *bɔ̀* *Màrí* *yì.*   Fongbe
  Rive *Jan* *rive,*   *(epi)* *Mari* *pati.*   Haitian
  arrive John arrive as-soon-as and-then Mary leave
  'As soon as John arrived, Mary left.'   (= (1) in Lefebvre 1994b)

b. CAUSAL ADVERBIAL

  Wá *Jan* *wá* *útú,* *Màrí* *yì.*   Fongbe
  Rive *Jan* *rive,*   *Mari* *pati.*   Haitian
  arrive John arrive cause Mary leave
  'Because John arrived, Mary left.'   (= (2) in Lefebvre 1994b)

c. FACTIVE

  Wá *ɖĕè* *Jan* *wá* *ɔ́,* *víví*   Fongbe
  Rive *ø* *Jan* *rive* *a,* *fè*   Haitian
  arrive OP John arrive def make(-happy)
  nú *nɔ̀* *tɔ̀n.*
  manman *li* *Ø* *kòntan.*
  for mother his GEN happy
  'The fact that John arrived made his mother happy.'
          (= (3) in Lefebvre 1994b)

d. PREDICATE CLEFT

  Wá *wè* *Jan* *wá.*   Fongbe
  Se **rive** *Jan* *rive.*   Haitian
  it-is arrive it-is John arrive
  'It is arrive that John did (not, e.g., leave).'
          (= (4) in Lefebvre 1994b)

The striking fact about the Haitian data is that they replicate the substrate constructions in a remarkable way, with the following minor exceptions. In contrast to Fongbe, Haitian Creole does not have clause-final lexical items meaning 'as soon as' or 'cause' (see (55a) and (55b), respectively). While Fongbe factive clauses manifest an overt nominal operator (the same as the one that participates in relative clause structures; Lefebvre & Brousseau 2002: 118–120), Haitian Creole has a null nominal operator in these constructions (Lefebvre 1998). Finally, in the predicate cleft constructions, while the Fongbe morpheme meaning 'it-is' is constituent-final, it is constituent-initial in Haitian.

The four constructions involving verb-doubling phenomena also exist in Saramaccan, as is shown in (56).

(56) a. TEMPORAL ADVERBIAL

Kó   Rohit kó   a   wósu pálá,   hen
arrive Rohit arrive LOC house as-soon-as and.then

Rowe gó.   SARAMACCAN
Rowe leave

'As soon as Rohit arrived at the house, Rowe left.'

(Lefebvre's field notes)

b. CAUSAL ADVERBIAL

Wáka a   wáka, a   kó   wéi.   SARAMACCAN
walk   3SG walk   3SG get tire

'Because she walked, she got tired.'   (Lefebvre's field notes)

c. FACTIVE

Dí **wáka** a   wáka, hen mei   a   kó   wéi.   SARAMACCAN
DEF walk   3SG walk   it   cause 3SG get tire

'The fact that she walked caused her to get tired.'

(Lefebvre's field notes)

d. PREDICATE CLEFT

Wáka a   wáka lóntu   dí   wósu.   SARAMACCAN
walk   3SG walk go around DEF house

'He really walked around the house.'

(= (11b) in Van den Berg 1987: 104)

Like the Haitian data in (55), the Saramaccan data closely parallel the Fongbe data in (53). Note that in contrast to Haitian (55a), in the temporal adverbial construction, Saramaccan has a constituent-final word *pálá* 'as soon as' that corresponds to Fongbe *tróló* 'as soon as' in (53a). As in Haitian (see (55b), however, in causal adverbial clauses, Saramaccan lacks the clause-final 'cause' lexical item of Fongbe (see (53b)). In factive clauses, Saramaccan has a null nominal operator, as does Haitian (see (55c)). And as in both Fongbe and Haitian, the factive clause requires the definite determiner. However, in Saramaccan, the determiner is constituent-initial, *dí* N 'the N,' and that is where it appears in factive clauses (see (56c)).

The four constructions involving verb-doubling phenomena are also manifested in Papiamentu, as shown in (57).

(57) a. TEMPORAL ADVERBIAL

    Yega ku   Juan a   yega, Maria a   bai.   PAPIAMENTU
    arrive COMP John PERF arrive Mary   PERF go
    'As soon as John arrived, Mary left.'   (Kearns 2008a)

    b. CAUSAL ADVERBIAL

    E **yega** ku   Juan a   yega, Maria a   bai.   PAPIAMENTU
    DEF arrive COMP John PERF arrive Mary   PERF go
    'Because John has arrived, Mary left.'   (Kearns 2008a)

    c. FACTIVE

    E **yega**   ku   Juan a   yega a   hasi
    DEF arrive   COMP John PERF arrive PERF make
    su   mama felis.   PAPIAMENTU
    POSS mother happy
    'The fact that John has arrived made his mother happy.'

    (Kearns 2008a)

    d. PREDICATE CLEFT

    Ta **kome** *el   a   kome.*   PAPIAMENTU
    it.is eat   3SG PERF eat
    'He has eaten.'   (= (332) in Maurer 1988a: 141)

Again, these constructions are built on the model of the Fongbe constructions in (53). As is the case in Saramaccan, the definite determiner in Papiamentu is constituent-initial, *e* N 'the N,' including in factive constructions.

Within the P&P model, the four constructions discussed in this section can only be mentioned as an available parametric option. It is not clear, however, how the parameter should be formulated. Lefebvre (1998: 363–374) tentatively suggests that availability of these phenomena may correlate with the properties of the determiner system. The fact remains that, in this model, the structure of each of the constructions involved is not provided as a whole unit in the grammar. Within the RCxG model, however, these four constructions are listed in the lexicon-syntax continuum, in a way similar to (54). We assume that, as the creators of the Caribbean creoles were building their respective creole lexicons, they retained the structures in (54) from their original lexicon. The similarity between the three creoles, and their similarity with Fongbe in this respect, cannot be a coincidence. The facts reported on in this section strongly support an analysis along the lines of our main proposal.

6. Conclusion

The objective of this chapter was to compare the predictions of two different approaches to the lexicon, P&P, and RCxG, for a relabeling-based account of creole genesis on the basis of data drawn from a subset of Caribbean creoles and their contributing languages. The results of this study show that, for all the constructions presented in this chapter, the RCxG framework presents clear advantages over the P&P model with respect to relabeling. First, constructions are listed in the grammar in the RCxG framework, so this framework allows for an account of the retention, from the substrate languages, of subsystems of the grammar such as the TMA system (section 2) and constructions involving verb-doubling phenomena (section 5). Second, since in the RCxG framework, constructions that involve more than one word may be listed in the lexicon, it allows for an account of the fact that a single lexical item in a creole may correspond to a complex construction in the substrate language. As we saw in section 3, the Fongbe imperfective construction involves two items: *ɖò . . . wè*. In RCxG, these two items constitute the imperfective construction. The fact that they can be listed together as a construction makes it possible to relabel them with a single superstrate lexical item. This explains why the imperfective markers, *ap* in Haitian Creole and *tá* in Saramaccan, present the same properties as the complex imperfective construction *ɖò . . . wè* in Fongbe. Similar data drawn from locative constructions were also discussed (e.g., *ɖò . . . mè* '(be) at . . . in' and *ɖò . . . jí* '(be) at . . . on') from a relabeling point of view. It was also shown that two different lexical items may be relabeled by the same superstrate label, which explains why the locative prepositions of Haitian correspond to more than one locative construction in its substrate languages.

CHAPTER 5 | Relabeling and Word Order

A Construction Grammar Perspective

CLAIRE LEFEBVRE AND RENÉE LAMBERT-BRÉTIÈRE

1. Introduction

1.1. The Puzzle of Word Order in Creoles and in Creole Genesis

Word order in creoles and in creole genesis has long been, and still is, a puzzle for researchers.* While the vast majority of creoles are subject-verb-object (SVO) languages (e.g., Caribbean creoles, see Muysken 1988a: 85), some are subject-object-verb (SOV) (e.g., Hiri Motu), and some even have both SOV and object-subject-verb (OSV) order (e.g., Pigin Yimas (-Arafundi)). While the vast majority of creoles derive their word order from their superstrate languages (e.g., Plag 2008; Siegel 2008), some appear to constitute counterexamples to this generalization. For example, Berbice Dutch is SVO in spite of the fact that both of its contributing sources, Dutch and Ijo, are SOV languages (e.g., Kouwenberg 1996; Muysken 1988a). While Saramaccan is generally an SVO language, like its superstrate languages, English and Portuguese, it has postpositions, a feature of OV languages, like its substrate Gbe languages (e.g., Essegbey 2005).

*The content of this chapter was presented at the 2012 SPCL/LSA meeting in Portland; we would like to thank the participants, particularly Clancy Clements and Tonjes Veenstra, for their valuable questions, comments, and suggestions. The content of this chapter was also presented at the Max Planck Institute for Evolutionary Anthropology in Leipzig and at the English Departments of the Universities of Düsseldorf and of Erlangen in November 2012. Questions and comments by participants, in particular Martin Haspelmath, Susanne Michaelis, Ingo Plag, Jürgen Lang, and Angelika Lutz, were much appreciated.

In some cases, it may look as if the respective contributions of the source languages to a creole's word order are split between lexical and functional categories.[1] For example, the structures in (1), (2), and (3) provide an overview of constituent and word order in the nominal structures of Fongbe, Haitian, and French (OBJP = objective phrase, GENP = genitive phrase, RC = relative clause).

(1)

OBJP N ADJ { GENP / RC } ADJ NUM { DEM / INDEF } DEF PL Q RC   FONGBE

(Lefebvre & Brousseau 2002: 56)

(2)

Q { NUM / INDEF } ADJ N OBJP GENP { ADJ / RC } DEM DEF PL RC   HAITIAN

(3)

Q { DEF / DEM / POSS } NUM ADJ N OBJP OBJP { ADJ / RC }   FRENCH

As can be seen from these structures, the constituent and word orders of Haitian correspond partially to those of Fongbe, a substrate language, and partially to those of French, the lexifier language. Apart from relative clauses, which appear to the right of the head noun in all three languages, it looks as though major category lexical items—adjectives, numerals, and quantifiers—follow the word order of French, whereas functional category lexical items—demonstrative terms, definite determiners, and plural markers—follow the word order of Fongbe. For example, while adjectives, numerals, and quantifiers follow the noun in Fongbe, they all precede it in Haitian, on the model of French. Furthermore, in Haitian, adjectives may either precede or follow the noun, as in French. By contrast, Haitian definite determiners (DEM DEF PL) all follow the noun, as in Fongbe, and unlike in French, where these items all precede the noun.

The generalization that lexical categories follow the word order of the superstrate language, and functional categories that of the substrate languages, is only partially correct, however, as the word order of some functional categories in creoles departs from that of their substrate languages. For example, unlike Haitian and Fongbe, where the plural marker follows the noun, in Martinican Creole it precedes it. This is illustrated in (4).

---

[1] For a proposal along these lines, see Lefebvre and Lumsden (1992).

(4) a. *liv*   *la*   *yo*   HAITIAN
         wèmá   *ɔ́*   *lé*   FONGBE
         book   DEF   PL   (Lefebvre's field notes)
         'these books'

     b. *se*   *liv*   *la*   MARTINICAN
         PL   book   DEF
         'these books'   (Lefebvre's field notes)

A similar example is provided by Saramaccan where, in contrast to Martinican, Haitian, and Fongbe, the definite determiner precedes the noun, as shown in (5).

(5) a. *liv*   *la*   HAITIAN & MARTINICAN
         wèmá   *ɔ́*   FONGBE
         book   DEF
         'the book'   (Lefebvre's field notes)

     b. *di*   *búku*   SARAMACCAN
         DEF   book
         'the book'   (Lefebvre's field notes)

Other similar examples can be found in Lefebvre (1998). Thus, the hypothesis that the contributions of the source languages to a creole's word order are divided between lexical and functional categories falls short in view of counterexamples of the type in (5b) (see also the discussion in Plag 2000).

Another avenue, explored in Lefebvre (2007), is that word order in creoles is established on the basis of the position of the form that provides the label for a lexical entry in the creole in question. For lexical categories, this is illustrated by the surface position, in Haitian, of adjectives, numerals, and quantifiers (see (2)), with respect to that of the same categories in Haitian's source languages (see (1) and (3)) (see also Aboh 2006). For functional categories, this is illustrated by the position of the definite determiners in (5). The form of the Haitian and Martinican definite determiners is derived from the French postnominal adverbial deictic form *là*; the definite determiner is thus postnominal in these creoles (see (5a)) (for details, see Lefebvre 1998: 78–79, and the references cited therein). The form of the Saramaccan definite determiner *di* (< *di(si)*) is derived from the English prenominal form *this*; the definite determiner is thus prenominal in this creole (see (5b)) (for details, see Lefebvre 2012). In some cases, lexical items have been retained from the substrate languages. For example, in Saramaccan, the Fongbe focus marker *wὲ* has been retained as such, including its low tone (e.g., Smith 1996). In this case, there is also a link between the label and the word order. As is shown in (6), the position of the creole lexical entry is the same as that of the substrate language form (see also Smith 1996: 126).

(6) a. *Masὲ   ví   lέ   wὲ,   wá*   FONGBE
         Massὲ   child PL   it.is arrive
         'It is the people of Massὲ who have arrived.'

                                              (from Hounkpatin 1985: 218)

    b. *Andí   wὲ   i   bói.*   SARAMACCAN
        what   FOC   you   cook
        'What did you cook?'   (= (11b) in Smith 1996: 117)

In this chapter, we will argue in support of the generalization that word order in creole genesis is mainly determined by that of the form (from either the superstrate or the substrate language) that provides the label for the creole lexical item. We will show, however, that this proposal is not sufficient to account for all cases of word order. For example, while both the definite determiner and the plural marker in Haitian are individually derived from French postnominal forms—*là* and *eux*, respectively—as we saw in Chapter 3, there is nothing in the French nominal structure that could account for the surface order of these morphemes with respect to one another in the creole (see (4)). Furthermore, some data appear to constitute counterexamples to the above generalization. For example, the fact that there are postpositions in Saramaccan such as *báka* 'behind' from English *back* and *déndu* 'in' from Portuguese *dentro* 'in' constitutes a counterexample, as *back* and *dentro* in English and Portuguese are not postpositional but prepositional. At first glance, then, it looks as if there were no principled way in which word order would be established in creoles.

In addition to the general problem posed by word order in creole genesis, as outlined above, there is the specific problem posed by the choice of a theoretical framework. For example, the relabeling-based account of creole genesis advocated in Lefebvre (1998, and related literature) was formulated within a theoretical model in which directionality properties are specified as part of individual lexical entries (e.g., the notation V__ specifies that the verb takes its complement to the right). Since a creole's word order does not necessarily reproduce that of its substrate languages, as we saw above, word order phenomena constitute systematic counterexamples to a relabeling-based account of creole genesis in such a model (see, e.g., the discussion in DeGraff 2002: 355–367). Since relabeling was otherwise shown to account for a vast amount of creole data, we would not want to falsify a relabeling-based account of creole genesis on the basis of word order alone. Instead, we conclude that word order should not be included in individual lexical entries. The account of word order in creole genesis proposed in this chapter is thus set within a theoretical framework in which word order is not specified as part of individual lexical entries, namely Croft's (2001) Radical Construction Grammar (RCxG).

In the last three decades, a large body of research on word order in creoles and in creole genesis has been carried out from various perspectives. For example, Kouwenberg (1996) addressed the problem from a functionalist point of view, Déprez (2007) from a generativist point of view, and Plag (2008) from a second language acquisition point of view. The goal of this chapter is to address this topic from yet another perspective: a relabeling-based account of creole genesis cast within the RCxG framework (Croft 2001).

1.2. Relabeling and Word Order within Croft's RCxG Model

Recall from Chapter 4 that, within the RCxG framework, word order is not specified as part of individual lexical entries, but rather as part of the constructions in which words occur. Throughout this chapter, we will assume that the RCxG lexicon has the features described in section 1.2.2 of Chapter 4. Second, we will assume that non-atomic constructions of the substrate lexicon-syntax continuum—that is, complex constructions—are all available to the incipient creole. Third, we will assume that substrate atomic structures—that is, lexical entries per se—are relabeled on the basis of superstrate forms, as discussed in Chapter 1.

With these assumptions in mind, we hypothesized that relabeling proceeds in one of two ways. It is either bound to a linguistic context, as in the case of modifiers and determiners, or it is free from a linguistic context, as in the case of denotational nouns and verbs. Lexical entries that are bound to a linguistic context are those that cannot appear in isolation. These are hypothesized to be relabeled on the basis of superstrate forms that are bound to a linguistic context. For example, determiners (e.g., definite/indefinite) and modifiers (e.g., adjectives, adverbs) cannot be relabeled outside a linguistic context. Indeed, a superstrate form can only be identified as a potential form for a determiner if it occurs with a noun that it relates to; likewise, a superstrate form can only be identified as a modifier if it occurs with a noun or a verb that it modifies, and so on. We therefore assume that, in these cases, relabeling proceeds on the basis of the minimal constructions in which eligible forms for determiners and modifiers occur in the superstrate language (e.g., [DET NP], [ADJ N]). In these cases, relabeling triggers the word order of the superstrate language in the creole. For example, in the genesis of Haitian, the postnominal quantifiers of the Gbe languages were relabeled on the basis of French prenominal quantifiers identified from the construction [Q NP]. The initial substrate structure [NP Q] thus had to be revised to [Q NP] in the creole, on the model of the superstrate language. This is illustrated in (7).

(7)   a.   FONGBE
           [NP Q]
      b.   FONGBE/FRENCH
           [NP Q]/[Q NP]
      c.   HAITIAN
           [Q NP]

However, the Fongbe postnominal definite determiner *ɔ́* was relabeled on the basis of the French postnominal deictic form *là,* yielding the Haitian postnominal definite determiner *la.* Thus, the substrate construction [NP DEF] could be retained unchanged in the creole. This is illustrated in (8).

(8)   a.   FONGBE
           [NP *ɔ́*]
      b.   FONGBE/FRENCH
           [NP *ɔ́*]/[NP *là*]
      c.   HAITIAN
           [NP *la*]

Lexical entries that are free from a linguistic context may appear in isolation. These are hypothesized to be relabeled on the basis of superstrate forms that are also free from a linguistic context. In this case, the semantic overlap between the two words that are associated in relabeling is identified on the basis of the pragmatics of the situation (Lefebvre & Lumsden 1994a). This is the case, for example, with denotational nouns such as *table, chair, child,* and so on; verbs such as *come, go, eat,* and so on; and deictic terms such as *here/there,* and so on. Lexical items that are relabeled free of linguistic context will be able to associate with the syntactic constructions of the substrate lexicon-syntax continuum that are available to the creators of a creole. For example, relabeled verbs will be able to associate with the substrate V . . . V structure of the serial verb construction, with the structures involved in verb-doubling phenomena (discussed in Chapter 4, section 5), and so on.

We therefore assume that, in creole genesis, relabeling applies throughout the lexicon-grammar continuum. It will be argued that the way in which word order is established is derivable from how relabeling is hypothesized to apply in creole genesis. Our proposal is summarized in (9).

(9)   a.   Word order in creoles is derivable from how relabeling applies in creole genesis.

       b.   Relabeling may be linguistically context-bound, in which case it triggers the superstrate word order, and this word order appears in the creole. This follows from the fact that labels and their positions are associated.

       c.   Relabeling may also be linguistically context-free, in which case relabeled lexical items may associate with substrate structures, and substrate word order appears in the creole.

1.3. Corpus

The bulk of our data is based on Caribbean creoles: Haitian (Haiti), Saramaccan (Surinam, French Guyana), and, to a lesser extent, Martinican Creole (Martinique). These creoles share the same pool of West African substrate languages, including the Gbe cluster of the Kwa family, which in turn is part of the larger Niger-Congo language family (e.g., Lefebvre 1998: 52–62). These creoles have different superstrate languages: French for Haitian and Martinican, English and Portuguese for Saramaccan.[2] Data from other creoles will also be discussed whenever they contribute something different to the discussion.

1.4. Organization of the Chapter

The chapter is organized as follows. Section 2 provides an account of word order for the linguistically bound lexical items such as modifiers and determiners. Section 3 presents an account of the position of demonstrative

---

[2] The Gbe languages and Saramaccan are tone languages. The representation of tones in Fongbe is phonemic and follows the notation adopted in Lefebvre and Brousseau (2002, Chapter 2). Given the variation in the notation of Saramaccan tones in the literature, the tones have been standardized for all the Saramaccan examples based on Rountree et al.'s Word List (2000).

terms in nominal structures. Section 4 discusses the position of numerals. Section 5 accounts for the availability of postpositions in Saramaccan. Section 6 addresses various potential counterexamples to our proposal, all involving OV/VO structures. Section 7 discusses the position of the Haitian negation marker *pa*. Section 8 concludes the chapter.

2. Deriving the Order of Modifiers and Determiners

In this section, we show how the proposal presented in the preceding section can be implemented for word order phenomena that are linguistically context-bound. We begin with the order of modifiers, summarized in (10) (from (1) to (3)).

(10) a.   N ADJ Q   FONGBE
      b. Q ADJ N ADJ   FRENCH
      c. Q ADJ N ADJ   HAITIAN

Fongbe speakers participating in the creation of the Haitian lexicon-grammar would relabel the quantifiers and adjectives of their own lexicon, on the basis of French forms. The modifiers of the superstrate language must occur in combination with nouns in order to be identified as such by the creators of a creole. By hypothesis, the creators of Haitian would have identified the French modifiers on the basis of the French constructions depicted in (11). Since the order of linguistically context-bound morphemes is determined by that of the forms that have provided the labels for the creole constructions, the Haitian constructions in (11) show the same word order as the corresponding French constructions. The formalism in (11) reflects the fact that the semantics of the Haitian construction replicates that of Fongbe, while the word order replicates that of French, whence the crossed lines in the representations of the Haitian constructions.

(11)

a. Quantifiers

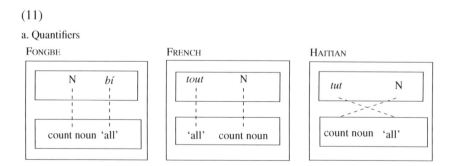

b. Adjectives

| FONGBE | FRENCH | HAITIAN |

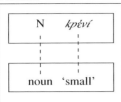 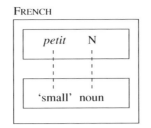 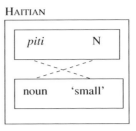

The relabeling of the substrate modifiers (see (10a)) on the basis of the French modifiers (see (10b)) created a creole construction that reflects French word order (see (10c)).

The surface order of definite determiners in Haitian and Saramaccan is derived in a similar fashion. A superstrate form has to occur in combination with a noun in order to be identified as a potential form to relabel a determiner. The pertinent data are summarized in (12a) and (12b) for Haitian and Saramaccan, respectively.

(12)   a.   N   DEF   FONGBE
               DEF   N   *là*   FRENCH
                    N   DEF   HAITIAN

       b.   N   DEF   FONGBE
           this   N   ENGLISH
               DEF   N   SARAMACCAN

Lefebvre (1998: 78–79) shows that French prenominal definite determiners were not identified as such by the creators of Haitian, who identified the postnominal deictic form *là* as a suitable item to relabel the substrate postnominal definite determiner. By hypothesis, they identified this form on the basis of the French construction in (13) Since the order of linguistically context-bound morphemes is determined by that of the form that provided the label for the creole lexical entry, and since the form that was selected from French is postnominal, the position of the definite determiner in Haitian is postnominal, as shown in (13).

(13)

| FONGBE | FRENCH | HAITIAN |

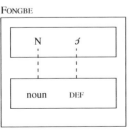 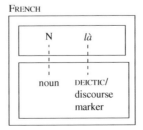 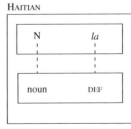

In this case, the superstrate construction manifests the same word order as the substrate construction. For Saramaccan, however, the Fongbe postnominal definite determiner *ɔ́* was relabeled on the basis of the English prenominal form *this,* yielding the prenominal definite determiner *di(si)*, as shown in (14).

(14)

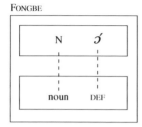
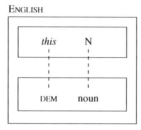
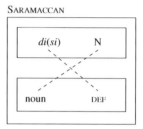

The relabeling of the substrate postnominal definite determiner on the basis of an English prenominal form resulted in the creation of a creole construction [DEF NP] that reflects the word order of English (see (12b)).

The derivation of the differential positions of the Haitian and Martinican plural markers in (4a) and (4b), respectively, may be accounted for in a similar way. As is discussed in Lefebvre (1998: 79–84, and the references cited therein), several Haitian substrate languages, including Ewegbe (but not Fongbe), have a single morpheme that serves both as a third-person plural pronoun and as a plural marker in nominal structures. Speakers of such a grammar would have relabeled this morpheme on the basis of the French third-person plural personal pronoun *eux* that may, in some contexts, occur postnominally as an emphatic form. This yielded the Haitian form *yo* depicted in (15). (For details, see Lefebvre 1998: 79–84; Lefebvre 2004b: 241–245).

(15)

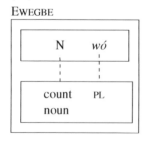
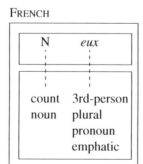
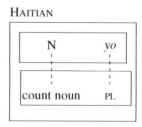

Note that, in this case, the Ewegbe and French forms have the same word order, and thus the creole also manifests the initial substrate construction [NP PL]. Such correspondences between the substrate and the superstrate word orders do not always exist, however. For example, consider the Martinican plural marker *se* illustrated in (4b). In this case, the substrate postnominal plural form was relabeled on the basis of the French prenominal forms *ces* (demonstrative plural determiner) or *ses* (possessive plural determiner), both pronounced [se]/[sɛ], yielding the Martinican prenominal plural form *se*, depicted in (16).

(16)

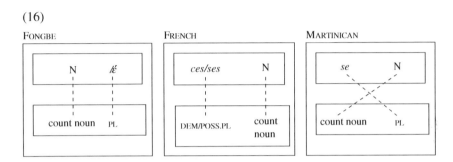

In this case, relabeling created the construction [PL NP] in the creole.[3]

Finally, the order of the Saramaccan focus marker *wɛ̀*, retained from Fongbe, can be derived as follows.

(17)

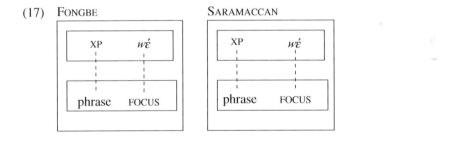

In this case, the substrate lexical entry is retained in the creole, as is the construction in which it occurs, [XP *wɛ̀*], as illustrated in (17).

To summarize, the preceding examples all illustrate the fact that a creole's word orders are established on the basis of the forms that provided

---

[3] The fact that the creators of Haitian chose the French postpositional form *eux* to relabel the Fongbe postnominal plural form, while the creators of Martinican chose the French prenominal forms *ces/ses*, illustrates the possibility that, when presented with more than one possible superstrate form to relabel a substrate lexical entry, different communities may make different choices. Relabeling choices are discussed in Chapter 6.

the labels for the creole lexical entries. Accordingly, labels that were retained in their original form (e.g., Fongbe *wὲ* in Saramaccan), keep their original surface position in the creole. Likewise, labels that come from context-bound lexical items (see (11)–(16)) keep their original superstrate surface position in the creole. If the position of the new form is the same as that of the corresponding form in the substrate language, the creole word order complies with that of both the substrate and the superstrate (see (13) and (15)). If the position of the new form is not the same as that of the corresponding form in the substrate language, a new construction reflecting a new word order is created by relabeling (see (11), (14), and (16)). Assuming this line of analysis to be valid, one may ask whether it is sufficient to account for all cases of word order in creole genesis. As the following sections will show, it is not.

3. Deriving the Position of Demonstrative Terms in Nominal Structures

Abstracting away from major category lexical items, the nominal structures of Fongbe, Haitian, and French are as in (18).

(18)   a.   N   DEM   DEF   PL   FONGBE

        b.   N   DEM   DEF   PL   HAITIAN

        c. $\left\{ \begin{array}{c} \text{DEF.PL} \\ \text{DEM.PL} \end{array} \right\}$ N.PL   FRENCH

One difference between these constructions lies in the expression of plural. In French, plural is realized on determiners, rather than as a free morpheme, as it is in Fongbe and in Haitian. Plural is also expressed on the noun in French, but not in Fongbe or Haitian. This difference need not concern us at this point. What is at stake here is the position of demonstrative terms. As can be seen in (18), demonstrative terms are postnominal in Haitian, as in Fongbe, not prenominal as in French. Given our proposal, we would expect them to be prenominal on the model of French. How can this situation be accounted for?

As Lefebvre (1998: 89–101; 2004b: 250–257) discusses in detail, the two Fongbe demonstrative terms occurring in nominal structures were relabeled on the basis of two French forms, yielding the Haitian paradigm of two demonstrative terms. These facts are summarized in (19).

(19)	FONGBE	FRENCH	HAITIAN
	élɔ́	*ça* [sa]	*sa*
	énɛ́	*cela* [sɔla]/*celui-là* [sɥila]	*sila*

Since the demonstrative terms' labels are drawn from French, we would expect Haitian demonstratives to occur in the position where demonstrative terms surface in that language. However, not only do demonstrative terms not occur prenominally in Haitian, as they do in French, but they in fact occur postnominally, as they do in Fongbe. This is illustrated in (20), exemplifying the constructions in (18).

(20) a. *àsɔ́n* *élɔ́/énɛ́* *ɔ́* *lɛ́*   FONGBE

      b. *krab* *sa/sila* *a* *yo*   HAITIAN
          crab DEM   DEF PL

      c. *ces*   *crabes*   FRENCH
         DEM.PL crab.PL
         'these/those crabs'

At first glance, this state of affairs may seem to constitute a counterexample to our proposal. As is argued in the subsequent discussion, however, this situation follows from it naturally.

On the one hand, the Fongbe demonstrative terms that occur in the nominal structures in (18) may also occur either in isolation, as in (21a) (possibly simultaneously with pointing), in topic position with emphasis, as in (21b), or in an argument position, as in (21c).[4]

(21) a. *élɔ́* / *énɛ́*   FONGBE
         DEM / DEM
         'this / that'

      b. *Énɛ́* *ɔ́,* *wɛ́* *zɔ́n* . . .   FONGBE
         that TOP it.is command
         'That, it is what causes . . .'   (Segurola & Rassinoux 2000)

      c. *Énɛ́* *wá* *yì*   FONGBE
         DEM come go
         'That has passed.'   (Segurola & Rassinoux 2000)

---

[4] Several patterns of interpretation are associated with these forms (for details, see Lefebvre 2004b: 250–257). Only one is shown here. The same remark applies to the Haitian data in (28).

Since the two Fongbe demonstrative terms may occur in isolation, they constitute atomic constructions that can be relabeled as such. On the other hand, the French forms selected to relabel the substrate lexical entries in (19) are not part of the paradigm of demonstrative terms that occur prenominally in nominal structures. Indeed, the demonstrative terms that occur prenominally in French nominal structures are *ce(t)* (masculine singular), *cette* (feminine singular), and *ces* (plural). Haitian *sa/sila* are not derived from these forms. Rather, they are derived from pronominal forms that occur in isolation (again, possibly simultaneously with pointing), as in (22a), or in topic position with emphasis, as in (22b), or even in argument position, as in (22c).

(22)   a.   *ça   / cela / celui-là*   FRENCH
           'that /   that /   that one'

       b.   *Ça / cela / celui-là,   je   le   veux.*   FRENCH
           that /   that /   that one,   1SG   3SG want
           'That/that one, I want it.'

       c.   *Je   veux ça   / cela / celui-là.*   FRENCH
           1SG   want that /   that   /   that one
           'I want that one.'

Presumably, these forms were identified as suitable to relabel the two substrate lexical entries. Since the two French forms selected to relabel the Fongbe forms occurring in isolation were themselves identified in isolation, the new Haitian lexical entries resulting from relabeling could also occur in isolation, as shown in (23a), in topic position, as in (23b), or in argument position, as in (23c).

(23)   a.   *sa   /   sila*   HAITIAN
           DEM   DEM

       b.   *sa/sila a,   m'   vle*   HAITIAN
           DEM   DEF   1SG   want
           'This/that, I want.'

       c.   *M   wè sa   / sila*   HAITIAN
           1SG see DEM   DEM
           'I saw this/that.'   (= (4) in Lefebvre 1997)

The two Fongbe lexical entries that were relabeled as *sa* and *sila*, respectively, also occur in nominal structures, as shown in (24). Since the two French forms used to relabel Fongbe *éné* and *éló* were identified in isolation, the only way to associate the new Haitian lexical entries with nominal structures involved associating them with the substrate nominal structure, yielding (18b) on the model of (18a), depicted in (24).

(24) *krab* *[mwen ø]* *sa* *a* *yo*   HAITIAN
      àsón *[nyè tòn]* *éló* *ó* *lé*   FONGBE
      crab   1SG   GEN   DEM DEF PL

'these/those crabs of mine (in question/that we know of)'

(Lefebvre's field notes)

Interestingly, in the nominal structures of Martinican Creole and Saramaccan, where some functional categories occur prenominally (see (14) and (16)), demonstrative terms also follow the noun as in Fongbe. This is illustrated in (25a) and (25b), respectively.

(25) a. *fanm...* *ta* *la*   MARTINICAN
          woman   DEM   DEF
          'this woman'   (= (1824) in Bernabé 1983: 707)

      b. *dí* *físi* *u* *mi* *akí*   SARAMACCAN
          DEF   fish   of   1SG   DEM
          'this fish of mine'   (Lefebvre's field notes)

The above data show that the word order of substrate lexical items that have been relabeled on the basis of superstrate forms identified in isolation is not constrained by that of the superstrate structure. Because they are freed from the superstrate word order, these lexical items may associate with the relevant position in a substrate construction.

To summarize, the data discussed in this section, like the TMA system and verb-doubling phenomena discussed in Chapter 4, show that substrate language constructions are available to the creators of a creole. The data in (11), (14), and (16) show that relabeling may trigger a change in word order to make the new creole label comply with the surface position of the superstrate form from which it is derived. The data in (24) and (25) show, however, that, when superstrate labels are identified in isolation, as the demonstrative terms discussed here were, they are word-order-free. In such cases, the new creole lexical items may associate with the relevant position of the substrate construction, resulting in structures such as (18b) in Haitian. In light of this analysis, we now turn to the position of numerals.

4. Deriving the Position of Numerals

Numerals may occur in isolation: *one, two, three,* and so on.[5] They may also occur with nouns, as in *two books.* Given this situation, our proposal on word order predicts that there should be two possible word orders for numerals in creoles. In the first case, numerals occurring in isolation would be able to associate with the substrate nominal construction available in the incipient creole; hence, the order of a noun and a numeral in the early creole would reflect the word order of the substrate language. In the second case, a numeral occurring with a noun would trigger the superstrate word order in the creole. This prediction is borne out by the data.

Fa d'Ambô (Post 2013) has postnominal numerals following the word order of its substrate languages (N NUM) rather than that of its Portuguese superstrate (NUM N). In Santome (Hagemeijer 2013), low numbers may occur postnominally, as in the substrate languages. This position appears to be rare, however, as in the synchronic data, numerals are mainly prenominal, as in the superstrate language. In Principense (Maurer 2013), all numerals formerly followed the noun, as in the substrate languages. Now, however, they all precede the noun, as in the superstrate language. According to Maurer, there is one exception to this general rule: the numeral 'one,' which also functions as the indefinite article, still occurs postnominally. In Haitian, all numerals occur prenominally, as in the superstrate language; we do not know whether there was a stage when numerals occurred postnominally, as in the substrate languages.

5. Deriving the Postpositions of Saramaccan

In addition to a few prepositions, Saramaccan has several postpositions. The latter correspond to Fongbe items. For example, a postposition meaning 'surface' is used both in Fongbe (*wú* in (26a)) and in Saramaccan (*sinkíi* (< Eng. *skin*) in (26b)).

(26) a. *Zɔgbè ɔ́ ɖò àzàn ɔ́ **wú.***   FONGBE
           lamp DEF be.at ceiling DEF surface

      b. *Dí lámpu dɛ a dí plafond **sinkíi.***   SARAMACCAN
           DEF lamp be.at LOC DEF ceiling surface
           'The lamp is on the ceiling.'   (from (23) in Essegbey 2005)

---

[5] The detailed content of this section was made possible by Susanne Michaelis, who generously provided us with data yet to appear in APICS at the time we were working on this chapter.

In (27), a postposition meaning 'on' is used both in Fongbe (*jí* in (27a)) and in Saramaccan (*líba* (< Port. *(ar)riba*) in (27b)).

(27) a. *Wěmá   ɔ́   ɖò   távò   ɔ́   jí.*   FONGBE
          book   DEF   be.at table DEF   on

      b. *Dí   búku   dɛ   a   dí   táfa   líba.*   SARAMACCAN
          DEF book   be.at LOC DEF   table on
          'The book is on the table.'   (from (39) in Essegbey 2005)

The labels of the Saramaccan postpositions are derived from English and Portuguese. Since, as we saw above, in the case of linguistically context-bound morphemes, word order is established on the basis of the forms that provided the labels for the creole lexical entries, and since neither English nor Portuguese features postpositions, the fact that Saramaccan has them is unexpected. One would instead expect a situation similar to that in Haitian, where superstrate prepositional forms are used to express locations (see Chapter 4). How can the presence of postpositions in Saramaccan be accounted for?

In Saramaccan, all postpositions can also be used as nouns. An inventory of Saramaccan nouns/postpositions, identified from the available literature, is presented in Table 5.1, along with the sources of their labels (from Muysken 1987; Smith & Cardoso 2004).

With the possible exception of Portuguese *dentro,*[6] the English and Portuguese lexical items that provided the forms of the Saramaccan

TABLE 5.1 Saramaccan Nouns/Postpositions and Their Putative Sources

	SOURCE	CATEGORY	MEANING
líba	< Port. *(ar)riba*	N, P	sky, on, above
sinkíi	< Eng. *skin*	N, P	skin, body, surface
(h)édi	< Eng. *head*	N, P	head, top
báka	< Eng. *back*	N, P	backside, back, behind
fési	< Eng. *face*	N, P	face, forehead, in front
básu	< Port. *(de)baixo*	N, P	bottom, under, underneath
déndu	< Port. *dentro*	N, P	inside, in
bándja	< Port. *banda*	N, P	side, near, next to

[6.] Although a Portuguese-English dictionary provides examples in which *dentro* may be interpreted as functioning as a noun, Jürgen Lang (p.c.) informs us that *dentro* basically belongs to the category P in Portuguese. He adds, however, that this lexical item may be used in isolation: *Dentro!* meaning 'Get inside!'

TABLE 5.2 English and Portuguese Lexical Items That Provided the Labels of the Saramaccan Nouns/Postpositions

	CATEGORY	MEANING
Port. *(ar)riba*	N,?P	up
Eng. *skin*	N, *P	skin
Eng. *head*	N, *P	head
Eng. *back*	N,?P	back, backside
Eng. *face*	N, *P	Face
Port. *(de)baixo*	N, P	under, underneath
Port. *dentro*	?N, P	inside, in
Port. *banda*	N, *P	Side

nouns/postpositions are all denotational nouns. Only a few may also be used as prepositions. This information is summarized in Table 5.2.

A quick comparison of the data in Tables 5.1 and 5.2 reveals that the creole lexical items all have the double function of nouns and postpositions, whereas the closest lexical items in the superstrate languages function either as nouns (in most cases) or as prepositions (in only a few cases). Furthermore, the semantics of the creole lexical items covers a wider scope than their superstrate language counterparts.

The discrepancies between the creole and the superstrate lexical items can be accounted for straightforwardly in a relabeling-based account of creole genesis. As Table 5.3 reveals, each of the Saramaccan nouns/postpositions has a Fongbe counterpart. Furthermore, the semantic scope of these lexical items is the same in Saramaccan and Fongbe (compare Tables 5.1 and 5.3).

The following examples illustrate the striking parallel between the Fongbe and the Saramaccan data. Example (28) shows the use of Fongbe *nùkɔ̀n* 'face, forehead, in front' as a postposition in (a) and a noun in (b).

TABLE 5.3 Saramaccan and Fongbe Nouns/Postpositions

SARAMACCAN N/POST	FONGBE N/POST	MEANING
líba	*jí*	sky, on, above
sinkíi	*wú*	skin, body, surface
hédi	*tà*	head, top
báka	*gúdò*	backside, back, behind
fési	*nùkɔ̀n*	face, forehead, in front
básu	*gló*	bottom, under, underneath
déndu	*mɛ̀*	inside, in
bándja	*àkpá*	side, near, next to

(28)   a.   *Àvún   ɔ́   ɖò   xwé   nùkɔ̀n.*   FONGBE
         dog   DEF   be.at   house   front
         'The dog is in front of the house.'   (= (76a) in Lefebvre &
                                              Brousseau 2002: 325)

      b.   *Xwé   (sín)   nùkɔ̀n   ɔ́   wì.*   FONGBE
         house   of   front   DEF   be.black
         'The front of the house is black.'   (= (76b) in Lefebvre &
                                              Brousseau 2002: 325)

Example (29) illustrates the use of Saramaccan *báka* 'backside, back, behind' as a postposition in (a), and as a noun in (b).

(29)   a.   *. . . a   dí   wósu   báka*   SARAMACCAN
         . . . LOC   DEF   house   back
         'behind the house'   (= (41a) in Muysken 1987)

      b.   *a   dí   báka   (f)u   dí   wósu*   SARAMACCAN
         LOC   DEF   back   of   DEF   house
         'the back of the house'   (based on Bally 2005: 75)

It thus appears that the Fongbe lexical items in Table 5.3 were relabeled on the basis of the English and Portuguese forms identified in Table 5.2, yielding the Saramaccan lexical entries in Table 5.1. But how can the [NP POST] order be derived, given that the superstrate languages do not have postpositions?

We propose that the Fongbe nouns/postpositions in Table 5.3 were relabeled from their nominal function on the basis of superstrate denotational nouns that could be identified in isolation. Example (30) illustrates the relabeling of the Fongbe noun/postposition *àkpá* 'side, near, next to' by the Portuguese noun *bánda* 'side,' yielding the Saramaccan noun/postposition *bándja* 'side, near, next to.'

(30)

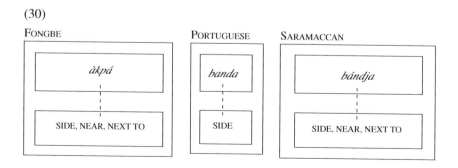

FONGBE	PORTUGUESE	SARAMACCAN
àkpá	*banda*	*bándja*
SIDE, NEAR, NEXT TO	SIDE	SIDE, NEAR, NEXT TO

The creole lexical entries so formed could be associated with the NP position in substrate constructions containing a NP. They could also be associated with the POST position in the substrate construction [NP POST], yielding the Saramaccan construction [NP POST], exemplified in (31).[7]

(31)
NP	V	PREP	NP	POST	
É	dò		xɔ̀	mὲ	FONGBE
A	dε	a	wósu	déndu	SARAMACCAN
3SG	be.at	LOC	house	inside	

'He/she is inside a house.'

To sum up, at first glance, the presence of postpositions in Saramaccan appears to constitute a potential counterexample to the generalization that the word order of a context-bound phrase/word/morpheme in a creole is determined by the superstrate language. In our analysis, however, the relevant substrate lexical items in this case were relabeled on the basis of superstrate forms identified in isolation. As a result, they were word-order-free and could associate with the postnominal position of the substrate constructions.

6. Deriving Potential OV/VO Counterexamples

Berbice Dutch is often cited as an example of a creole that has SVO order even though both its source languages—Ijo, its West African substrate, and Dutch, its European superstrate—are SOV languages (e.g., Kouwenberg 1996; Muysken 1988a). Since the word order of Berbice Dutch does not follow that of its superstrate language, this creole is a potential counterexample to our proposal. Our solution to this potential problem is as follows. Dutch is identified as SOV because OV is the surface order in embedded clauses. However, Dutch is a verb second language, which means that in main clauses the verb surfaces between the subject and the object, resulting in SVO order (e.g., Koster 1978). Examples are shown in (32a) and (32b), respectively.

---

[7] A difference between the Fongbe and Saramaccan constructions is the presence in the latter of a general locative preposition, *a*. The etymology of this preposition is "obscure" (Muysken 2008: 198). Essegbey (2005), following Bruyn (1996), proposes that locative phrases in Saramaccan (and Sranan) are always treated as adjuncts, and as such, must always be introduced by a preposition. This is not the case in Fongbe, where locative complements (as in (30)) do not need to be introduced by a locative preposition. We leave further discussion of this matter to future work.

(32) a. *Ik denk dat Mary het boek las.*   DUTCH
          I think that Mary the book read
          'I think that Mary read the book.'   (= (165a) in Koster 1978: 204)

      b. *Ik haat Mary.*   DUTCH
          I hate Mary
          'I hate Mary.'   (= (158a) in Koster 1978: 199)

We hypothesize that the creators of Berbice Dutch were more likely to have been exposed to Dutch main clauses manifesting an SVO word order than to embedded clauses with an SOV order. In this view, the creators of Berbice Dutch interpreted Dutch clauses as being SVO. Assuming this scenario to be correct, Berbice Dutch word order does follow that of its superstrate language, just like other creoles, and in conformity with our proposal.

Pidgin Yimas(-Arafundi) is an SOV/OSV language.[8] Its two word orders replicate those of Arafundi, its substrate language. Again, this might appear to constitute a counterexample to our proposal. A look at the word order of the superstrate language, however, suggests a solution for this potential problem. The superstrate language of Pidgin Yimas is Yimas, a language known to have free word order. In this case, then, the superstrate language was unable to determine the word order of the incipient pidgin. Consequently, the creators of the pidgin had to use the constructions of their native grammar to establish word order in the creole, hence the SOV and OSV word orders modeled on those of the substrate language.

As an SOV creole, Hiri Motu is often cited as an exception to the claim that the vast majority of creoles are SVO. However, Hiri Motu does not constitute a counterexample to our proposal since, in addition to its Papuan and Austronesian substrate languages, which are SOV, its superstrate language, Motu, is also an SOV language.

Finally, there are a few cases in which the word order of creoles follows that of the substrate languages rather than that of the superstrate languages. For example, Siegel (2008) reports that Fiji Hindi is an SOV language like Hindi, its substrate, in spite of the fact that its superstrate, standard Fijian, is an SVO language. A similar example is reported by Ansaldo (2009): Sri Lanka Portuguese Creole is SOV, on the model of its substrate languages, Tamil and Sinhala, instead of SVO like its superstrate language. Yet

---

[8] We are indebted to William Foley (p.c.) for providing us with the pertinent facts on Pidgin Yimas and on Hiri Motu.

another example is reported by Clements (2001) in the case of Korlai, a Portuguese-based creole with an SOV word order based on Marathi, the substrate language. It is our contention that such cases do not constitute counterexamples to our proposal. The aforementioned authors all note that, at the time when these creoles were formed, their word order conformed to that of their superstrate languages. Furthermore, all three authors account for their synchronic word orders as resulting from a word order change due to the pressure of the substrate languages on speakers who were fluent in both the creole and its substrate languages.

In summary, then, it appears that potential counterexamples to our proposal involving the order of the verb and its complement can in fact be accounted for unproblematically.

7. Deriving the Position of the Haitian Negation Marker *Pa*

Another potential counterexample to our proposal is the position of the Haitian negation marker *pa* < French *pas* [pa]. Lefebvre (1998: 208–211) argues at some length that, although Haitian *pa* was labeled by French *pas*, the two morphemes do not have the same properties (see also De-Graff 1993). While *pa* is the negation marker in Haitian, French *pas* 'not' is a negative adverb. In French, it is *ne* that is the negation marker (Pollock 1989). Lefebvre (1998) also argues that Haitian *pa* has the properties of the substrate negation marker, *mà* in Fongbe, and that Fongbe *mà* was relabeled on the basis of French *pas,* yielding Haitian *pa*. We refer the interested reader to the published literature on this topic. Here, we will concentrate on the surface position of Haitian *pa* with respect to that of French *pas*.

In Haitian, *pa* systematically occurs before the lexical verb, as in (33).

(33) *Jan   pa   vini.*   HAITIAN
      John   NEG   come
      'John did not come.'   (Lefebvre's field notes)

In French, the negative adverb *pas* may occur either before the lexical verb, as in (34a), or after it, as in (34b).

(34) a. *Jean   n'   était   pas   venu.*   FRENCH
        John   NEG   AUX   NEG-ADV   come
        'John had not come.'

b. *Jean ne vient pas.* FRENCH
John NEG come NEG-ADV
'John does not come.'

In a model of grammar in which variable surface order is accounted for by movement rules (e.g., Chomsky 1989), the variable position of the lexical verb with respect to negation in French is due to verb raising to INFL(ection). Pollock (1989) accounts for the difference between the positions of *pas* in (34a) and (34b) as follows. In French, tense and person morphology require a bearer. In complex tenses, involving an auxiliary ('be' or 'have'), the morphology bearer is the auxiliary, as in (34a). In this case, the lexical verb remains in its basic position and *pas* precedes it. Simple tenses do not require auxiliaries. In such cases, the lexical verb must move to INFL so it can bear tense and person morphology. As a result of verb movement to INFL, over the negative adverb, *pas* now follows the lexical verb, as in (34b). Within the same framework, the invariable position of the lexical verb with respect to *pa* in Haitian would be due to the absence of verb raising to INFL over the negation marker because of the lack of tense and person morphology on the verb (DeGraff 1993; Lefebvre 1998: 351–355).

Returning to the order of *pas* and the lexical verb in French, the order V *pas* is observed only in the context of simple tenses and imperatives. The order *pas* V is much more frequent, as it appears in all the complex tenses. It is therefore likely that the creators of Haitian were exposed to the word order *pas* V, as in (34a), much more frequently than V *pas*, as in (34b). The position of Haitian *pa* thus follows the most salient position for French *pas*. In agreement with our proposal, the position of Haitian *pa* corresponds to that of the form that provided the label for the creole lexical entry. Hence, the position of *pa* does not contradict our proposal.

This account of word order involving Haitian *pa* would not be complete if the item's surface position with respect to tense, mood, and aspect markers were not considered. While French uses auxiliaries and morphology on the verb to encode tense, mood, and aspect, as we saw in (34), Haitian, like its substrate languages, lacks auxiliaries and verb morphology and uses preverbal markers. The inventories of preverbal tense, mood, and aspect (TMA) markers for Haitian and Fongbe are summarized in Table 5.4.

TMA markers in Haitian and Fongbe are similar not only with respect to inventory but also with respect to semantics and to the way the various markers combine to form complex tenses (for details, see Lefebvre 1998:

TABLE 5.4 Preverbal TMA Markers in Haitian and Fongbe

ANTERIOR	IRREALIS		NON-COMPLETE	
• Past/Past perfect	• Definite future		• Habitual	• Imperfective
H F	H	F	H F	H F
te kò	ap	ná	— nɔ̀	ap ɖò...wὲ
	• Indefinite future			
	H	F		
	a-va	ná-wá		
	• Subjunctive			
	H	F		
	pou	ní		

SOURCE: Lefebvre (1998: 112).

111–140). In both languages, the negation marker precedes the TMA markers, as is illustrated in (35a) and (35b), respectively.

(35) a. *Jan pa pou ale nan mache.*   HAITIAN
          John NEG SUB go in   market
          'John does not have to go to the market.'

      b. *Kɔ̀kú mà ní wá àxì   mὲ.*   FONGBE
          Koku NEG SUB go market in
          'Koku does not have to go to the market.'

In both Haitian and Fongbe, negation markers precede TMA markers in their basic and unmarked position, such that, in both languages, the word order is as in (36).

(36) a. NEG T M A V   HAITIAN
      b. NEG T M A V   FONGBE

Now, how does the fact that the Haitian negation marker precedes TMA markers, as in the substrate languages, fit with our proposal?

Recall that subsystems of the substrate grammars are available to the creators of a creole. Hence, we hypothesize that the subsystem in (36b) was available to the creators of Haitian. Once *pa* became part of the Haitian lexicon, as depicted above, it needed to find its position with respect to the TMA markers. Since the structure in (36b) was readily available, the creators of Haitian simply used it for Haitian, as is attested by the structure in (36a).

In summary, Haitian *pa* entered the Haitian lexicon via the relabeling of Fongbe *mà* on the basis of French *pas,* which occurred preverbally. It was then associated with a substrate structure that specified the surface order of negation with respect to TMA markers.

8. Conclusion

Within a model in which word order is not specified as part of individual lexical entries, such as the RCxG model, the fact that creoles' word order generally does not reflect that of their substrate languages is no longer a problem for a relabeling-based account of creole genesis. In this chapter, we proposed that a relabeling-based account of creole genesis within the framework of RCxG would proceed as follows. Substrate constructions are available to the creators of the creole. The phonological representations of lexical items are relabeled on the basis of superstrate forms. Relabeling is either linguistically context-free or context-bound. In the latter case, the position of the relabeled word is determined by that of the superstrate label in the minimal construction in which it appears. In the former case, the relabeled lexical item may associate with the relevant position in the substrate construction. Word order in creole genesis then follows from how relabeling works. This proposal was illustrated by various constructions (section 2). Potential counterexamples were considered, leading to the conclusion that the data involved can, in fact, be accounted for straightforwardly within our proposal (sections 3, 4, 5, 6, and 7). Our conclusion is therefore that our proposal can provide a principled account of how word order is established in creole genesis.

CHAPTER 6

Relabeling Options: On Some
Differences Between Haitian
and Saramaccan

1. Introduction

Although Haitian and Saramaccan share a common Gbe substrate, there
are differences between them.* Some of them are due to differences between their superstrate languages. For example, as we saw in Chapter 3,
the fact that the determiner is prenominal in Saramaccan, while it is postnominal in Haitian, as shown in (1), is the result of differences between
their superstrate languages.

(1) SARAMACCAN   HAITIAN

     DEF   N   N   DEF

     di   buku   liv   la   'the book'

Other differences were shown to be due to differing exposure by the creoles' creators to their respective superstrate languages (see Chapter 3, section 2.5). For example, the creators of Saramaccan had less exposure to
their superstrate languages than did the creators of Haitian. Consequently,
Saramaccan is generally closer to its substrate languages than Haitian is.
Other differences between the two creoles, however, may not be explain-
able in terms of these two factors. For example, consider the items listed
in (2).

---

*A preliminary version of this chapter was presented at the SPCL meeting held in Lisbon in June
2013. Thanks to the participants for their most useful questions and comments.

(2) F ONGBE   S ARAMACCAN   H AITIAN
    • postpositions   • postpositions   • —
    • ɖò 'be at'   • dɛ 'be at'   • —
    • morphological   • morphological   • —
      reduplication   reduplication

While Saramaccan has postpositions, a locative copula, and morphological reduplication, on the model of its substrate languages, Haitian does not. These differences must be accounted for (Smith 2001). This chapter shows that the creators of creoles have relabeling options; they may choose different ones, resulting in differences between creoles that share the same substrate. The availability or unavailability of postpositions and morphological reduplication in Saramaccan versus Haitian illustrate this possibility.

2. The Availability/Unavailability of Postpositions

Recall from Chapter 5 (section 5) that Saramaccan has postpositions that are modeled on those of Fongbe. This was shown in Table 5.3, reproduced here as Table 6.1 for convenience.

This situation was shown to result from the relabeling of the substrate lexical items on the basis of English/Portuguese denotational nouns that could be identified in isolation. In Chapter 5, it was also shown that Saramaccan has a locative copula *dɛ* 'to be at' modeled on the Fongbe locative copula *ɖò* 'to be at.' In both languages the locative copula co-occurs with the locative postpositions, as illustrated in (3).

TABLE 6.1 Saramaccan and Fongbe Nouns/Postpositions

SARAMACCAN N/POST	FONGBE N/POST	MEANING
líba	*jí*	sky, on, above
sinkíi	*wú*	skin, body, surface
hédi	*tà*	head, top
báka	*gúdò*	backside, back, behind
fési	*nùkɔ̀n*	face, forehead, in front
básu	*gló*	bottom, under, underneath
déndu	*mὲ*	inside, in
bándja	*àkpá*	side, near, next to

(3) a. *Wèmá* *ɔ́* ***ɖò*** *távò* *ɔ́* ***jí.*** FONGBE
     book DEF be.at table DEF on

b. *Dí* *búku* ***dɛ*** *a* *dí* *táfa* ***líba.*** SARAMACCAN
     DEF book be.at LOC DEF table on
     'The book is on the table.' (from (39) in Essegbey 2005)

Several authors have noted the similarity between Saramaccan *dɛ* and Fongbe *ɖò* (e.g., Essegbey 2005; Kramer 2002; Migge 2003). This situation was shown to follow from the relabeling of Fongbe *ɖò* on the basis of English *there,* yielding the Saramaccan locative copula *dɛ* 'to be at.'[1]

By hypothesis, Haitian could have had similar outcomes to Saramaccan with respect to these lexical entries, but it did not: there are no postpositions and no lexical item corresponding to Fongbe *ɖò* 'be at' in this language. Why not? Recall from Chapter 4 (section 4) that Haitian has mega-prepositions derived from the relabeling with French prepositions of Fongbe simple and complex locative constructions. This is summarized in (4) for the Haitian mega-preposition *nan* (<Fr. *dans*) 'in,' and in (5) for the Haitian mega-preposition *sou* (<Fr. *sur*) 'on.'

(4)	FONGBE	FRENCH	HAITIAN
	. . . *mὲ*	*dans* . . .	*nan* . . .
	'in'	'in'	'in'
	ɖò . . . *mὲ*	*dans* . . .	*nan* . . .
	'be at . . . in'	'in'	'be at in . . .'
(5)	FONGBE	FRENCH	HAITIAN
	. . . *jí*	*sur* . . .	*sou* . . .
	'on'	'on'	'on'
	ɖò . . . *jí*	*sur* . . .	*sou* . . .
	'be at . . . on'	'on'	'be at on . . .'

Thus, it appears that the creators of Haitian made different relabeling choices from the creators of Saramaccan. First, instead of using denotational nouns as postpositions, they relabeled the substrate postpositions with French prepositions, yielding the Haitian prepositions *nan* and *sou.* Second, they chose to relabel complex locative constructions involving both the locative copula and a postposition (see (4) and (5)) with a single lexical item. The fact that relabeling involved the conflation of *ɖò* and postpositions explains why *ɖò* was not relabeled as such in this language.

---

[1] The same authors also discuss the changes undergone by *dɛ* in modern Saramaccan.

TABLE 6.2 Relabeling Options Chosen for Saramaccan and Haitian

	SARAMACCAN	FONGBE	HAITIAN
Locative copula	*dɛ*	*ɖò*	—
	'be at'	'be at'	
Postpositions	. . . *líba*	. . . *jí*	*sou* . . .
	'on'	'on'	'on'
	. . . *déndu*	. . . *mὲ*	*nan* . . .
	'inside'	'inside'	'inside'
Complex locative	—	*ɖò* . . . *jí*	*sou* . . .
constructions		'be at . . . on'	'be at on . . .'
	—	*ɖò* . . . *mὲ*	*nan* . . .
		'be at . . . in'	'be at in . . .'

The different relabeling options chosen by the creators of Saramaccan and Haitian are summarized in Table 6.2.

In light of this discussion, I now turn to another striking difference between Saramaccan and Haitian: the availability or otherwise of morphological reduplication.

3. The Availability of Morphological Reduplication

This section explores the idea that the availability/unavailability of morphological reduplication in these two Caribbean creoles correlates with the selection of a position for the morphological head. Morphological reduplication[2] involves cases of full or partial reduplication of the base that can be stated as a word formation rule. For example, in some languages, reduplication changes the syntactic category of the base from v to N. Such phenomena are analyzed in terms of a word formation rule involving a base and an affix, realized as a full or partial copy of the base.[3] In Fongbe, morphological reduplication is a very productive process. For example, the verb *gbà* 'to construct' can be nominalized by reduplication of its base, yielding *gbì-gbà*, a resultative adjective meaning 'constructed' or an action nominal meaning 'construction.' Both Saramaccan and Sranan also manifest morphological reduplication. In (6a), reduplication of the verbal base yields a deverbal resultative adjective. In (6b), reduplication of the verbal base yields a deverbal action nominal.

---

[2] See Kouwenberg (ed.) (2003) and the references cited therein for a thorough discussion of the differences between morphological reduplication and other types of reduplication.
[3] Like Brousseau (1993) and Marantz (1982), for example, I consider morphological reduplication to be a kind of affixation.

(6) a. *fon*   *fonfon*   SARAMACCAN
       'to pound'   'pounded'

   b. *fumm*   *fumfum*
       'to beat'   'beating'   SRANAN
       (= (12b) in Braun & Plag 2003: 91)

By contrast, Haitian and Papiamentu both lack morphological reduplication. The discrepancy between the two subsets of Caribbean creoles requires an explanation (Smith 2001: 72).

In this section, I further explore the proposal made by Brousseau et al. (1989) and Lefebvre (1998: 330–332) regarding the position of the morphological head. The morphological head of a word is the constituent that determines the category of that word. Languages vary as to the position of the morphological head in a word (e.g., left, right, or both). The proposal is as follows. During Haitian genesis, the position of the morphological head was set as the rightmost position of a derived word. As a consequence, reduplication, a morphological process that creates left-headed structures, had to be abandoned. In contrast, during the creation of Saramaccan (and Sranan), the position of the morphological head was not assigned a fixed position. Consequently, morphological reduplication, which creates left-headed structures, could be retained as a productive means of deriving words. The following paragraphs substantiate this proposal, beginning with Haitian.

Table 6.3 contains the list of Haitian productive affixes based on the analysis in Lefebvre (1998: 331) and DeGraff (2001) for *-ion*. The morphological head is underlined.

TABLE 6.3 The Productive Affixes of Haitian and the Position of the Morphological Head

	HAITIAN	FRENCH	FONGBE
Agentive	V-*è*	V-*eur*	V/N-*tɔ́*
Attributive	N-*è*	N-*eur*	N/V-*nɔ́*
Verbalizing	V-*e*	N/A-*er* / -*é*	—
Inversive	*de*-V	*dé*-V/A	*mà*-V/A
Diminutive	*ti*-N	N/A-*et* / -*ot* / -*on*	N-*vǐ*
Nominalizing	V-*ay* / -*syon* / *ø*[4]	V-*age* / -*ion*	*RE*-V
Adverbial	A-*man*	A-*ment*	—
Place of origin	N-*wa* / -*yen*	N-*ois* / -*ien*	N-*tɔ́* / -*nù*
Ordinal	Q-*yèm*	Q-*ième*	Q-*gɔ́ɔ́*

SOURCE: (45) in Lefebvre (1998: 331).

---

[4] Brousseau and Nikiema (2001: 313f) consider morphological conversion to involve a phonologically null affix, which they treat as a suffix.

As can be seen in, the position of the morphological head in Haitian is systematically the rightmost position in a word. This suggests that the creators of Haitian set the position of the morphological head as the rightmost position of a word (Brousseau et al. 1989). With one exception—the diminutive affix, to which I will return below—this corresponds to the position of the morphological head in French. In French, the morphological head is generally the rightmost constituent of a word, as suffixes generally determine a word's category (Brousseau & Nikiema 2001, and the references therein). There are two exceptions to this generalization. The first involves the diminutive and depreciative suffixes, which do not change the category of a word. These are listed in (7) to (13) (from Brousseau & Nikiema 2001: 283–284).

(7) a. **-eau/elle**: masculine/feminine, "small BASE"
     b. [N ___] - N = mainly animal
     c. *chevreau* 'kid'

(8) a. **-on/onne** (and their allomorphs): masculine/feminine, "small BASE"
     b. [N ___] - N
     c. *capuchon* 'hood'

(9) a. **-âtre**: "a bit BASE"—negative connotation
     b. [A ___] - A = feminine
     c. *blanchâtre* 'whitish'

(10) a. **-aud**: "BASE"—negative connotation
     b. [A ___]
     c. *noiraud* 'swarthy'

(11) a. **-aill**: "BASE often"—negative connotation
     b. [V ___]
     c. *courailler* 'to chase women'

(12) a. **-et/ette** (and their allomorphs): masculine/feminine, "small/a bit BASE"
     b. [N/A ___] –
     c. *bâtonnet* 'short stick'

(13) a. **-asse**: feminine, "BASE"—negative connotation
     b. [N/A/V ___]
     c. N: *paillasse* 'straw mattress'
         A: *bonasse* 'meek'
         V: *rêvasser* 'to daydream'

The second exception involves three prefixes that are claimed to change the category of a word, even though prefixes do not generally do so in French. These are listed in (14) to (16) (from Brousseau & Nikiema 2001: 289).

(14) a. **a$_V$ -**: "make like BASE / arrive at BASE / put in BASE"
      b. [___ A/N]
      c. *agrandir* 'to make bigger'

(15) a. **é$_V$-**: "deprive of BASE / make BASE"
      b. [___ A/N/V]
      c. *ébrancher* 'to prune'
          élargir 'to enlarge'

(16) a. **en$_V$-**: "put in BASE / put BASE in / make BASE"
      b. [___ N/A]
      c. *encadrer* 'to frame'

Interestingly, it appears that the affixes involved in both types of exceptions to the general rule concerning the position of the morphological head in French went unnoticed by the creators of Haitian. Indeed, the French diminutive and depreciative suffixes do not figure in the inventory of Haitian productive affixes (see Table 6.3). Furthermore, very few Haitian words contain these French affixes. For example, Freeman's (1988) inverse dictionary of Haitian Creole contains only a handful of words ending in /o/ corresponding to the diminutive/depreciative suffixes in French (*-eau, -aud*). Nor are there many Haitian words ending in *-on, -at, -ail, -et,* or *-asse*. Similarly, the French prefixes in (14) to (16) were not identified as such by the creators of Haitian. None of them appear in the inventory of Haitian productive affixes in Table 6.3. Furthermore, many Haitian labels drawn from French have been incorporated into Haitian without these prefixes. For example, the Haitian label derived from the French verb *associer* 'to associate' was incorporated into Haitian as *sosye* 'to associate,' that derived from *assécher* 'to dry' as *seche* 'to dry,' that derived from *élargir* 'to widen' as *laji* 'to widen,' *égrener* 'to shell' as *grennen* 'to shell,' *encercler* 'to encircle' as *sèkle* 'to encircle,' *endommager* 'to damage' as *domaje* 'to damage,' *envoyer* 'to send' as *voye* 'to send,' and so on (Valdman et al. 2007). It therefore appears that the only French affixes that were identified by the creators of Haitian all occupy the rightmost position of the word in French. This strongly suggests that the creators of Haitian established the position of the morphological head as the rightmost position of a word.

The selection of this option had two major consequences for the morphological inventory presented in Table 6.3. The first one concerns the position of the diminutive affix. As Table 6.3 shows, this affix is a suffix in French. Even if the creators of Haitian perceived this affix as a potential diminutive suffix for the creole they were creating, they did not retain it. The reason is that this suffix does not change the category of the base it attaches to. Hence, it is not a morphological head, despite its position as the rightmost constituent of the word it is part of. The Haitian diminutive affix therefore had to be a prefix, even though, in both source languages, the corresponding affix is a suffix. Accordingly, the creators of Haitian used a reduced form of the prenominal adjective *petit* 'small,' pronounced [pəti], [pti], or [ti] in colloquial French, to create a diminutive prefix. The second consequence of establishing the morphological head as the rightmost position of a word concerns morphological reduplication. Morphological reduplication creates a prefix that changes a word's syntactic category. That prefix is not the rightmost constituent of the word it is part of. Thus, the retention of morphological reduplication in the incipient creole would have let a non-rightmost constituent of a word establish the word's category. Hence, in the genesis of Haitian, morphological reduplication had to be abandoned.[5]

Morphological conversion (or zero affixation) and the nominalizing suffixes *-ay* and *-syon* were developed to fulfill the functions of Fongbe RE-. For example, Fongbe RE- and Haitian *-ay* derive nouns from two-place verbal predicates, as is illustrated in (17).

(17) a. *kèn*   *kì-kèn*   FONGBE
          'to bet'   'bet or action of betting'

      b. *pary-e*   *pary-ay*   HAITIAN
          'to bet'   'bet or action of betting'   (from Lefebvre 1998: 322)

Fongbe RE- and Haitian *-ion* also derive nouns from two-place verbal predicates, as shown in (18).

(18) a. *gbá*   *gbìgbá*   FONGBE
          'to construct'   'construction'

      b. *konstri*   *konstrik-syon*   HAITIAN
          'to construct'   'construction'

---

[5] Papiamentu is like Haitian in that all the constituents that change the category of the base are suffixes or tonal/accent modifications that affect the last syllable of the word (Dijkhoff 1993; Kouwenberg & Murray 1994). The question of whether a similar scenario to that suggested for Haitian would apply to Papiamentu must nevertheless await further detailed research.

Fongbe RE- and Haitian morphological conversion derive nouns from one-place verbal predicates, as is illustrated in (19).

(19) a. *yì*   *yì-yì*   FONGBE
          'to leave'   'action or result of leaving'

      b. *pati*   *pati*   HAITIAN
          'to leave'   'action or result of leaving'   (from Lefebvre 1998: 322)

Finally, Fongbe RE- and Haitian morphological conversion also derive deverbal resultative adjectives, as shown in (20).

(20) a. *ḍì*   *ḍìḍà*   FONGBE
          'to cook'   'cooked'

      b. *kwit*   *kwit*   HAITIAN
          'to cook'   'cooked'   (from Védrine 1992: 167–168)

As for Saramaccan and Sranan, it appears that their creators did not identify any of the derivational affixes of English since none of them was retained in the formation of these creoles (e.g., Braun & Plag 2003: 99; Migge 2003: 40f).[6] As a result, the position of the morphological head was not set in the early creoles. Both languages were therefore able to retain the process of morphological reduplication from the substrate languages, in which RE- is a left-headed derivational prefix. At the same time, they could develop a right-headed derivational suffix derived from the English free morpheme *man* 'man.' These two sets of facts will be discussed in turn, using data from Saramaccan. (For similar data in Sranan, see Braun & Plag 2003.)

To a great extent, the properties of Saramaccan RE- replicate those of Gbe RE-. Like Fongbe RE-, Saramaccan RE- derives deverbal resultative adjectives, as shown in (21) and (22), respectively.

---

[6] The reason for this absence is still unclear. Braun and Plag (2003: 99) propose two avenues for further research. "Two factors are in principle possible, structural or socio-historical. For example, it is remarkable that both Spanish and French have a tendency of placing stress on their suffixes, which would make these elements more salient and more easily borrowable. However, this does not explain why English auto-stressed suffixes like -*ation* did not make it into the creole and why prefixes, which mostly have secondary stress in English, French and Spanish, did only survive in the said Romance-based creoles. Such considerations point to the non-structural direction . . . ," that is, to "the nature and length of contact between the superstrate and the creole." For English Maroon Creoles, Migge (2003: 37) establishes that "[b]oth the sociohistorical and the linguistic evidence suggest that most of the agents of creole formation had only little access to relatively reduced varieties of English." So it is likely that the difference in exposure to the superstrate languages played a role in the creation of this discrepancy between the two subgroups of creoles.

(21) só   súsó   FONGBE
    'pound'   'pounded'

(22) fon   fonfon   SARAMACCAN
    'pound'   'pounded'

In Fongbe, in other Gbe languages, and in English Maroon Creoles (EMC), including Saramaccan, these derived forms are found in adjectival passive clauses, as is shown in (23) to (25).

(23) Làn   ɔ́   ɖò   ɖìɖà   FONGBE
    meat   DEF   be.at   cooked
    'The meat is cooked.'
    [Lit.: 'The meat is at cooked.']   (from Brousseau 1993)

(24) Nyɔnu   vi   a   le   blɔ̀-blɔ̀.   GBE
    woman   small DET   COP   thin-thin
    'The girl is in a thin state.'
    [Lit.: 'The girl is at thin.']   (= (24a) in Migge 2003)

(25) A   dagu   ya   de   fatu-fatu.   EMC
    DET   dog   here   COP   fat-fat
    'This dog is in a fat state.'
    [Lit.: 'The dog is at fat.']   (= (23a) in Migge 2003)

In all three languages, these derived forms are also found as participial adjectives in noun phrases, as shown in (26) to (28).

(26) làn   ɖìɖà   ɔ́   FONGBE
    meat   cooked   DEF
    'the meat is cooked.'
    [Lit.: 'The cooked meat']   (from Brousseau 1993)

(27) mɔ̀tó   kpùkpó   ɔ́   GBE
    car   old   DET
    'the old car'
                                              (= (32) in Migge 2003)

(28) wan   fonfon   alisi   EMC
    DET   pounded   rice
    'a quantity of pounded rice'
                                              (= (31) in Migge 2003)

Smith (2001: 71) notes: "Fon and Saramaccan also share the property that such participial adjectives are virtually the only adjectives in the two languages in the strict sense of the word. Virtually all adjectives in European languages are translated by stative verbs in both these languages. There are very few exceptions in either language."

Fongbe RE- is also found in verbal passives, as illustrated in (29).

(29) Làn   ɔ́   nyì   ɖìɖà   FONGBE
      meat   DEF   be   cooked
      'The meat has been cooked.'

Note that the verbal passive construction involves the copula *nyì* 'to be,' as in (29), whereas the adjectival passive construction involves the locative copula *ɖò* 'to be at,' as in (23). In Saramaccan, RE- is not found in verbal passives. Kramer (2002) proposes the following explanation for this fact. While the Saramaccan locative copula *dɛ* in (24b) replicates the properties of Fongbe *ɖò* 'to be at,' there is no Saramaccan counterpart for Fongbe *nyì* 'to be.' Because of the unavailability of a general copula in this language, the verbal passive could not involve RE-. This is because, as Bakker (2003: 77f) shows convincingly, a copula is obligatory with deverbal predicates. Hence, while RE- can be involved in adjectival passives in Saramaccan due to the locative copula *dɛ*, it cannot be involved in verbal passives due to the lack of a general copula. (For further discussion of this topic, see Kramer (2002), Chapters 3 and 6.)

Apart from the difference discussed above, Saramaccan RE- replicates the properties of Fongbe RE-. On the basis of this fact and of the fact that morphological reduplication is not part of the grammar of the superstrate language of the Surinamese creoles, English, and to a lesser extent Portuguese, Bakker (2003: 79), Kramer (2002), Migge (2003: 63–70), and Smith (2001) all conclude that morphological reduplication of verbs in the Surinamese creoles must be the result of retention from the Gbe languages. Smith also remarks that, in contrast to the Gbe languages, Kikongo and Twi, two other substrate languages of the Surinamese creoles, lack such morphological structures.

So, as a consequence of not setting the position of the morphological head, the creators of Saramaccan could retain morphological reduplication from their substrate languages, thereby deriving left-headed structures. At the same time, they were able to develop a very productive derivational suffix, *-ma* (<En. *man* 'man'), deriving right-headed structures. From a semantic point of view, this suffix corresponds to English *-er*, as it derives nouns from verbs yielding the meaning 'one who VERBs,' as in (30).

(30) *fufúu* 'to steal' *fufúu-ma* 'thief' Saramaccan

(Rountree et al. 2000)

The suffix *-ma* also attaches to adjectival bases yielding the meaning 'one who has the characteristic ADJ,' as in (31).

(31) *laú* 'crazy' *laú-ma* 'crazy person' Saramaccan

(Rountree et al. 2000)

Migge (2003: 81) shows that *-ma* in (30) and (31) has the same function as the Gbe suffixes *-tɔ́* and *-nɔ̀*, respectively. As Brousseau (1990) reports, the agentive suffix *-tɔ́* derives agentive nouns from dynamic verbs, as in (32a), and the attributive suffix *-nɔ̀* derives nouns meaning 'one who possesses or uses NOUN,' as in (32b).[7]

(32) a. *wà-àzɔ̀* *àzɔ̀-wà-tɔ́* Fongbe

'do work' 'worker' (= (16) in Brousseau 1990)

b. *xɛ̀sì* *xɛ̀sì-nɔ̀* Fongbe

'fright' 'coward' (= (14) in Brousseau 1990)

In summary, as a consequence of having selected the rightmost position of a word for the morphological head, the creators of Haitian had to abandon the process of morphological reduplication, which creates left-headed structures. On the other hand, because they did not select a fixed position for the morphological head (possibly due to insufficient exposure to the superstrate language, see note 6), the creators of Saramaccan and Sranan were able to retain morphological reduplication, as well as developing right-headed morphological structures.

4. Conclusion

The aim of this chapter was to show that creoles' creators have options when it comes to relabeling. They may choose different ones, creating differences between creoles that share the same substrate languages. The different relabeling choices that were made by the creators of Saramaccan and Haitian, as discussed in this chapter, are summarized in Table 6.4.

---

[7] In addition to the suffix *-man*, Sranan (though not Saramaccan) also developed the suffixes *-sanni*, from English *something*, and *-fasi*, from English *fashion*, as productive derivational affixes (Braun & Plag 2003: 86).

TABLE 6.4 Relabeling Choices Made for Saramaccan and Haitian

	SARAMACCAN	FONGBE	HAITIAN
Locative copula	*dε*	*ḍò*	—
	'be at'	'be at'	
Postpositions	*. . . líba*	*. . . jí*	*sou . . .*
	'on'	'on'	'on'
	. . . déndu	*. . . mὲ*	*nan*
	'inside'	'inside'	'inside'
Complex locative constructions	—	*ḍò . . . jí*	*sou. . .*
		'be at . . . on'	'be at on . . .'
	—	*ḍò . . . mὲ*	*nan . . .*
		'be at . . . in'	'be at in . . .'
Position of morphological head	left or right	left or right	right
Availability of morphological reduplication	RE-	RE-	—

Parkvall (2003) considers the lack of morphological reduplication in French-based Caribbean creoles to be a potential counterexample to a relabeling-based account of creole genesis. Referring to Haitian, he writes: "If Haiti FC [French Creole] really arose through relexification of Fon and related languages, as claimed by Lefebvre (1998), then this is certainly one of the features we would expect it to have inherited, since there are no obvious constraints on transferring reduplication as such in creolization" (30). As was argued in this chapter, there appears to be an independent reason that some creoles did not keep the morphological process of reduplication while others did.

CHAPTER 7 | Relabeling and the Contribution of
the Superstrate Languages to Creoles

1. Introduction

A review of the literature on the contribution of superstrate languages to creoles reveals that the topic has seldom been studied. An extreme position is held by authors who claim that creole languages are dialects of their superstrate languages (e.g., Chaudenson 2003); this position will be discussed in Chapter 8. All authors agree that the core contribution of superstrate languages to creoles consists in providing the labels for the creolfes' lexical entries. Some authors mention their contribution to a creole's word order (e.g., Mufwene 1990; Mühlhäusler 1986a). Some authors also mention the contribution of superstrate languages to the semantics of creole lexical entries (e.g., Siegel 2008). Bao (2005) proposes that a major role of the superstrate language in creole genesis is to act as a filter, sifting out substrate features that have been brought into a creole by means of transfer but that do not conform to the superstrate. Other than that, not much has been said on the topic. The contribution of superstrate languages to creoles is mainly discussed in comparison to that of the substrate languages. Some authors emphasize the contribution of either the substrate or the superstrate languages. However, there does not seem to have been any attempt to characterize the contribution of each source in a principled way, or to identify domains of contribution of the sources languages to a creole. I shall begin this chapter with an overview of the major publications examining the respective contributions of creoles' source languages.

A first major publication is the edited book by Muysken and Smith (1986) entitled *Substrata versus Universals in Creole Genesis*. The contribution of the superstrate languages is not discussed in this publication, or in the edited book by Lefebvre (2011c), *Creoles, Their Substrates and*

Language Typology. In an edited volume by Neumann-Holzschuh and Schneider (2001), *Degrees of Restructuring in Creole Languages*, some of the contributors propose that creoles are restructured varieties of both their substrate and superstrate sources (e.g., Alleyne 2001; Chaudenson 2001a). With this approach, it is not possible to identify the respective contributions of the superstrate and substrate languages. Moreover, in their introduction to the collection of papers, the editors point out the confusion regarding the definition of "restructuring" and related concepts. In her book *Creole Formation as Language Contact: The Case of the Suriname Creoles*, Migge (2003) investigates the respective input of European (her Chapter 4) and African (her Chapters 5 and 6) languages to these creoles. Migge presents evidence showing that the creators of these creoles had little access to English, the superstrate language. Consequently, it comes as no surprise that the positive input from the superstrate language resided mainly in providing the labels for the creoles' lexical entries and contributing the basis for establishing word order. As for the African input, there are a few retentions of African words, but Migge's study emphasizes the contribution of the African substrate languages to the semantic and syntactic properties of lexical items with English-derived labels. Migge's study also identifies the contribution of the African substrate languages with respect to syntactic constructions, such as the Tense-Mood-Aspect subsystem of the grammar, verb-doubling phenomena, serial verb constructions, locational constructions, and so on. This study is extremely rich from many points of view, as it lists the substrate and superstrate languages' contributions to Surinamese creoles. However, it does not provide a principled account of the respective contributions of substrate and superstrate languages to creoles. The recent collection of papers edited by Michaelis (2008), *Roots of Creole Structures: Weighing the Contribution of Substrates and Superstrates,* was intended to provoke an in-depth discussion on the respective roles of substrate and superstrate languages in creole formation. However, very few chapters in this book actually address the contribution of the superstrate languages to creoles; most of them bear on substrate features in a subset of creoles. Lefebvre's (2008b) chapter in this volume documents the claim that, in creole genesis, the contribution of substrate and superstrate languages is principled. However, the only contribution of the superstrate language to a creole discussed in that chapter is the source of creole labels.

About the position taken in Lefebvre (1998), DeGraff (2002: 355) writes: "...the contribution of French to the development of Haitian Creole was exclusively limited to phonetic strings deprived of abstract properties."

While it is true that, in a relabeling-based account of creole genesis such as mine, the substrate languages provide important input to creoles, it is not the case that the superstrate languages' contribution is limited to providing phonetic strings. In Lefebvre (1998), several contributions of French to the creation of Haitian are identified. One major contribution was providing the phonetic strings from which the labels of the creole lexical entries are derived; this follows from a relabeling-based account of creole genesis. However, French is also shown to have constrained relabeling, as this process is limited by what the superstrate language has to offer in relabeling the lexical entries of the substrate languages (see Chapter 1; see also Lefebvre & Lumsden 1994a). French is also shown to have determined most surface orders of elements in Haitian (Lefebvre 1998: 38–40, 89, 107, 180; Lefebvre & Lumsden 1992; Lumsden 1991) (see also Chapter 5 of this volume). The creation of a large class of intransitive verbs in Haitian is attributed to French as well (Lefebvre 1998: 280–283; 1999). The form of the resumptive pronoun *ki* (<Fr. *qui*) in contexts of Wh-extractions out of subject position, in complementary distribution with the form *li* in other contexts, is also derived from French (Lefebvre 1998: 193–203). This partial list invalidates DeGraff's statement. However, while the items enumerated here were identified as contributions of French to Haitian, no principled explanation was provided as to why these various items should belong in the same list.

The aim of this chapter is to identify the domains in which the superstrate languages make a contribution to creoles. I will set my discussion within the relabeling-based account of creole genesis that I have developed so far, and assume, as in my previous work (e.g., Lefebvre & Lumsden 1994a; Lefebvre 1998, 2004b, 2008b), that the respective contributions of substrate and superstrate languages to creole genesis are not random but principled. I will use the contributions of French to Haitian Creole mentioned above as a starting point, documenting and analyzing them in more detail. Hence, the following contributions of French to Haitian will be examined in turn. First, the superstrate language provides the bulk of the labels for the creole lexical entries (section 2). Second, the superstrate language determines the bulk of the surface orders of elements in a creole. Affix order, basic word order in tensed clauses, and word order in nominal and nominalized structures will be discussed in turn. It will be shown that the creation of a large class of intransitive verbs in Caribbean creoles is surface-order-related, and that, consequently, the presence of intransitive verbs in the creole manifests the superstrate language's contribution to the creation of a creole (section 3). Third, the superstrate language constrains relabeling (section 4). This will be shown on the basis of certain specific constructions. Finally, the superstrate language contributes the morphological material used to spell out grammatical features of the substrate languages (section 5). Bao's proposal will be evaluated in section 6 on the basis of the data discussed in sections 2 through 5. Section 7 is an attempt to characterize the nature of superstrate languages' contribution in creole genesis; the question of why the items identified as superstrate contributions to a creole should belong in the same list will be addressed in that section. Section 8 concludes the chapter.

From a methodological point of view, the comparison of creoles sharing the same substrate languages but differing in their superstrate languages provides us with a wealth of data for exploring the contribution of the superstrate languages. In the various sections of this chapter, I will therefore compare, as much as possible, three Caribbean creoles that share the same substrate, mainly the Gbe dialect cluster,[1] but have different superstrate languages: Haitian, a French-based creole; Saramaccan, an English- and Portuguese-based creole; and Papiamentu, a Portuguese- and Spanish-based creole. By hypothesis—other things being equal—the majority of the similarities between these creoles should be attributable to their shared substrate, and most of the differences between them should stem from their different superstrate languages. As will be shown throughout this chapter, this expectation is borne out.

The content of this chapter is limited to lexicon and syntax. The phonological component of the grammar (phonological inventories, syllable structures, tonal/accentual systems) is not discussed here. I leave the discussion of this component of the grammar to phonologists. However, for the sake of completeness, it should be mentioned that this is a component where the superstrate has significant input.

2. The Superstrate Language Provides the Bulk of the Labels for the Creole Lexical Entries

Scholars agree that, although individual creole languages may exhibit words of different origins, most of the labels in a creole's lexicon are derived from its superstrate language(s). For example, the Haitian lexicon contains some 350 West African words—mainly nouns, referring to religious beliefs, objects, persons or activities, body parts, food, animals, plants, kinship relationships,

---

[1] The similarity between the Gbe languages/dialects is discussed in Lefebvre (1998: 58–62, and the references cited therein).

some verbs, and a few exclamations—that have been retained from the substrate languages (e.g., Ewe, Fongbe, Mandingo, and Kikongo) (Hilaire 1993).[2] It also contains some 200 nouns designating local objects, such as plants and place names, borrowed from local Amerindian languages (Hilaire 1992), a few borrowings from Spanish (Hilaire 1992), and a few from English (Valdman et al. 1981) (for further discussion, see Lefebvre 2002). Nevertheless, the vast majority of the labels in the Haitian lexicon is derived from French. However, as has been shown in several instances, the Haitian lexical entries that have labels derived from French do not necessarily share all the semantic or syntactic properties of the corresponding French lexical entries (e.g., Lefebvre 1998, and the references cited therein). There is thus a discrepancy between the properties of French and Haitian lexical entries that have related labels.

It has been suggested that the study of nonstandard dialects of the superstrate language, in this case French, might shed light on this discrepancy (e.g., Chaudenson 2001b: 171). As Neumann-Holzschuh (2008: 364) points out, however, although the nonstandard dialects of the superstrate language may provide us with information on the form of the lexical items that the creators of a creole were exposed to and, consequently, the form of some creole labels, the study of nonstandard superstrate dialects cannot explain the semantic discrepancies that exist between lexical entries in the superstrate and the creole. For example, Neumann-Holzschuh documents the fact that the third-person plural personal pronoun in North American French dialects may have the following forms: *eusse* [øs], *ieusses* [yøs], *zeux* [zø]. This may shed light on the historical derivation of the form of the third-person plural personal pronoun of Haitian, *yo*. But, as she points out (367), North American French dialects do not account for the fact that the form *nou*, for example, refers to both first- and second-person plural in Haitian. Lefebvre (1998: 141–142) shows that the semantic properties of Haitian *nou* follow those of the substrate languages, such as Fongbe, where the same pronominal form is used to refer to both first- and second-person plural. Interestingly enough, in the Surinamese creoles, the same form, *unu/u* is also used for first- and second-person plural, following the Gbe pattern (Migge 2003: 49). It is worth noting that, in the Indian Ocean

---

[2] Cases of lexical retention from substrate languages mainly involve words from major categories. A few cases involving functional categories have been reported, however, showing that words from these categories are not excluded. For example, Smith (2001) reports that, in Saramaccan, the Wh-words *ambé* 'who' and *andí* 'what' have been retained from the Gbe substrate languages. Furthermore, Smith (1996) argues that the Gbe focus marker *wè* has been retained in Saramaccan (see Chapter 5, example (6)).

creoles, which are also French-based, the form *zot* is used to refer to both second- and third-person plural. Chaudenson points out that this fact cannot be traced to French dialects. He suggests that it is attributable to Malagasy, one of the substrate languages of these creoles, in which the same form is used to refer to both second- and third-person plural (e.g., Chaudenson 2001b: 183–184, 2003: 307–308).

Neumann-Holzschuh (2008: 369) further points out that the lexifier languages of Atlantic creoles cannot account for the distribution of personal pronouns in those creoles. For example, personal pronouns are also used to encode possession in nominal structures in these creoles. A case in point is the Haitian possessive construction, which involves a personal pronoun and a case marker, either *a* or null, depending on the dialect: for example, *ti-mounn (a) mwen* [Lit.: child CASE me] 'my child.' Lefebvre (1998, Chapter 6) argues that the distribution of pronouns in Haitian follows that of its Gbe substrate languages. In Fongbe, for instance, the possessive construction involves a personal pronoun and a case marker: for example, *ví nyè tɔ̀n* [Lit.: child me CASE] 'my child.' So both Haitian and Fongbe lack a paradigm of possessive determiners and use personal pronouns to encode possession. This contrasts with French, which has a full paradigm of possessive determiners *mon* 'my,' *ton* 'your,' *son* 'his/her,' and so on. Likewise, Saramaccan, an English-based creole, lacks possessive determiners and encodes possession by means of a personal pronoun and a case marker: *míi u hén* [Lit.: child of he] 'his child.' This is like Fongbe and contrasts with English, which has a full paradigm of possessive determiners such as *my*, *your*, *his/her*, and so on. It has been pointed out more than once in the literature that, in French, there is an emphatic possessive construction involving a case marker and a personal pronoun: *mon enfant à moi* [Lit.: my child of me] '*my* child' (with emphasis). Likewise, English allows for a nominal structure of the type *this child of mine*. Whether the availability of these structures, which exhibit a postnominal possessive phrase in French and in English, reinforced the substrate in determining the structure of the Haitian and of the Saramaccan possessive construction remains an open question. The fact is, however, that, like Fongbe, both Haitian and Saramaccan lack a paradigm of possessive determiners and encode possession only by personal pronouns related to the head noun of the construction by a case marker. In the unmarked case in both French and English, possessive constructions are encoded by means of a prenominal possessive determiner. In the French emphatic construction, the possessive determiner is required, as **enfant à moi* [Lit.: child of me] is ungrammatical, unlike in Fongbe. In the marked construction in English, the possessive determiner is excluded (*my child of mine) and a demonstrative determiner is required (this child of mine). The phrase introduced by of takes a possessive pronoun instead of a personal pronoun as in Fongbe, Haitian, and Saramaccan. It thus appears that, while the possessive constructions in Haitian and Saramaccan are exactly like Fongbe, they are not exactly like the marked constructions in the superstrate languages. Like Neumann-Holzschuh, then, I conclude that the lexifier languages of Atlantic creoles cannot account for the distribution of personal pronouns in those creoles. The source of the distribution pattern of personal pronouns in these creoles is clearly the substrate languages.

In conclusion, while the bulk of the semantic and syntactic properties of creole lexical entries come from their substrate languages, the majority of their labels are derived from the superstrate languages. This division of properties between the source languages follows in a principled way from the nature of relabeling, and from the claim that this process plays a central role in the formation of creoles (see Chapter 3).

3. The Superstrate Language Determines the Bulk of the Surface Orders in a Creole

The fact that the superstrate language makes a major contribution to a creole's word order has been acknowledged on several occasions in the literature (e.g., Aboh 2009; DeGraff 1999; Lefebvre & Lumsden 1992; Lefebvre 1998). In Chapter 5, a specific proposal was implemented, showing how word order can be established in creole genesis.[3] This section addresses the

---

[3] This proposal may be summarized as follows. In creole genesis, relabeling proceeds in one of two ways: it is either free of linguistic context, as in the case of denotational nouns, some verbs, demonstrative terms, etc., or it is bound to a linguistic context, as in the case of modifiers and determiners. In the former case, lexical items are relabeled in isolation. As such, they may be associated with a substrate position, an available option because the substrate subsystems of the grammar are available to the creators of a creole. Hence, as we saw in Chapter 5, the position of demonstrative terms in Haitian and Saramaccan and that of locative adpositions in Saramaccan result from the relabeling of lexical entries that are free of linguistic context and that have been associated with a substrate subsystem position. The latter case concerns modifiers and determiners, which must occur in combination with nouns in order to be identified as such in the superstrate language by the creators of a creole. In these cases, relabeling has to proceed on the basis of the minimal constructions in which these lexical items appear in the superstrate language, and the creole word order is determined by that of the superstrate language. This is the case, for example, of quantifiers and adjectives in Haitian, which manifest French rather than Fongbe word order. This is also true of most Haitian determiners, including the definite determiner and the plural marker, which derive their surface position from that of the superstrate form that provided the creole label. As we saw in Chapter 5, the French forms that provided the labels for the definite determiner and the plural marker are postnominal; consequently, the definite determiner and the plural marker are postnominal in Haitian. By contrast, the English forms that provided the labels for the definite determiner and the plural marker in Saramaccan are prenominal, and so the definite determiner and plural marker are prenominal in this language.

surface word order phenomena that were not discussed in that chapter. Affix order, word order in tensed clauses, and word order in nominal and nominalized structures will be discussed in turn. It will be shown that the superstrate language plays a major role in determining the surface order of these constituents in a creole. It will also be shown that conflicting orders in the superstrate and substrate languages may lead the creators of a creole to abandon certain substrate structures in the emerging creole.

3.1. Affix Order

Building on the work of Brousseau et al. (1989), Lefebvre (1998: 330–332, 381) shows that the derivational affixes of Fongbe were relabeled on the basis of French affixes, yielding the core of the derivational affixes in Haitian. The relabeling of substrate affixes on the basis of French affixes must be linguistically bound since French affixes can only be identified with respect to the stem that they attach to. The position of the superstrate affixes is thus expected to determine the position of the creole affixes. This is indeed the case. For example, the Haitian agentive suffix -è (e.g., *dechouk-è* 'insurgent') is derived from the French agentive suffix -*eur* (e.g., *vol-eur* 'thief'). The Haitian verbalizing suffix -*e* (e.g., *betiz-e* 'to talk nonsense') is derived from the French suffix -*er* [e] (e.g., *fêt-er* 'to celebrate'), and so on. The same situation obtains in Papiamentu. According to Dijkhoff (1993: 74), the two most productive suffixes of this language are -*mentu* and -*dó*. For example, the form of the deverbal nominalizing suffix -*mentu*, as in *batisa-mentu* 'baptism,' is derived from that of the Spanish suffix -*miento*, as in *conoci-miento* 'knowledge.' The form of the Papiamentu agentive suffix -*do(r)*, as in *bringa-dó* 'fighter,' is derived from that of the Spanish agentive suffix -*dor*, as in *vende-dor* 'salesman,' and so forth.

In all cases, the superstrate has determined the surface position of the creole affix. This is true even in cases of conflicting affix orders between the substrate and superstrate languages. For example, as we saw in Chapter 6, the Fongbe nominalizing affix is a prefix, produced by morphological reduplication, henceforth referred to as RE-, as in (1a). By contrast, Haitian does not have morphological reduplication. In this language, three affixes fulfill the functions of Fongbe RE-: a null affix (also referred to as morphological conversion), and the affixes -*ay* and -*syon* (DeGraff 2001; Lefebvre 1998, 2003). The Haitian affixes that correspond to the Fongbe prefix RE- are suffixes. For example, the Haitian affix -*ay* is a suffix (see (1b)), because it is derived from the French nominalizing suffix -*age*, illustrated in (1c).

(1) a. *àvɔ̀-lìlì*   FONGBE
       'ironing'

   b. *repasay*   HAITIAN
       'ironing'

   c. *repassage*   FRENCH
       'ironing'

Likewise, the Haitian counterpart of the Fongbe diminutive suffix *-ví* in (2a) is a prefix, as shown in (2b). This is because the form of the Haitian diminutive affix *ti-* is derived from the French prenominal adjective *petit* 'small' in (2c). *Petit* is pronounced [pəti], [pti], or [ti] in colloquial French.

(2) a. *àwí-ví*   FONGBE
       'kitten'

   b. *ti-chat*   HAITIAN
       'kitten'

   c. *petit chat*   FRENCH
       'kitten'

So affix order in a creole is determined by the order of the superstrate form that provided the label for the affix.[4]

3.2. Basic Word Order in Tensed Clauses and the Creation of a Large Class of Intransitive Verbs in Caribbean Creoles

Gbe tensed clauses are SVO. French, Spanish, and English tensed clauses are also SVO. It therefore comes as no surprise that tensed clauses in Caribbean creoles are also SVO. There is a difference, however, between basic word orders in the substrate and superstrate languages of these creoles: while the superstrate languages also manifest SV order, due to a large class of intransitive verbs, the substrate languages seldom show this combination, because they have very few, if any, intransitive verbs. All three creoles follow their superstrate languages in having many intransitive

---

[4] In both Haitian and Papiamentu, however, the size of the productive morphological inventories is much smaller than those of their superstrate languages and tends to correspond to those of the substrate languages (for Haitian, see Lefebvre 1998; for Papiamentu, see Dijkhoff 1993; Kouwenberg & Murray 1994). This suggests that the creators of these creoles identified, in the superstrate languages, almost exclusively those affixes that corresponded to the ones they already had in their native languages. As Lefebvre (1998, Chapter 10) discusses extensively, this follows naturally from a relabeling-based account of creole genesis.

verbs and thus manifesting SV order frequently. By hypothesis, the creation of a large class of intransitive verbs in the Caribbean creoles is linked to the availability of SV word order in the superstrate languages. The following paragraphs expand on this hypothesis.

Fongbe has very few intransitive verbs (Lefebvre & Brousseau 2002: 241–245). In addition to having a relatively large class of genuine transitive verbs, it has a large class of inherent and cognate object verbs (Lefebvre & Brousseau 2002: 247–250). These are illustrated in (3a) and (3b), respectively.

(3)　　FONGBE

a.　*gbɔ̀*　　*àzɔ̀n*　　'to heal'
　　　'calm　　disease'

　　　nyà　　*gbé*　　'to hunt'
　　　'hunt　　animals'

　　　ɖùn　　*sín*　　'to draw (water)'
　　　'draw　　water'

　　　kùn　　*hún*　　'to drive'
　　　'drive　　vehicle'

　　　ɖù　　*nú*　　'to eat'
　　　'eat　　something'

　　　zà　　*àyí*　　'to sweep'
　　　'sweep　　ground'　　(from Lefebvre & Brousseau 2002: 247–248)

b.　*nɔ̀*　　*ànɔ̀*　　'to suckle'
　　　'suck　　breast'

　　　ɖɔ̀　　*àɖɔ̀*　　'to pee'
　　　'pee　　piss'

　　　kpén　　*àkpén*　　'to cough'
　　　'cough　　cough'

　　　ɖì　　*àɖì*　　'to believe'
　　　'believe　　belief'

　　　kwín　　*àkwín*　　'to whistle'
　　　'whistle　　whistle'　　(from Lefebvre & Brousseau 2002: 248–249)

Inherent and cognate object verbs are semantically autonomous. Unlike the objects of light verbs, their objects do not contribute to the meaning of the verb itself. These verbs can take different types of objects, but they cannot surface without an overt object of some kind. When no specific object is referred to, these verbs appear with the typical object that is appropriate for a given verb (e.g., *nɔ̀ ànɔ̀* [Lit.: 'suck breast'] 'to suckle,' *kùn hún* [Lit.: 'drive vehicle'] 'to drive'), or with an object meaning 'thing' (e.g., *ɖù nú* [Lit.: 'eat thing'] 'to eat'). The objects of inherent object verbs have the properties of ordinary direct objects (e.g., Brousseau 1998), and so do the objects of cognate object verbs (e.g., Massam 1990).

Taking an inherent or cognate object is a property of verbs. We would therefore expect that, in relabeling, the Haitian verbs corresponding to inherent and cognate object verbs in the substrate would reproduce this property. This prediction is only partially borne out by the data, however. As can be seen in (4), only three Haitian verbs follow the pattern of the substrate language in requiring an inherent object (see (4a)). In (4b) the inherent objects of the substrate verbs are not reproduced in the creole, and nor are the cognate objects in (4c).

(4)

		FONGBE		HAITIAN	
a.	*gbɔ̀* 'calm	*àzɔ̀n* disease'	*kalme doulè*	'to heal'
	nyà 'hunt	*gbé* animals'	*chase bèt*	'to hunt'
	ɖùn 'draw	*sín* water'	*tire dlo*	'to draw (water)'
b.	*kùn* 'drive	*hún* vehicle'	*kòndwi*	'to drive'
	ɖù 'eat	*nú* something'	*manje*	'to eat'
	zà 'sweep	*àyí* ground'	*bale*	'to sweep'
c.	*nɔ̀* 'suck	*ànɔ̀* breast'	*tete*	'to suckle'
	ɖɔ̀ 'pee	*àɖɔ̀* piss'	*pise*	'to pee'
	kpén 'cough	*àkpén* cough'	*touse*	'to cough'
	ɖì 'believe	*àɖì* belief'	*kwè*	'to believe'
	kwín 'whistle	*àkwín* whistle'	*sifle*	'to whistle'

(= (63) in Lefebvre 1998: 200–201)

Lefebvre (1998: 280–283) proposes that the difference between the Fongbe verbs in (4) and their corresponding Haitian verbs may best be stated in terms of their transitivity properties: whereas the Fongbe verbs are necessarily transitive, the corresponding Haitian verbs may also be used intransitively. It is suggested that this discrepancy is attributable to the creole's superstrate language. In French, some transitive verbs may also be used intransitively. For example, along with *il a mangé une pomme* 'he ate an apple,' we find *il a mangé* 'he ate.' With three exceptions (see (5a)), Haitian follows the pattern of French in licensing an intransitive version of an otherwise transitive verb (see (5b) and (5c)).

(5)

		Fongbe		French	Haitian	
	a.	gbɔ	àzɔn	calmer la douleur	kalme doulè	'to heal'
		'calm	disease'			
		nyà	gbé	chasser X	chase bèt	'to hunt'
		'hunt	animals'			
	b.	kùn	hún	conduire	kòndwi	'to drive'
		'drive	vehicle'			
		ɖù	nú	manger	manje	'to eat'
		'eat	something'			
		zà	àyí	balayer	bale	'to sweep'
		'sweep	ground'			
	c.	nɔ	ànɔ	téter	tete	'to suckle'
		'suck	breast'			
		ɖɔ	àɖɔ	pisser	pise	'to pee'
		'pee	piss'			
		kpɛn	àkpɛn	tousser	touse	'to cough'
		'cough	cough'			
		ɖì	àɖì	croire	kwè	'to believe'
		'believe	belief'			
		kwín	àkwín	siffler	sifle	'to whistle'
		'whistle	whistle'			

(= (63) in Lefebvre 1998: 280–281)

Presumably, the creators of Haitian perceived that the French verbs in (5) could occur without an object in a structure of the type SV. On this basis, they abandoned the requirement that objects of inherent and cognate object verbs be projected in the syntax, thus producing SV-type structures.

The same situation obtains in Saramaccan and Papiamentu. Aboh (2009: 333f) shows that Saramaccan has also developed a class of intransitive verbs on the model of English, as illustrated in (6).

(6)   *I   njan   kaa   no?*   SARAMACCAN
       2SG eat   already Q
       'Have you already eaten?'
                               (= (14a) in Aboh 2009, citing Rountree & Glock 1982: 43)

Maurer (1988b) provides several examples of Papiamentu verbs, such as *kanta* 'to sing,' *kome* 'to eat,' and so on, used intransitively.

In summary: the superstrate languages of the Caribbean creoles appear to be responsible for the creation of a large class of intransitive verbs in these creoles, even though intransitive verbs are practically nonexistent in the substrate languages. This is linked to word order phenomena.[5]

3.3. Word Order in Nominal Structures

The superstrate language also determines the positions of arguments in nominal structures. For example, in Fongbe nominal structures, possessive phrases may occur prenominally, marked for objective case *sín*, or postnominally, marked for genitive case *tɔ̀n* (Brousseau & Lumsden 1992). This is illustrated in (7).

(7)   a.   *[Kɔ̀kú sín]   fɔtóó   lέ*   FONGBE
           Koku OBJ   picture PL
           'the pictures of Koku'   (= (6b) in Brousseau & Lumsden 1992)

      b.   *fɔtóó   [Kɔ̀kú tɔ̀n]   lέ*   FONGBE
           picture Koku GEN   PL
           'Koku's pictures'   (= (6a) in Brousseau & Lumsden 1992)

Lumsden (1991) shows that, in Haitian Creole, the prenominal position is not available for possessive phrases, which can only occur in postnominal position, as is shown in (8).

(8)   *pòtre   [pèche   ø]   a*   HAITIAN
       portrait fisherman CASE   DEF
       'the portrait of the fisherman'   (= (4) in Lumsden 1991)

---

[5] See Aboh (2009: 332) for a different account of these phenomena.

He proposes that, in the creation of Haitian, the prenominal position for possessive phrases in the Gbe languages had to be abandoned because, in French, possessive phrases only occur postnominally, as is illustrated in (9).

(9) *le*   *portrait* [*du*   *pêcheur*]   FRENCH
     DEF   portrait   of.the   Fisherman
     'the portrait of the fisherman'

The plausibility of this proposal is further reinforced by data from Saramaccan. Unlike Haitian, Saramaccan has two positions available for possessive phrases, one following the noun and one preceding it, as shown in (10).

(10) a. *dí*   *míi*   [*u*   *Kofi*]   SARAMACCAN
          DEF   child   CASE   Kofi
          'the child of Kofi'   (Kearns 2011)

      b. *dí*   [*u*   *Kofi*]   *míi*   SARAMACCAN
          DEF   CASE   Kofi   child
          'Kofi's child'   (Kearns 2011)

This parallels the two Fongbe surface positions (see (7)), but also the two English surface positions. Indeed, in English, the possessive phrase may either follow or precede the head noun, as is illustrated in (11).

(11) a. *The picture* [*of John*]   ENGLISH
      b. [*John's*] *picture*   ENGLISH

Building on Lumsden's (1991) proposal based on Haitian, we can hypothesize that, in the creation of Saramaccan, the Fongbe prenominal position for possessive phrases was retained due to the availability of the prenominal position for possessive phrases in English.

The contrastive data from Haitian and Saramaccan show that the superstrate language is determinative in preventing a substrate constituent order from manifesting itself in a creole, as in Haitian, or in letting a substrate constituent order manifest itself in a creole, as in Saramaccan.

3.4. Word Order in Nominalized Structures

In Gbe languages, the imperfective construction involves two lexical items: the locative copula, *ɖò* 'to be at' in Fongbe, and a locative postposition generally meaning 'in,' or *wè*, otherwise the focus marker in Fongbe, and a nominalized VP. This nominalized VP is characterized by two components. First, it involves morphological reduplication of the verb, which, in this case, converts the verb into an action nominal, as illustrated in (12).

(12) É ḍò yìyì wè.   FONGBE
    3SG be.at RE.leave POST
    '(S)he is leaving.'   (= (35b) in Lefebvre & Brousseau 2002: 196)

Second, although Fongbe word order is VO in tensed clauses, in nominalized VPs, as in nominal structures (see (7a)), the constituent order is OV, as shown in (13).

(13) É ḍò mì kpɔ́n wè.   FONGBE
    3SG be.at me RE-look.at POST
    'He is looking at me.'   (Segurola & Rassinoux 2000: 153)

The contrast between (12) and (13) with respect to reduplication of the verb illustrates the fact that reduplication is overt with objectless verbs but covert with overt objects (for an extensive discussion of these facts, see Lefebvre & Brousseau 2002: 195–215).

In Haitian, the imperfective marker is *ap,* which, as we saw in Chapter 4, corresponds to the conflation of Fongbe *ḍò . . . wè.* In spite of the fact that the language has morphological means of nominalizing verbs (e.g., morphological conversion and nominalizing affixes such as *-ay* and *-syon,* as we saw in section 3.2), the VP in the imperfective construction is not nominalized. Instead, the verb appears in its verbal form and the canonical VO order is maintained. This is illustrated in (14).

(14) *Mari Ap manje krab la.*   HAITIAN
    Mary IMP eat crab DET
    'Mary is eating the crab.'   (= (18) in Lefebvre 1996)

Thus, it appears that, in the creation of Haitian, the nominalization of VPs in the imperfective construction was abandoned. Why? Lefebvre (1998) proposes that it was abandoned due to conflicting word orders in the substrate and the superstrate languages. Indeed, in French, deverbal nominalizations do not involve a shift in word order from VO to OV, as is shown in (15).

(15) a. *construire* [*la*   *maison*] FRENCH
     build   DEF   house
     'to build the house'

   b. *la*   *construction* [*de*   *la*   *maison*] FRENCH
     DEF   construction   of   DEF   house
     'the construction of the house'

   c. **la*   [*maison*]   *construction* FRENCH
     DEF   house   construction

In fact, excluding rare holdovers from Old French, French presents no instantiation of OV word order. We can therefore hypothesize that, in the creation of Haitian, the nominalization of VPs in the imperfective construction was abandoned because the substrate language construction involved a word order that was not compatible with that of the superstrate language.

A similar explanation could also account for the lack of nominalized VPs in the Saramaccan imperfective construction. As was pointed out in Chapter 4, the Saramaccan imperfective construction is similar to the Haitian construction. It involves only one lexical item: *tá*, illustrated in (16).

(16) *Dí*   *ganía*   *tá*   *fá.* SARAMACCAN
     DEF   chicken   IMP   fat
     'The chicken is getting fat.' (= (5a) in Kramer 2002: 52)

Just like Haitian *ap*, Saramaccan *tá* corresponds to the complex substrate construction involving a locative predicate and a postposition, *ɖò . . . wὲ* in Fongbe. Even though the focus marker *wὲ* was retained from Fongbe in Saramaccan (Smith 1996), as is illustrated in (17), this morpheme does not participate in the Saramaccan imperfective construction.

(17) *Andí*   *wὲ*   *i*   *bói.* SARAMACCAN
     what   FOC   you   cook
     'What did you cook?' (= (11b) in Smith 1996: 117)

Furthermore, although the language uses reduplication to form adjectives and past participles (e.g., *kuakua* 'fresh') or nouns (e.g., *pikipiki* 'a little bit')—as do the substrate languages, as we saw in Chapter 6—the VP involved in the imperfective construction is not nominalized. The verb occurs in its verbal form and the canonical VO word order is maintained, as shown in (18).

(18) *Nómo   a   tá   toóbi   mi.*   SARAMACCAN
       always   3SG   IMP   annoy   1SG
       'He is always annoying me.'   (= (25a) in Byrne 1987: 47)

It thus appears that, in the creation of Saramaccan, VP nominalization was abandoned. Again, a likely explanation of this fact may be formulated in terms of the conflicting word orders in the substrate and superstrate constructions. In English, deverbal nominalizations do not involve a shift in word order from VO to OV, as is shown in (19).

(19)   a.   *to construct [a house]*   ENGLISH
       b.   *the construction [of the house]*
       c.   **the house construction*

We can therefore hypothesize that, in the creation of Saramaccan, the nominalization of VPs in the imperfective construction was abandoned because the original substrate construction involved a constituent order that was not licit in the superstrate language.

3.5. Summary

Based on the discussion in this section, it is clear that the superstrate language plays a major role in determining the surface ordering of elements in creole genesis. This includes affix order, word order, and constituent order. It even includes word order in compounds, discussed at length in Lefebvre (1998: 339–342), based on Brousseau (1989, 1994), but not re-examined here. The surface order of elements was shown to have repercussions for the syntax, such as the creation of a large class of intransitive verbs and the loss of certain nominalized constructions. Thus, it appears that, via its contribution to the setting of word order in creole genesis, the superstrate language has a role to play in the retention or loss, in the creoles, of some substrate language constructions.

4. The Superstrate Language Constrains Relabeling

Since relabeling proceeds on the basis of superstrate forms, it is constrained by what the superstrate language has available to relabel a substrate lexical entry. Comparative work on creole languages that have the same substrate languages but different superstrate languages provides us with the pertinent data to illustrate how the superstrate can constrain relabeling. In this section, I discuss three sets of data that illustrate this role of the superstrate language. The first one involves reflexives, the second the semantics of verbs, and the third deverbal resultative adjectives.

4.1. The Expression of the -SELF Anaphor in Atlantic Creoles

Gbe languages and Caribbean creoles offer several possibilities for encoding reflexivity (e.g., Lefebvre 1998: 159–171; Lefebvre & Brousseau 2002; Muysken 1993). One of them is the -SELF anaphor. In Fongbe, the form of the -SELF anaphor is *-ɖéè* (Hazoumê 1990). This form has semantic and distributional properties that are similar to those of English *-self* (Kinyalolo 1994). For example, as in English, where pronouns combine with *-self* (e.g., *he washes himself*), in Fongbe, pronouns combine with *-ɖéè,* yielding a reflexive interpretation of the pronoun, as is illustrated in (20).

(20) a. N_i ná   hù   nyὲ-ɖéè$_i$ FONGBE
      1SG   DEF.FUT kill   me-SELF
      'I will kill myself.'   (= (45) in Brousseau 1995)

    b. *Bàyí$_i$*   mɔ̀   é-ɖéè$_i$ FONGBE
      Bayi   see   she-SELF
      'Bayi saw herself.'   (= (45) in Brousseau 1995)

Atlantic creoles vary as to how they realize the lexical entry corresponding to Fongbe *-ɖéè*. Creoles, such as Dutch- and English-based creoles, whose lexifier language has an overt -SELF anaphor, have an overt -SELF anaphor as well. For example, Berbice Dutch has the form *-selfu* derived from Dutch *-zelf* (Robertson 1993: 307), Gullah has *-self* from English *-self* (Mufwene 1992: 169), and Saramaccan has *-seéil-seépi* (Veenstra 1996a: 43) from English *-self*. Papiamentu has the form *mes* derived from the Spanish intensifier *mismo*. This form occurs with pronouns, yielding a reflexive interpretation, as is shown in (21). The various authors who have written about Papiamentu gloss *mes* as 'self' and analyze it as a reflexive anaphor (e.g., Kouwenberg & Murray 1994: 40–41; Muysken 1993: 300f).

(21) *Mi ta weta mi mes*   PAPIAMENTU
     'I look at myself.'   (= (33a) in Muysken 1993: 291)

Haitian differs from these creoles. In this language, no lexical item can be identified as having the function of a -SELF anaphor. Nevertheless, a bare personal pronoun may be interpreted as reflexive anaphor, as is shown by the two possible interpretations of the sentence in (22).

(22) *Li*_i *wè* *li*_{i/j}   HAITIAN
     he   see   himself/him/it
     'He saw himself/him/it.'   (= (1a) in Déchaine & Manfredi 1994)

The possibility of assigning a reflexive anaphor interpretation to a bare personal pronouns suggests that in Haitian Creole the -SELF anaphor is covert, that is, it does not have a phonological representation.[6] This situation is attributable to the fact that French does not have a lexical anaphor. Rather, French expresses reflexivity by means of pronominal clitics, including the reflexive clitic *se*. (For an extensive discussion of this topic, see Lefebvre 1998: 159–171.) Consequently, the Haitian lexical entry corresponding to Fongbe -*ɖéè* remained phonologically null. Practically speaking, this means that the lexical entry is available but is not pronounced. (For arguments supporting an analysis along those lines, see Lefebvre 1998: 160–167, and the references therein.) The discrepancy between the Atlantic Creoles with respect to overt/covert lexical entries constitutes one type of example showing how the superstrate language may constrain relabeling.

4.2. Verbs of CUTTING in Haitian

Another way in which the superstrate may constrain relabeling involves a situation in which the substrate languages lexically encode semantic distinctions that are not lexically encoded in the superstrate language. Verbs of CUTTING in Haitian and Surinamese creoles and in their source languages exemplify this situation. As is shown in (23), there are several verbs of cutting in Fongbe. The semantics of these verbs includes manner.

(23) *sèn gàn*   'cut iron'   FONGBE
     mà kwíkwí 'cut/slice banana'
     vló wò   'cut/separate paste'
     kàn làn   'cut meat' (animal or human)
     já làn   'cut meat (in pieces)'
     gbó àtín   'cut tree'
     kpá ɖà   'cut hair'
     zè nàkí   'cut/chop wood'   (= (54) in Lefebvre 1989: 335)

---

[6] This idea is attributable to John Lumsden (research seminar, Fall 1993).

In Haitian Creole, all these verbs can be translated by *koupe* 'to cut' (< French *couper* 'to cut') (also Valdman et al. 1981). The Haitian verb appears to lack the manner component of the Fongbe verbs of cutting. Essegbey and Ameka (2007) discuss parallel data for Sranan, showing that, in this English-based creole as well, the manner component of the substrate verbs of cutting appears to be lacking. They conclude that, in these cases, relabeling has failed to apply; in fact, they take these data to constitute counterexamples to a relabeling-based account of creole genesis. In my view, the relabeling-based account of creole genesis provides us with an alternative proposal. It is possible that the superstrate language has fewer verbs of cutting than the substrate languages. As a result, the creators of the creole would not have found, in the superstrate language, all the different forms they needed to relabel each pertinent lexical item of their own lexicons. Consequently, several substrate verbs of cutting would have been relabeled on the basis of a single superstrate form, in this case *couper* 'to cut.' The result would be exactly what the data show: the creole has fewer verbs of cutting than the substrate lexicons.[7] This situation illustrates yet another way in which the superstrate language constrains relabeling.

4.3. Deverbal Resultative Adjectives

Consider the pairs of predicates in Table 7.1.

TABLE 7.1 Pairs of Stative Predicates and Deverbal Resultative Adjectives in Fongbe, Haitian, and French

FONGBE		HAITIAN		FRENCH	
fà	'to be cold'	*frèt*	'to be cold'	*froid*	'cold'
fifà	'state cold'	*fwadi*	'state cold'	*refroidi*	'state cold'
gbló	'to be wide'	*laj*	'to be wide'	*large*	'wide'
gbìgbló	'state wide'	*laji*	'state wide'	*élargi*	'state wide'
gblɔ́	'to be lukewarm'	*tièd*	'to be lukewarm'	*tiède*	'lukewarm'
gblɔ́gblɔ́	'state lukewarm'	*tyedi*	'state lukewarm'	*tiédi*	'state lukewarm'
kló	'to be big'	*gwo*	'to be big'	*gros*	'big'
kìkló	'state big'	*grosi*	'state big'	*grossi*	'state big'
wí	'to be black'	*nwa*	'to be black'	*noir*	'black'
wìwí	'state black'	*nwasi*	'state black'	*noirci*	'state black'

---

[7] It is also possible that, regardless of the number of verbs of cutting that the superstrate language had, the creators of the creole might have been exposed to only one or two such verbs. Consequently, more than one substrate verb of cutting would have been relabeled on the basis of the same superstrate form. The result would be exactly the same: the creole lexicon would contain fewer verbs of cutting than the substrate lexicons.

The Fongbe pairs involve a stative verb and a deverbal resultative adjective derived by morphological reduplication. This type of pair is illustrated in (24a) and (24b), respectively, on the basis of the stative verb *fà* 'to be cold.'

(24) a. *É   fà.*   FONGBE
          3SG   be.cold
          'It is cold.'

      b. *É   ɖò   fifà.*   FONGBE
          3SG   BE.AT   state.cold
          'It has become cold.'
          [Lit.: 'It is at state cold']

The Haitian pairs also involve a stative verb and a morphologically related deverbal resultative adjective. This type of pair is illustrated in (25a) and (25b), respectively. Recall from Chapter 4 that the Fongbe copula meaning 'to be at' was not relabeled as such in Haitian. As a result, the sentence in (25b) does not contain an overt copula.

(25) a. *Li   frèt.*   HAITIAN
          3SG   be.cold
          'It is cold.'

      b. *Li   fwadi.*   HAITIAN
          3SG   cold
          'It has become state.cold.'
          [Lit.: 'It is at state cold']

Finally, the French pairs involve a stative adjective and a morphologically related resultative participle. This type of pair is illustrated in (26). Note that, in French, the stative adjective in (25a) is introduced by the auxiliary *être* 'to be,' whereas the resultative participle is introduced by the auxiliary *avoir* 'to have.'

(26) a. *Il   est   froid.*   FRENCH
          3SG   be.3SG   cold
          'It is cold.'

      b. *Il   a   refroidi.*   FRENCH
          3SG   have.3SG   state.cold
          'It has become cold.'
          [Lit.: 'It is at state cold']

Within a relabeling-based account of Creole genesis, how were the Haitian data derived, given the data from Fongbe, on the one hand, and French, on the other hand?

First, the Fongbe stative predicates (e.g., *fà* 'to be cold') would have been relabeled on the basis of the semantically closest French adjective (e.g., *froid* 'cold,' pronounced [frεt] in colloquial French), yielding the Haitian stative verb *frèt* [frεt] 'to be cold.' This is schematized in (27).

(27) FONGBE   FRENCH   HAITIAN
      fà   *froid* [frεt] *frèt* [frεt]
      'to be cold'   'cold'   'to be cold'

Second, the Fongbe deverbal resultative adjective (e.g., *fìfà* 'state cold') would have been relabeled with the form of the French resultative participle (e.g., *refroidi* 'state cold'), yielding the Haitian resultative adjective (e.g., *fwadi* 'state cold'), as is schematized in (28).

(28) FONGBE   FRENCH   HAITIAN
      fìfà   *refroidi*   *fwadi*
      'state cold'   'state cold'   'state cold'

What is new about this derivation, in terms of a relabeling-based account of creole genesis, is that it takes a derived word, *fìfà*, rather than a root or a stem, as the basis for relabeling.[8]

The derivation in (28) is made possible by properties of the French lexicon that do not exist in the English lexicon. Indeed, the French lexicon contains numerous pairs of lexical items similar to those listed in Table 7.1. The correspondence between the two lexical items in each pair is systematic throughout. This is what made the type of derivation in (28) possible in Haitian. By contrast, English does not have such systematically related pairs of lexical items. For example, although it does have the pairs *black/blackened* and *wide/widened,* it does not have **cold/coldened,* **big/biggened,* and so on. English resultative participles often require recourse to a circumlocution of the type *x has become y* (e.g., *it has become cold, it has become big, it has become lukewarm,* etc.). Consequently, speakers of West African languages who were relabeling their lexicon on the basis of English did not find a form to relabel the second item of the substrate pairs of lexical items in Table 7.1. As we saw in Chapter 6, however, morphological reduplication, which is available in Saramaccan,

[8] I would like to thank Renée Lambert-Brétière for a very useful discussion of these data.

though not in Haitian, provided a means of deriving deverbal resultative adjectives in this language.

The contrasting Haitian and Saramaccan data constitute yet another example illustrating the constraints the superstrate language imposes on relabeling.

4.4. Summary

In this section, three sets of data were presented to illustrate different ways in which the superstrate language may constrain relabeling. The first one involved the reflexive anaphor, which is overt in English- and Spanish-based creoles and covert in French-based creoles of the Caribbean. The second set of data involved verbs of CUTTING in Haitian and Saramaccan and in their source languages. The third set of data involved deverbal resultative adjectives in Haitian and Saramaccan and their source languages. Another similar set of data involving the semantic case system will be presented in Chapter 8, section 5.5.

5. The Superstrate Language Contributes the Morphological Material Used to Spell Out Grammatical Features of the Substrate Languages

Building on Lefebvre (1998: 262–269), this section documents the fact that the superstrate language contributes the morphological material used to spell out, in the creoles, grammatical features of the substrate languages. This phenomenon will be illustrated with the forms of resumptive pronouns in contexts of extraction out of subject position in two Atlantic creoles, Haitian and Papiamentu, and in their source languages. I will begin with one of their shared substrate languages: Fongbe.

In Fongbe, there are two contexts of extraction out of subject position: subject raising and Wh-movement. A resumptive pronoun is required in the extraction site. This resumptive pronoun has the same form in all contexts: the form of the personal pronoun, which is singular or plural depending on the number of the referent. The first context of extraction out of subject position involves raising verb constructions. For example, the verb *ɖì* 'to seem, to resemble' (Segurola & Rassinoux 2000: 146) is a raising verb that takes a tensed clause complement. The subject of this clause may be realized in situ, in which case an expletive pronoun optionally fills the subject position of *ɖì*, as in (29a). The subject of the embedded clause may also be raised to the subject position of *ɖì*, in which case a resumptive pronoun must occur in the extraction site, as in (29b). When the raised subject is singular, the resumptive pronoun is singular, as in (29b). When it is plural, the resumptive pronoun is plural, as in (29c).

(29) a. (É)   ɖì   ɖɔ̀   Kɔkú   j'àzɔ̀n.   FONGBE
          3SG   seem   Koku   be.sick
          'It seems that Koku is sick.'

      b. Kɔkú   ɖì   mɛ́   ɖè-é   j'àzɔ̀n   ɔ́.   FONGBE
          Koku   seem   person   OP-RES.SG be.sick   DEF
          'Koku seems to be sick.'

      c. Yé   ɖì   mɛ̆   ɖè-yé   j'àzɔ̀n   ɔ́.   FONGBE
          3PL   seem   person   OP-RES.PL be.sick   DEF
          'They seem to be sick.'

The presence of the operator ɖè, which only occurs in tensed clauses in Fongbe, argues that subject raising in (29b) and (29c) has taken place out of a tensed clause.

The second context of extraction out of subject position involves Wh-movement, which occurs in questions. As Law (1994) shows, short-distance movement does not allow a resumptive pronoun in the extraction site of the subject (compare (30a) and (30b)), but long-distance movement requires one (compare (31a) and (31b)).[9]

(30) a. Mɛ̆$_i$ wɛ̀   t$_i$ yì?   FONGBE
          person   it-is   leave
          'Who is it that left?'

      b. *Mɛ̆$_i$ wɛ̀   é$_i$ yì   FONGBE
          person   it.is   RES.SG   Leave
          'Who is it that left?'

                                          (= (58) in Lefebvre 1998: 202)

(31) a. Mɛ̀$_i$ tɛ́   (wɛ̀)   Kɔkú   ɖì   ɖɔ̀   é$_i$ mɔ̀   Àsíbá?   FONGBE
          person   which   it-is   Koku   think that RES.SG see   Asiba
          'Who is it that Koku thinks saw Asiba?'

      b. *Mɛ̀$_i$ tɛ́   wɛ̀   Kɔkú   ɖì   ɖɔ̀   t$_i$ mɔ̀   Àsíbá   FONGBE
          person   which   it-is   Koku   think COMP   see   Asiba
                                          (= (54) in Lefebvre 1998: 201)

---

[9] This discrepancy still remains to be explained.

When the extracted subject is plural, the third-person plural form *yé* shows up in the extraction site instead of the third-person singular form *é*. This is shown in (32).

(32) [*Mέ lέ*]ᵢ (*wὲ*) *Kɔ́kú ɖì ɖɔ̀ yé*ᵢ *mɔ̀ Àsíbá?*   FONGBE
      person PL it-is Koku think that RES.PL see Asiba
      'Who (PL) is it that Koku thinks saw Asiba?'

                               (= (56) in Lefebvre 1998: 201)

Wh-movement also plays a role in relative clause formation. In this case, the resumptive pronoun in subject position is pied-piped by the operator *ɖé*. Again, when the subject is singular, the resumptive pronoun is singular, as in (33a), and when the subject is plural, the resumptive pronoun is plural, as in (33b).

(33) a. *súnù ɖè-é*ᵢ tᵢ *wá ɔ́*   FONGBE
          man OP-RES.SG come DEF
          'the man who came' (= (80) in Lefebvre & Brousseau 2002: 161)

    b. *súnù*ᵢ *ɖè-yé*ᵢ tᵢ *wá lέ ɔ́*
          man OP-RES.PL come PL DEF
          'the men who came' (= (89) in Lefebvre & Brousseau 2002: 163)

To sum up, in Fongbe, subjects can be raised or Wh-moved; when this happens, with one exception (see (30)), a resumptive pronoun is required in the extraction site. In both contexts, this pronoun is a personal pronoun, which may be singular or plural depending on the number of the referent.

Like Fongbe, Haitian also requires a resumptive form in the extraction site of subjects. However, this resumptive can be realized in two ways: the form of the personal pronoun, either singular or plural depending on the number of the referent (*li* SG and *yo* PL), and the form *ki* (<French *qui* [ki]), which is invariant in number, in the context of Wh-extraction. Building on Lefebvre (1998: 193f), I present arguments supporting the analysis whereby these forms are allomorphs of a resumptive form in the contexts of extraction out of subject position. Crucially, the French form *qui* ([ki]), which is the phonetic source of Haitian *ki*, is not a resumptive pronoun but a complementizer.

Like Fongbe, Haitian allows subject raising out of a tensed clause. For example, the verb *sanble* 'to seem, to resemble' (Valdman et al. 2007: 650) is a raising verb that takes a tensed clause complement. The subject of this clause may be realized in situ, in which case an expletive optionally fills the subject position of *sanble*, as in (34a). Alternatively, the subject of the embedded clause may be raised to the subject position of *sanble*,[10] in which case a resumptive pronoun must occur in the extraction site, as is shown in (34b) (Massam 1989). When the raised subject is singular, the resumptive pronoun occurs in its singular form *li*, as in (34b); when the raised subject is plural, the resumptive pronoun occurs in its plural form *yo*, as in (34c).

(34) a.   *(Li)*   *sanble*   *Jan*   *te*   *malad.*   HAITIAN
          it   seem   John   PA   sick
          'It seems that John has been sick.'

    b.   *Jan*   *sanble*   *li*   *te*   *malad.*   HAITIAN
          John   seem   RES.SG   PA   sick
          'John seems to have been sick.'   (= (1) in Law 1992)

    c.   *Yo*   *sanble*   *yo*   *te*   *malad.*   HAITIAN
          they   seem   RES.PL   PA   sick
          'They seem to have been sick.'   (= (50) in Lefebvre 1998: 199)

Two basic facts show that the complement clause of *sanble* is tensed. First, as Dumais (1988) points out, the clause embedded under *sanble* may contain the marker of anteriority *te,* which can only occur in tensed clauses (Lefebvre 1998: 116–118). Second, as we will see below, when the embedded subject is questioned, the form *ki* must be used. Haitian *ki* is inherently nominative and thus it can only occur in tensed clauses (e.g., Déprez 1992b; Law 1991, 1992). This contrasts with French, where subject raising is only possible out of infinitival clauses, as the sentences in (35) show. In (35a), the subject of the embedded clause is realized in situ and the subject position of the matrix verb is obligatorily filled by the expletive *il.* In (35b), the subject of the tensed embedded clause has been raised to the subject position of the matrix clause and the resulting sentence is ungrammatical. In (35c), the subject of the infinitival embedded clause has been raised to the subject position of the matrix clause and the resulting sentence is grammatical. The infinitival character of the embedded sentence in (35c) is revealed by the lack of a [+tensed] complementizer, by the infinitival morphology on the verb, and the lack of an overt subject in the embedded clause.

---

[10] Déprez (1992b) makes several arguments showing that movement is involved in this construction.

(35) a. *Il semble que Jean soit malade.*   FRENCH
          it   seem   that John be   sick
          'It seems that John is sick.'   (= (37a) in Lefebvre 1998: 267)

      b. **Jean semble qu' il soit malade*   FRENCH
          John   seem   that he be   sick   (= (37c) in Lefebvre 1998: 267)

      c. *Jean   semble être   malade.*   FRENCH
          John   seem   be   sick
          'John seems to be sick.'   (= (37b) in Lefebvre 1998: 267)

The contrast in grammaticality between (35b) and (35c) shows that the option of subject raising out of an embedded clause is available in French, provided that the clause is infinitival. This is in direct contrast with Haitian and Fongbe, which allow subject raising out of tensed complements (see (34b) and (29b)).

In the context of Wh-movement out of subject position, the morpheme *ki* appears instead of *li*. This is shown in (36a) for short Wh-movement[11] and in (36b) for long-distance Wh-movement (Law 1992).

(36) a. *(Se) ki   mounn$_i$ ki$_i$ vini?*   HAITIAN
          it-is which person   KI   come
          'Who is it that came?'   (= (41b) in Lefebvre 1998: 195)

      b. *(Se) ki   mounn$_i$, Jak   di   ki$_i$ wè   Mari?*   HAITIAN
          it-is which person   James say KI   see Mary
          'Who is it that James said saw Mary?'
                                                (= (42b) in Lefebvre 1998: 196)

Law (1994) provides evidence showing that the morpheme *ki* appears only in contexts where the subject has been extracted by Wh-movement.[12] As Lefebvre (1998: 193–195) discusses at some length, the Haitian morpheme *ki* derives its form from French *qui*, pronounced [ki], which occurs in contexts of Wh-movement out of subject position. French *qui* only occurs when the subject of a clause has been extracted, as in (37a). This form contrasts with *que* [kə], which appears when a non-subject argument has been extracted, as in (37b).

---

[11] The discrepancy between (36a) in Haitian and (30a) in Fongbe still remains to be explained.
[12] All authors (e.g., Koopman 1982b; Koopman & Lefebvre 1982; Law 1994) but one (DeGraff 1992a) link the presence of *ki* in this context to *that*-trace effects, restated as ECP (Empty Category Principle) effects in Chomsky (1981). To the best of my knowledge, DeGraff (1992a) is the only researcher to have proposed an analysis claiming that Haitian lacks *that*-trace effects.

(37) a. *Qui*_i *penses-tu qui*_i t_i *est venu?*   FRENCH
who   think-2SG COMP   AUX come
'Who do you think came?'

b. *Qui*_i *crois-tu que*_i *Marie a vu* t_i*?*   FRENCH
who   believe-2SG COMP Mary AUX See
'Who do you believe Mary saw?'   (= (32) in Lefebvre 1998: 193)

In the literature on French syntax, it has been argued that the first occurrence of *qui* in the sentences in (37a) is a Wh-pronoun meaning 'who,' but the second one is not. Indeed, the form of *qui* that occurs in the latter context also shows up in relative clauses whose subject has been relativized, as shown in (38). Since (38) does not involve a question, *qui* in this context cannot possibly be an interrogative pronoun (Moreau 1971).

(38) *l' homme qui est venu*   FRENCH
DET man   COMP AUX come
'the man that came'   (= (33) in Lefebvre 1998: 193)

Kayne (1976) also argues that the second *qui* in (37a) is not a relative pronoun either, and demonstrates that genuine relative pronouns do not occur in this context. The ungrammaticality of the (b) sentence in (39), as opposed to the grammaticality of (39a), supports this claim.

(39) a. *L' homme que Jean croit qui est venu.*   FRENCH
DET man   COMP John believe COMP AUX come
'The man that John believes came.'

b. **L' homme que Jean croit à qui Marie*
DET man   COMP John believe to whom Mary
a parlé   FRENCH
AUX speak
[Lit.: 'The man that John believes Mary spoke to.']

On the basis of its distributional properties, it has been proposed that the second *qui* in (37a) is a special form of the [+tense] complementizer (Kayne 1976; Moreau 1971). For one thing, it occurs only in tensed clauses, such as (37a). When the subject of an infinitival clause is questioned, as in (40a), *qui* is not licit, as is shown by the ungrammaticality of (40b).

(40) a. *Qui*_i *crois-tu*   t_i *être* *arrivé?*   FRENCH
         who believe-2SG   be arrive

   'Who do you believe to have arrived?'

   b. **Qui*_i *crois-tu*   *qui*_i *être* *arrivé*   FRENCH
         who believe-2SG   COMP be arrive

   [Lit.: 'Who do you believe to have arrived?']

Second, as shown in (37), in tensed clauses, *qui* is in complementary distribution with the [+tense] complementizer *que*: when the subject has been extracted, *qui* appears; when a non-subject has been extracted, *que* appears. Third, as Law (1994) points out, *qui* is also in complementary distribution with the subjunctive complementizer *que*, which requires that the embedded clause be in the subjunctive mood. As shown in (41), in this context as well, *que* introduces the embedded clause when a non-subject has been fronted, but *qui* introduces it when a subject has been fronted.

(41) a. *Qui*   *veux-tu*   *que*   *Jean*   *voie?*   FRENCH
         Who want-2SG COMP John see-SUB

   'Who do you want John to see?'

   b. *Qui*_i   *veux-tu*   *qui*_i   *vienne?*   FRENCH
         who want-2SG COMP come-SUB

   'Who do you want to come?'

So, the second *qui* in (37a) has the same distribution as the complementizer *que*, except that it occurs when a subject has been extracted. Thus, *que* and *qui* are allomorphs of the [+tense] complementizer *que* (Kayne 1976; Moreau 1971). Hence, the French form that provided the morphological material for Haitian *ki* is a special form of the complementizer that occurs when the subject has been extracted.

This raises the question of whether Haitian *ki* is also a special form of the complementizer, like its superstrate counterpart, or whether it is a special kind of resumptive pronoun occurring in the extraction site of the embedded subject in questions and relative clauses. There are two competing views in the literature on this matter. Koopman (1982a, 1982b) takes the position that Haitian *ki* is in COMP. Aboh (2006) and DeGraff (1992a, 1992b) also adopt this view. Law (1994), Lumsden (1990), and Manfredi (1993) all defend the position that Haitian *ki* occurs in the extraction site of the Wh-moved subject. Both proposals are thoroughly reviewed in Lefebvre (1998: 193–203). The conclusion of this discussion is that Haitian *ki* is not a complementizer occurring in COMP, as is advocated by the first group of authors. The proposal that Haitian *ki* is a resumptive form occurring in the position of a subject extracted by Wh-movement is retained based on the following three major arguments.

First, consider the data in (42) involving complements of the verb *vle* 'want' introduced by the complementizer *pou*. (For the properties of *pou* as a complementizer, see, e.g., Koopman & Lefebvre 1981; Sterlin 1988.) Law (1992) points out that *ki* in the (b) sentence is in the same surface position as the lexical subject *Mari* in the (a) sentence, and that therefore both *ki* and *Mari* must be in the same surface position, that is, the subject position of the embedded clause.

(42) a. *Jan   vle   pou   Mari   vini.*   HAITIAN
          John   want   COMP   Mary   come
          'John wants Mary to come.'   (= (28) in Law 1992)

      b. *Ki   mounn$_i$ Jan   vle   pou   ki$_i$ vini?*   HAITIAN
          which   person   John   want   COMP   RES   come
          'Who does John want to come?'   (= (29) in Law 1992)

Second, verbs of the *want* class subcategorize for the complementizer *pou* (Lefebvre 1998: 271); thus, *pou* in (42) is the complementizer of the embedded clause. Given that, in this context, *pou* must be in COMP and *ki* follows *pou*, Law (1992) concludes that *ki* is in the subject position of the extracted subject, as in (43).

(43) Ki   mounn$_i$ Jan   vle   [$_{CP}$ pou   [$_{IP}$ ki$_i$ [$_{VP}$ vini]]]   HAITIAN
                                                              (= (29) in Law 1992)

Third, Law (1992) shows that, in raising contexts, when the embedded subject is questioned, *ki* appears in both the embedded extraction site and the subject position of *sanble*, as shown in (44).

(44) *Ki   mounn   ki   sanble   ki   entèlijan?*   HAITIAN
      which   person   seem   intelligent
      'Who seems to be intelligent?'   (= (8) in Law 1992)

The most embedded *ki* in (44) is in the same position as *Jan* in the embedded clause in (34a), and the *ki* before *sanble* in (44) is in the same position as *Jan* in (34b). Thus, in subject-raising constructions, the embedded subject moves to the subject position of the matrix verb; moreover, when the embedded subject is questioned, *ki* appears in both subject positions. These facts support the analysis that *ki* is a resumptive occurring in the position of the extracted subject. It therefore appears that, while in Fongbe there is only one form of resumptive pronoun, in Haitian there are two.

The fact that *ki* occurs, instead of *li*, in the subject position left empty by Wh-movement out of subject position led Law (1994) to conclude that these data constitute a counterexample to the relabeling-based account of creole genesis. My own conclusion differs from his, however. Haitian is like Fongbe in terms of the contexts that require resumptive pronouns. In both languages, a resumptive pronoun has to occur in the extraction site of a subject left empty either by subject raising out of a tensed clause or by Wh-movement out of the subject position of a tensed clause. Unlike these two languages, French offers no context for a resumptive pronoun in subject position. For one thing, French does not allow subject raising out of a tensed clause, as was shown above by the ungrammaticality of (35b). The absence of subject raising out of the tensed complement of *sembler* 'to seem' ex-cludes the possibility of a resumptive pronoun. Furthermore, in French, subject raising is only possible out of infinitival complements, as was shown in (35c). French infinitival clauses exclude overt subjects. Finally, as we saw above, Wh-movement out of subject position in French requires a spe-cial form of the complementizer *qui* rather than a resumptive pronoun in subject position. So, with respect to the distribution of resumptive pro-nouns, Haitian contrasts with French and pairs with Fongbe. With respect to the form of the resumptive pronoun, Haitian partially departs from Fongbe. While Fongbe has only one kind of resumptive pronoun for both contexts, namely a form corresponding to a personal pronoun, Haitian has two: a form corresponding to a personal pronoun in subject-raising contexts, and a form derived from the French complementizer *qui* > *ki* in Wh-movement contexts. In fact, these two forms may be seen as contextually conditioned allomorphs of the resumptive pronoun. The fact that Haitian has *ki* as a form of resumptive pronoun is undoubtedly attributable to French. Since French *qui* is invariant with respect to number, so is Haitian *ki*. This illus-trates the fact that the superstrate language contributes the morphological material used to spell out grammatical features of the substrate languages.

In summary: subjects in Haitian can be raised or Wh-moved. Without exception, in both contexts, a resumptive pronoun is required in the extrac-tion site of the subject. The resumptive pronoun has two allomorphs: a personal pronominal form in the context of subject raising, and the form *ki* derived from a special form of the French complementizer *qui* in contexts in which Wh-movement has taken place out of subject position. With the exception of short Wh-movement (see (30a) and (36a)) (which still remains to be accounted for), the Haitian data parallel the Fongbe data and contrast with French. I assume the following scenario for the creation of the Haitian structures discussed in this section. Since French does not have subject raising out of tensed clauses, the creators of Haitian would have simply used the forms of the third-person singular or plural personal pronouns as resumptive pronouns in subject-raising contexts, on the model of their native languages. Since French has a special form of the complementizer in the context of Wh-moved subjects, the creators of Haitian would have adopted this form as an allomorph of the resumptive pronoun in subject positions left empty by Wh-movement. This illustrates one way the superstrate language may contribute the morphological material used to spell out the grammatical features of the substrate languages.

Papiamentu offers us yet another example of the contribution the superstrate language can make in determining the morphological material used to spell out grammatical features of the substrate languages. In Papiamentu, the verb *parse* means both 'to seem' and 'to resemble' (Maurer 1988b: 60). Sentences containing this verb may have two surface realizations. In the first, the subject of the embedded clause is realized in the embedded clause and the subject position of the matrix clause is empty. In the second one, the subject of the embedded clause occurs in the subject position of the matrix clause and a resumptive pronoun must occur in the embedded subject position. These two surface realizations are illustrated in (45).

(45) a.   — *parse*   *ku*   *Juan*   *tabata*   *malu.*   PAPIAMENTU
           seem   COMP   Juan   ASP   sick
           'It seems that Juan has been sick.'   (Kearns 2008b)

      b.   *Juan*   *parse*   *ku*   *e*   *tabata*   *malu.*[13]   PAPIAMENTU
           Juan   seem   COMP   RES   ASP   sick
           'Juan seems to have been sick.'   (Kearns 2008b)

---

[13] Kouwenberg (1990) points out that *parse* 'seem' is not a raising verb in Papiamentu. Furthermore, Martha Dijkhoff (p.c.) observes that (45b) is not grammatical for her. However, in the course of our fieldwork on Papiamentu our informants did produce or accept (45b) as grammatical (e.g., Kearns 2008b; Olguín 2006). This situation suggests that there are two Papiamentu grammars for this feature: one in which *parse* is a raising verb and one in which it is not. A possible explanation for the division between speakers could be formulated in terms of closeness to, versus distance from, the superstrate language. By hypothesis, for speakers whose grammar is closest to the superstrate, *parse* would not be a raising verb, since raising out of tensed clauses is not grammatical in Spanish. For speakers whose grammar is farthest from the superstrate, *parse* would be a raising verb, allowing subject raising out of tensed clauses, as in the substrate languages.

There is a gap in our data regarding the possibility of a raised plural subject, so I cannot provide Papiamentu data corresponding to the Fongbe structure in (29c).[14] The sentence in (45a) contains the complementizer *ku*. The fact that this complementizer is restricted to tensed clauses (Lefebvre & Therrien 2007b) argues that the embedded clause in (45b) is in fact tensed. Papiamentu is thus like Fongbe in allowing subject raising out of tensed clauses and in requiring a resumptive pronoun in the extraction site of the subject (see (45b) and (29b) and (28c)).

In Spanish, sentences containing the verb *parecer* 'to seem, to resemble' can also have two surface realizations. In the first one, the embedded subject is realized in the embedded clause, and the subject position of the matrix clause is filled by an expletive realized as a suffix on the verb (see (46a)). In the second, the embedded subject occurs in the subject position of the matrix clause; the clause out of which the subject has been raised is infinitival (see (46b)). This contrasts with the ungrammaticality of (46c), where the embedded subject has been raised out of a tensed clause, showing that, in Spanish, subject raising out of a tensed clause is not possible (Zagona 2002: 130).

(46) a. *Parece   que   Juan está   enfermo.*   SPANISH
          seem.3SG COMP Juan be.3SG   sick
          'It seems that John is sick.'   (= (48) Olguín 2006: 23)

      b. *Juan   parece   estar   enfermo.*   SPANISH
          Juan   seem.3SG be.COMP sick
          'John seems to be sick.'   (from Olguín 2006: 30)

      c. **Juan* parece   que   está   enfermo*   SPANISH
          Juan   seem.3SG COMP be.3SG sick   (from Olguín 2006: 30)

Thus, Papiamentu allows for subject raising out a tensed clause, whereas Spanish does not. In allowing subject raising out of a tensed clause with a resumptive pronoun in the extraction site, Papiamentu differs from its superstrate language and pairs with its substrate languages.

Given the substrate and superstrate data, how did the Papiamentu grammar emerge for structures involving subject raising out of tensed clauses? Since such raising is not possible in Spanish, I assume that the creators of Papiamentu used the properties of their own grammar in establishing those of Papiamentu raising constructions. By hypothesis, like the creators of Haitian, they used the personal pronouns of the incipient creole as resumptive pronouns.

---

[14] To my knowledge, the literature on Papiamentu does not provide such data either.

In contexts involving Wh-movement out of subject position, at first glance, Papiamentu appears to differ from its substrate languages (and from Haitian). Indeed, there is no overt resumptive pronoun in the extraction site of a Wh-moved subject, in cases either of short- or long-distance Wh-movement, as illustrated in (47).

(47) a. *Ken — a bai fiesta?*   Papiamentu
who   ASP go party
'Who has gone to the party?'   (= (17) in Muysken 1979)

b. *Ken bo ta kere   ku — ta parse mi tata?* Papiamentu
who you ASP believe that   ASP look.like my father
'Who do you believe looks like my father?'
(= (27) in Muysken 1979)

c. *Ken b'a   bisa ku — a bai fiesta?*   Papiamentu
who you-ASP say that   ASP go party
'Who did you say went to the party?'
(= (105a) in Muysken 1979)

Due to the lack of resumptive pronoun in the subject extraction sites, data such as those in (47b) and (46c) contrast with those of Fongbe (see (31)), and Haitian (see (36)). Furthermore, the data in (47) appear to constitute violations of the *that-t* filter (e.g., Kouwenberg 1990; Muysken 1979; Veenstra 2008), which was formulated so as to exclude empty subject positions preceded by tensed complementizers from the licit configurations of natural languages (Chomsky 1981). Clearly, in the Papiamentu data in (47b) and (46c), the empty subject positions are preceded by the [+tense] complementizer *ku*. Should the *that-t* filter or any more principled version of it be ruled out on the basis of these Papiamentu data? Or is there another explanation for the Papiamentu data that would be compatible with the *that-t* filter?

Following on the discussion in this section, I would like to offer a solution based on the superstrate input. Spanish is a pro-drop language: because the verb is obligatorily marked for person and number of the subject, the subject position need not be filled in cases of extracted subjects any more than it does in simple sentences. *Quien crees que _ vendra?* [Lit.: Who believe.2SG that _ come.FUT.3SG] 'Who do you believe will come?' Although Papiamentu is not a pro-drop language (e.g., Kouwenberg 1990; but see Veenstra's 2008 discussion of this topic), it allows for empty subjects in the context of Wh-extractions. In light of the discussion on Haitian, this fact can be analyzed as follows. Just as the creators of Haitian

TABLE 7.2 The Distribution of Resumptive Pronouns in Fongbe, Haitian, and Papiamentu

	FONGBE	HAITIAN	PAPIAMENTU
Raising out of subject position	_é_	_li_	_e_
Wh-movement out of subject position	_é_	_ki_	_ø_

identified _qui_ in the environment of Wh-moved subjects in French, the creators of Papiamentu identified a null form in the same context in Spanish. And just as the former analyzed French _qui_ as a form of resumptive pronoun, the latter analyzed the null form as a null resumptive pronoun.[15] Thus, Papiamentu actually does resemble Haitian and Fongbe, except that, due to the pro-drop character of its superstrate language, the form identified as a resumptive pronoun is phonologically null.

In summary, both Haitian and Papiamentu manifest the syntax of their substrate languages in allowing subject raising out of tensed clauses, in contrast to their superstrate languages, which allow subject raising only out of infinitival clauses. Both creoles also share the syntax of their substrate languages in requiring a resumptive pronoun in the position of extracted subjects. However, the forms of the resumptive pronouns in the creoles appear to be dictated by their respective superstrate languages. The forms and distribution of resumptive pronouns in Fongbe, Haitian, and Papiamentu are summarized in Table 7.2.

In subject-raising contexts, the form of the resumptive pronoun corresponds to that of the personal pronouns. In Wh-movement contexts, the form of the resumptive pronoun varies according to the superstrate language. It is null in Papiamentu, on the basis of a null form in Spanish, and _ki_ in Haitian Creole, on the basis of the French complementizer _qui_ [ki] that appears in contexts of Wh-movement out of subject position.

6. Does the Superstrate Language Act as a Filter?

Recall from the introduction that, according to Bao (2005, 2010), the superstrate acts as a filter. Bao's proposal is threefold. First, there is a mechanism that he refers to as "system transfer"; it involves the transfer of entire grammatical subsystems (e.g., the Tense-Mood-Aspect system). System transfer "captures the clustering effect of substrate influence by stipulating that substrate transfer must involve an entire grammatical subsystem"

---

[15] For a much more detailed discussion on resumptive pronouns in Papiamentu, see Dijkhoff (1983).

(Bao 2005: 258).[16] Second, relabeling (which he refers to as relexification) is adopted as the basic generative mechanism of substrate transfer.[17] Third, the lexical-source language "acts like a filter, sifting out those categories of the transferred subsystem for which its grammar cannot provide straightforward morphosyntactic exponence" (Bao 2005: 238). The "morphosyntactic exponence" consists of "the morphological or syntactic materials used to express, or spell out, grammatical features transferred from the linguistic substratum" (Bao 2010: 795). The superstrate language must act as a filter because "the morphosyntactic exponence of the transferred system must meet the grammaticality requirements of the lexical-source language" (Bao 2005: 237). As Bao notes, the first and third components of the proposal are antagonistic, as they pull the emerging language in opposite directions: "System Transfer demands faithfulness to the substratum language, whereas Lexifier Filter demands faithfulness to the lexifier language" (Bao 2005: 261). In the following subsections, I evaluate the hypothesized filtering role of the superstrate language against the data discussed in sections 2 through 5 (section 6.1). I then present data showing that there are several superstrate filter violations in the three creoles under investigation (section 6.2). An overall evaluation of Bao's proposal is provided in the concluding section (section 6.3).

6.1. Evaluation of the Superstrate Language's Filtering Role

The filtering role of the superstrate language is evaluated on the basis of data discussed in sections 2 through 5 earlier.

The superstrate language's first contribution to a creole consists in providing the phonetic strings from which the labels of the creole's lexical entries are derived (section 2). This process has been referred to as relabeling. As we saw in section 4, this process is constrained by what the superstrate has to offer to provide new labels for the substrate lexical items. In this case, the superstrate may be viewed as constraining relabeling but not as filtering substrate lexical items in Bao's terms. I therefore consider that Bao's proposal does not apply to this feature.

The second contribution the superstrate language makes to a creole consists in determining the bulk of its surface orders (section 3). Affix order was shown to be determined by the superstrate (section 3.1). This follows from the more general principle that morpheme order in a creole is

---

[16] Recall from Chapter 4 that we prefer to characterize the phenomenon as "retention" of subsystems from the substrate rather than as "transfer."

[17] In our view, this is not an optimal formulation. See the discussion of this point in Chapter 4.

determined by the order of the superstrate form from which the creole form is derived. In this case again, I would say that Bao's proposal does not apply. Basic word order in tensed clauses was considered in section 3.3. It was shown that all the languages involved—namely substrate, superstrate, and the three creoles—manifest SVO word order in simple tensed clauses. There is one difference between the substrate and superstrate languages' basic word order: while the superstrate languages also have SV order, because they have many intransitive verbs, the substrate languages seldom show this combination, due to the extremely small class of intransitive verbs in these languages and the relatively large number of inherent and cognate object verbs. It was shown that all three creoles track their superstrate languages in having many intransitive verbs and thus manifesting SV order fairly frequently. It was hypothesized that the creation of a large class of intransitive verbs in the Caribbean creoles was linked to the availability of SV word order in their superstrate languages. This context appears to illustrate Bao's proposal in a straightforward way. Indeed, due to the availability of SV word order in the superstrate languages, the latter may be seen as filtering out of the creoles the obligatory objects of inherent and cognate object verbs (which might have been transferred into the creoles by means of relabeling) when no specific object is intended. As a result of this filtering, a relatively large class of intransitive verbs emerged in the creoles.

In section 3.4, it was shown that the contrasting data pertaining to the possible positions of the possessive phrase within the nominal structure in Haitian and Papiamentu versus Saramaccan argue that the superstrate language is instrumental in preventing a substrate constituent order from manifesting itself in a creole, as in Haitian and Papiamentu, or in allowing the substrate constituent order to appear in a creole, as in Saramaccan. In this case, the difference between Haitian/Papiamentu and Saramaccan pertaining to the possible position of the possessive phrase within the nominal structure can be straightforwardly explained by Bao's proposal that the superstrate language acts like a filter, sifting out of the creole features of the substrate languages that have no parallel in the superstrate language (the case of Haitian and Papiamentu), and letting into the creole the features of the substrate languages that do have a parallel in the superstrate language (the case of Saramaccan).

The loss of the substrate nominalization of VPs in the imperfective construction in the creation of Haitian and Saramaccan, discussed in section 3.5, was attributed to conflicting word orders in the substrate and superstrate languages. Indeed, while the deverbal nominalizations involved in the substrate imperfective construction require a word order shift from VO to OV_{nom}, deverbal nominalizations in the superstrate languages of the creoles under discussion do not require such a shift. It was hypothesized that the nominalization of VPs in the creole imperfective construction was abandoned because the original construction in the substrate languages involved a constituent order that was not licit in the superstrate languages. In this case, then, we can say that the similarity between Haitian, Papiamentu, and Saramaccan with respect to the lack of nominalized VPs in the imperfective construction can also be straightforwardly explained by Bao's filtering proposal.

Finally, in section 5, it was shown that, in Haitian and Papiamentu, most contexts of subject extraction out of a tensed clause (subject raising and Wh-movement out of subject position) require a resumptive pronoun in the extraction site. This follows the requirement of the substrate languages' grammar, illustrated on the basis of Fongbe, but not that of the superstrate languages, which require that the subject extraction site be phonologically empty. As summarized in Table 7.2, however, the superstrate languages may contribute the morphological material used to spell out the substrate languages' grammatical features. If Bao's proposal applied in this case, we would expect the superstrate languages of the two creoles to filter out the resumptive pronouns occurring in the position of extracted subjects since none of them have resumptive pronouns in this position. This is not what we observed, however. What we saw was that, although the superstrate languages contribute the forms of the resumptive pronouns, they do not filter out the categories transferred into the creole that do not meet the requirement of the superstrate grammar. I therefore conclude that, in this case, Bao's proposal does not apply.

A summary of the above discussion is presented in Table 7.3.

For the features in which the superstrate contribution is most important, Bao's filter does not apply, and there are other language-internal accounts for the observed phenomena. There are only three cases in which the superstrate languages do appear to act as a filter (see Table 7.3). Interestingly, all of them have to do with word order. Thus, it appears that the hypothesized filtering role of the superstrate language applies in only a subset of cases. The reason for this state of affairs will be addressed in section 7. First, though, in light of the discussion in this section, I will examine the lexifier filter violations manifested by the three creoles investigated in this chapter.

6.2. Lexifier Filter Violations

The three creoles examined in this chapter present several cases of lexifier filter violations. In the following paragraphs, I discuss three of these cases: verb-doubling phenomena, the double-object construction, and the serial verb construction.

TABLE 7.3 Summary of the Evaluation of the Superstrate Languages' Filtering Role
in Creole Genesis

ROLE OF THE SUPERSTRATE IN CREOLE GENESIS	FILTERING ROLE OF SUPERSTRATE?
– Superstrate provides creole's labels	n.a.
– Superstrate constrains relabeling	n.a.
– Superstrate determines affix order with respect to the base	n.a.
– Superstrate responsible for	
• loss of obligatory objects with inherent and cognate object verbs	yes
• loss of some substrate positions for the possessive phrase in creoles' nominal structures due to conflicting word orders between the substrate and superstrate	yes
• loss of some substrate nominalized structures due to conflicting word orders between the substrate and superstrate	yes
– Superstrate contributes the morphological material used to spell out grammatical features retained from the substrate languages	n.a.

n.a. = not applicable

Verb-doubling phenomena, also discussed in Chapter 4, are involved in the following four constructions: temporal adverbial, causal adverbial, factive clauses, and the predicate cleft construction. These exist in the substrate languages of Caribbean creoles but not in their superstrate languages, and yet the four constructions in the creoles are remarkably close to the structures in the substrate languages. The four constructions are illustrated in (48) for Fongbe and Haitian Creole.

(48) a. TEMPORAL ADVERBIAL

Wá *Jan wá (tróló)* bɔ *Màrí yì.*   FONGBE
Rive *Jan rive* epi *Mari pati.*   HAITIAN
arrive John arrive as-soon-as and-then Mary leave
'As soon as John arrived, Mary left.'   (= (1) in Lefebvre 1994b)

  b. CAUSAL ADVERBIAL

Wá *Jan wá útú Màrí yì.*   FONGBE
Rive *Jan rive Mari pati.*   HAITIAN
arrive John arrive cause Mary leave
'Because John arrived, Mary left.'   (= (2) in Lefebvre 1994b)

c. FACTIVE

Wá	*ɖěè*	*Jan*	*wá*	*ɔ́*	*víví*		*nú*	*nɔ̀*
Rive	*ø*	*Jan*	*rive*	*a,*	*fè*			*manman*
arrive	OP	John	arrive	DEF	make(-happy)		for	mother

tɔ̀n.		FONGBE
li	*kɔ̀ntan.*	HAITIAN
his	happy	

'The fact that John arrived made his mother happy.'

(= (3) in Lefebvre 1994b)

d. PREDICATE CLEFT

Wá	*wè*	*Jan*	*wá.*	FONGBE
Se	**rive**	*Jan*	*rive.*	HAITIAN
it-is	arrive	it-is	John arrive	

'It is arrive that John did (not, e.g., leave).'   (= (4) in Lefebvre 1994b)

As can be seen from the data in (48), the Haitian constructions involving verb-doubling are modeled on those of Fongbe. The data in (49) and (50) show that the Saramaccan and Papiamentu constructions are also modeled on the Fongbe structures.

(49) a. TEMPORAL ADVERBIAL

Ko	*Rohit*	*ko*	*a*	*wosu*	*pala,*	*hen*
arrive	Rohit	arrive	LOC	house	as-soon-as	and.then

Rowe	*go.*	SARAMACCAN
Rowe	leave	

'As soon as Rohit arrived at the house, Rowe left.'

(Lefebvre's field notes)

b. CAUSAL ADVERBIAL

Waka	*a*	*waka,*	*a*	*ko*	*wei.*	SARAMACCAN
walk	3SG	Walk	3SG	get	tire	

'Because she walked, she got tired.'   (Lefebvre's field notes)

c. FACTIVE

Di	**waka**	*a*	*waka,*	*hen*	*mei*	*a*	*ko*	*wei.*	SARAMACCAN
DEF	walk	3SG	walk	it	cause	3SG	get	tire	

'The fact that she walked caused her to get tired.'

(Lefebvre's field notes)

d. PREDICATE CLEFT

Waka *a* *waka* *loutu* *di* *wosu.* SARAMACCAN
walk 3SG walk go around DEF house
'He really walked around the house.'

(= (11b) in Van den Berg 1987: 104)

(50) a. TEMPORAL ADVERBIAL

Yega *ku* *Juan* *a* *yega, Maria* *a* *bai.* PAPIAMENTU
arrive LOC John PERF arrive Mary PERF go
'As soon as John arrived, Mary left.' (Kearns 2008b)

b. CAUSAL ADVERBIAL

E **yega** *ku* *Juan* *a* *yega,* *a* *hasi* *ku*
DEF arrive COMP John PERF arrive PERF make COMP
Maria *a* *bai.* PAPIAMENTU
Mary PERF go
'Because John has arrived, Mary left.' (Kearns 2008b)

c. FACTIVE

E **yega** *ku* *Juan* *a* *yega* *a* *hasi* *su*
DEF arrive COMP John PERF arrive PERF make POSS
mama *felis.* PAPIAMENTU
mother happy
'The fact that John has arrived made his mother happy.'

(Kearns 2008b)

d. PREDICATE CLEFT

Ta **kome** *el* *a* *kome.* PAPIAMENTU
it.is eat 3SG PERF eat
'He has eaten.' (= (332) in Maurer 1988b: 141)

Clearly, here, the superstrate languages have failed to filter out the substrate constructions that constitute part of the core features of the grammar of the three creoles under discussion.

The second case has to do with the double-object construction. While the West African substrate languages of Caribbean creoles allow the double-object construction, many of the lexifier languages of these creoles, including French and Spanish, do not present the construction. English is an exception since it does have the double-object construction. Yet all Caribbean creoles have this construction, as is shown in subsequent examples.

The sentence in (51) illustrates the Recipient-Theme construction for Haitian.

(51) *Mwen bay   Pòl   liv   la.*   HAITIAN
       I   give Paul   book   DEF
       'I gave Paul the book.'   (= (19) in Lumsden 1994)

French does not have the Recipient-Theme construction (Kayne 1984; Tremblay 1991), as is shown by the ungrammaticality of the sentence in (52).

(52) **J' ai   donné Paul   le   livre*   FRENCH
       I   AUX give   Paul   DEF   book

French only has a Theme-Goal construction in which the Goal is either assigned dative case by *à* or marked for dative case *à*, depending on one's analysis of *à*. This is illustrated in (53).[18]

(53) *J' ai   donné le   livre à   Paul.*   FRENCH
       I   AUX give   DEF book   to Paul
       'I gave the book to Paul.'

In Saramaccan, the Recipient-Theme construction is available, as is exemplified in (54).

(54) *Mi   da   Carlo   wan   fisi.*   SARAMACCAN
       1SG give Carlo   a   fish
       'I gave Carlo a fish.'   (= (188) in Bally et al. 2006: 48)

The Recipient-Theme construction is also available in English, as shown in (55).

(55) *I gave John a book.*   ENGLISH

---

[18] A reviewer remarks that French seems to have the NP NP construction when the two objects of the verb appear as clitics as in (i):

(i) *Je   le   lui   ai   envoyé*   FRENCH
      1SG 3SG   3SG   AUX   send
      'I sent it to him.'

The sentence in (i) cannot be an instantiation of the V NP NP construction. Typically, in the double-object construction (V NP NP), both NPs bear accusative case. This is visible in languages with overt case markers such as Quechua (Lefebvre & Muysken 1988). In French (i), *le* and *lui* are pronominal clitics marked for case: *le* is accusative (and refers to the Theme), whereas *lui* is dative (and refers to the Goal). The structure in (i) is thus not an instantiation of the V NP NP construction but rather of the V NP PP construction.

In Papiamentu, the Recipient-Theme construction is available, as shown in (56).

(56) B'a   duna Michael un doshi di lusafè.   PAPIAMENTU
     2SG.ASP give Michael a   box   of matches
     'You gave Michael a box of matches.'   (Maurer 1988b: 378)

However, it is not available in Spanish, as shown by the ungrammaticality of (57).

(57) *María le   dio   Juan el   libro   SPANISH
      Maria   3SG   give.3SG   Juan DEF   book   (Olguín 2006: 43)

Spanish is like French in having only a Theme-Goal construction, illustrated in (58).

(58) María le   dio   el   libro a   Juan   SPANISH
     Maria 3SG   give.3SG   DEF   book   to Juan
     'Maria gave the book to Juan.'   (Olguín 2006: 40)

In the case of Saramaccan, it could be argued that the double-object construction is available to the creole because it is compatible with the superstrate language, which also has the construction. However, in Haitian and Papiamentu, the construction is available, even though it does not exist in French or Spanish. Furthermore, as was extensively documented by Michaelis and Haspelmath (2003), the double-object construction is available only in those creoles whose substrate languages manifest the construction, regardless of whether or not their superstrate language has it. In this view, Saramaccan has the double-object construction for the same reason that Haitian and Papiamentu have it: all three creoles have inherited the construction from their substrate languages. The availability of the double-object construction in Haitian and Papiamentu, modeled on the substrate languages, constitutes another violation of the superstrate language's filtering role in creole formation.

A third case has to do with the serial verb construction. All Caribbean creoles, like their substrate languages, have serial verb constructions. None of their superstrate languages has these constructions. This cluster of facts constitutes yet another case of violation of the filtering role of the superstrate language in creole formation.

To account for similar cases of violation of the hypothesized superstrate filter, Bao (2005) appeals to the notion of weak lexifier violators, which he defines as basilectal features drawn from the substratum languages that violate some constraint in the lexifier language.[19] Using data drawn from Singapore English and its source languages, Bao (2010: 806) discusses the case of serial verbs as weak violators: "The Singapore English serial verb is severely restricted in structural and semantic range." He explains this fact by the filtering role of English: "The morphosyntax of English, the lexifier language, provides a ready explanation for the mismatch in usage. English is not a serializing language, and forms like take . . . v and v . . . go are ill-formed. Serial verbs are, by our definition, weak violators. The low frequency reflects the substratum-lexifier dynamic: the morphosyntactic exponence of the substratum grammatical feature—here verb serialization—is subject to the grammatical circumscription by the lexifier language."

According to Bao's definition, all three cases of lexifier violations discussed above would be identified as weak violators. However, the four substrate constructions involving verb-doubling phenomena are readily accessible in Haitian, Saramaccan, and Papiamentu. As for the double-object construction, although in Saramaccan the set of double-object verbs is similar to that of Fongbe—that is, a handful of verbs—in the other creoles the range of these verbs is much greater than in the substrate languages (e.g., Lefebvre 2009b). Finally, although the serial verb construction may be severely restricted in Singapore English compared to its substrate languages, as Bao states, it is not always the case that such constructions are "severely" restricted. For example, according to Hagemeijer and Ogie (2011) for Santome, Jacob and Grimes (2011) for Kupuang Malay, Donohue (2011) for Papuan Malay, and Ansaldo et al. (2011) for China Coast English, the concatenation of verbs in these creoles replicates to a large extent those found in their respective substrates.

Based on the above discussion, my conclusion is that even "weak lexifier violators" in Bao's terms constitute severe drawbacks to the hypothesized filtering role of the superstrate languages in creole genesis.

6.3. Summary

Bao's hypothesized lexifier filter was shown to be inapplicable in most cases where the superstrate language appears to play a role in creole genesis, except those involving word order (section 6.1). Furthermore,

---

[19] Bao (2005) also considers cases of strong violators, that is, cases that violate some grammatical constraint established in the contact language. Based on his discussion of such cases, I was not able to see how they contrast with weak violators. Although such cases may exist in the creoles under discussion in this chapter, they are not discussed here.

several cases of lexifier filter violations were reported, which casts doubt on the filtering role of the lexifier language in creole genesis. An intriguing question concerns the fact that, while the lexicon filter applies to word-order-related phenomena (see Table 7.2), it does not apply in the case of verb-doubling phenomena, double-object constructions, or serial verb constructions.

7. The Contribution of the Superstrate Language to a Creole Is Principled

As discussed in this chapter, the superstrate language's contribution to a creole appears to be restricted to two areas of the grammar. First, it provides the phonetic strings from which the creole labels are derived, as well as the morphological material used to spell out grammatical features kept from the substrate languages. Consequently, the superstrate language may also contribute to the phonological component of the grammar (not discussed here). Second, it plays an important role in establishing word order in creole genesis in two ways. As we saw in Chapter 5, relabeling is either linguistically context-free or context-bound. In the latter case, the position of the creole word is determined by that of the superstrate form that provided the creole label. Furthermore, as we saw in this chapter, superstrate word order phenomena may have a filtering effect on some structures of the substrate that are not compatible with them, yielding constituent order changes from the substrate to the creole, or even deletion of some substrate structures from the creole in cases in cases of conflicting order between the substrate and superstrate.

The two sets of facts just described suggest that labels and word order belong in the same area of the grammar, which could be characterized as the "form," as opposed to "meaning" and "function." Given a model of grammar in which form constitutes a component of the grammar, the contribution of the superstrate language could be said to be restricted to this component. In this view, the items in Table 7.2 constitute a coherent set: they all belong to the "form." Moreover, the fact that the filtering role of the superstrate language is restricted to word-order-related phenomena has a natural explanation.

In this line of thought, there is a principled division of labor between the substrate and superstrate languages in creole genesis. While the superstrate language would appear to determine the "form" of a creole—that is, the labels and most surface orderings—the substrate languages would appear to determine the "meaning" and "function," that is, the semantic and syntactic properties of the creole's lexical entries, as well as the general syntax of the creole language (e.g., the syntax of verb-doubling constructions, double-object constructions, extractions, etc.).

At the beginning of this chapter, I mentioned that some authors note that the superstrate language may also contribute to the semantics of creole lexical entries. This observation contradicts the conclusion I have just reached. In my view, these two contrary statements can be reconciled as follows. In Chapter 2, we saw that, in the Full Transfer/Full Access model of second-language acquisition, the entirety of the L_1 grammar (excluding the phonetic matrices of lexical/morphological items) represents the L_2 initial state—hence Full Transfer—and that Full Transfer can be restated in terms of relabeling (Sprouse 2006: 170). In Chapter 3, we saw that the formation of creoles is a special case of second-language acquisition with limited access to the superstrate language, and that relabeling is a central process in the formation of these languages. Assuming this line of thought, in the initial phase of creole formation, the semantics of creole lexical entries is provided by the substrate languages by virtue of the very nature of relabeling. I believe that the superstrate language contributes to the semantics of creole lexical entries only later, and that the importance of its contribution is determined by the amount of exposure to the superstrate language, as discussed in Chapter 3, section 2.5.

8. Conclusion

The aim of this chapter was to identify the domains where the superstrate languages make a contribution to creoles. Differences between three creoles that are lexically based on different languages but share the same pool of substrate languages enabled us to identify the areas of the grammar in which the superstrate languages have an input in creole genesis. These are the labels (including morphological material to spell out grammatical features retained from the substrate languages) and the surface order of constituents of various sorts. An in-depth analysis of a wide array of phenomena related to these two areas of the grammar led to the conclusion that the contribution of the superstrate language to a creole is principled, in that it appears to determine the "form" (labels and word order), while the substrate languages appear to determine what has been referred to as the "meaning" and "function."

CHAPTER 8 | Relabeling and the Typological
Classification of Creoles

1. Introduction

Based on the material in Lefebvre (ed.) (2011c), this chapter addresses the
problem of the typological classification of creoles.[*] The various positions
on this issue are summarized in section 2. Section 3 sets out the aims and
limitations of this study. The bulk of the chapter presents a synthesis of the
research contained in the various chapters in Lefebvre (ed.) (2011c). Section 4 outlines the ways in which the typological features of the substrate
languages are manifested in the creoles. Section 5 provides a global picture of the variation found among creoles in various subsystems of the
grammar. To a great extent, this variation reflects that displayed by the
creoles' substrate languages. Based on each author's proposals, section 6
reviews the processes that led to the current situation and the constraints
acting upon them. The chapter ends with my overall evaluation of the typological classification of creoles (section 7). Section 8 is the conclusion.

2. The Problem

Since creole languages derive their properties from both their substrate
and superstrate sources, the typological classification of creoles has long

[*]I would like to thank Renée Lambert-Bretière for her assistance in documenting various aspects of
the content of this chapter, and Annie Trudel for helping to produce the map showing the
distribution of the creoles under investigation. I am also grateful to the following colleagues for
their insightful comments on an earlier version of this chapter: Umberto Ansaldo, Mark Donohue,
Chuck Grimes, Harold Koch, Jürgen Lang, Lisa Lim, Stephen Matthews, Jeff Siegel, Armin
Schwegler, Peter Slomanson, and Bao Zhiming.

been a major issue for creolists, typologists, and linguists in general. Several proposals have been put forward in the literature.

Because the labels of the lexical entries of creoles are derived from their superstrate languages, creoles have often been genealogically classified with their superstrates. For example, Hall (1950: 203) classifies Haitian Creole as a Romance language: "Haitian Creole is to be classified among the Romance languages, and especially among the northern group of the Gallo-Romance branch, on the basis of its systematic phonological, morphological, syntactical and lexical correspondences." Goodman (1964: 136) makes a similar statement: "I do feel impelled to restate, however, that on the basis of no purely linguistic criteria for genetic relationship which have thus far been advanced, including that of 'parenté syntaxique' advanced by Sylvain (1936: 121–122), can Creole French be classified with any specific language other than French." Some authors have claimed that, even from a typological point of view, creoles pair with their superstrate languages. Chaudenson (2003: 38), for example, writes: "[Creoles are] idioms that emerged from European languages and were formed in colonial societies between the sixteenth and eighteenth centuries" [our translation from French]. He also writes: "From a typological point of view, the distance between French and the French creoles is quite small" (177) [our translation from French].

Because the properties of a creole's lexical entries are derived from those of its substrate languages, some scholars have classified creoles as hybrid languages. Adam (1883: 47) makes the following statement: "I go so far as to claim . . . that the so-called patois of Guyana and Trinidad constitute Negro-Aryan dialects. By that I mean that the Guinean Negroes who were transported to the colonies adopted the words of French but, as much as possible, kept the phonetics and grammar of their mother tongues. . . . Such a formation is clearly hybrid. . . . The grammar is no different from the general grammar of the languages of Guinea" [our translation from French]. Speaking of Haitian Creole, Sylvain (1936: 178) observes: "We are in the presence of a French that has been cast in the mold of African syntax or . . . of an Ewe language with a French vocabulary" [our translation from French]. Lefebvre (1998) shows at some length that, even though the phonological representations of Haitian Creole lexical entries are drawn from French phonetic strings, Haitian Creole shares its lexical properties, morphosyntax, concatenation principles, and the salient features of its parametric values with its West African substrate languages. In this approach, creole languages would pair typologically with their substrate languages rather than with their superstrates.

A third approach is Bickerton's (1984) proposal that children, who are exposed to the impoverished pidgin grammar and lexicon spoken by their parents, fill in the gaps by drawing on language universal principles, thus creating a creole. The resulting creole languages are claimed to manifest only the unmarked values of language. Further, due to the way they emerge, all creole languages have been claimed to be alike. This may suggest that, from a typological point of view, creole languages constitute an identifiable group of languages that can be set apart from other natural languages. To my knowledge, Bickerton never went so far as to make this claim. McWhorter (2001: 125), however, did, very specifically, as he wrote that "[c]reole grammars constitute a synchronically identifiable class." This claim builds on an earlier one (McWhorter 1998: 790) that creole languages constitute a "synchronically definable typological class."

As can be seen from this brief summary of the major positions on the typological classification of creole languages, the topic is a controversial one. It has been the subject of hot debates, as witnessed by the papers in, for example, the following volumes: Ansaldo et al. (2007), *Deconstructing Creole*; Michaelis (ed.) (2008), *Roots of Creole Structures: Weighing the Contribution of Substrates and Superstrates*; Muysken and Smith (eds.) (1986), *Substrata versus Universals in Creole Genesis*; the special issue of *Linguistic Typology: "Creoles: A Structural Type?"* (2001); and Neumann-Holzschuh and Schneider (eds.) (2001), *Degrees of Restructuring in Creole Languages.*[1]

3. Aims and Limitations of This Chapter

This chapter explores the problem of the typological classification of creole languages on the basis of a representative sample of some 30 creoles that have emerged from typologically different substrate languages. Creoles that have African languages as their substrates are Belizean Creole, Haitian Creole, Kriyol, Ndyuka, Nicaraguan, Palenque(ro), Pamaka, Papiamentu, Portuguese Creole of Santiago Island, Providence Island Creole, Saamaka, San Andrés Islands Creole, Santome, Saramaccan, Sranan Tongo, and St. Lucian. Those that have Asian languages as their substrates are China Coast Pidgin, Kupang Malay, Mindanao Chabacano, Singapore English or Singlish, Sri Lanka(n) Malay, and Ternate Chabacano. Those that have Pacific languages as their substrates are Bislama, Central Australian Aboriginal English (CAAE), Hawai'i Creole, Kriol, New South Wales Pidgin (NSWP), Papuan Malay, Solomon Islands Pijin, Tayo and Tok Pisin. The locations where these languages are spoken are indicated in the map on the next page.

---

[1] See also Lim and Gisborne (eds.) (2009), *The Typology of Asian Englishes.*

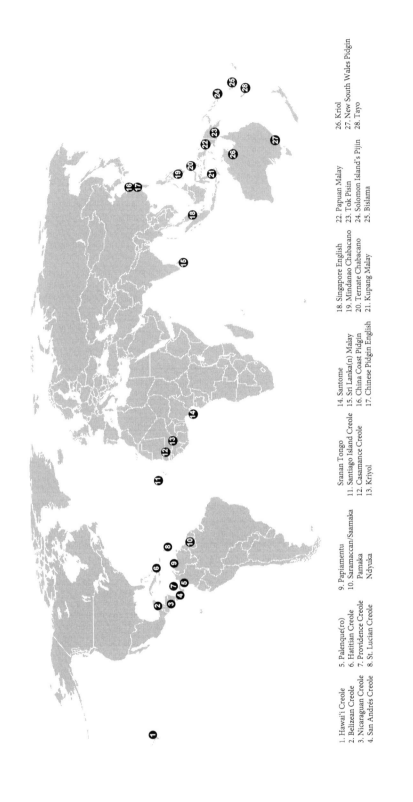

1. Hawai'i Creole
2. Belizean Creole
3. Nicaraguan Creole
4. San Andrés Creole

5. Palenque(ro)
6. Hattian Creole
7. Providence Creole
8. St. Lucian Creole

9. Papiamentu
10. Saramaccan/Saamaka
    Pamaka
    Ndyuka

Sranan Tongo
11. Santiago Island Creole
12. Casamance Creole
13. Kriyol

14. Santome
15. Sri Lanka(n) Malay
16. China Coast Pidgin
17. Chinese Pidgin English

18. Singapore English
19. Mindanao Chabacano
20. Ternate Chabacano
21. Kupang Malay

22. Papuan Malay
23. Tok Pisin
24. Solomon Island's Pijin
25. Bislama

26. Kriol
27. New South Wales Pidgin
28. Tayo

For ease of presentation, the creoles have been grouped by geographical area. In the case of creoles spoken in Africa or in the Caribbean, the substrate languages are all from the same language family: Niger-Congo. However, for creoles spoken in Asia and in the Pacific region, the situation is not as simple. For example, several Malay-based creoles are considered. While Malay itself is an Austronesian language (western branch), the substrate languages involved in the Malay-based creoles are varied. Kupang Malay has other Austronesian languages (central branch) as its substrate languages. Papuan Malay has various (non-Austronesian) Papuan languages as its substrate languages. Sri Lanka(n) Malay has substrate languages that belong in different language families, with Tamil, a Dravidian language, and Sinhala, an Indo-European language, as two major substrate languages (in Slomanson's 2011 view) or adstrate languages (in Ansaldo's 2011b view). CAAE, Kriol, and NSWP have Australian languages as their substrates. Tok Pisin, Bislama, Solomon Islands Pijin, and Tayo, spoken in the Pacific region, have mainly Austronesian languages as their substrate, as does Chabacano, which is spoken in the Philippines.

In the list of creole languages enumerated above, all except four are commonly referred to as creoles. China Coast Pidgin and NSWP are commonly referred to as pidgins because they do not have native speakers (as opposed to creoles, which do have native speakers). In the literature on the "New Englishes" of the world, Singapore English and CAAE are generally considered to be varieties of English. In this chapter, I will use the term "creole" as an overall term for the languages generally referred to as creoles, but also for these two pidgins and the two varieties of "New Englishes." In doing this, I do not want to open a debate on the status of these four contact languages. The reason for using the term "creole" is merely practical. But it is also in line with the fact that scholars have started referring to pidgins and creoles as PCs, suggesting that they fall within a single category (e.g., Hancock 1980; Mufwene 1990; Mühlhäusler 1980, 1986b). The rationale behind this grouping is that the creation of pidgins and of creoles involves the same processes (e.g., Lefebvre 1998). As for the two varieties of English referred to above, the context in which they emerged differs from that in which the plantation creoles were created. These two contexts do, however, share an important feature. They both involve multilingual communities in need of a lingua franca. Hence, Singapore English was created in a multilingual community—involving Malay and several Sinitic languages—that needed a lingua franca. Likewise, CAAE was also created in a multilingual community—involving several Australian languages—that needed a lingua franca. Furthermore, the creation of these New Englishes makes use of the same processes that are at work in the formation of pidgins and creoles (Bao 2011; Koch 2011b; Siegel 2011). Finally, this grouping is in line with the claim made by Koch (2011a), who considers the variety of CAAE he reports on in Lefebvre (ed.) (2011c) to be a post-pidgin variety that is quite distinct from other varieties also referred to as CAAE (such as those discussed in Eades 1991, 1996), which in fact constitute dialects of English.

Lefebvre's (2011c) edited book contains 25 chapters that set out detailed comparisons of subsystems of the above sample of creoles with their respective major substrate languages. The major subsystems of creoles' grammars and lexicons discussed in this book include segmental inventories, pronouns, case systems, the syntactic properties of verbs, copulas, Tense-Mood-Aspect (TMA) systems, negation, serial verbs, and discourse structures. The results of these comparisons constitute test cases for the different positions summarized above regarding the typological classification of creoles.

As will be seen below, the bulk of the data indicates that creoles are best typologically classified with their substrate languages. As will be further discussed in section 7.2, this may reflect the fact that, except for two chapters, all the chapters in Lefebvre (ed.) (2011c) discuss data that belong in the lexical or syntactic components of the grammar. These are two components in which we expect substrate features to manifest themselves in the creoles, given the processes that create creoles' lexicons and syntax (see section 6). As for phonology, it is discussed in only two chapters. Brousseau (2011) addresses the source of the segmental inventories of Haitian and St. Lucian creoles, and Lim (2011) discusses the source of tones in Singlish. For a thorough discussion of the typological features of creoles in this component of the grammar, more detailed comparisons of segmental inventories and prosodic and syllabic structures of creoles and their contributing languages will be needed. The same remark applies to word order. The fact that there are so few chapters on the phonological component of the grammar and none on word order is not intentional. It simply reflects the fact that few authors volunteered chapters on the phonology and none on word order. I now turn to a discussion of the results presented in Lefebvre (ed.) (2011c) from a global perspective.

4. Ways in Which the Typological Features of the Substrate Are Manifested in Creoles

This section summarizes the various ways in which the typological features of the substrates are manifested in creoles. Creoles spoken in Africa and the Caribbean area, those spoken in Asia, and those spoken in the Pacific region will be discussed in turn.

4.1. Creoles Spoken in Africa and the Caribbean Region

Hagemeijer and Ogie (2011) study the inventory of serial verb constructions (SVC) in Santome and Edo. They conclude that "pretty much the full range of types of SVCs in Edo can also be found in Santome" (57). They note, however, that "the languages often differ with respect to the more fine-grained properties of SVCs, which is expected from many centuries of independent development and, foremost, due to the creolisation process itself" (57).

Lang (2011) compares the manifestation of aspect in Santiago Creole and in Wolof. He shows that ". . . the Santiago Creole progressive has retained only the progressive meaning of the imperfective variety of the Wolof 'situative,' abandoning its 'situative' meaning" (61). He suggests that leveling accounts for the difference between the two: "This simplification would have occurred to ease the joining of other groups whose language may have had a progressive, but not a 'situative' with a progressive meaning in the imperfective" (78). In the same vein, Migge (2011) compares the tense, mood, and aspect systems of the Surinamese creoles with those of the Gbe languages. While the comparison between the two sets reveals many similarities, Migge notes that substrate influence is not a "unified process" since "its operation and outcomes appear to take different forms, most likely due to its interaction with other processes and sources" (155).

Escure (2011) studies the influence of the substrate languages of Belize Creole on its tense and mood system: ". . . maintenance of African elements, including the intact preservation of some essential verbal morphology such as ANT *me* and its counterfactual structure. Direct African antecedents have been found for this structure (Ibibio/Efik, Kituba, Swahili and generally Bantoid languages). Its anteriority morpheme, the specific shape of its futurity/irrealis marker and its related counterfactual combinations appear to closely mirror aspects of Bantu morphology, as well as the semantics of hypothetical events" (198).

In her chapter on the phonology of Haitian and St. Lucian, Brousseau (2011) compares the segmental inventories of the two creoles with those of French and Fongbe to evaluate the impact of the substrate languages on the development of these systems. She concludes that "[t]he influence of the substrate is pervasive in the inventories of the two creoles, even for cases where we could convincingly argue for the role of Universal Grammar" (123).

Lefebvre (2011b) compares the properties of verbs in three Atlantic creoles—Haitian, Saramaccan, and Papiamentu—with those of their contributing languages: Fongbe, an important substrate language, and French, English, and Spanish, the respective lexifier languages of the three creoles. The verbal properties compared are the following: BODY-state expressions, WEATHER verbs, raising verbs, control verbs, double-object verbs, and serial verbs. The three-way comparison shows that first, the properties of verbs in the three creoles often contrast with those of the corresponding verbs in their respective superstrate languages; second, these properties systematically parallel those of the corresponding verbs in their substrate languages; and third, the properties of the substrate verbs manifest themselves in all three creoles, even though they have different superstrate languages.

Bartens (2011) compares some 30 phonological, morphosyntactic, and lexical features in Twi and in the English-based creoles spoken on San Andrés and Old Providence (Colombia) and on the Atlantic coast of Nicaragua. Her conclusion is as follows: "In a number of cases, it was impossible to make a case for exclusive substrate influence and it seems preferable to speak of convergence. However, there are also many language structures for which substrate influence offers the most likely explanation" (201).

Meanwhile, Schwegler (2011) compares Palenquero and Kikongo. His assessment of the situation is as follows: ". . . We have noted that substratal influence can be detected in multiple domains: in the creole's *lexicon*, where dozens of words are traceable to Kikongo etyma; in its *phonology*, where several features (including prenasalisation, the free [d], [ɾ] and [l] alternations, and peculiar intonational patterns) point to Kikongo roots; and in its *morphosyntax*, where nominal pluralisations with *ma* and reiterative P/N marking in the singular (e.g., *yo i kelé-lo* 'I want it'), and a host of other traits are similarly suggestive of Kikongo input" (243). However, Palenquero has not preserved the class-concord agreement system that characterizes many Bantu languages.

To sum up, the creoles with a Niger-Congo substrate discussed in the first part of Lefebvre (ed.) (2011c) all appear to manifest features of their substrate languages. As some authors note, however, certain substrate features may not appear in the creole due to interaction between different processes (e.g., transfer and leveling in Lang's chapter, several processes in Migge's chapter) (see also section 6). Kriyol, spoken in Guinea-Bissau, departs from this general tendency. Kihm's (2011) explanation of why this is so will be discussed in section 6.

4.2. Creoles Spoken in Asia

Two chapters concern Singapore English/Singlish (two appellations for the same language variety), one on syntax, the other on phonology. Bao (2011) compares the patterns of the passive constructions in the Singaporean component of the International Corpus of English with the substrate passive constructions. He shows that the substrate passives are adversative and that Singapore English passives also exhibit a clear adversative bias. Furthermore, he shows that the quantitative analysis supports two distinct mechanisms of substratum influence: "the abrupt substratum transfer (the locally derived passives) and the gradual convergence-to-substratum (the English-derived passives)" (254). Lim's (2011) chapter focuses on the origin of tones in Singlish, the mesolectal/basilectal variety of English spoken in Singapore. Singlish has two major substrate languages: the Sinitic substrate languages, which have tones, and Malay, which does not. At first blush, one would posit that the tone observed in Singlish must originate in the Sinitic substrate languages. As Lim points out, however, the situation is more complex. As she puts it, "even when the *feature* of tone may be ascribed to the tone language substrates, the actual *realisation* in terms of prosodic patterns—for instance, in the case of Singlish, the location of the H tone at word or phrase level—can be influenced by the prosody of a non-tone language; in the case of Singlish, this is Malay. What is also significant is that this is the language of a population—the Peranakans—that is recognised as having been an earlier or founder population in the ecology, which therefore exerts a significant influence on the structure of the emergent contact language" (284).

In their comparative study of serial verbs, classifiers, properties of verbs, copulas, negation, TMA, pronouns, Wh-interrogatives, topic-comment structures, and compounds, Ansaldo et al. (2011) argue that Cantonese typological features are reproduced in China Coast Pidgin.

Grant (2011) and Sippola (2011) study two creole varieties spoken in the Philippines: Mindanao Chabacano (MC) and Ternate Chabacano (TC). Grant concludes that "between Spanish, Central Philippine languages and some sort of Manila Bay Creole, almost all the grammar of MC could be included as 'substrate features'" (311). As for Sippola, she concludes her study of negation as follows: ". . . It can be affirmed that the main pattern of Ternate Chabacano negation follows its adstrate language Tagalog when distinguishing the standard clausal negation and the negation of existentials and possession" (335).

The chapter by Jacob and Grimes (2011) describes serial verb constructions in Kupang Malay and its substrate languages. The parallel between the structures, functions, and semantics of SVCs in Kupang and those in the substrate languages is quite striking, whereas there are simply no parallels found with standard Malay grammar.

There are two chapters on Sri Lanka(n) Malay (SLM). Ansaldo (2011b) shows that the Lankan case system has been reproduced in SLM: "SLM has developed agglutinative morphology with incipient fusional tendencies in the nominal system, which indicates a typological shift away from the isolating type" (370). As for tense and aspect, the results are split between the two contributing languages. While tense reflects the Lankan tense system, the aspectual system retains some of the aspectual categories of Malay. Slomanson's (2011) study of the morphosyntax of SLM leads him to the following conclusion: ". . . The morphosyntax of SLM substantially reflects influence from the Sri Lanka(n) *sprachbund* [. . .] While a small number of features and processes from vehicular Malay persist in SLM, such as the fixed pre-verbal position of those functional contrasts directly marked on lexical verbs and the categorial flexibility of adjectives, the language's morphosyntax has incorporated more features from its Sonam model language than it has retained from vehicular Malay" (408).

To sum up, the creoles spoken in Asia all appear to manifest features of their substrate languages.

4.3. Creoles Spoken in the Pacific Region

Donohue (2011) investigates the serial verb constructions of Papuan Malay and its substrate languages and concludes that Papuan Malay SVCs manifest the properties of its New Guinea Papuan substrate languages.

In his first chapter, Koch (2011a) discusses data from three areas of the grammar of CAAE, and compares it with Kaytetye, one of the Arandic substrate languages. It shows how two relatively exotic grammatical categories found in Kaytetye (and other Arandic languages)—"dyadic" in kinship nouns and "associated motion" in verbs—are replicated in CAAE using formal material derived from English. Koch also compares the use of CAAE prepositions, whose forms are from English, with Kaytetye case functions. He concludes that "the organisation of the semantic 'functions' of the cases is replicated in considerable detail in the use of the CAAE prepositions" (437) (see section 5.5).

Munro (2011) considers pronouns, TMA markers, and case in Kriol and its substrate Australian languages. She reaches a conclusion similar to that of the aforementioned authors: the properties of the lexical items involved in the Kriol subsystems of the grammar reproduce those of its substrate languages. She emphasizes that Aboriginal languages are agglutinating languages and discusses how the properties of the affixes are reproduced in free morphemes in the creole (see section 7.3).

In his study of NSWP and its contributing languages, Koch (2011b) shows that the grammatical features of zero expression third-person singular objects and Noun Phrase head nouns are indirectly reflected in *-im* and *-fela*, respectively.

Siegel (2011) considers pan-Pacific Pidgin features in modern contact varieties. Many grammatical features of Pacific Pidgin English, NSWP, and Chinese Pidgin English were attested in the New Hebrides (now Vanuatu), Solomon Islands, New Guinea Islands, Hawai'i, and the Northern Territory of Australia in the late nineteenth and early twentieth centuries. The creoles that later developed in each of these locations retained a different subset of these "Pan-Pacific" features. Siegel examines nine of these features to see whether their presence or absence in each of the five modern contact varieties can be accounted for by the presence or absence of the same features in the substrate languages. The results show that "for at least seven of the nine Pan-Pacific features, when the feature is present in the contact variety, a corresponding feature is also present in the substrate languages, and when it is absent in the contact variety, it is absent in the substrate languages" (553).

The chapter by Roberts (2011) "presents comparative and diachronic evidence indicating that substrate patterns played a significant role in the development of the copula in Hawai'i Creole English (HCE). The predominantly Cantonese, Portuguese, Hawaiian, and Japanese substrate did not contribute much to the innovation of lexical forms since HCE drew on a preexisting pidgin, but the transference and reinforcement of semantic and syntactic properties from these languages—with the exception of Japanese—is detectible in the copula system that arose in HCE" (557).

About Tayo, Sandeman (2011) writes: "Research carried out to date on Tayo indicates that many of its structures depart radically from what has been considered a 'typical' creole pattern; instead, they appear to more closely resemble structures in the substrate languages" (575). Her specific study of the TMA subsystem illustrates this more general claim.

To sum up, here again the creoles appear to manifest the properties of their substrate languages. Since the last chapter in this section of

Lefebvre (ed.) (2011c), Terrill's (2011) work on Solomon Islands Pijin, is dedicated to constraints on transference, it will be discussed in section 6.

4.4. Summary

The data reported on in this section show that, to a great extent, creoles reproduce the features of their substrate languages. This conclusion becomes even more evident when we compare subsystems of grammar across creoles.

5. Subsystems of the Grammar across Creoles with Different Substrates

This section considers subsystems of the grammar across creoles with typologically different substrates. The following subsystems will be discussed: pronominal forms, classifiers, TMA systems, negation, semantic case systems, transitivity markers, the properties of verbs, serial verbs, verb-doubling phenomena, and discourse structures. In the following paragraphs, it will be shown that typological differences between subsystems of the grammar across creoles reflect typological differences between their respective substrate languages.

5.1. Pronominal Forms

Creole languages have different kinds of pronominal inventories. For example, Kriol has a pronominal system that distinguishes between singular, dual, and plural pronouns, and also between first-person plural and dual inclusive and exclusive. These forms are all constructed from English pronominal forms (e.g., *mi < me, yu < you*, etc.), or some combination thereof (e.g., *yunmi < you and me*). This is shown in Table 8.1.

TABLE 8.1 The Pronominal System of Kriol

	SINGULAR	DUAL	PLURAL
1	*ai/mi*		
2	*yu*	*yundubala*	*yumop*
3	*im*	*dubala*	*olabat*
1 inclusive		*yunmi*	*wi*
1 exclusive		*mindubala/minbala*	*melabat/mela*

SOURCE: Adapted from Munro (2004: 123).

(See also Keesing 1988 for similar data based on Solomon Islands Pijin.)

This pronominal system contrasts with that of, say, Haitian Creole, which has only five pronominal forms, because first- and second-person plural are encoded by the same morpheme, as shown in Table 8.2.

The pronominal system of Kriol reproduces that of its substrate languages, illustrated with Alawa in Table 8.3, and summarized in Table 8.4 for all the Kriol substrate languages that Munro has documented.

TABLE 8.2 The Pronominal System of Haitian Creole

mwen	'I, me'	HAITIAN
ou/[wu]	'you (SG)'	
li	'he/she/it/him/her'	
nou	'we/us/you (PL)'	
yo	'they/them'	

SOURCE: Valdman et al. (1981); Fattier (1998, vol. 2: 850).

TABLE 8.3 The Pronominal System of Alawa

	SINGULAR	DUAL	PLURAL
1	*ngina*		
2	*nyagana*	*wurru*	*wulu*
3	*nurla* (m.)	*yirrurla*	*yilurla*
	nga durla (f.)		
1 inclusive		*nyarru*	*nyalu*
1 exclusive		*ngarru*	*ngalu*

SOURCE: Munro (2004: 122).

TABLE 8.4 The Pronominal System of Kriol Substrate Languages

	SINGULAR	DUAL	PLURAL
1	√		
2	√	√	√
3	√	√	√
1 inclusive		√	√
1 exclusive		√	√

SOURCE: Adapted from Munro (2004: 121).

TABLE 8.5 The Pronominal System of Fongbe

nyὲ	'I, me'	FONGBE
hwὲ	'you (SG)'	
é(yὲ)	'he/she/it/him/her'	
mí	'we/us/you (PL)'	
yé	'they/them'	

SOURCE: (18) in Brousseau (1995).

Likewise, the pronominal system of Haitian Creole reproduces that of its Fongbe substrate, shown in Table 8.5.[2]

Other creoles with substrates that are typologically different as regards their pronominal system do not make the same distinctions. For example, Palenquero (Schwegler 2011) possesses a different pronominal system, modeled on that of substrate languages such as Kikongo. Both the creole and its substrate distinguish between a first-person emphatic and a first-person topic pronoun. In the same vein, Mindanao Chabacano (Grant 2011) distinguishes between different levels of politeness for second-person singular and plural, and it makes a first-person plural inclusive/exclusive distinction, like the Philippine languages.

5.2. Classifiers

Not all creole languages have classifiers. As expected, classifiers are found only in creoles whose substrate languages have them. For example, noun phrases in China Coast Pidgin (Ansaldo et al. 2011) have the patterns [NUM-CL-N] and [DEM-CL-N], reproducing the classifiers of its Sinitic substrate languages.

5.3. TMA Systems

The TMA systems of creole languages exhibit considerable variation. This is supported by the comparison of the Kriol TMA system reproduced in Table 8.6, from Munro (2011), with that of Haitian Creole in Table 8.7, from Lefebvre (1996).

---

[2] Note that, as is reported in Lefebvre (1998: 142), traditional Fongbe grammars (e.g., Anonymous 1983) sometimes represent the form meaning 'we' as *mǐ* (bearing a complex low-high tone) and the form meaning 'you (PL)' as *mī* (bearing a mid-tone). Mid- and low-high tones are phonetic variants (Capo 1991); the distinction between the two is thus phonemically irrelevant. Furthermore, extensive fieldwork by Brousseau (1995) on the tonological specification of the form *mí* reveals that this form always bears a phonological high tone.

TABLE 8.6 The TMA System of Kriol

REALIS		ASPECT		IRREALIS	
bin	Past	*oldei*	Continuative	*garra*	Obligatory (Future)
Ø	Present	*stil*	Durative	*−l*	Definite 1SG
		stat	Incipient	*mait*	Potential
		onli	Limitational	*gin*	Abilitive
		jes	Proximal	*gan*	Inabilitive
		−bat	Progressive	*lafda*	Necessary
		yusdu	Habitual		

SOURCE: Table 6 in Munro (2011).

In the chapters of Lefebvre (ed.) (2011c), TMA systems are documented for the following creoles: Surinamese (Migge 2011), Tayo (Sandeman 2011), Sri Lanka(n) Malay (Ansaldo 2011b; Slomanson 2011), Kriyol (Kihm 2011), China Coast Pidgin (Ansaldo et al. 2011), Santiago Creole (Lang 2011), and Kriol (Munro 2011). Again, all authors agree that the features of the TMA systems of these creoles most resemble those of their respective substrates, such that the typological differences between them manifest the typological differences between their substrate languages.

Munro (2011) shows that the semantics associated with the categories of tense, mood, and aspect reflects substrate features, such as the distinction between past punctual and past continuous aspects, and the expression of future and potential mood. She remarks that "evitative" mood, found in TMA systems of the substrate languages, does not appear in Kriol. She explains this absence by the unavailability of an appropriate form in the superstrate language to transfer evitative mood to (see section 6).

TABLE 8.7 The TMA System of Haitian Creole

ANTERIOR	IRREALIS	NON-COMPLETE
Past or Past perfect	Definite future	Imperfective
te	*ap*	*ap*
	Indefinite future	
	a-va	
	Subjunctive	
	pou	

SOURCE: Lefebvre (1996: 239).

TABLE 8.8 Inventories of TMA Markers in Haitian Creole and Fongbe

ANTERIOR		IRREALIS		NON-COMPLETE			
Past or Past perfect		Definite future		Habitual		Imperfective	
H	F	H	F	H	F	H	F
te	*kò*	*ap*	*ná*	—	*nɔ̀*	*ap*	*ɖò...wɛ̀*
		Indefinite future					
		H	F				
		a-va	*ná-wá*				
		Subjunctive					
		H	F				
		pou	*ní*				

SOURCE: (115) in Lefebvre (1996: 263).

The TMA systems of Atlantic creoles reproduce the characteristics of their West African substrate languages. This is illustrated in Table 8.8 for Haitian Creole and Fongbe from Lefebvre (1996, and the references therein).

Except for the fact that it does not distinguish between definite and indefinite future, the TMA system of Saramaccan is very similar to those of Haitian and Fongbe. It encodes tense, mood, and aspect by means of an inventory of TMA markers comprising the marker of anteriority *bì* (< English *been*), the future marker *ó* (< English *go*), the subjunctive marker *fu* (< English *for*), and the imperfective marker *ta* (< Portuguese *esta*, according to Byrne 1987; < English *stand*, according to Veenstra 1996a) (for *fu*, see Lefebvre & Loranger 2006, and the references therein; for the other markers, see Rountree 1992). As in Haitian and Fongbe, these markers combine with each other to form complex tenses (Bally 2004; Rountree 1992). Furthermore, Saramaccan, like Haitian and Fongbe but unlike English, allows for bare sentences. Saramaccan bare sentences are assigned a temporal-aspectual interpretation in the same way that Haitian and Fongbe bare sentences are (for Haitian and Fongbe, see Lefebvre 1996; for Saramaccan, see Bally 2004). In their comparison of Surinamese creoles and Gbe languages, Winford and Migge (2007) expand the inventory of TMA markers to include aspectual and modal verbs. Their conclusion is that the properties of the TMA markers and of the aspectual and modal verbs of these creoles are very similar to those of the Gbe languages. The chapter by Migge (2011) extends the demonstration to all Surinamese creoles. She shows that some parts of the TMA system are clear calques of forms in the substrate languages (e.g., perfective aspect expressed by the unmarked verb), whereas others are partial calques. For example, the marker that encodes imperfective aspect extends to habitual, an extension not found in Gbe since Gbe languages have an independent marker encoding habitual, as shown in Table 8.8.[3] Note that in Haitian Creole, the marker that encodes imperfective aspect also extends to habitual (Lefebvre 1998: 120).

Kriyol has a different West African substrate from the Caribbean creoles. Indeed, while the substrate languages of the latter are Kwa and predominantly Gbe languages, Kriyol's substrates are mainly Atlantic languages, including Wolof and Balanta. Kihm (2011) shows that, unlike the other West-African-based creoles, Kriyol has a postverbal, as opposed to preverbal, morpheme *ba* encoding anteriority. According to Kihm, this is attributable to Wolof and Balanta, in which the marker of anteriority is also postverbal.

Sandeman (2011) states that the Tayo TMA system differs radically from those of the Caribbean creoles. She shows that this system reflects the properties of substrate languages such as Cèmuhî, Drubéa, and Xârâcùu. For example, Tayo has a marker *va* that encodes unrealized events/situations; this marker thus appears in contexts of future and potential events/situations. Both Cèmuhî and Drubéa have a future marker and a potential marker. Marking future and potential events in Tayo comes from the substrate languages, with the difference that, while Cèmuhî and Drubéa have two different markers, Tayo has only one to encode both meanings. Another example of similarity between Tayo and its Pacific substrate languages lies in the marking of asserted and insisted reality. Cèmuhî, Drubéa, and Xârâcùu all possess a specific marker encoding asserted reality. Cèmuhî and Xârâcùu also have another marker to express insisted reality. Tayo has a mood marker *ke*, which encodes emphasis and is also used to encode asserted and insisted reality.

In his comparison of SLM with its superstrate and adstrate (Sinhala) languages, Ansaldo (2011b) concludes that the TMA system of SLM draws from both its sources. Slomanson (2011) argues in his comparison of SLM with its superstrate and its Sonam substrate language, that, in SLM, TMA categories are preverbal bound markers modeled on Sonam: "There are clear parallels in the functional contrasts that are explicitly morphologized in SLM, using processes comparable or identical to those

---

[3] The TMA system of Papiamentu used to be seen as different from that of the other Caribbean creoles (e.g., Muysken 1981b). The analysis in Kouwenberg and Lefebvre (2007), however, shows that the TMA system of this language is in fact quite similar to those of the other Caribbean creoles and thus to those of its Gbe substrate languages. See Chapter 3, section 2.1.3.2, for further discussion.

that we find in Sonam, such as inflection and agglutination [. . .]" (388). Furthermore, he shows that SLM manifests contrastive tense marking, just as Sonam does. The fact that Ansaldo and Slomanson do not reach exactly the same conclusion appears to result from the fact that they do not evaluate the role of the various contributing languages in the same way. While Ansaldo emphasizes the role of Sinhala and Tamil, Slomanson focuses on Sonam.

5.4. Negation

Negation, which is discussed for several creoles—Ternate Chabacano (Sippola 2011), China Coast Pidgin (Ansaldo et al. 2011), Belizean Creole (Escure 2011), Mindanao Chabacano (Grant 2011), and Sri Lanka(n) Malay (Slomanson 2011)—is another subsystem of the grammar in which creoles manifest the typological differences of their substrates. For example, Sippola shows that the properties of the negation system in Ternate Chabacano, namely standard clausal negation and negation of existentials and possession, are analogous to what is observed in Tagalog. Another example comes from Belizean Creole, which encodes past negation by a different morpheme (*neva*) from that used to encode general negation. Past negation markers are also found in the African substrate languages of Belizean Creole such as Ibibio, Mandinka, and Swahili.

In Sri Lanka(n) Malay, the expressions of negation and finiteness interact. Slomanson (2011) shows that SLM has two etymologically unrelated negation markers, the choice of which is solely determined by the finiteness of an associated verb. He also shows that overt tense morphology is suppressed when a lexical verb is negated. Both these features of negation are attributed to Sonam. As Slomanson mentions, the second feature is not found in SLM's other substrate languages such as Sinhala.

5.5. Semantic Case Systems

Some creoles manifest overt semantic cases and some do not. Creoles that do have overt semantic cases are those whose substrate languages do so as well. In Lefebvre (ed.) (2011c), the case systems of three creoles are documented: Sri Lanka(n) Malay and its Sinhala adstrate (Ansaldo 2011b), Kriol and its Australian substrate languages such as Alawa (Munro 2011), and CAAE and its Australian substrate languages such as Kaytetye (Koch 2011a). As will be seen, all three reproduce the case inventories of their respective substrate languages.

TABLE 8.9 The Semantic Case Systems of SLM and Sinhala

FUNCTIONS EXPRESSED	SINHALA CASE SUFFIXES (FORMS NOT GIVEN)	SRI LANKA(N) MALAY CASE SUFFIXES	
Agent	Nominative	Nominative	-ϕ
Experiencer	Dative	Dative	-nang
Goal	Dative	Dative	-nang
Beneficiary	Dative	Dative	-nang
Possessor	Dative	Dative	-nang
Patient	Accusative	Definite object marking	-yang
Possession	Genitive/locative	Genitive	-pe
Location	Genitive/locative	Locative	-ka
Instrument	Instrumental/ablative	Instrumental/ablative	-ring
Source	Instrumental/ablative	Instrumental/ablative	-ring
Association	Comitative	Comitative	-le

SOURCE: Adapted from Table 2 in Ansaldo (2011b).

Ansaldo shows that the semantic case system of SLM reproduces the Sinhala semantic case system almost to perfection. This is shown in Table 8.9.

Ansaldo sees one difference between the creole and Sinhala case systems: "In SLM, Genitive and Locative receive different marking; SLM therefore has a specialized Possessive marker, an innovation in relation to the adstrates" (371).

Koch (2011a) and Munro (2011) both show that the Australian creoles they study reproduce the semantic case inventories of their respective substrate languages. In this case, however, the inventories are realized as prepositions instead of as suffixes. Table 8.10, from Munro, shows the similar case systems of Kriol and Alawa. There is one difference: In Alawa, "[a]ccompaniment is [. . .] not marked through a case suffix as such. The fact that Accompaniment is expressed with the same form as Instrument in Kriol is therefore unexpected" (481).[4]

Table 8.11 from Koch (2011a) shows the similarity in the semantic case systems of CAAE and Kaytetye.

---

[4] Harold Koch (p.c.) comments: "I believe the Location function should be -rri 'locative' (Sharpe 1972: 62)—the same form as Instrument. If this is correct, a second difference between Alawa and Kriol is the fact that Location and Instrument are expressed differently in the latter. (This may reflect the grammar of other substrate languages rather than Alawa: Australian languages differ as to whether they express Instrument by a form identical to Locative or something else (usually Ergative or the 'having' case); it seems that Kriol garra (from gott'em) reflects the latter strategy, which was probably present in some of the Kriol substratum languages."

TABLE 8.10 The Semantic Case Systems of Kriol and Alawa

FUNCTIONS EXPRESSED	ALAWA CASE SUFFIXES	KRIOL PREPOSITIONS
Location	*–rru* 'allative'	*langa, la*
Goal	*–rru* 'allative'	*langa, la*
Source	*–yunu* 'ablative'	*burrum, brom*
Possession	*–ja* 'genitive'	*blong, bla*
Purpose	*–ja* 'genitive'	*blong, bla*
Instrument	*–rri* 'instrumental'	*garra*
Accompaniment	(no case; nominal suffix *-wanji*)	*Garra*

SOURCE: Munro (2011).

TABLE 8.11 The Case Systems of CAAE and Kaytetye

FUNCTIONS EXPRESSED	KAYTETYE CASE SUFFIXES	CAAE PREPOSITIONS
Location	*–le, -nge* 'locative'	*longa*
Instrumental	*–le, -nge* 'locative'	*longa*
Goal	*–warle* 'allative'	*longa*
Purpose	*–warle* 'allative'	*longa*
Specific location/goal	x N-*le*/-*ngel*-*warle*	x *longa*
Terminative	*–wartetye* 'terminative'	*right up longa*
Perlative	*–angkwerre* 'perlative'	*through longa*
Source	*–theye* 'ablative'	*from*
Cause	*–theye* 'ablative'	*from*
Comparison	*–theye* 'ablative'	*from*
Material source	*–penhe* 'sequential'	*from*
Prior condition	*–penhe* 'sequential'	*from*
Aversive	*–ketye* 'aversive'	*from*
Possessive	*–arenge* 'possessive'	*blong(int)a*
Purpose	*–warle* 'allative'	*blong(int)a*
Purpose	*–we* 'dative'	*for*
Recipient	*–we* 'dative'	*for*
Proprietive	*–akake* 'proprietive'	*with*
Proprietive	*–akake* 'proprietive'	*gottem, got*
Privative	*–wanenye* 'privative'	*(got) no*

SOURCE: Table 3 in Koch (2011a: 18).

As Table 8.11 shows, however, some CAAE prepositions may correspond to more than one form in the substrate language. As Koch (2011a: 457) comments: "The syncretism in the expression of the Locative and Allative by *longa* and the use of *from* to express a number of semantic functions that are distinguished in Kaytetye does not seem to indicate a simplification of the system of semantic functions so much as the lack of available lexical items in English that could be recruited for their expression" (see section 6).

To sum up, the data on semantic case discussed above show that SLM, Kriol, and CAAE feature different subsets of semantic cases. Each subset in the creoles corresponds to the respective subset of the creoles' substrate languages, within the limits imposed by the constraints that act on the processes responsible for this state of affairs (for further discussion, see section 6).

5.6. Transitivity Markers

Creole languages vary with respect to the availability of transitivity markers, which attach to intransitive verbs to make them transitive, thus allowing for a grammatical distinction between transitive and intransitive verbs. By hypothesis, transitivity markers should manifest themselves in creoles whose substrate languages make a grammatical distinction between transitive and intransitive verbs. Thus, this feature is expected not to appear in creole languages with West African substrates since West African languages do not mark this distinction. This expectation is borne out by the data, as no Caribbean or West African creole has been reported to have transitivity markers. However, these markers are expected to appear in creole languages with Austronesian substrate languages such as Tangoan, Kwaio, or Tolai, which do make this distinction. Siegel (2011) identifies the availability of transitivity markers as a Pan-Pacific Pidgin feature. For example, they are found in the three dialects of Melanesian Pidgin reported on in (1)–(3) (= (82)–(84) in Siegel 2011: 551).

(1)   *stil* 'commit theft'   *stil-**im*** 'steal [something]'   BISLAMA
      kuk 'cook'   *kuk-**um*** 'cook [something]'
      bon 'be burning'   *bon-**em*** 'burn [something]'   (Crowley 2004: 77)

(2)   *luk* 'look'   *luk-**im*** 'see'   PIJIN
      stil 'commit theft'   *stil-**im*** 'steal [something]'
      dig 'dig'   *dig-**im** siton* 'dig up a stone'   (Keesing n.d.)

(3)   *bruk* 'break, be broken'   *bruk-**im*** 'break, tear'   TOK PISIN
      kuk 'cook'   *kuk-**im*** 'cook [something]'
      wok 'work, be busy'   *wok-**im*** 'to make [something], build'
                                        (Mosel 1980: 41)

The presence of a transitivity marker in these dialects of Melanesian Pidgin reproduces the pattern of their substrate languages, as is shown in (4)–(6) (= (86)–(88) in Siegel 2011: 551).

TANGOAN

(4) For Bislama:

    sua 'to paddle'   *sua-i* 'paddle [something]'

    inu 'drink'   *inu-mi* 'drink, swallow [something]'

    keco 'be hanging' *keco-ci* 'hang [something]'   (Camden 1979: 90)

KWAIO

(5) For Pijin:

    aga 'look'   *aga-si-a* 'see (it)'

    beri 'commit theft'   *beri-a* 'steal it'

    takwe 'dig'   *takwe-a fou* 'dig up a stone'   (Keesing n.d.)

TOLAI

(6) For Tok Pisin:

    gumu 'dive, bathe' *gumu-e* 'dive for [something]'

    tangi 'cry, weep'   *tani-e* 'mourn for [someone or something]'

    ngarau 'be afraid' *ngarau-ane* 'be afraid of [someone or something]'

(Mosel 1980: 42–43)

This would appear to be just like the other cases discussed so far, were it not for the fact that some creoles spoken in the Pacific region have transitivity markers, while their substrate languages do not. The creoles that have Australian languages as their substrate languages are among them. For example, Kriol has a transitivity marker, as shown in (7) (= (85) in Siegel 2011: 551).

KRIOL

(7) *rid* 'read'   *rid-im* 'read [something]'

    kuk 'cook'   *kuk-um* 'cook [something]'

    barn 'be burning' *barn-im* 'burn [something or someone]'

(Sandefur & Sandefur 1979)

CAAE and NSWP also have transitivity markers (Koch 2011a, 2011b). All three of these creoles have Australian substrate languages that do not manifest transitivity markers. A possible conclusion is that, in these cases, the presence of transitivity markers on the verb cannot be claimed to reproduce a feature of the substrate languages. Nevertheless, Koch (2011b) argues that the development of transitivity markers on verbs in these creoles *was* motivated by the properties of their substrate languages. His argument can be summarized as follows: Australian languages have a syntactic ergative case system whereby the subject of a transitive verb bears ergative case and that of an intransitive verb bears nominative case (Blake 1987; Koch 2007). This case system reflects a deeper typological characteristic of Australian languages: every verb "is either strictly transitive . . . or strictly intransitive" (Dixon 1980: 378). Koch (2011b: 503) thus suggests that

> ergative case-marking of NPs is a surface manifestation of a deep lexico-grammatical principle of language organisation, namely the rigid distinction between transitive and intransitive verbs (and hence clause types). And it is this grammatical principle, ingrained in the consciousness of AL speakers, that was influential in promoting, in the developing pidgin, the polarisation in form between transitive verbs (*VERBim*) and intransitive verbs (*VERB*). The existence of a recognisable termination -*im* (and perhaps its minor variant -*it*) was exploited by native speakers of "ergative" languages to keep separate the two categories of verbs which their internalised grammars led them to expect in the pidgin they were learning, and whose distinctiveness could not otherwise be signalled.

Siegel (2011: 552) further comments: "It seems clear that having a marked distinction between transitive and intransitive verbs may have reinforced the use of the feature."

At the end of this discussion, there remains the question of whether the syntactic ergative case system of these Australian languages has been reproduced in the relevant creoles. The answer to this question is no, as will be shown in section 6.

5.7. The Properties of Verbs

In the same vein, verbs and verb classes do not have the same properties in all creoles. Again, the properties of creole verbs manifest those of their substrate languages. This is evidenced by data presented by Bartens (2011) and Lefebvre (2011b) for Caribbean creoles, by Koch (2011a) for CAAE, and by Ansaldo et al. (2011) for China Coast Pidgin. For example, CAAE has associated motion verbs modeled on its substrate Australian languages (Koch 2011a). Creoles without such substrate languages do not manifest this feature. Caribbean creoles have double-object verbs, like their substrate languages (Lefebvre 2011b). As Michaelis and Haspelmath (2003) note, double-object verbs are found only in creoles whose substrates have the construction.

5.8. Serial Verbs

Serial verb constructions are available in some creoles but not in others. They exist in creoles whose substrate has the construction (e.g., creoles with a West African or Sinitic substrate). They are not available in creoles whose substrate does not have the construction (e.g., creoles with an Australian substrate). Furthermore, although there might be some overlap between the concatenation of verbs in different languages that feature this construction, by hypothesis, this feature might not necessarily be the same for all the languages that have the construction. In Lefebvre (ed.) (2011c), serial verbs are documented for Santome (Hagemeijer & Ogie 2011), Kupuang Malay (Jacob & Grimes 2011), Papuan Malay (Donohue 2011), and China Coast English (Ansaldo et al. 2011). According to all these authors, the concatenations of verbs in the above-mentioned creoles replicate those found in their respective substrates. While these authors do provide the possible concatenations of verbs in the languages they study, they do not list the impossible ones (a task which would have gone far beyond what could have been expected of them). The fuller identification of differential concatenations of verbs among the creoles under investigation will therefore have to await future research.

5.9. Verb-Doubling Phenomena

Creole languages also vary with respect to the availability of verb-doubling phenomena, which are partially discussed in Bartens (2011), and in Hagemeijer and Ogie (2011). As we saw in Chapter 4, they involve four constructions: temporal adverbial, causal adverbial, and factive clauses, as well as the predicate cleft construction. The full range of these constructions is shown in (8) for Haitian Creole and Fongbe.

(8) a. TEMPORAL ADVERBIAL

Wá	Jan	wá	(tróló)	bɔ̀	Màrí	yì.	FONGBE
Rive	Jan	rive		epi	Mari	pati.	HAITIAN

arrive John arrive as-soon-as and-then Mary leave
'As soon as John arrived, Mary left.'   (= (1) in Lefebvre 1994b)

 b. CAUSAL ADVERBIAL

Wá	Jan	wá	útú	Màrí	yì.	FONGBE
Rive	Jan	rive		Mari	pati.	HAITIAN

arrive John arrive cause Mary leave
'Because John arrived, Mary left.'   (= (2) in Lefebvre 1994b)

c. FACTIVE

Wá ɖè Jan wá ɔ́ víví nú
Rive ∅ Jan rive a, fè
arrive OP John arrive DEF make(-happy) for

nɔ̀ tɔ̀n. FONGBE
manman li kòntan. HAITIAN
mother his happy

'The fact that John arrived made his mother happy.'

(= (3) in Lefebvre 1994b)

d. PREDICATE CLEFT

Wá wè Jan wá. FONGBE
Se **rive** Jan rive. HAITIAN
it-is arrive it-is John arrive

'It is arrive that John did (not, e.g., leave).' (= (4) in Lefebvre 1994b)

Saramaccan also exhibits these four constructions, as is illustrated in (9).

(9) a. TEMPORAL ADVERBIAL

Ko Rohit ko a wosu pala, hen Rowe
arrive Rohit arrive LOC house as-soon-as and.then Rowe

go. SARAMACCAN
leave

'As soon as Rohit arrived at the house, Rowe left.' (Lefebvre's field notes)

b. CAUSAL ADVERBIAL

Waka a waka, a ko wei. SARAMACCAN
walk 3SG walk 3SG get tire

'Because she walked, she got tired.' (Lefebvre's field notes)

c. FACTIVE

Di **waka** a waka, hen mei a ko wei. SARAMACCAN
DEF walk 3SG walk it cause 3SG get tire

'The fact that she walked caused her to get tired.' (Lefebvre's field notes)

d. PREDICATE CLEFT

Waka a waka loutu di wosu. SARAMACCAN
walk 3SG walk go around DEF house

'He really walked around the house.'

(= (11b) in Van den Berg 1987: 104)

And Papiamentu exhibits the same four constructions, as shown in (10).

(10) a. TEMPORAL ADVERBIAL

    Yega *ku Juan a yega, Maria a bai.* PAPIAMENTU
    arrive LOC John PERF arrive Mary PERF go
    'As soon as John arrived, Mary left.' (Kearns 2008a)

  b. CAUSAL ADVERBIAL

    E **yega** *ku Juan a yega, a hasi*
    DEF arrive COMP John PERF arrive PERF make
    ku Maria a bai. PAPIAMENTU
    COMP Mary PERF go
    'Because John has arrived, Mary left.' (Kearns 2008a)

  c. FACTIVE

    E **yega** *ku Juan a yega a hasi*
    DEF arrive COMP John PERF arrive PERF make
    su mama felis. PAPIAMENTU
    POSS mother happy
    'The fact that John has arrived made his mother happy.' (Kearns 2008a)

  d. PREDICATE CLEFT

    Ta **kome** *el a kome.* PAPIAMENTU
    it.is eat 3SG PERF eat
    'He has eaten.' (= (332) in Maurer 1988b: 141)

The fact that verb-doubling phenomena are available in Haitian Creole, Saramaccan, Papiamentu, and other Caribbean creoles such as Martinican Creole (Bernabé 1983), as well as in Santome (Hagemeijer & Ogie 2011), cannot be attributed to their superstrate languages (French, English, Portuguese, Spanish), which do not manifest these constructions. Most probably, Caribbean creoles and Santome manifest verb-doubling phenomena because of their substrate languages, in which verb-doubling is a typological feature. Not surprisingly, these phenomena are found only in creoles that have a West African substrate; they are not found in creoles spoken in Asia or in the Pacific.

5.10. Discourse Structures

Discourse structures also vary among creoles. Once again, creoles reflect the typological differences of their substrate languages. For example, China Coast Pidgin reproduces the pattern of Cantonese, whereas Papuan Malay reproduces that of Melanesian languages. While China Coast

Pidgin has a topic-comment discourse structure similar to that found in Cantonese (Ansaldo et al. 2011), Papuan Malay makes use of tail-head linkage, a discourse strategy widely observed in the languages of Melanesia (Donohue 2011).

5.11. Summary

The sample of data discussed in this section shows that creole languages vary with respect to their typological features and that this variation reflects the typological differences manifested by the respective substrate languages. I now turn to a discussion of the processes identified by the various authors to account for this state of affairs.

6. Processes and Constraints

Various authors in Lefebvre (ed.) (2011c) have posited several different processes as the means by which substrate features are reproduced in creoles. The review of these processes is followed by an overview of the various constraints invoked by authors to explain why some substrate features did or did not make their way into the creoles. (This section should be read in light of the content of Chapter 2 of this book.)

Most authors claim that the process of interference/transfer plays a role (Ansaldo, Bao, Brousseau, Hagemejier and Ogie, Ansaldo et al., Munro, Roberts, Schwegler, Siegel, and Terrill). This process, which dates back to Weinreich (1953: 1), refers to the use of features of their first language by learners who are speaking a second language. For Andersen (1983: 7), this process may also manifest itself in second language acquisition: "*Transfer* from a learner's previously acquired language [. . .] is assumed to interact with the normal acquisitional process by causing the learner to perceive input in terms of certain aspects of the structure of the previously acquired language." For Siegel (1997: 120), transfer is the main process involved in the formation of creole languages: "Here I am defining substrate influence as the evidence of transfer (or interference) at an earlier stage of development. Transfer refers to speakers unconsciously carrying over features from one language (usually their first) when speaking (or trying to speak) another language" (see also Siegel 2001).

Other authors refer to the process of calquing (Ansaldo, Hagemejier and Ogie, Jacob and Grimes, Ansaldo et al., Migge). Keesing (1988) defines *calquing* as the process by which creole speakers copy the properties of their native languages when speaking a creole. A similar definition is given by Holm (1988: 86): "Calquing is a process whereby words or idioms in one language are translated word-for-word (or even morpheme-by-morpheme) into another."

Jacobs and Grimes invoke the process of relexification discussed in Chapter 2. Lefebvre (2011b) also appeals to relexification, which, she argues, is best characterized as relabeling (see Chapters 1 and 2).

Migge (2011: 156) uses the term *reinterpretation*: ". . . Substrate influence emerged in creoles because the creators of creoles structurally reinterpreted the kinds of superstrate structures that they encountered on the plantations according to the grammatical patterns and strategies of their L_1s." I believe that her use of "reinterpretation" corresponds to the process referred to as relexification/relabeling above.

Are all these processes equivalent? From a cognitive point of view, transfer/calquing and relexification/relabeling are not entirely equivalent. While the former means that L_1 material (e.g., phonological, semantic, syntactic properties) is carried along into the L_2 versions of individual speakers, the latter entails that L_2 material (the labels of lexical entries) is incorporated in the L_1 lexicon as parallel labels. In spite of this difference, the processes are similar in that the individual, that is, the second-language learner, is the locus where they take place. Furthermore, these processes are semantically driven; indeed, the lexical items that are associated in these processes must share at least partial semantics. For example, Fongbe *hù* 'to murder, to mutilate' was relabeled as *ansasine* in Haitian on the basis of French *assassiner* 'to murder.' Fongbe *hù* 'to murder, to mutilate' and French *assassiner* 'to murder' overlap semantically, though they are not entirely equivalent. The relevance of this situation will be further explored in section 6. Another process, "restructuring" (of the target language), is referred to by a few authors in Lefebvre (ed.) (2011c) (e.g., Ansaldo, Donohue, and Slomanson). In my view, "restructuring" is conceptually different from the other processes discussed above. First, it refers to the learner acting upon the structure of L_2 (see also Mufwene 2006, and the references therein). Thus, the process is defined not in terms of the individual but in terms of the second language itself. Second, the semantic condition applying to the first group of processes is absent from the concept of "restructuring." Since the nature of the processes that determine the presence of substrate features in a given creole is still a matter of debate in the literature (see the references in section 2), I shall leave further discussion of this issue to future research.

In light of the above review, I now turn to a discussion of the constraints that favor or hinder transfer/relabeling. I shall use the terms *transfer/relabeling* to refer to all the processes discussed previously except *restructuring*. The first constraint imposed on transfer/relabeling stems from the very nature of the processes themselves. As we saw earlier, these processes are semantically driven. Consequently, items that have semantic content can be transferred/relabeled. Those that do not, cannot be. A striking example of this constraint is provided by data pertaining to case. As we saw in section 5.5, the semantic case systems of creoles' substrate languages were transferred/relabeled in the creoles either as suffixes (e.g., Sri Lanka(n) Malay) or as prepositions (e.g., Kriol and CAAE). By contrast, the syntactic case systems of substrate languages did not make their way into the creoles. Koch (2011a), Munro (2011), and Siegel (2011) all mention that the ergative case system of Australian languages has no parallel in Kriol, CAAE, or NSWP. Speaking of Mindanao Chabacano, Grant (2011: 318) writes:

> Up till now, as Nolasco (2005) points out, MC and other varieties of PCs have not developed an ergative model of syntax despite the fact that Austronesian Philippine languages, in which many MC speakers are fully bilingual, customarily use ergative syntactic models which are more complex than the Spanish and MC nominative-accusative syntax.

The contrast between the transfer/relabeling of semantic and syntactic cases follows straightforwardly from the fact that this process is semantically driven. In this account, semantic cases are predicted to be transferred/relabeled, and so they are (see section 5.5). In contrast, syntactic cases, which have no semantic content, are predicted not to be transferred/relabeled, and they are not. Note, however, that, as we saw in section 5.6, the creators of creoles who were native speakers of syntactic ergative case languages found a way to maintain the distinction between transitive and intransitive verbs that pervades their native languages by developing transitivity markers in their respective creoles.

In section 5.2. we saw that the classifiers of the Sinitic substrate languages have been reproduced in China Coast Pidgin. Was this done by means of transfer/relabeling, which are semantically driven processes? The answer to this question can only be positive if classifiers have some semantics. Stephen Matthews (p.c.) informs me that classifiers in Sinitic languages do have semantic content, that is, they are not arbitrary. Hence, their presence in China Coast Pidgin may be accounted for by means of transfer/relabeling.

The fact that the processes of transfer/relabeling are semantically driven requires the substrate item to have semantic content, as we just saw above. It also requires that there be a form in the superstrate language that can be semantically associated with the substrate item. Transfer/relabeling is thus constrained by whether the superstrate language has a form available to transfer or relabel a substrate lexical entry. The first formulation of this constraint is Andersen's (1983) "transfer to somewhere principle." This inspired Siegel's (1999) Availability Constraint, which states that the superstrate language must have a form that is available for a substrate feature to transfer to (see also Munro 2011). Likewise, relexification/relabeling is constrained by what the superstrate language has to offer to relexify/relabel a substrate lexical entry (see Lefebvre 1998 for an extensive discussion of this point).

The chapter by Terrill (2011) on Solomon Islands Pijin (SIP) illustrates this constraint. Terrill addresses the following question: "What grammatical elements of a substrate language find their way into a creole?" She writes: "Grammatical features of the Oceanic substrate languages have been shown to be crucial in the development of Solomon Islands Pijin and of Melanesian Pidgin as a whole (Keesing 1988), so one might expect constructions which are very stable in the Oceanic family of languages to show up as substrate influence in the creole" (513). Terrill's chapter investigates three Oceanic language constructions that have remained stable over thousands of years and persist throughout a majority of the Oceanic languages spoken in the Solomon Islands. She shows that, in the case of the locative, possessive, and transitive constructions, "there was no congruent construction or available lexical item to be brought in to express any of these distinctions" (528). She therefore concludes that "despite the ubiquity, stability and uniformity of the locative, possessive and transitive constructions in the substrate languages, none of them appear in SIP" (528). She argues that the constraint imposed by the superstrate language in terms of availability of linguistic material is more important than the ubiquity, stability, or uniformity of the structure in the substrate languages as a predictor of linguistic transfer from a substrate into a creole. Munro (2011) also appeals to this constraint in accounting for why "evitative" mood does not exist in Kriol although it is part of the TMA system of its substrate languages. As we saw in section 5.5, Koch (2011a) appeals to the same constraint in explaining the range of meanings covered by a single creole form when the substrate languages have different forms to encode these various meanings.

The convergence of substrate and superstrate languages on a particular feature is assumed to favor transfer/relabeling of a substrate feature in a creole (Bartens 2011; Escure 2011; Kihm 2011; Sandeman 2011; Siegel 2011). In that case, semantic and phonological features are conflated to produce a creole's lexical entry. An example of conflation is given by Kihm in his account of the sources of the negation marker *ka* in Kriyol.

This word has a form similar to the negative form *nunca* 'never' in Portuguese. The reason why the form of the negation is *ka* can be explained by the presence of this syllable as a negative morpheme in substrate languages, such as *kaka* 'negative imperfective imperative' in Mandinka, *kë* 'negation marker' in Balanta, and *dika* 'negative imperfective' in Manjaku. Kihm goes so far as to claim that substrate influence in creoles occurs precisely in cases of semantic and phonological conflation.

The typological congruence of the substrate languages (Ansaldo 2011b) is also claimed to favor transfer of a substrate feature into a creole. Siegel (2011: 532) speaks of substrate reinforcement: "Substrate reinforcement occurs when a particular variant has a corresponding feature in a numerically or socially dominant substrate language or languages. By a corresponding feature, I mean one that occurs in the same surface syntactic position and that can be interpreted (or misinterpreted) as having the same or a closely related function." In his study of the nine Pan-Pacific features, Siegel finds that when a feature is present in the contact variety, a corresponding feature is also present in the substrate languages, and when it is absent from the contact variety, it is absent from the substrate languages. He concludes that "the presence or absence of substrate reinforcement during levelling can account for the retention of particular features" (553).

A final constraint on transfer is discussed by Kihm (2011). This one appears to be social rather than linguistic. Kihm shows that, in contrast to other creoles with African substrates, which reproduce the typological features of their respective substrates (e.g., Haitian Creole), Kriyol does not reproduce many features of its African substrate: "In fact, substrate influence, although readily visible, turns out to be limited as can be shown by comparing core grammatical phenomena between Kriyol and a selection of local languages (Balanta, Diola, Manjaku, Mankanya)" (81). Kihm proposes that there are two main reasons for this state of affairs: first, the creole-creating *grumetes* soon formed a tightly united group with its own culture; second, they were perfectly bilingual in Kriyol and one or more local languages and therefore were able to keep their grammars separate. He claims that, if the creators of a creole are very bilingual, speaking both creole and substrate languages fluently, this will constrain (negatively) the amount of transfer from substrate languages into a creole.

In summary, the cognitive processes of transfer/calquing or relexification/relabeling were identified as means by which substrate features enter creole languages. These processes were shown to be constrained in various ways, both linguistically and socially, such that not all the features of substrate languages can be reproduced in the creoles. As a result, creole languages cannot be claimed to be exact replicas of their substrate languages.[5] Some authors identified other processes as playing a role in the development of creoles. For example, leveling and its interaction with transfer are briefly discussed by Lang (2011), Migge (2011), and Siegel (2011), while reanalysis and its role in creole development are discussed by Koch (2011b).

7. Creoles and Language Typology

Based on the data and analyses presented in sections 4, 5, and 6, this section addresses three questions: Do creoles constitute an identifiable typological class? To what extent do creoles replicate the typological features of their substrate languages? Why are creole languages typologically isolating?

7.1. Do Creoles Constitute an Identifiable Typological Class?

In section 5, it was shown that pronominal forms, classifiers, TMA systems, negation, case systems, transitivity markers, the properties of verbs, serial verbs, verb-doubling phenomena, and discourse structures are not the same in creoles from different places. This argues that creoles cannot be claimed to be "alike." Furthermore, we saw that the variation among creoles reflects the variation observed among their respective substrate languages, and that creoles largely reproduce the typological features of their substrate languages. This argues that creoles as a group *cannot* be claimed to constitute an identifiable typological class. Assuming this general conclusion, I will now turn to further discussion of the typology of creole languages.

7.2. To What Extent Do Creoles Replicate the Typological Features of Their Substrate Languages?

The data discussed in Lefebvre (ed.) (2011c) show that creoles massively replicate the typological features of their substrate languages. This conclusion may, however, reflect the fact that most of the chapters in that book consider data related to the lexicon and to syntactic constructions (e.g., serial verb constructions, verb-doubling phenomena, etc.). The fact that the

---

[5] Creoles cannot be said to be exact replicas of their substrate languages not only because some substrate features cannot be transferred/relabeled, but also because, as in other languages, creoles may innovate and diverge from their contributing languages.

properties of creole lexicons replicate those of their respective substrate languages follows from the analysis that creole lexical entries are, to a great extent, created by means of transfer/calquing or relexification/relabeling (see section 6). And the fact that the syntactic constructions of creoles copy those of their substrate languages follows from the fact that these structures are generally adopted wholesale by creoles (see Chapter 4 of this book).[6] Does the same conclusion apply to the phonological component of the grammar or to word order? I will briefly discuss these two areas of the grammar and identify topics for future research.

The phonological inventories of creoles are derivable in a straightforward way from those of their respective substrate languages. This is what Brousseau (2011) convincingly shows on the basis of Haitian Creole, St. Lucian, and their contributing languages. However, it cannot be claimed that these creoles are typologically similar to their Gbe substrate languages in all aspects of their phonology. For example, Brousseau shows that, in the formation of the Haitian and St. Lucian creoles, the complex consonants (/kp/, /gb/, etc.) of the substrate languages were abandoned. For this feature, at least, the creoles diverge typologically from their substrate languages. Likewise, the prosodic systems of substrate languages are not necessarily reproduced in the creoles. For example, most West African languages have tones. Saramaccan has tones, but its tonal system does not reproduce that of its substrate languages, according to the analyses in Good (2004) (see also Ham 1999). In contrast, Haitian Creole does not have tones, but it has a complex accentual system (Brousseau 2003). Another complexity of the prosodic systems of creoles is addressed by Lim (2011) in her study of tones in Singlish; she investigates the possibility that the presence of a high tone in Singlish might not be attributable only to its tonal substrate languages, but also to the intonation pattern of Malay, a non-tonal substrate.

In the same vein, the syllable structures of creoles pose a problem for typologists. For example, Saramaccan and Haitian Creole both have Gbe languages as their main substrate languages. Gbe languages exhibit V and CV but no *CVC syllable structures (Capo 1991). While the syllable structures of Saramaccan are identical to those in the Gbe languages (Smith 1987), Haitian Creole exhibits CVC structures as well as V and CV syllables (e.g., Brousseau & Nikiema 2006). So, with respect to syllable structure, Saramaccan is typologically like its Gbe substrate languages,

---

[6] See also Aboh (2006); Gerrit Dimmendaal (p.c.) made some valuable comments on this issue.

but Haitian Creole is not. It therefore seems that, in the phonological component of the grammar, creoles do not reproduce the typological features of their substrate languages as straightforwardly as they do in the lexicon and the syntax.

Word order is another area of creole grammars that presents a challenge for the typological classification of these languages. Although none of the chapters in Lefebvre (ed.) (2011c) is dedicated entirely to word order, some of them present some observations on word order. For example, in China Coast Pidgin, some word orders follow Cantonese, the substrate language (Ansaldo et al. 2011). Likewise, Sri Lanka(n) Malay has adopted the OV ordering of its adstrate languages Sinhala and Tamil (Ansaldo 2011b). Koch (2011a, 2011b) and Munro (2011), however, claim that creoles' word order generally follows that of their superstrate languages. Kihm (2011) shows that this claim is borne out in some cases but that in other cases the word order seems to follow that of the substrate languages. So, as with the phonological component of the grammar, word order in creoles does not appear to straightforwardly reflect the properties of the substrate languages. (An account of how word order is established in creoles is proposed in Chapter 5.)

It therefore appears that creole languages do not reflect the typological features of their substrate languages equally in all components of the grammar. While they reflect their substrate languages' typological features that are related to "meaning" and "function," they are more permeable to superstrate features that are related to the "form" (labels and word order). This is congruent with the conclusion of Chapter 7, according to which the substrate languages of a creole determine what has been referred to as "meaning" and "function," whereas the superstrate language determines the "form."

7.3. Why Are Creoles Typologically Isolating?

Recall from Chapter 3 that a striking feature of creoles is that they tend to be isolating languages. In this chapter, we have seen that with a few exceptions (e.g., Ansaldo 2011b, on case suffixes; Koch 2011b, on -im and –fela; Siegel 2011, on -im), creoles are typologically isolating, regardless of whether their substrates are isolating or agglutinating. The three creoles— CAAE, NSWP, and Kriol—that evolved from a hundred agglutinating Aboriginal languages in Australia, discussed by Koch (2011a, 2011b) and Munro (2011), illustrate this clearly. For example, the bulk of the TMA suffixes of the Australian languages have been reproduced as preverbal periphrastic markers in Kriol. Likewise, the properties of the case suffixes of the Australian languages have been reproduced in prepositions in both CAAE and Kriol. In the same vein, Bartens (2011) shows that Twi affixes were not reproduced as affixes in the Caribbean creoles that she studies. The fact that substrate affixes are generally realized as free morphemes in creoles follows from the way the processes that play a role in their formation apply in creole genesis (see section 6). All the authors who contribute to Lefebvre (ed.) (2011c) agree that the superstrate forms that are selected for transfer/calquing or for relexification/relabeling must be free forms. Hence, person markers are transferred/relabeled with personal pronouns, case markers with prepositions, and so on. This explains why creoles are isolating languages (see also Chapter 3 of this book).

8. Conclusion

As we saw throughout this chapter, there is a great deal of variation among creoles. Thus, they cannot be claimed to be "alike" in any sense of the word or to constitute a typological class as such. As regards the semantic and syntactic properties of their lexical entries and syntactic constructions, creoles generally manifest the typological features of their substrate languages. This rules out the claim that creole languages should be typologically classified with their superstrate languages. As for the phonological component of the grammar (segmental inventories, tonal/prosodic systems, and syllable structures), the extent to which the creoles reproduce (or not) the typological features of their substrate languages remains to be further documented.

My general conclusions open up a whole new set of questions. For example, from a typologist's perspective, are substrate features in a given creole substantial enough to lead one to conclude that creoles should be typologically classified with their substrate languages? What parameters should be involved in measuring the weight of features favoring one view or the other? These are just a few of the questions raised by the results of the research discussed in this chapter.

CHAPTER 9

Conclusion

A Strong Alternative to the Bioprogram
Hypothesis

THE MAIN GOAL OF this book has been to bring to light the progress that
has been made over the last fifteen years concerning the relabeling-based
account of creole genesis. In this concluding chapter, I highlight the major
points that have been made in this book. The following themes will be
discussed: relabeling and exceptionalism (section 1); relabeling and the
principled contribution of substrate and superstrate languages to creoles
(section 2); relabeling and theories of the lexicon (section 3); relabeling
and types of morphemes (section 4); relabeling and variation among creoles (section 5); relabeling and other approaches to creole genesis, including the feature pool (section 6); relabeling and the relevance of pidgins and
creoles in the debate on language origins (section 7).

1. Relabeling and Exceptionalism

The relabeling-based theory of creole genesis is based on the premise that,
because creoles are natural languages, it must be possible to account for
their properties, and for their emergence and development, within the
framework of the major processes at work in language creation and language change in general.

    In Chapter 2, we saw that relabeling is a major process in language con-
tact/genesis, as it plays a role in several such situations: during the first
phase of second language acquisition, in the creation of mixed languages,
in the formation of New Englishes, and in language death. The extent of
recourse to the process across various language contact situations attests to

its importance. The fact that relabeling appears to be a central process in the creation of creoles is therefore not just an exception since it also applies in other cases of language contact/genesis. In Chapter 2, we also saw that the output of relabeling is not necessarily uniform in different situations. A key variable in determining the output is the extent of relabeling across lexicons: which major categories have been relabeled (all in Media Lengua, only nouns in Michif), whether functional categories have been relabeled (none in Media Lengua, some in Ma'a), and whether the whole lexicon has been relabeled (as in creoles and New Englishes). In turn, the variable extent of relabeling across lexicons correlates with several factors that define the situations in which the process applies, including the number of languages involved (two in the case of mixed languages, several in the case of New Englishes), whether speakers are bilingual (bilingual in the case of mixed languages, but not in the case of New Englishes), the amount of access to the "lexifier"/"target"/L_2 language (full in cases of bilingualism, variable in other cases), whether code switching is involved (e.g., Michif), whether language shift is involved (e.g., Angloromani), and whether the new language was created with the purpose of setting the community apart from neighboring ones (e.g., mixed languages) or in order to create a lingua franca for a multilingual community (e.g., New Englishes).

Situations in which creoles are formed involve several languages and restricted access to the target language. The purpose of their creation is to produce a lingua franca that will ease communication among speakers who have no common language. Given this cluster of features, relabeling, in the case of creole genesis, must cover the entire lexicon. The general approach taken in Chapter 2 shows that it possible to make a unified analysis of the contribution of a single process to different language varieties arising in different language contact situations, including those resulting in the creation of creoles, and thus to link a number of contact phenomena and situations that would otherwise remain separate. By its very nature, and given that it is used in various contexts that do not necessarily involve creole formation, the relabeling-based account of creole genesis speaks against an exceptionalist approach to these languages.

The relabeling-based theory of creole genesis developed here states that other processes known to play a role in language change in general also play a role in the further development of creoles (Chapter 3). These processes include grammaticalization and reanalysis, which play a role in language change in general; diffusion across the lexicon, a process that consists in the spreading of a feature to a wider range of lexical items; and leveling, which entails the reduction of variation between dialects or idiolects of the same language in situations where they come into contact. The relabeling-based account of creole genesis makes a specific proposal as to how these processes interact in creole genesis. In the account presented in this book, relabeling is a primary tool for creating new lexicons. The other processes then apply to its output. Our proposal is thus an integrated theory of how the processes apply in situations in which creole genesis occurs. This second aspect of our theory also speaks against an exceptionalist approach to creole genesis.

2. Relabeling and the Principled Contribution of Substrate and Superstrate Languages to Creoles

The very nature of relabeling specifies the principled contribution of the substrate and superstrate languages to a creole. The process of relabeling, as schematized in Chapter 1, predicts that the lexical entries it forms will have the semantic and syntactic properties of the substrate languages, and labels derived from phonetic strings drawn from the superstrate language. As was shown in detail in Chapter 3, this prediction is borne out. Furthermore, in Chapter 5, we saw that the labels from the superstrate language retain their relative position when identified in linguistic contexts (this excludes cases in which lexical items are relabeled in isolation), such that the superstrate language contributes the bulk of a creole's word orders. Moreover, as we saw in Chapter 7, superstrate word order phenomena may have a filtering effect on certain substrate structures that are not compatible with them, yielding constituent order changes from the substrate to the creole. In fact, in cases of conflicting orders between the substrate and superstrate, certain substrate structures may not appear in the creole at all. Finally, as we saw in Chapter 7, all the superstrate language's contributions to a creole can be argued to be related in one way or another to labels and word order. These elements constitute the form of a language, whereas semantic and syntactic properties constitute the meaning and function. In light of this state of affairs, it is possible to characterize the division of labor between the substrate and superstrate languages in creole genesis as follows: while the substrate contributes the meaning and function, the superstrate contributes the form. The contribution of the source languages to a creole is thus very principled, and this follows from the very nature of relabeling.

The fact that the respective contributions of the source languages divide up as they do predicts the source of the typological features of a creole: the typological features of the superstrate language will be found in the form, that is, the labels and word order; and the typological features of the substrate languages will be found in the meaning and function, that is, in the semantics and syntax. This prediction is borne out, as was discussed in depth in Chapter 8, on the basis of a significant sample of creoles from Africa, the Caribbean area, Asia, Australia, and the Pacific region.

This discovery pertaining to the source languages' contributions to a creole has a major theoretical consequence. It argues for a model of grammar with two major components: form (labels and word order), on the one hand, and meaning and function, on the other hand.

The principled division of properties between a creole's two (or more) sources highlights the fact that, while the superstrate language's contributions are "visible," those of the substrate languages are "invisible," so to speak. This is probably why, historically, creoles have been classified with their superstrate languages, since labels and word order are what one sees. But of course, this association is quite superficial. The progress achieved in creole studies over the last forty years has revealed the important contributions substrate languages make to creoles, as we saw in Chapters 3, 4, 7, and 8.

3. Relabeling and Theories of the Lexicon

By its very nature, relabeling takes place in the lexical component of the grammar. By hypothesis, different theories of the lexicon should make different predictions as to the nature of the lexical items that are pertinent for relabeling. The evaluation of the consequences of two different theories of the lexicon—Principles and Parameters (P&P) and Radical Construction Grammar (RCxG)—for a relabeling-based account of creole genesis in Chapter 4 shows that the RCxG framework presents clear advantages over the P&P model. First, constructions are listed in the lexicon in the RCxG framework, so this framework allows for an account of the retention, from the substrate languages, of grammatical subsystems such as the TMA system and complex constructions involving verb-doubling phenomena. Second, since constructions that involve more than one lexical item are listed in the lexicon in the RCxG framework, this framework allows for their relabeling. This accounts for the fact that a single lexical item in the creole may correspond to the combination of two lexical items in the substrate languages. For example, the imperfective construction in Fongbe comprises two lexical items. The fact that the latter are listed together as a single construction makes it possible to relabel them with a single superstrate lexical item, resulting in a one-word imperfective in Haitian. Similar data involving locative constructions made up of two lexical items were also discussed, showing that complex constructions of this type may be relabeled with a single superstrate language lexical item. Third, within a model where word order is not specified as part of individual lexical entries, such as the RCxG model, the fact that creoles' word orders generally do not reflect those of their substrate languages is no longer a problem for a relabeling-based account of creole genesis. In Chapter 5, we proposed that relabeling is either linguistically context-free or context-bound. In the latter case, the position of the relabeled word is determined by that of the superstrate label in the minimal construction in which it appears. In the former case, the relabeled lexical item may associate with the substrate position. Word order in creole genesis thus follows from how relabeling applies. In short, the RCxG framework allows for an account for certain creole data that were problematic in the P&P model, in at least three areas of the lexicon.

Within the RCxG model, the starting point of relabeling is the individual speakers' lexicon-syntax continuum. The creators of a creole thus have their own lexicon-syntax continuum as an available resource. They relabel atomic structures on the basis of phonetic strings found in the superstrate language, using the new lexical items so formed within the subsystems of their grammar (e.g., the TMA system, serial verb construction, verb-doubling constructions, etc.). Some changes with respect to the word orders of the original grammar may be triggered by the order of the superstrate language when relabeling is linguistically bound. Thus, this scenario accounts straightforwardly for the principled contributions of a creole's source languages.

4. Relabeling and Types of Morphemes

As we saw in Chapter 2, the fact that creoles are created to provide a lingua franca for a multilingual community that does not have a common language requires that the entire substrate lexicons be relabeled. This raises the question of whether relabeling may apply to any type of morpheme. In Chapter 3, it was argued that all types of morphemes—functional as well as lexical, bound as well as free—may undergo relabeling, provided that they have some semantic content. The latter proviso is required because relabeling is semantically driven, in that the two items that are associated in the process must share at least some semantics. Shared semantics is identified in pragmatic contexts. In the following paragraphs, I will summarize how relabeling proceeds for each type of morpheme, on the basis of the discussions in Chapter 3. Recall from Chapters 3 and 7 that relabeling is always constrained by what the superstrate has to offer to relabel a lexical item of the substrate languages.

Major category lexical items that are free, that is, Ns, Vs, As, and Ps, as well as complex constructions involving two lexical items (e.g., a pre- and a postposition) are relabeled on the basis of major category lexical entries (Chapter 3, section 2.1, and Chapter 1, section 1). Major category lexical items that are bound, that is, affixes that determine the syntactic category of a word, are relabeled by superstrate affixes on the basis of minimal pairs of lexical items (e.g., *work* versus *work-er* 'one who works') (Chapter 3, section 2.1.2). Functional categories that are free (e.g., determiners, TMA markers, etc.) are relabeled with superstrate free morphemes that are salient (Chapter 3, section 2.2). Finally, functional categories that are bound, or inflectional affixes, are relabeled by salient free morphemes. For example, person and number affixes are relabeled with strong personal pronouns (Chapter 3, section 2.2.4).

The fact that functional bound affixes can be relabeled with salient free forms was brought to our attention by Munro's work on Kriol, a creole that emerged from the contact between some hundred agglutinative Australian Aboriginal languages and English. Munro (2004) shows in great detail that the bulk of the agglutinative morphology of the substrate languages of Kriol was relabeled by free morphemes (Chapter 3, section 2.2.4). This finding provides us with new information to revisit the question of the role of Bantu speakers in the makeup of Caribbean creoles. As we saw in several chapters, the Caribbean creoles discussed in this book ended up much like their Gbe, and more generally their Kwa, substrate languages. In part, this is because the languages of this family were predominant at the time the creoles were formed (Lefebvre 1998, Chapter 3). Nevertheless, Bantu speakers were also present when the creoles were formed, and there were many of them around before and after the formation of these creoles. This raises the question of what happened to the Bantu speakers' contributions as these creoles were formed. In Lefebvre (1998: 390–394), I addressed this question on the basis of the information I had at that time. One piece of information needed to fully reply to this question was missing, however. Thanks to Munro, this information is now available. There is no reason to believe that the Bantu speakers did not do exactly the same thing in the formation of Caribbean creoles as the Australian Aboriginal language speakers did in the formation of Kriol, that is, relabel their agglutinative morphology with free forms from the superstrate languages. Assuming that this was the case, the Bantu speakers' relabeled lexicons would have been isolating, just like those of the Gbe/Kwa speakers. Hypothetically, leveling led these speakers to abandon categories that the other speakers did not have, such as nominal classes.

5. Relabeling and Variation among Creoles

As we saw throughout this book, creoles present variation. This variation may be minimal, similar to the type distinguishing between dialects of the same language. An example of this kind of variation was provided in Chapter 3. While some Fongbe and some Haitian speakers allow the plural marker to co-occur with the definite determiner, other speakers of the two languages do not accept the co-occurrence of these two morphemes. The variation may also be maximal—of the type that distinguishes between typologically different languages. Several examples of this kind of variation were provided in Chapter 8. While some creoles manifest the serial verb constructions, for instance, others do not. A great deal of this variation is due to typological differences between the contributing languages. For example, serial verbs are found in creoles whose substrates manifest this typological feature (e.g., Caribbean creoles); they are not found in creoles whose substrates do not have the typological feature (e.g., Kriol).

The process of relabeling makes predictions regarding how creoles might vary with respect to their contributing languages. First, creoles that evolved from the same substrate languages are predicted to share the semantic and syntactic properties of grammatical subsystems, regardless of their superstrate languages. This is borne out. For example, both Haitian and Saramaccan have a paradigm of five person pronouns, in which the same form encodes first- and second-person plural. This has nothing to do with the superstrate languages—French and English, respectively—but is derived from Fongbe, one of their substrate languages, which has a paradigm of personal pronouns comprising five forms in which the same form encodes both first- and second-person plural (Chapter 3, section 2.4.). The corollary prediction is that creoles with different substrates will reproduce the semantic and syntactic properties of the subsystems of their respective substrate languages, even if they share the same superstrate language. This prediction, too, is borne out. For example, Saramaccan and Kriol were shown to have very different pronominal systems, even though English is the superstrate language of both. As predicted, Saramaccan reproduces the features of its substrate languages in having only five pronominal forms, as we saw above. And Kriol reproduces the semantic specifications of its substrate languages in having 11 forms encoding singular, dual, plural, and first-person plural and dual inclusive and exclusive (see Chapter 8, section 5, for numerous examples of this type).

A second prediction is that creoles that evolved from the same substrate languages will reproduce any variation existing in these substrate languages, at least in the incipient creole, before leveling has applied. This prediction has been confirmed. For example, with respect to plural marking, the substrate languages of the Caribbean creoles offer two options: the Ewegbe type, in which the same morpheme encodes both the third-person plural personal pronoun and plural in nominal structures; and the Fongbe type, in which the third-person plural personal pronoun and plural in nominal structures are encoded by two separate morphemes. Both these patterns were reproduced in the Caribbean creoles. Haitian and Saramaccan, for instance, manifest the first pattern, while Martinican Creole has reproduced the second one (Chapter 3, section 3.1). Other similar examples may be found in Lefebvre (1998, Chapter 8; 2001) and Lefebvre and Therrien (2007b).

A third prediction of relabeling with respect to variation among creoles is that creoles with the same lexifier language will manifest the word order of this superstrate language for lexical items that are linguistically bound (e.g., modifiers), and that of their substrate languages for those that are linguistically free, regardless of what their substrate languages may be. This prediction is borne out. For example, while Haitian and Seychellois share the same superstrate language (French), they have different substrates: West African languages for Haitian and Eastern Bantu languages for Seychellois. Both creoles manifest the ADJ N ADJ word order of their superstrate in spite of their respective substrates, which have only the N ADJ word order. (For Haitian, see Chapter 5; for Seychellois, see Bollée 1977: 42ff; for Gbe, see Lefebvre & Brousseau 2002; for Eastern Bantu, see Dryer 2005: 354–358.[1])

While the variation found among creoles is due in many cases to the differences between their contributing languages, some of it is simply due to different possible relabeling choices. For example, as we saw in Chapter 4, the relabeling of the plural morpheme in nominal structures in Caribbean French-based creoles involved two different French forms. The creators of Haitian chose the French postnominal form *eux,* yielding the Haitian postnominal *yo*; meanwhile, the creators of Martinican Creole chose the French

---

[1] I thank Susanne Michaelis and Robert Papen for discussing the Seychellois data with me.

prenominal form *ces,* yielding the Martinican prenominal *se.* Another example of this type of variation involves the levels at which relabeling may apply. As we saw in Chapter 6, in some cases, creoles' creators had a choice between relabeling atomic or conflated complex structures. The relabeling of Fongbe atomic structures yielded postpositions in Saramaccan, while the relabeling of Fongbe complex structures led to mega-prepositions in Haitian. Finally, we saw that variation among creoles may result from different choices as to the position of the morphological head. As we saw in Chapter 6, the choice made for this feature is linked to the availability/unavailability of morphological reduplication.

6. Relabeling and Other Approaches to Creole Genesis

At the end of Chapter 3, we saw that the relabeling-based theory of creole genesis can account for all the features that any theory of creole genesis must be able to account for. It accounts for the fact that creole languages emerge in multilingual societies where a lingua franca is needed. It accounts for the fact that the creators of a creole have limited access to the superstrate language. It accounts for the fact that creole languages are created in a relatively short period of time, as only one generation of speakers is required to create a new language by means of relabeling. The fact that creoles are generally isolating languages also follows from the proposal. Since the functional categories of creole languages derive their labels from major category lexemes in the superstrate language or from grammaticalization, and since they are typically free morphemes, it follows that creoles will tend to be isolating languages, even when they evolved from agglutinative languages, as in the case of Kriol, discussed in Chapter 3, section 2.2.4. By virtue of the nature of relabeling, creole lexical entries are predicted to have the same semantic and syntactic properties as the corresponding lexical entries in the substrate languages but phonological representations derived from phonetic strings found in the superstrate language. The relabeling-based account of creole genesis therefore accounts for the fact that creoles reflect the properties of both their superstrate and substrate source languages in the way they do.

Some scholars have questioned whether this theory would hold as straightforwardly if other features were selected instead of the ones that were chosen here. The features we selected are the most important ones, and they are at the heart of what any scientific theory of creole genesis must be able to account for. Scholars who believe that other features belong in this list should introduce them and justify their presence. Pending further development on this matter, I assume that the relabeling-based theory of creole genesis does account for all the features that any theory of creole genesis must account for.

In Lefebvre (2004b, Chapter 2), I review the theories of creole genesis that were proposed before the one advocated in Lefebvre (1998): pidgins and creoles as reduced codes, creoles as "nativized" pidgins, pidgins and creoles as crystallized varieties of "imperfect" second-language acquisition, pidgins and creoles as restructured varieties of their substrate and/or superstrate languages, as well as the theory that creoles reflect the properties of Universal Grammar. I have evaluated these theories against the set of features discussed above. My review shows that none of these theories can account for all the features that need to be accounted for. The account of creole genesis proposed in Siegel (2008) is not very different from the one advocated here and in Lefebvre (1998). The main difference is that it characterizes the main process in creole genesis as transfer, rather than as relabeling. In Lefebvre (2009b), I compare the two approaches, showing that the relabeling-based account of creole genesis predicts the data more precisely than Siegel's theory.

The most recent proposal, inspired by genetics, is being called "the feature pool" hypothesis of creole genesis (e.g., Aboh 2009; Aboh & Ansaldo 2007; Mufwene 2001). According to this hypothesis, in the multilingual contexts where creoles emerge, the linguistic features of the competing languages form a feature pool (Mufwene 2001). These features enter into a competition and selection process. Factors that play a role in the competition and selection process are prominence, markedness/transparency, frequency, and salience. Furthermore, information about the typological input provides the means of explaining the structural output (Aboh & Ansaldo 2007: 44, 2007: 63; Mufwene 2001: 57). In this approach, creolization consists in recombining features of the available languages in a way that differs from their original combinations. In summary: "A feature pool can be defined as the total set of linguistic variables available to speakers in a contact environment in which a process of competition, selection and exaptation takes place" (Aboh & Ansaldo 2007: 44, based on Mufwene 2001). In the following paragraphs, I discuss the major—indeed, fundamental—problems I see with this hypothesis.

The first problem concerns the content of the feature pool. Mufwene (2001: 4) writes: "While interacting with each other, speakers contribute features to a pool." How do we determine/know what is in the pool? Is it on the basis of what linguists know about the languages involved? Probably not. Is it on the basis of what speakers know about the languages involved? If so, how do we know what they know? We know that, in creole genesis, the speakers of the substrate languages generally have limited access to the superstrate language. Are the features of this language as important in the pool as those of the substrate languages? These are just a few of the problems that are related to the content of the feature pool.

The second problem concerns the competition process. What kinds of features are likely to enter the competition and on what basis? Aboh and Ansaldo (2007: 45) suggest the following answer to this question on the basis of a hypothetical scenario involving word order.

> Suppose, for instance, a scenario where two strictly SVO languages compete with one strictly SOV language. Our working hypothesis is that the congruent (or converging) SVO-type features will reinforce each other and therefore become more regular/frequent in the feature pool. This, in turn, makes such features acquire a high competitiveness, which may favour their selection in the emerging language. Being marked in such a feature pool, however, the SOV-type features appear disfavoured or less competitive because their selection (even though possible) is subject to the huge pressure of more competitive SVO-type features.

In this view, frequency and (un)markedness play a role. Let us look at this hypothetical scenario in light of real data. We know, for example, that the Caribbean creoles have substrate languages that have OV word order in a number of constructions (e.g., nominal structures, the imperfective construction, locative constructions involving postpositions, etc.), and that this word order pattern is consistent across the numerous West African languages that were represented when the Caribbean creoles were created. We also know that the superstrate languages of these creoles only present VO structures and that, at the time of creole genesis in the Caribbean area, speakers of the superstrate languages were far outnumbered by speakers of the substrate languages in all early creole communities. According to Aboh and Ansaldo's proposal, this constellation of facts should be assigned the following analysis: OV structures are numerous and frequent, hence unmarked; the corresponding VO structures are less numerous and less frequent, thus marked. Consequently, the configuration of facts considered here should have favored the retention of the substrate OV structures in Caribbean creoles. This is not what happened, however. As we saw in Chapter 7, OV structures were virtually eliminated from the Caribbean creoles (except for Saramaccan postpositional structures). So, it appears that the least frequent and most marked word order structures (with the exception, once again, of the Saramaccan postpositional structures) won the competition. This is the opposite of Aboh and Ansaldo's scenario.

The selection process constitutes yet a third problem for the feature pool hypothesis. As we saw above, frequency and unmarkedness are among the factors that play a role in the competition and selection processes. Another important factor is the typological features of the languages involved. As Aboh and Ansaldo (2007: 43) put it: "we show that the differences across creoles can be accounted for if one assumes a theory of genesis that primarily takes into account typological properties of the languages in contact as well as the process of competition and selection as the driving force in language creation." However, these authors do not specify exactly how the typological properties of the languages in contact are to play a role in the selection process. In his critique of the feature pool hypothesis, Plag (2011: 91) remarks that "[t]ypological information does not suffice to understand the emergence of new structure." Regarding the selection process, Plag also says: "The feature pool approach neglects processing constraints: one can only select from what one can process" (107). Therefore, "any feature pool account would have to incorporate insights concerning the role of processing in order to explain feature selection and creation of new structure" (102).

A fourth problem for the feature pool hypothesis has to do with how the contributing languages manifest themselves in creoles. Aboh (2009: 319) remarks: "[. . .] creoles appear more mixed than often assumed in the literature." Based on my research experience, I can only agree with this statement. My question for Aboh is the following: What kind of a mix do we find in creoles? In his study of the nominal structure of Saramaccan, Aboh (2009) concludes that the definite determiner has the semantics of the substrate languages, but the syntax (word order) of the superstrate language. "Gbe-type languages won on the semantic side and English won on the syntax side" (Aboh 2009: 327). Very rightly, Aboh and Ansaldo (2007: 49) raise the following question: "Assuming that this is the right characterisation, one may wonder what principle allows such apparently peculiar recombination in the emerging language." However, they provide no clear answer to this question. Given the feature pool, is there a principled reason that the substrate languages provide the semantics of the Saramaccan definite determiner, while the superstrate provides its word order? Why do the properties of the Saramaccan definite determiner divide in this way between the contributing languages? Furthermore, how does the feature pool hypothesis account for the fact that, in the Haitian and Martinican creoles, the definite determiner has both the semantics and the word order (post-nominal) of its substrate languages? While Aboh does not have a principled way of explaining these facts, we do. Recall from Chapter 5 that the Saramaccan definite determiner has the properties it has because it was produced by relabeling. As such, it has the semantic properties of the substrate definite determiner, but a surface position corresponding to that of the English form that provided its label (the phonetic string and the label are tied together in cases of linguistically bound lexical items). In our analysis, it is possible to account for the fact that the Haitian definite determiner has the semantics of its substrate languages but the postnominal position of the French form that provided its label; this position happens to coincide with that of the substrate position for definite determiners. In Aboh's analysis, both Saramaccan and Haitian should have prenominal determiners, since in both their superstrate languages, determiners are prenominal.

These are just a few questions that one can direct at the feature pool hypothesis of creole genesis in its present form. (For further discussion, see Plag 2011; see also McWhorter 2012, on the simplicity/complexity issue.) In light of these remarks, I will now evaluate the feature pool hypothesis against the basic features that were selected as those that any theory of creole genesis must be able to account for.

The first feature is the fact that creoles only develop in multilingual communities. Since creoles "emerge from the recombination of linguistic features from different languages" (Aboh 2009: 317), the feature pool hypothesis accounts for this feature. The second feature is that creoles develop in multilingual situations where there is a need for a lingua franca. To my knowledge, the feature pool hypothesis does not say anything about the need for a lingua franca in communities where creoles develop. The third feature is that the creators of a creole have relatively little access to the superstrate language. It is not clear how the feature pool hypothesis in its present form can account for this feature. The fourth feature has to do with the fact that creoles are created in a relatively short period of time. Again, it is not clear how the feature pool hypothesis handles this feature. The fifth feature is the fact that creoles are typologically isolating languages. I have not seen anything so far in the feature pool hypothesis that accounts for this feature. The last feature has to do with the fact that a theory of creole genesis must be able to account for the type of mix that creoles manifest. Aboh (2009: 320) remarks that "[. . .] creoles share significant similarities with both their superstrate and substrate languages." He does not, however, tell us the principles that govern how the two linguistic sources contribute to a creole. As we saw throughout this book, the contribution of the substrate and superstrate languages is principled: the substrate languages contribute the semantics and syntax (including some word orders), and the superstrate language contributes the form, that is, the labels and some word orders. The feature pool hypothesis does not predict this division of contributions of the source languages to a creole.

The feature pool hypothesis thus accounts for only one of the features that must be accounted for by any theory of creole genesis. To be fair to the proponents of this hypothesis, however, I should report that they themselves are critical of their own hypothesis. For example, Aboh and Ansaldo (2007: 64) write: "While this approach to language creation appears promising, a number of principles that govern the competition and selection of linguistic features need further elaboration."

7. Relabeling and the Relevance of Pidgins and Creoles in the Debate on Language Origins

In the literature on the origins and the evolution of language, the general assumption is that language started as a restricted code, referred to as "protolanguage." Since there is no direct access to data manifesting the nature of incipient human language, it is inferred that the restricted linguistic codes that are presently available can inform us about the nature of protolanguage. Pidgin languages feature among the restricted codes that have been identified in the literature (e.g., Bickerton 1984). Furthermore, it is hypothesized that the pidgin–creole sequence may provide us with a window on the protolanguage–language sequence. As we saw throughout this book, pidgins and creoles reproduce the properties of their substrate languages. This is achieved through relabeling. This calls into question the relevance of the pidgin–creole sequence in understanding the protolanguage–language sequence. Lefebvre (2013) discusses these issues in detail. The conclusion is twofold: first, pidgins and protolanguage are not alike. Second, the pidgin–creole sequence does not open a window on the protolanguage–language sequence. Major arguments include the fact that pidgins, even restricted ones, are too elaborate to be analogues of protolanguage (see also Botha 2006), and the fact that pidgins and creoles are not created *ex nihilo* (Botha 2006; Comrie 2000; Mufwene 2008; Slobin 2002).

REFERENCES

Aboh, Enoch O. 2006. The role of the syntax-semantic interface in language transfer. In Lefebvre, White, and Jourdan (eds.), 221–253.

Aboh, Enoch O. 2007. La genèse de la périphérie gauche du Saramaka: un cas d'influence du substrat? *Grammaires créoles et grammaire comparative*, ed. by Karl Gadelii and Anne Zribi-Hertz, 73–79. Paris: Presses Universitaires de Vincennes.

Aboh, Enoch O. 2009. Competition and selection. That's all! *Complex processes in new languages* [Creole Language Library 35], ed. by Enoch O. Aboh and Norval Smith, 317–344. Amsterdam/Philadelphia: John Benjamins Publishing.

Aboh, Enoch O., and Umberto Ansaldo. 2007. The role of typology in language creation. *Deconstructing creole*, ed. by Umberto Ansaldo, Stephen Matthews, and Lisa Lim, 39–66. Amsterdam: John Benjamins Publishing.

Adam, Lucien. 1883. *Les idiomes négro-aryen et maléo-aryen*. Paris: Maisonneuve et Cie.

Agbidinoukoun, Cosme Christian. 1991. Analyse contrastive des syntagmes nominaux du fongbe et du français. Doctoral dissertation, Université Paris III (Sorbonne Nouvelle), Paris.

Alleyne, Mervyn C. 1966. La nature du changement phonétique à la lumière du créole français d'Haïti. *Revue de linguistique romane* 30: 279–303.

Alleyne, Mervyn C. 1971. Acculturation and the cultural matrix of creolisation. In Hymes (ed.), 169–187.

Alleyne, Mervyn C. 1981. *Comparative Afro-American: An historical-comparative study of English-based Afro-American dialects of the New World*. Ann Arbor, MI: Karoma.

Alleyne, Mervyn C. (ed.). 1987. *Studies in Saramaccan language structure* [Caribbean Culture Series 2]. Amsterdam: Universiteit von Amsterdam.

Alleyne, Mervyn C. 2001. Opposite processes in "creolization." In Neumann-Holzschuh and Schneider (eds.), 125–133.

Allsop, Richard. 1980. How does the creole lexicon expand? In Valdman and Highfield (eds.), 89–107.

Andersen, Roger W. 1980. Creolisation as the acquisition of a second language as a first language. In Valdman and Highfield (eds.), 273–295.

Andersen, Roger W. 1983. A language acquisition interpretation of pidginisation and creolisation. *Pidginisation and creolisation as language acquisition*, ed. by Roger W. Andersen, 1–59. Rowley, MA: Newbury House.

Anonymous. 1983. *Éléments de recherche sur la langue Fon*. Cotonou, Bénin: [No indication of publisher].

Ansaldo, Umberto. 2009. *Contact languages: Ecology and evolution in Asia* [Cambridge Approaches to Language Contact 7]. Cambridge: Cambridge University Press.

Ansaldo, Umberto. 2011a. Metatypy in Sri Lanka Malay. *Annual review of South Asian languages and linguistics 2011*, ed. by G. Sharma and R. Singh, 3–16.Berlin/Boston: Walter de Gruyter GmbH.

Ansaldo, Umberto. 2011b. Sri Lanka Malay and its Lankan adstrates. In Lefebvre (ed.), 367–382.

Ansaldo, Umberto, Stephen Matthews, and Lisa Lim. 2007. *Deconstructing creole* [Typological Studies in Language 73]. Amsterdam: John Benjamins Publishing.

Ansaldo, Umberto, Stephen Matthews, and Geoff P. Smith. 2011. The Cantonese substrate in China Coast Pidgin. In Lefebvre (ed.), 289–301.

Arends, Jacques. 1986. Genesis and development of the equative copula in Sranan. In Muysken and Smith (eds.), 103–127.

Arends, Jacques. 1993. Towards a gradualist model of creolization. *Atlantic meets Pacific: A global view of pidginization and creolization*, ed. by F. Byrne and J. Holm, 371–380. Amsterdam: John Benjamins Publishing.

Arends, Jacques. 1995. Demographic factors in the formation of Sranan. *The early stages of creolization* [Creole Language Library 13], ed. by Jacques Arends, 233–285. Amsterdam: John Benjamins Publishing.

Arends, Jacques. 1997. The development of complementation in Saramaccan. *Proceedings of the 16th International Congress of Linguistics* [CD-Rom, paper no. 0389], ed. by B. Caron. Oxford: Pergamon.

Arends, Jacques, Pieter C. Muysken, and Norval Smith (eds.). 1995. *Pidgins and creoles: An introduction* [Creole Language Library 15]. Amsterdam/Philadelphia: John Benjamins Publishing.

Arends, Jacques, and Matthias Perl (eds.). 1995. *Early Suriname Creole texts: A collection of 18th-century Sranan and Saramaccan documents*. Frankfurt/Madrid: Iberoamericana.

Baker, Philip. 1996. Productive *fellow*. In Wurm, Mühlhäusler, and Tryon (eds.), 533–536.

Baker, Philip, and Chris Corne. 1982. *Isle de France Creole*. Ann Arbor, MI: Karoma.

Baker, Philip, and Anand Syea (eds.). 1996. *Changing meanings, changing functions* [Westminster Creolistics Series 2]. London: University of Westminster Press.

Bakker, Peter. 1989. Relexification in Canada: The case of Métif (French-Cree). *La créolisation*. Special issue of *Revue canadienne de linguistique* 34.3: 339–350.

Bakker, Peter. 1992. A language of our own: The genesis of Mitchif, the mixed Cree-French language of the Canadian Metis. Doctoral dissertation, University of Amsterdam, Amsterdam.

Bakker, Peter. 1994. Michif, the Cree-French mixed language of the Métis buffalo hunters in Canada. In Bakker and Mous (eds.), 13–33.

Bakker, Peter. 2003. Reduplication in Saramaccan. In Kouwenberg (ed.), 73–82.

Bakker, Peter, and Maarten Mous (eds.). 1994. *Mixed languages: 15 case studies in language intertwining* [Studies in Language and Language Use 13]. Dordrecht: ICG Printing.

Bakker, Peter, Norval Smith, and Tonjes Veenstra. 1995. Saramaccan. In Arends, Muysken, and Smith (eds.), 165–178.

Bally, Anne-Sophie. 2004. L'interprétation aspectuo-temporelle des énoncés en Saramaccan. Master's thesis, Université du Québec à Montréal, Montreal.

Bally, Anne-Sophie. 2005. Corpus saramaka du terrain en Guyane française du 11/01/2005 au 02/04/2005. Université du Québec à Montréal, Montreal. Unpublished manuscript.

Bally, Anne-Sophie. 2007a. Les catégories fonctionnelles du Saramaccan. Unpublished research report. Université du Québec à Montréal.

Bally, Anne-Sophie. 2007b. Quelques caractéristiques de la structure nominale en Saramaccan et leur origine. Unpublished research report. Université du Québec à Montréal.

Bally, Anne-Sophie. 2011. Structure nominale et expression du temps, du mode et de l'aspect en saramaka: Analyse synchronique et diachronique. Doctoral dissertation, Université du Québec à Montréal, Montreal.

Bally, Anne-Sophie, Claude Dionne, and Maribel Olguín. 2006. Les constructions verbales dans quatre langues créoles de l'Atlantique et leurs langues contributrices. Research report on the project "La genèse des langues créoles." Université du Québec à Montréal, Montreal.

Bao, Zhiming. 2005. The aspectual system of Singapore English and the systemic substratist explanation. *Journal of Linguistics* 41: 237–267.

Bao, Zhiming. 2010. A usage-based approach to substratum transfer: The case of four unproductive features in Singapore English. *Language* 86.4: 798–821.

Bao, Zhiming. 2011. Convergence-to-substratum and the passives in Singapore English. In Lefebvre (ed.), 253–270.

Bao, Zhiming, and Hui Min Lye. 2005. Systemic transfer, topic prominence, and the bare conditional in Singapore English. *Journal of Pidgin and Creole Languages* 20.2: 269–291.

Bao, Zhiming, and Lionel Wee. 1999. The passive in Singapore English. *World Englishes* 18.1: 1–11.

Bao, Zhiming, and Lionel Wee. 2005. The aspectual system of Singapore English and the systemic substratist explanation. *Journal of Linguistics* 41.2: 237–267.

Bartens, Angela. 2011. Substrate features in Nicaraguan, Providence and San Andrés Creole Englishes: A comparison with Twi. In Lefebvre (ed.), 201–224.

Bernabé, Jean. 1983. *Fondal-Natal* [Grammaire basilectale approchée des créoles guadeloupéen et martiniquais 3]. Paris: L'Harmattan.

Bickerton, Derek. 1981. *Roots of language*. Ann Arbor, MI: Karoma.

Bickerton, Derek. 1984. The language bioprogram hypothesis. *The Behavioral and Brain Sciences* 7: 173–221.

Bickerton, Derek. 2006. On Siegel on the bioprogram. *Language* 82: 230–232.

Blake, Barry J. 1987. *Australian Aboriginal grammar*. London: Croom Helm.

Bollée, Anegret. 1977. *Le créole français des Seychelles*. Tübingen: Niemeyer.

Booij, Geert E., and Jaap van Marle (eds.). 2003. *Yearbook of morphology 2002*. Dordrecht: Kluwer.

Boretzky, Norbert, and Birgit Igla. 1994. Romani mixed dialects. In Bakker and Mous (eds.), 35–68.

Boretzky, Norbert, Werner Enninger, and Thomas Stolz (eds.). 1988. *Bochum-Essener Beiträge zur Sprachwandelforschung.* Bochum: Studienverlag Brockmeyer.

Botha, R. 2006. Pidgin languages as a putative window on language evolution. *Language and Communication* 26: 1–14.

Bouchard, Denis. 2002. *Adjectives, number and interfaces: Why languages vary.* Oxford: North-Holland Linguistics Series, Elsevier.

Braun, Maria, and Ingo Plag. 2003. How transparent is creole morphology? A study of Early Sranan word-formation. In Booij and van Marle (eds.), 81–105.

Brousseau, Anne-Marie. 1989. De 'nù-fló' à 'po-bouche': hypothèses sur l'origine des composés en haïtien. *La créolisation.* Special issue of the *Revue canadienne de linguistique* 34.3: 285–312.

Brousseau, Anne-Marie. 1990. Panorama de la morphologie du Fongbe. *Journal of West African Languages* 20: 27–45.

Brousseau, Anne-Marie. 1993. Représentations sémantiques et projections syntaxiques des verbes en F¿ngbè. Doctoral dissertation, Université du Québec à Montréal, Montreal.

Brousseau, Anne-Marie. 1994. Morphological structure and relexification. In Lefebvre and Lumsden (eds.), 30 pages.

Brousseau, Anne-Marie. 1995. Les pronoms en créole haïtien, en français et en fongbé. Research report prepared for FCAR on the project *L'organisation des lexiques et des entrées lexicales* [4 volumes], ed. by Claire Lefebvre, volume IV, 33 pages. Université du Québec à Montréal, Montreal.

Brousseau, Anne-Marie. 1998. *Réalisations argumentales et classes de verbes en fongbe* [Langues et cultures africaines 22]. Paris: Peeters.

Brousseau, Anne-Marie. 2003. The accentual system of Haitian Creole: The role of transfer and markedness values. *The phonology and morphology of creole languages,* ed. by Ingo Plag, 3–23. Tübingen: Niemeyer.

Brousseau, Anne-Marie. 2011. One substrate, two creoles: The development of segmental inventories in St. Lucian and Haitian. In Lefebvre (ed.), 105–125.

Brousseau, Anne-Marie. In preparation. *The genesis of the phonological system of Haitian Creole* [provisional title].

Brousseau, Anne-Marie, Sandra Filipovich, and Claire Lefebvre. 1989. Morphological processes in Haitian Creole: The question of substratum and simplification. *Journal of Pidgin and Creole Languages* 4.1: 1–36.

Brousseau, Anne-Marie, and John S. Lumsden. 1992. Nominal structure in Fongbe. *Journal of West African Languages* 22: 5–26.

Brousseau, Anne-Marie, and Emmanuel Nikiema. 2001. *Phonologie et morphologie du français.* Montreal: Fides.

Brousseau, Anne-Marie, and Emmanuel Nikiema. 2006. From Gbe to Haitian: The multistage evolution of syllable structure. In Lefebvre, White, and Jourdan (eds.), 295–330.

Bruyn, Adrienne. 1995. *Grammaticalization in Creoles: The development of determiners and relative clauses in Sranan* [Studies in Language and Language Use 21]. Amsterdam: IFOTT.

Bruyn, Adrienne. 1996. On identifying instances of grammaticalization in Creole languages. In Baker and Syea (eds.), 29–46.

Bruyn, Adrienne. 2003. Grammaticalisation, réanalyse et influence substratique: quelques cas du sranan. In Kriegel (ed.), 25–48.

Bruyn, Adrienne. 2009. Grammaticalisation in creoles: Ordinary and not-so-ordinary cases. *Studies in Language* 33.2: 112–138.

Bybee, Joan. 2006. From usage to grammar: The mind's response to repetition. *Language* 82: 711–734.

Byrne, Francis. 1987. *Grammatical relations in a radical creole: Verb complementation in Saramaccan* [Creole Language Library 3]. Amsterdam/Philadelphia: John Benjamins Publishing.

Byrne, Francis, and Donald Winford (eds.). 1993. *Focus and grammatical relations in creole languages* [Creole Language Library 12]. Amsterdam/Philadelphia: John Benjamins Publishing.

Cadely, Jean-Robert. 1994. Aspects de la phonologie du créole haïtien. Doctoral dissertation, Université du Québec à Montréal, Montreal.

Camden, Pastor Bill. 1979. Parallels in structure of lexicon and syntax between New Hebrides Bislama and the South Santo language as spoken at Tangoa. *Papers in Pidgin and Creole Linguistics no.2* [Pacifics Linguistics A-57], ed. by P. Mühlhäusler et al., 51–117. Canberra: Australian National University.

Capo, Hounkpati B. C. 1991. *A comparative phonology of Gbe* [Publications in African Languages and Linguistics 14]. Dordrecht: Foris Publications.

Chaudenson, Robert. 1977. Toward the reconstruction of the social matrix of creole language. *Pidgin and Creole Linguistics*, ed. by Albert Valdman, 259–277. Bloomington/London: Indiana University Press.

Chaudenson, Robert. 1993. De l'hypothèse aux exemples. Un cas de créolisation: selon la formation des systèmes de démonstratifs créoles. *Études créoles* 16: 17–38.

Chaudenson, Robert. 2001a. Créolisation du français et francisation du créole: les cas de Saint-Barthélemy et de la Réunion. In Neumann-Holzschuh and Schneider (eds.), 361–381.

Chaudenson, Robert. 2001b. *Creolisation of language and culture*. Routledge: London.

Chaudenson, Robert. 2003. *La créolisation: Théorie, applications, implications*. Paris: l'Harmattan.

Chomsky, Noam. 1981. *Lectures on government and binding*. Dordrecht: Foris Publications.

Chomsky, Noam. 1989. Some notes on the economy of derivation and representation. *Functional heads and clause structure* [MIT Working Papers in Linguistics 10], ed. by Itziar Laka Mugarza and Anoop Mahajan, 43–74. Cambridge, MA: Department of Linguistics and Philosophy, MIT.

Chomsky, Noam. 1995. *The minimalist program*. Cambridge, MA: MIT Press.

Clements, J. Clancy. 2001. Word order shift and natural L2 acquisition in a Portuguese creole. *Romance syntax, semantics and L2 acquisition* [Current Issues in Linguistic Theory 216], ed. by Joaquim Camps and Caroline R. Wiltshire, 73–87. Amsterdam/Philadelphia: John Benjamins Publishing.

Comrie, B. 2000. From potential to realization: An episode in the origin of language. *Linguistics* 38.5: 989–1004.

Croft, William. 2001. *Radical construction grammar*. Oxford: Oxford University Press.

Crowley, Terry. 2004. *Bislama reference grammar*. Honolulu: University of Hawai'i Press.

d'Ans, André-Marcel. 1968. *Le créole français d'Haïti*. The Hague: Mouton.

da Cruz, Maxime. 1994. Contribution à l'étude de la négation en F¿ngbè. In Lefebvre and Lumsden (eds.), volume III, 69–111.

Déchaine, Rose-Marie. 1988. Opérations sur les structures d'arguments: le cas des constructions sérielles en Haïtien. Master's thesis, Université du Québec à Montréal, Montreal.

Déchaine, Rose-Marie, and Victor Manfredi. 1994. Binding domains in Haitian. *Natural Language and Linguistic Theory* 12: 203–257.

DeGraff, Michel A. F. 1992a. Is Haitian Creole a pro-drop language? *Travaux de recherche sur le créole haïtien* 11: 1–22 [UQAM].

DeGraff, Michel A. F. 1992b. Creole grammars and acquisition of syntax: The case of Haitian. Doctoral dissertation, University of Pennsylvania, Philadelphia.

DeGraff, Michel A. F. 1992c. The syntax of predication in Haitian. *Proceedings of the 22nd Annual Meeting of the Northeastern Linguistics Society*. Amherst: University of Massachusetts, Graduate Linguistics Students Association.

DeGraff, Michel A. F. 1993. A riddle on negation in Haitian. *Probus* 5: 63–93.

DeGraff, Michel A. F. 1999. Empirical quicksand: Probing two recent articles on Haitian Creole. *Journal of Pidgin and Creole Languages* 14.2: 359–377.

DeGraff, Michel A. F. 2001. Morphology in creole genesis: A prolegomenon. *Ken Hale: A life in language*, ed. by Michael J. Kenstowicz, 53–121. Cambridge, MA: MIT Press.

DeGraff, Michel A. F. 2002. Relexification: A reevaluation. *Anthropological Linguistics* 44: 321–414.

DeGraff, Michel A. F. 2003. Against creole exceptionalism. *Language* 79: 391–411.

De Groot, Adrianus H. P. 1977. *Woordregister Nederlands-Saramakkaans*. Paramaribo: VACO.

Denis, Marie-Josée. 2004. *-syon, -ès* et *-te* sont-ils des affixes productifs en créole haïtien? Master's thesis, Université du Québec à Montréal, Montreal.

Déprez, Viviane. 1992a. Is Haitian Creole really a pro-drop language? *Travaux de recherche sur le créole haïtien* 11: 23–40 [UQAM].

Déprez, Viviane. 1992b. Raising constructions in Haitian Creole. *Natural Language and Linguistic Theory* 10: 191–231.

Déprez, Viviane. 2005. Morphological number, semantic number and bare nouns. *Lingua* 115: 857–883.

Déprez, Viviane. 2006. On the conceptual role of number. In C. Nishida and J. P. Montreuil (eds.). *Proceedings of LSRL 2006*, 61–85.

Déprez, Viviane. 2007. Probing the structuring role of grammaticalization: Nominal constituents in French lexifier creoles. *Journal of Pidgin and Creole Languages* 22.2: 263–307.

Detges, Ulrich. 2003. La notion de réanalyse et son application à la description des languages créoles. In Kriegel (ed.), 49–68.

Dijkhoff, Marta. 1983. Movement rules and the resumptive pronoun strategy in Papiamentu. Master's thesis, University of Groningen, Groningen, Netherlands.

Dijkhoff, Marta. 1993. Papiamentu word formation. A case study of complex nouns and their relation to phrases and clauses. Doctoral dissertation, Curaçao.

Dixon, Robert M. W. 1980. *The languages of Australia*. Cambridge: Cambridge University Press.

Donohue, Mark. 2011. Papuan Malay of New Guinea: Melanesian influence on verb and clause structure. In Lefebvre (ed.), 413–435.

Dryer, Matthew S. 2005. Order of adjective and noun. *The world atlas of language structures*, ed. by Martin Haspelmath, Matthew S. Dryer, David Gil, and Bernard Comrie, 354–358. Oxford: Oxford University Press.

Dubois, Jean. 1962. *Étude sur la dérivation suffixale en français moderne et contemporain*. Paris: Larousse.

Dumais, Danielle. 1988. INFL en créole haïtien. *Études syntaxiques, morphologiques et phonologiques*, ed. by Claire Lefebvre, 242–265. Research report prepared for SSHRCC, FCAR and PAFAC on the *Haiti-Fon* project, Université du Québec à Montréal, Montreal.

Dumais, Danielle. 2007. La détermination et l'expression du nombre en Fongbe. Université du Québec à Montréal, Montreal. Unpublished manuscript.

Eades, Diana. 1991. Aboriginal English: An introduction. *Vox: Journal of the Australian Advisory Council on Languages and Multicultural Education (AACLAME)* 5: 55–61.

Eades, Diana. 1996. Aboriginal English. In Wurm, Mühlhäusler, and Tryon (eds.), 133–141.

Escure, Geneviève. 2011. African substratal influence on the counterfactual in Belizean Creole. In Lefebvre (ed.), 181–200.

Essegbey, James. 2005. The "basic locative construction" in Gbe languages and Surinamese creoles. *Journal of Pidgin and Creole Languages* 20.2: 229–267.

Essegbey, James, and Félix K. Ameka. 2007. "Cut" and "break" verbs in Gbe and Sranan. *Journal of Pidgin and Creole Languages* 22.1: 37–55.

Étienne, Gérard. 1974. Le créole du nord d'Haïti: Étude des niveaux de structure. Doctoral dissertation, Université des sciences humaines de Strasbourg, Strasbourg.

Faine, Jules. 1937. *Philologie créole: études historiques et étymologiques sur la langue créole d'Haïti*. Port-au-Prince: Imprimerie de l'État.

Fattier, Dominique. 1998. Contribution à l'étude de la genèse d'un créole: l'Atlas linguistique d'Haïti, cartes et commentaires [volume 2]. Thèse à la carte. ANRT (Atelier national de reproduction des thèses). 6 volumes.

Férère, Gérard A. 1974. Haitian Creole sound-system, form-classes, texts. Doctoral dissertation, University of Pennsylvania, Philadelphia.

Fillmore, Charles J., and Paul Kay. 1993. Construction grammar coursebook. Manuscript, University of California at Berkeley, Department of linguistics.

Fillmore, Charles J., Paul Kay, and Mary Catherine O'Connor. 1988. Regularity and idiomaticity in grammatical constructions: The case of *let alone*. *Language* 64: 501–538.

Foley, William A. 1988. Language birth: The processes of pidginisation and creolisation. *Language: The socio-cultural context* [Linguistics: The Cambridge Survey 4], ed. by Frederick J. Newmeyer, 162–183. Cambridge: Cambridge University Press.

Fournier, Robert. 1977. N ap fè yun ti-kose su la (La grammaire de la particule *la* en créole haïtien). Master's thesis, Université du Québec à Montréal, Montreal.

Freeman, Bryant C. 1988. Dictionnaire inverse de la langue haïtienne. Lawrence, KS: Unpublished manuscript.

Furetière, Antoine. 1984. *Le dictionnaire universel d'Antoine Furetière* [3 volumes]. Paris: Le Robert.

Gilbert, Glenn G. (ed.). 1987. *Pidgin and Creole languages: Essays in memory of John E. Reinecke*. Honolulu: University of Hawaii Press.

Gilles, Rolande. 1988. Réalisation du Cas en créole haïtien dans trois environnements: les prépositions, les marqueurs de Cas et les noms. Master's thesis, Université du Québec à Montréal, Montreal.

Goldberg, Adele E. 1995. *Constructions. A construction grammar approach to argument structure*. Chicago: University of Chicago Press.

Goldberg, Adele E. 2006. *Constructions at work: The nature of generalizations in language*. Oxford: Oxford University Press.

Good, Jeff. 2004. Tone and accent in Saramaccan: Charting a deep split in the phonology of a language. *Lingua* 114: 575–619.

Goodman, Morris F. 1964. *A comparative study of Creole French dialects*. The Hague: Mouton de Gruyter.

Goodman, Morris F. 1987. The Portuguese element in the American creoles. In Gilbert (ed.), 361–405.

Gougenheim, Georges. 1973. *Grammaire de la langue française au seizième siècle*. Paris: A. et J. Picard.

Grant, Anthony P. 2011. Substrate influences in Mindanao Chabacano. In Lefebvre (ed.), 303–324.

Güldemann, Tom. 2001. Quotative constructions in African languages: A synchronic and diachronic survey. Doctoral dissertation, Leipzig University, Leipzig.

Güldemann, Tom. 2002. When 'say' is not *say*: The functional versatility of the Bantu quotative marker *ti* with special reference to Shona. *Reported discourse, a meeting ground for different linguistic domains*, ed. by Tom Güldemann and Manfred von Roncador, 253–287. Amsterdam: John Benjamins Publishing.

Hagège, Claude. 1985. *L'homme de parole*. Paris: Librairie Arthème Fayard.

Hagemeijer, Tjerk. 2013. Santome language structure dataset. *Atlas of Pidgin and Creole language structures online*, ed. by Susanne Michaelis, Philippe Maurer, Martin Haspelmath, and Magnus Huber, Chapter 6. Leipzig: Max Planck Institute for Evolutionary Anthropology.

Hagemeijer, Tjerk, and Ota Ogie. 2011. Èdó influence on Santome: Evidence from verb serialisation. In Lefebvre (ed.), 37–60.

Hall, Robert A. 1950. The genetic relationships of Haitian Creole. *Ricerche Linguistiche* 1: 194–203.

Hall, Robert A. 1958. Creolized languages and genetic relationships. *Word* 14: 367–373.

Ham, William H. 1999. Tone sandhi in Saramaccan: A case of substrate transfer? *Journal of Pidgin and Creole Languages* 14.1: 45–91.

Hancock, Ian F. 1980. Gullah and Barbadian: Origins and relationships. *American Speech* 55: 17–35.

Hancock, Ian F. 1987. A preliminary classification of the anglophone Atlantic creoles with syntactic data from thirty-three representative dialects. In Gilbert (ed.), 264–333.

Haspelmath, Martin. 1998. Does grammaticalization need reanalysis? *Studies in Language* 22: 315–351.

Hazoumê, Marc Laurent. 1990. *Essai de classification synchronique. Étude comparative des parles Gbe du Sud-Bénin*. Cotonou, Bénin: Centre national de linguistique appliquée.

Heath, Jeffrey. 1981. *Basic materials in Mara: Grammar, texts and dictionary*. Canberra: Pacific Linguistics c/60.

Heine, Bernd. 1997. *Cognitive foundations of grammar*. Oxford: Oxford University Press.

Heine, Bernd, and T. Kuteva. 2005. *Language contact and grammatical change*. Cambridge: Cambridge University Press.

Hérault, Georges (ed.). 1983. *Atlas des langues kwa de Côte d'Ivoire* [vol. 1, 2nd edition]. Paris: Agence de coopération culturelle et technique/Abidjan, Ivory Coast: Université d'Abidjan, Institut de linguistique appliquée.

Hesseling, Dirk Christiaan. 1933. Een Spaans boek over het Papiaments. *TNTL* 52: 40–57; review of Rodolfo Lenz *El Papiamento, la lengua criolla de Curazao (la grammatica mas sencilla)*, Anales de la Unive. de Chile, Seperatum (Santiago, 1928).

Heurtelou, Maude, and Fequiere Vilsaint. 2004. *Guide to learning Haitian Creole* (2nd edition). Coconut Creek, FL: Educa Vision.

Hilaire, Jeannot. 1992. *Soubassements amérindiens* [L'édifice créole en Haïti 1]. Fribourg, Switzerland: Edikreyol.

Hilaire, Jeannot. 1993. *Soubassements africains* [L'édifice créole en Haïti 2]. Fribourg, Switzerland: Edikreyol.

Hill, Jane, and Kenneth Hill. 1977. Language death and relexification in Tlaxcalan Nahuatl. *Journal of the Sociology of Language* 12: 55–69.

Holm, John A. 1988. *Pidgins and creoles. Vol 1: Theory and structure*. Cambridge: Cambridge University Press.

Hopper, Paul J., and Elizabeth C. Traugott. 1993. *Grammaticalisation* [Cambridge Textbooks in Linguistics]. Cambridge: Cambridge University Press.

Hounkpatin, Basile. 1985. Le verbal et le syntagme verbal du fon-gbe parlé à Massè. Doctoral dissertation, Université de la Sorbonne nouvelle, Paris III.

Hudson, Carla L., and Elissa L. Newport. 1999. Creolization: Could adults really have done it all? *Proceedings of the 23rd Annual BUCLD*, ed. by A. Greenhill, H. Littlefield, and C. Tano, 265–276. Boston: Cascadilla Press.

Hudson, Carla L., and Elissa L. Newport. 2005. Regularizing unpredictable variation: The roles of adult and child learners in language formation and change. *Language Learning and Development* 1: 151–195.

Hulk, Aafke. 1986. Subject clitics and the PRO-drop parameter. *Formal parameters of generative grammar*, ed. by P. Coopmans, I. Bordelois, and B. D. Smith, 107–120. Dordrecht: ICG Printing.

Huttar, George L. 1975. Sources of creole semantic structures. *Language* 51: 684–695.

Hymes, Dell. 1971a. Introduction. In Hymes (ed.), 65–91.

Hymes, Dell (ed.). 1971b. *Pidginization and creolization of languages*. Cambridge: Cambridge University Press [Proceedings of a conference held at the University of West Indies, Mona, Jamaica, April 1968].

Jacob, June, and Charles E. Grimes. 2011. Aspect and directionality in Kupang Malay serial verb constructions: Calquing on the grammars of substrate languages. In Lefebvre (ed.), 337–366.

Jaeggli, Osvaldo A. 1984. Subject extraction and the null subject parameter. *Proceedings of NELS 14*, ed. by C. Jones and P. Sells, 132–153. Amherst: University of Massachusetts at Amherst, GLSA.

Johnson, Kyle. 1991. Object positions. *Natural Language and Linguistic Theory* 9: 577–639.

Joseph, Frantz. 1988. La détermination nominale en créole haïtien. Doctoral dissertation, Université Paris VII (Denis Diderot), Paris.

Joseph, Sauveur Joseph. 1994. De l'étude sémantico-syntaxique de la locution *nan* du créole haïtien. Master's thesis, Université du Québec à Montréal, Montreal.

Joseph, Sauveur Joseph. 1995. La négation en créole Haïtien: un cas de relexification. Université du Québec à Montréal, Montreal. Unpublished manuscript.

Kay, Paul, and Charles J. Fillmore. 1999. Grammatical constructions and linguistic generalizations: The *What's X doing Y?* construction. *Language* 75.1: 1–33.

Kayne, Richard S. 1976. French relative que. *Current studies in romance linguistics*, ed. by Fritz Hensey and Marta Luján, 255–299. Cambridge, MA: MIT Press.

Kayne, Richard S. 1984. *Connectedness and binary branching*. Dordrecht: Foris Publications.

Kearns, Lucie. 2008a. *Terrain sur la langue Papiamentu (par Internet-Curaçao)*.

Kearns, Lucie. 2008b. Papiamentu data base. Research report 2008, 2009, SSHRCC. Université du Québec à Montréal, Montreal.

Kearns, Lucie. 2011. Fieldnotes on Saramaccan. Research report. Université du Québec à Montréal, Montreal.

Kearns, Lucie. In progress. Saramaccan *fu*: preposition ou marqueur de cas? UQAM.

Keesing, Roger M. n.d. Solomons Pijin and the Malaita languages: Kwaio grammar and Pijin grammar. Unpublished manuscript.

Keesing, Roger M. 1988. *Melanesian pidgin and the Oceanic substrate*. Stanford, CA: Stanford University Press.

Kihm, Alain. 1989. Lexical conflation as a basis for relexification. In Lefebvre and Lumsden (eds.), 351–376.

Kihm, Alain. 1994. French-Gbe lexical conflations in the genesis of Haitian. In Lefebvre and Lumsden (eds.), 24 pages.

Kihm, Alain. 2011. Substrate influences in Kriyol: Guinea-Bissau and Casamance Portuguese-related Creole. In Lefebvre (ed.), 81–103.

Kinyalolo, Kasangati K. W. 1994. Pronouns and relexification. In Lefebvre and Lumsden (eds.), volume III, 259–293.

Koch, Harold. 2000. The role of Australian Aboriginal languages in the formation of Australian Pidgin grammar: Transitive verbs and adjectives. In Siegel (ed.), 13–46.

Koch, Harold. 2007. An overview of Australian traditional languages. *The habitat of Australia's aboriginal languages: Past, present, and future* [Trends in Linguistics. Studies and Monographs 179], ed. by Gerhard Leitner and Ian G. Malcolm, 23–56. Berlin: Mouton de Gruyter.

Koch, Harold. 2011a. The influence of Arandic languages on Central Australian Aboriginal English. In Lefebvre (ed.), 437–460.

Koch, Harold. 2011b. Substrate influences on New South Wales Pidgin: The origin of *-im* and *-fela*. In Lefebvre (ed.), 489–512.

Koopman, Hilda. 1982a. Les constructions relatives. In Lefebvre, Magloire-Holly, and Piou (eds.), 167–203.

Koopman, Hilda. 1982b. Les questions. In Lefebvre, Magloire-Holly, and Piou (eds.), 204–233.

Koopman, Hilda. 1986. The genesis of Haitian: Implications of a comparison of some features of the syntax of Haitian, French and West African languages. In Muysken and Smith (eds.), 231–258.

Koopman, Hilda, and Claire Lefebvre. 1981. Haitian Creole "pu." In Muysken (ed.), 201–221.

Koopman, Hilda, and Claire Lefebvre. 1982. PU: marqueur de mode, préposition et complémenteur. In Lefebvre, Magloire-Holly, and Piou (eds.), 64–91.

Koster, Jan. 1978. *Locality principles in syntax* [Studies in Generative Grammar 5]. Dordrecht: Foris Publications.

Kouwenberg, Silvia. 1990. Complementiser *PA*, the finiteness of its complements, and some remarks on empty categories in Papiamentu. *Journal of Pidgin and Creole Languages* 5.1: 39–51.

Kouwenberg, Silvia. 1996. Grammaticalization and word order in the history of Berbice Dutch Creole. In Baker and Syea (eds.), 207–218.

Kouwenberg, Silvia (ed.). 2003. *Twice as meaningful: Reduplication in pidgins, creoles and other contact languages*. London: Battlebridge Publications.

Kouwenberg, Silvia, and Claire Lefebvre. 2007. A new analysis of the Papiamentu clause structure. *Probus* 19: 37–75.

Kouwenberg, Silvia, and Eric Murray. 1994. *Papiamentu* [Languages of the World Materials 83]. Munich/Newcastle: Lincom Europa.

Kouwenberg, Silvia, and Pieter C. Muysken. 1995. Papiamento. In Arends, Muysken, and Smith (eds.), 205–218.

Kramer, Marvin. 2002. Substrate transfer in Saramaccan Creole. Doctoral dissertation, University of California at Berkeley.

Kriegel, Sibylle (ed.). 2003. *Grammaticalisation et réanalyse: Approches de la variation créole et française*. Paris: CNRS.

Labov, William. 2007. Transmission and diffusion. *Language* 83.2: 344–388.

Lafage, Suzanne. 1985. *Français écrit et parlé en pays Ewé (Sud-Congo)*. Paris: SELAF.

Lambert-Brétière, Renée. 2009. Serializing languages as satellite-framed: The case of Fon. *Annual Review of Cognitive Linguistics* 7: 1–29.

Lambert-Brétière, Renée. 2010. *Les constructions sérielles en fon: approche typologique* [Afrique et langage 15]. Louvain/Paris: Peters.

Lang, Jürgen. 2011. A Wolof trace in the verbal system of the Portuguese Creole of Santiago Island (Cape Verde). In Lefebvre (ed.), 61–80.

Langacker, Ronald. 1987. *Foundations of cognitive grammar. Vol I: Theoretical prerequisites*. Stanford, CA: Stanford University Press.

Langacker, Ronald. 1991. *Foundations of cognitive grammar. Vol II: Descriptive application*. Stanford, CA: Stanford University Press.

Langacker, Ronald. 2005. Construction grammars: Cognitive, radical and less so. *Cognitive linguistics: Internal dynamics and interdisciplinary interaction* [Cognitive Linguistics Research 32], ed. by Francisco J. Ruiz de Mendoza Ibáñez and Sandra Peña Cervel, 101–159. Berlin/New York: Mouton de Gruyter.

Lardière, Donna. 2006. Comparing creole genesis with SLA in unlimited-access contexts: Going beyond relexification. In Lefebvre, White, and Jourdan (eds.), 401–428.

Larson, Richard K., and Claire Lefebvre. 1991. Predicate clefting in Haitian Creole. *Proceedings of the North East Linguistic Society*, ed. by Tim Sherer, 247–262. Montreal,
Université du Québec à Montréal: GLSA.

Larson, Richard K., and Gabriel Segal. 1995. *Knowledge of meaning: An introduction to
semantic theory*. Cambridge, MA: MIT Press.

Law, Paul. 1991. Verb movement, expletive replacement, and head-government. *The Linguistic Review* 8: 253–285.

Law, Paul. 1992. What is a null subject language? *Travaux de recherche sur le créole
haïtien* 11: 41–58 [UQAM].

Law, Paul. 1994. Resumptives in Haitian and relexification. In Lefebvre and Lumsden
(eds.), 36 pages.

Lefebvre, Claire. 1982. Introduction. In Lefebvre, Magloire-Holly, and Piou (eds.), 1–20.

Lefebvre, Claire. 1984. Grammaires en contact: définition et perspectives de recherche.
Revue québécoise de linguistique 14: 11–49.

Lefebvre, Claire. 1986. Relexification in creole genesis revisited: The case of Haitian
Creole. In Muysken and Smith (eds.), 279–301.

Lefebvre, Claire. 1989. Instrumental *take* serial constructions in Haitian and in Fon. *La
créolisation*. Special issue of the *Revue canadienne de linguistique* 34.3: 319–339.

Lefebvre, Claire. 1990. Establishing a syntactic category P in Fon. *The Journal of West
African Languages* 20.1: 45–63.

Lefebvre, Claire. 1991. *Take* serial verb constructions in Fon. *Serial verbs: Grammatical,
comparative and cognitive approaches* [Studies in the Sciences of Language Series
8], ed. by Claire Lefebvre, 37–78. Amsterdam/Philadelphia: John Benjamins Publishing.

Lefebvre, Claire. 1993. The role of relexification in creole genesis: The case of functional
categories. *Travaux de recherche sur le créole haïtien* 14: 23–52 [UQAM].

Lefebvre, Claire. 1994a. The role of relexification in creole genesis: The case of functional categories. Arbeitsstelle für Mehrsprachigkeit, Hamburg.

Lefebvre, Claire. 1994b. On spelling out E. *Travaux de recherche sur le créole haïtien* 23:
1–33 [UQAM].

Lefebvre, Claire. 1994c. New facts from Fongbe on the double object constructions.
Lingua 94.2–3: 69–123.

Lefebvre, Claire. 1996. The tense, mood and aspect system of Haitian Creole and the
problem of transmission of grammar in creole genesis. *Journal of Pidgin and Creole
Languages* 11.2: 231–313.

Lefebvre, Claire. 1997. Relexification in creole genesis: The case of demonstrative terms
in Haitian Creole. *Journal of Pidgin and Creole Languages* 12.1: 181–203.

Lefebvre, Claire. 1998. *Creole genesis and the acquisition of grammar: The case of Haitian Creole* [Cambridge Studies in Linguistics 88]. Cambridge: Cambridge University Press.

Lefebvre, Claire. 1999. Substratum semantics in the verbal lexicon of Haitian Creole.
Studies in Language 23.1: 61–103.

Lefebvre, Claire. 2001. The interplay of relexification and levelling in creole genesis and
development. *Linguistics* 39: 371–408.

Lefebvre, Claire. 2002. The field of pidgin and creole linguistics at the turn of the millennium: The problem of the genesis and development of PCs. *Pidgin and creole linguistics in the twenty-first century*, ed. by Glenn Gilbert, 247–287. New York: Peter Lang.

Lefebvre, Claire. 2003. The emergence of productive morphology in creole languages: The case of Haitian Creole. In Booij and van Marle (eds.), 35–81.

Lefebvre, Claire. 2004a. Coordinating constructions in Fongbe with reference to Haitian Creole. *Coordinating constructions: Typological studies in language*, ed. by Martin Haspelmath, 123–165. Amsterdam/Philadelphia: John Benjamins Publishing.

Lefebvre, Claire. 2004b. *Issues in the study of pidgin and creole languages*. Amsterdam: John Benjamins Publishing.

Lefebvre, Claire. 2007. A theory of creole genesis. Plenary speaker at the 18th International Conference on Historical Linguistics. Université du Québec à Montréal. August 6–11, 2007.

Lefebvre, Claire. 2008a. Relabelling: A major process in language contact. *Journal of Language Contact* 2. http://www.jlc-journal.org.

Lefebvre, Claire. 2008b. On the principled nature of the respective contribution of substrate and superstrate languages to a creole's lexicon. In Michaelis (ed.), 197–225.

Lefebvre, Claire. 2009a. A note on lexical diffusion in the development of creole: The case of double-object verbs. *Gradual creolization: Studies celebrating Jacques Arends* [Creole Language Library], ed. by R. Selback, H. C. Cardoso, and M. van den Berg, 101–113. Amsterdam: John Benjamins Publishing.

Lefebvre, Claire. 2009b. The contribution of relexification, grammaticalization, and reanalysis to contact-induced language change. *Studies in Language* 33.2: 277–312.

Lefebvre, Claire. 2011a. The problem of the typological classification of creoles. In Lefebvre (ed.), 3–33.

Lefebvre, Claire. 2011b. Substrate features in the properties of verbs in three Atlantic creoles: Haitian Creole, Saramaccan and Papiamentu. In Lefebvre (ed.), 127–153.

Lefebvre, Claire (ed.). 2011c. *Creoles, their substrates, and language typology*. [Typological Studies in Language 95]. Amsterdam: John Benjamins Publishing.

Lefebvre, Claire. 2012. A comparison of the nominal structures of Saramaccan, Fongbe and English with reference to Haitian Creole: Implications for a relabeling-based account of creole genesis. *Lingua*, in press, corrected proof.

Lefebvre, Claire. 2013. On the relevance of pidgins and creoles in the debate on the origins of language. *New perspectives on the origins of language*, ed. by C. Lefebvre, B. Comrie, and H. Cohen, 441–486. Amsterdam: John Benjamins Publishing.

Lefebvre, Claire, and Anne-Marie Brousseau. 2002. *The structure of Fongbe* [Mouton Grammar Library 25]. Berlin/New York: Mouton de Gruyter.

Lefebvre, Claire, and Jonathan Kaye. 1985–1989. Créole haïtien: Langues africaines relexifiées? Grant application. FCAR.

Lefebvre, Claire, and Renée Lambert-Brétière. 2014. A note on the Haitian double-object construction and the relabelling-bases account of creole genesis. *Journal of Pidgin and Creole Languages* 29.1: 136–146.

Lefebvre, Claire, and Virginie Loranger. 2006. On the properties of Saramaccan *fu*: Synchronic and diachronic perspectives. *Journal of Pidgin and Creole Languages* 21.2: 275–337.

Lefebvre, Claire, and Virginie Loranger. 2008. A diachronic and synchronic account of the multifunctionality of Saramaccan *táa*. *Linguistics* 46.6: 1109–1167.

Lefebvre, Claire, and John S. Lumsden. 1989a. Les langues créoles et la théorie linguistique. *La créolisation*. Special issue of *Revue canadienne de linguistique* 34.3: 249–272.

Lefebvre, Claire, and John S. Lumsden (eds.). 1989b. Aspects de la grammaire du créole haïtien. Special issue of *Revue québécoise de linguistique* 18.2: 189 pp.

Lefebvre, Claire, and John S. Lumsden. 1992. On word order in relexification. *Travaux de recherche sur le créole haïtien* 10: 1–22 [UQAM].

Lefebvre, Claire, and John S. Lumsden. 1994a. Relexification in creole genesis. In Lefebvre and Lumsden (eds.), 28 pages.

Lefebvre, Claire, and John S. Lumsden (eds.). 1994b. *The central role of relexification in creole genesis: The case of Haitian Creole*. Research report prepared for SSHRCC on the project "La genèse du créole haïtien: un cas particulier d'investigation sur la forme de la grammaire universelle" [3 volumes]. Université du Québec à Montréal, Montreal.

Lefebvre, Claire, Hélène Magloire-Holly, and Nanie Piou (eds.). 1982. *Syntaxe de l'haïtien*. Ann Arbor, MI: Karoma Publishers.

Lefebvre, Claire, and Diane Massam. 1988. Haitian Creole syntax: A case for DET as head. *Journal of Pidgin and Creole Languages* 3: 213–243.

Lefebvre, Claire, and Pieter C. Muysken. 1988. *Mixed categories: Nominalizations in Quechua* [Studies in Natural Languages and Linguistic Theory]. Dordrecht: Kluwer Academic Publishers.

Lefebvre, Claire, and Elizabeth Ritter. 1993. Two types of predicate doubling adverbs in Haitian Creole. In Byrne and Winford (eds.), 65–91.

Lefebvre, Claire, and Isabelle Therrien. 2007a. On the properties of Papiamentu *pa*: Synchronic and diachronic perspectives. *Synchronic and diachronic perspective on contact languages* [CLL 32], ed. by M. Huber and V. Velupillai, 257–278. Amsterdam: John Benjamins Publishing.

Lefebvre, Claire, and Isabelle Therrien. 2007b. On Papiamentu *ku*. *Language description, history and development: Linguistic indulgence in memory of Terry Crowley*, ed. by Jeff Siegel, John Lynch, and Diana Eades, 169–182. Amsterdam: John Benjamins Publishing.

Lefebvre, Claire, Lydia White, and Christine Jourdan (eds.). 2006. *L2 acquisition and creole genesis. Dialogues* [Language Acquisition and Language Disorders 42]. Amsterdam: John Benjamins Publishing.

Leland, C. G. 1874. *The Gypsies and their language*. London: Trübuer.

Lenz, Rodolfo. 1928. *El Papiamento, la lengua criolla de Curazao (la grammatica mas sencilla)*. Santiago de Chile: Imprenta Balcells.

Lightfoot, David. 1979. *Principles of diachronic syntax* [Cambridge Studies in Linguistics 23]. Cambridge: Cambridge University Press.

Lim, Lisa. 2011. Tone in Singlish: Substrate features from Sinitic and Malay. In Lefebvre (ed.), 271–287.

Lim, Lisa, and Nikolas Gisborne (eds.). 2009. *The typology of Asian Englishes*. Special issue of *English World-Wide* 30.2.

Lumsden, John S. 1989. On the distribution of determiners in Haitian Creole. *Le créole haïtien*. Special issue of *Revue québécoise de linguistique* 18.2: 64–93.

Lumsden, John S. 1990. The bi-clausal structure of Haitian clefts. *Linguistics* 28: 741–760.

Lumsden, John S. 1991. On the acquisition of nominal structures in the genesis of Haitian Creole. *Travaux de recherche sur le créole haïtien* 4: 37–61 [UQAM].

Lumsden, John S. 1994. Possession: Substratum semantics in Haitian Creole. *Journal of Pidgin and Creole Languages* 9: 25–51.

Lumsden, John S. 1999. Language acquisition and creolization. *Language creation and language change*, ed. by Michel A. DeGraff, 129–157. Cambridge, MA/London: MIT Press.

Lumsden, John S., and Claire Lefebvre. 1994. The genesis of Haitian Creole. In Lefebvre and Lumsden (eds.), 15 pages.

Manfredi, Victor. 1993. Verb focus in the typology of Kwa/Kru and Haitian. In Byrne and Winford (eds.), 3–51.

Marantz, Alec. 1982. Re reduplication. *Linguistic Inquiry* 13: 435–483.

Massam, Diane. 1989. Predicate argument structure in Haitian Creole. In Lefebvre and Lumsden (eds.), 95–130.

Massam, Diane. 1990. Cognate objects as thematic objects. *Canadian Journal of Linguistics* 35.2: 161–190.

Maurer, Philippe. 1988a. Les réitérations et reduplications lexicalisées du Papiamento: Influence du substrat Africain? In Boretzky, Enninger, and Stolz (eds.), 95–118.

Maurer, Philippe. 1988b. *Les modifications temporelles et modales du verbe dans le papiamento de Curaçao (Antilles néerlandaises).* Hamburg, Kreolische Bibliothek: Helmut Buske Verlag.

Maurer, Philippe. 2013. Principense. In Michaelis, Maurer, Haspelmath, and Huber (eds.), 72–80.

McWhorter, John H. 1992. Substratal influence in Saramaccan serial verb constructions. *Journal of Pidgin and Creole Languages* 7: 1–54.

McWhorter, John H. 1998. Identifying the creole prototype: Vindicating a typological class. *Language* 74: 788–818.

McWhorter, John H. 2001. The world's simplest grammars are creole grammars. *Linguistic Typology* 5: 125–166.

McWhorter, John H. 2008. Hither and thither in Saramaccan. *Studies in Language* 32.1: 163–195.

McWhorter, John H. 2012. Case closed? Testing the feature pool hypothesis. *Journal of Pidgin and Creole Languages* 27.1: 171–182.

McWhorter, John H., and J. Good. 2012. *A grammar of Saramaccan Creole* [Mouton Grammar Library 56]. The Hague: Mouton de Gruyter.

Merlan, Francesca. 1983. *Ngalakgan grammar, texts and vocabulary.* Canberra: Pacific Linguistics B/89.

Michaelis, Susanne (ed.). 2008. *Roots of creole structures: Weighing the contribution of substrates and superstrates* [Creole Language Library 33]. Amsterdam/Philadelphia: John Benjamins Publishing.

Michaelis, Susanne, and Martin Haspelmath. 2003. Ditransitive constructions: Creole languages in a cross-linguistic perspective. *Creolica* 2003-04-23. Online journal: www.creolica.net.

Michaelis, Susanne, Philippe Maurer, Martin Haspelmath, and Magnus Huber (eds.). 2013. *Survey of Pidgin and Creole languages. Vol II: Portuguese-based, Spanish-based and French-based languages.* Oxford: Oxford University Press.

Migge, Bettina M. 1998. Substrate influence in the formation of the Surinamese Plantation Creole: A consideration of sociohistorical data and linguistic data from Ndyuka and Gbe. Doctoral dissertation, Ohio State University, Columbus.

Migge, Bettina. 2003. *Creole formation as language contact: The case of the Suriname Creoles* [Creole Language Library 25]. Amsterdam/Philadelphia: John Benjamins Publishing.

Migge, Bettina. 2011. Assessing the nature and role of substrate influence in the formation and development of the creoles of Suriname. In Lefebvre (ed.), 155–179.

Moreau, Marie-Louise. 1971. L'homme que je crois qui est venu: *que, qui* relatifs et conjonctions. *Langue française* 11: 77–90.

Mosel, Ulrike. 1980. *Tolai and Tok Pisin: The influence of the substratum on the development of New Guinea Pidgin.* Canberra: Australian National University.

Mous, Maarten. 1994. Ma'a or Mbugu. In Bakker and Mous (eds.), 175–200.

Mous, Maarten. 1995. Language intertwining. Paper presented at the Amsterdam Creole Workshop: Creole Genesis and Language Contact, Amsterdam.

Mous, Maarten. 2001. Ma'a as an ethno-register of Mbugu. *Sprache und Geschichte in Afrika* 16/17; *Historical language contact in Africa*, ed. by Derek Nurse, 293–320. Cologne: Rüdiger Köppe.

Mufwene, Salikoko S. 1986. The universalist and substrate hypotheses complement one another. In Muysken and Smith (eds.), 129–162.

Mufwene, Salikoko S. 1990. Transfer and the substrate hypothesis in creolistics. *Studies in Second Language Acquisition* 12.1: 1–23.

Mufwene, Salikoko S. 1992. Africanisms in Gullah: A re-examination of the issues. *Old English and new: Studies in language and linguistics in honor of Frederic G. Cassidy*, ed. by Joan H. Hall, Nick Doane, and Dick Ringler, 156–182. New York: Garland.

Mufwene, Salikoko S. 2001. *The ecology of language evolution.* Cambridge: Cambridge University Press.

Mufwene, Salikoko S. 2006. *The ecology of language evolution.* Cambridge: Cambridge University Press (re-edition).

Mufwene, S. S. 2008. What do creoles and pidgins tell us about the evolution of language? *Origin and evolution of languages: Approaches, models, paradigms*, ed. by B. Laks, S. Cleuziou, J.-P. Demoule, and P. Encrevé, 272–297. London/Oakville: Equinox.

Mühlhäusler, Peter. 1980. Structural expansion and the process of creolisation. In Valdman and Highfield (eds.), 19–56.

Mühlhäusler, Peter. 1986a. *Bonnet blanc* and *blanc bonnet*: Adjective-noun order, substratum and language universals. In Muysken and Smith (eds.), 41–55.

Mühlhäusler, Peter. 1986b. *Pidgin and Creole linguistics* [Language in Society II]. Oxford: Basil Blackwell.

Munro, Jennifer. 2000. Kriol on the move: A case of language spread and shift in Northern Australia. In Siegel (ed.), 245–270.

Munro, Jennifer. 2004. Substrate language influence in Kriol: The application of transfer constraints to language contact in Northern Australia. Doctoral dissertation, University of New England, Armidale, NSW.

Munro, Jennifer. 2011. Roper River Aboriginal language features in Australian Kriol: Considering semantic categories. In Lefebvre (ed.), 461–487.

Muysken, Pieter C. 1979. Movement rules in Papiamentu. *Amsterdam Creole Studies* 1: 80–201.

Muysken, Pieter C. 1981a. Half-way between Quechua and Spanish: The case for relexification. *Historicity and variation in creole studies*, ed. by Arnold R. Highfield and Albert Valdman, 52–79. Ann Arbor, MI: Karoma.

Muysken, Pieter C. 1981b. Creole tense/mood/aspect system: The unmarked case? In Muysken (ed.), 181–201.

Muysken, Pieter C. (ed.). 1981c. *Generative studies on creole languages* [Studies in Generative Grammar 6]. Dordrecht: Foris Publications.

Muysken, Pieter C. 1987. Prepositions and postpositions in Saramaccan. In Alleyne (ed.), 89–102.

Muysken, Pieter C. 1988a. Are creoles a special type of language? *Linguistic theory: Extensions and implications* [Linguistics: The Cambridge Survey 2], ed. by Frederick J. Newmeyer, 285–301. Cambridge: Cambridge University Press.

Muysken, Pieter C. 1988b. Media Lengua and linguistic theory. *The Canadian Journal of Linguistics* 33.4: 409–422.

Muysken, Pieter C. 1988c. Lexical restructuring in creole genesis. In Boretzky, Enninger, and Stolz (eds.), 799–210.

Muysken, Pieter C. 1993. Reflexes of Ibero-Romance reflexive clitic + verb combinations in Papiamentu: Thematic grids and grammatical relations. In Byrne and Winford (eds.), 285–301.

Muysken, Pieter C. 2007. Mixed codes. *Handbook of multilingualism and multilingual communication* [Handbooks of Applied Linguistics 5], ed. by Peter Auer and Li Wei, 303–328. Berlin: Mouton de Gruyter.

Muysken, Pieter C. 2008. *Functional categories* [Cambridge Studies in Linguistics 117]. Cambridge: Cambridge University Press.

Muysken, Pieter C., and Norval Smith (eds.). 1986. *Substrata versus universals in creole genesis* [Creole Language Library 1]. Amsterdam/Philadelphia: John Benjamins Publishing.

Naro, Anthony J. 1978. A study of the origins of pidginisation. *Language* 54: 314–347.

Navarro, Tomás. 1953. Observaciones sobre el Papiamento. *Nueva revista de filología hispanica* 7: 183–189.

Neumann-Holzschuh, Ingrid. 2008. À la recherche du "superstrat": What North American French can and cannot tell us about the input to creolization. In Michaelis (ed.), 357–383.

Neumann-Holzschuh, Ingrid, and Edgar W. Schneider (eds.). 2001. *Degrees of restructuring in creole languages* [Creole Language Library 22]. Amsterdam/Philadelphia: John Benjamins Publishing.

Nolasco, Ricardo M. 2005. The Chabacano challenge to Philippine ergativity. *Linguistics and language education in the Philippines and beyond: A festschrift in honor of Ma*, ed. by Danilo Dayag, John S. Quakenbush, and Maria Lourdes S. Bautista, 401–433. Manila: De La Salle University Press.

Olguín, Maribel. 2006. Analyse comparative des propriétés lexicales de dix classes de verbes en papiamentu et en espagnol. Master's thesis, Université du Québec à Montréal, Montreal.

Papen, Robert. 1988. Convergence et divergence en métif. Paper presented at the Department of Linguistics, Université du Québec à Montréal, Montreal.

Parkvall, Mikael. 2000. *Out of Africa: African influences in Atlantic Creoles*. London: Battlebridge.

Parkvall, Mikael. 2003. Reduplication in the Atlantic Creoles. In Kouwenberg (ed.), 19–37.

Pienemann, Manfred. 2000. Psycholinguistic mechanisms in the development of English as a second language. *Language use, language acquisition and language history: (Mostly) Empirical studies in honour of Rüdiger Zimmermann*, ed. by Ingo Plag and Klaus P. Schneider, 99–118. Trier: Wissenschaftlicher Verlag Trier.

Plag, Ingo. 2000. Review of Claire Lefebvre, *Creole genesis and the acquisition of grammar* [Cambridge Studies in Linguistics 88]. Cambridge: Cambridge University Press 1998. *Journal of Linguistics* 36: 176–180.

Plag, Ingo. 2008. Creoles as interlanguages: Inflectional morphology. *Journal of Pidgin and Creole Languages* 23.1: 114–135.

Plag, Ingo. 2011. Creolization and admixture: Typology, feature pools, and second language acquisition. *Journal of Pidgin and Creole Languages* 26.1: 89–110.

Pollock, Jean-Yves. 1989. Verb movement, Universal Grammar, and the structure of IP. *Linguistic Inquiry* 20: 365–424.

Post, Marike. 2013. Fa d'Ambô. In Michaelis, Maurer, Haspelmath, and Huber (eds.), 81–89.

Potsma, Johannes. 1990. *The Dutch in the Atlantic slave trade, 1600–1815*. Cambridge: Cambridge University Press.

Rassinoux, Jean. 2000. *Dictionnaire français-fon*. Cotonou, Bénin: Société des Missions africaines.

Rawley, James A. 1981. *The transatlantic slave trade: A history*. New York/London: W. W. Norton & Company.

Riemer, Johann Andreas. 1779. *Wörterbuch zur Erlernung der Saramakka-Neger-Sprache*. Published with an English translation in Arends and Perl (eds.), vol. 49, 251–374.

Ritter, Elizabeth. 1992. Cross-linguistic evidence for number phrase. *Functional categories*, ed. by C. Lefebvre, J. Lumsden, and L. Travis, 197–219. Special issue of *Revue canadienne de linguistique* 37.

Rizzi, Luigi. 1997. The fine structure of the left periphery. *Elements of grammar: A handbook in generative syntax*, ed. by Liliane Haegeman, 281–337. Dordrecht: Kluwer Academic Publishers.

Roberge, Yves. 1990. *The syntactic recoverability of null arguments*. Kingston, ON: McGill-Queen's University Press.

Roberts, Sarah J. 2011. The copula in Hawai'i Creole English and substrate reinforcement. In Lefebvre (ed.), 557–573.

Robertson, Ian. 1993. The Ijo element in Berbice Dutch and the pidginisation/creolisation process. *Africanisms in Afro-American language varieties*, ed. by Salikoko S. Mufwene, 296–316. Athens, GA/London: The University of Georgia Press.

Ross, Malcolm. 2007. Calquing and metatypy. Paper presented at the Symposium on Language Contact and the Dynamics of Language: Theory and Implications. Max Planck Institute for Evolutionary Anthropology, Leipzig, May 10–13, 2007.

Rountree, Catherine S. 1992. *Saramaccan grammar sketch*. Paramaribo: Summer Institute of Linguistics.

Rountree, Catherine S., Jajo Asodanoe, and Naomi Glock. 2000. *Saramaccan-English word list* (with idioms). Paramaribo: Institut voor Taalwetenschap.

Rountree, Catherine S., and Naomi Glock. 1982. *Saramaccan for beginners: A pedagogical grammar of the Saramaccan language*. Paramaribo: Instituut voor Taalwetenschap and Summer Institute of Linguistics.

Sandefur, John R., and Joy L. Sandefur. 1979. *Beginnings of a Ngukurr-Bamyili Creole dictionary*. [Work Papers of SIL-AAB B4]. Darwin: Summer Institute of Linguistics.

Sandeman, Barbara. 2011. "On traduit la langue en français": Substrate influence in the TMA system of Tayo. In Lefebvre (ed.), 575–595.

Sankoff, Gillian. 1991. Using the future to explain the past. *Development and structures of creole languages* [Creole Language Library 10], ed. by Francis Byrne and Thom Huebner, 61–74. Amsterdam: John Benjamins Publishing.

Sankoff, Gillian, and Suzanne Laberge. 1973. On the acquisition of native speakers by a language. *Kivung* 6: 32–47.

Schuchardt, Hugo. 1979. *The ethnography of variation: Selected writings on Pidgins and Creoles*, edited and translated by T. L. Markey. Ann Arbor, MI: Karoma.

Schuchardt, Hugo (ed.). 1914. *Die Sprache der Saramakkaneger in Surinam*. Amsterdam: Johannes Müller.

Schumann, Christian Ludwig. 1778. *Saramaccanish Deutsches Wörter-Buch*. Ms. In Schuchardt (ed.), 6–116.

Schumann, John H. 1978. *The pidginisation process: A model for second language acquisition*. Rowley, MA: Newbury House.

Schwartz, Bonnie D., and Rex A. Sprouse. 1996. L2 cognitive states and the full transfer/full access model. *Second Language Research* 12.1: 40–72.

Schwegler, Armin. 2011. Palenque(ro): The search for its African substrate. In Lefebvre (ed.), 225–249.

Segurola, R. P. B. 1963. *Dictionnaire fon-français*. Cotonou, Bénin: Procure de l'Archidiocèse.

Segurola, Basilio, and Jean Rassinoux. 2000. *Dictionnaire fon-français*. Cotonou, Bénin: Société des missions africaines.

Sharpe, Margaret C. 1972. *Alawa phonology and grammar*. Canberra: Australian Institute of Aboriginal Studies.

Siegel, Jeff. 1997. Mixing, levelling and pidgin/creole development. *The structure and status of Pidgins and Creoles* [Creole Language Library 19], ed. by Arthur K. Spears and Donald Winford, 111–149. Amsterdam/Philadelphia: John Benjamins Publishing.

Siegel, Jeff. 1999. Transfer constraints and substrate reinforcement in Melanesian Pidgin. *Journal of Pidgin and Creole Languages* 14: 1–44.

Siegel, Jeff. 2000a. Introduction: The processes of language contact. In Siegel (ed.), 1–12.

Siegel, Jeff (ed.). 2000b. *Processes of language contact: Studies from Australia and the South Pacific* [Collection Champs linguistiques]. Montreal: Fides.

Siegel, Jeff. 2001. Koine formation and creole genesis. In Smith and Veenstra (eds.), 175–197.

Siegel, Jeff. 2008. *The emergence of pidgin and creole languages*. Oxford: Oxford University Press.

Siegel, Jeff. 2011. Substrate reinforcement and the retention of Pan-Pacific Pidgin features in modern contact varieties. In Lefebvre (ed.), 531–556.

Singler, John V. 1988. The homogeneity of the substrate as a factor in pidgin/creole genesis. *Language* 64: 27–51.

Singler, John V. 1996. Theories of creole genesis, sociohistorical considerations, and the evaluation of evidence: The case of Haitian Creole and the relexification hypothesis. *Journal of Pidgin and Creole languages* 11.1: 185–231.

Sippola, Eeva. 2011. Negation in Ternate Chabacano. In Lefebvre (ed.), 325–336.

Slobin, D. I. 2002. Language evolution, acquisition and diachrony: Probing the parallels. *The evolution of language out of pre-language*, ed. by T. Givón and B. F. Malle, 375–392. Amsterdam/Philadelphia: John Benjamins Publishing.

Slomanson, Peter. 2011. Dravidian features in the Sri Lankan Malay verb. In Lefebvre (ed.), 383–409.

Smith, Norval. 1987. The genesis of the creole languages of Surinam. Doctoral dissertation, University of Amsterdam, The Netherlands.

Smith, Norval. 1996. WE-focus in Saramaccan / substrate feature or grammaticalisation? In Baker and Syea (eds.), 113–129.

Smith, Norval. 2001. Voodoo Chile: Differential substrate effects in Saramaccan and Haitian. In Smith and Veenstra (eds.), 43–81.

Smith, Norval, and Hugo Cardoso. 2004. A new look at the Portuguese element in Saramaccan. *Journal of Portuguese Linguistics* 3.1: 115–147.

Smith, Norval, and Tonjes Veenstra (eds.). 2001. *Creolisation and contact* [Creole Language Library 23]. Amsterdam/Philadelphia: John Benjamins Publishing.

Sprouse, Rex A. 2006. Full transfer and relexification: Second language acquisition and creole genesis. In Lefebvre, White, and Jourdan (eds.), 169–182.

Steele, Jeffrey, and Anne-Marie Brousseau. 2006. Parallels in process: Comparing Haitian Creole and French learner phonologies. In Lefebvre, White, and Jourdan (eds.), 331–354.

Sterlin, Marie-Denise. 1988. Les différentes caractéristiques de *pou* en créole haïtien. *Travaux de recherche sur le créole haïtien* 3: 1–34 [UQAM].

Sterlin, Marie-Denise. 1989. Les caractéristiques de *pou*: un modal en position de complémenteur. *Le créole haïtien*. Special issue of *Revue québécoise de linguistique* 18.2: 131–147.

Sylvain, Suzanne. 1936. *Le créole haïtien: morphologie et syntaxe*. Wetteren, Belgium: Imprimerie De Meester/Port-au-Prince: By the author.

Terrill, Angela. 2011. Limits of the substrate: Substrate grammatical influence in Solomon Islands Pijin. In Lefebvre (ed.), 513–529.

Terrill, Angela, and Michael Dunn. 2006. Semantic transference: Two preliminary case studies from the Solomon Islands. In Lefebvre, White, and Jourdan (eds.), 67–86.

Thomason, Sarah G., and Terrence Kaufman. 1991. *Language contact, creolisation, and genetic linguistics*. Berkeley/Los Angeles/Oxford: University of California Press.

Tinelli, Henri. 1970. Generative phonology of Haitian Creole. Doctoral dissertation, University of Michigan, Ann Arbor.

Trask, Robert L. 1993. *A dictionary of grammatical terms in linguistics.* London/New York: Routledge.

Tremblay, Mireille. 1991. Possession and datives: Binary branching from lexicon to syntax. Doctoral dissertation, McGill University, Montreal.

Trudgill, Peter. 1986. *Dialects in contact* [Language in Society 10]. Oxford: Basil Blackwell.

Valdman, Albert. 1978. *Le créole: structure, statut et origine.* Paris: Klincksieck.

Valdman, Albert. 1980. Creolisation and second language acquisition. In Valdman and Highfield (eds.), 297–311.

Valdman, Albert. 1993. Matrice et diffusion culturelle dans le développement des créoles français. Paper read at the Université du Québec à Montréal.

Valdman, Albert. 1996. *A learner's dictionary of Haitian Creole.* Bloomington: Indiana University, Creole Institute.

Valdman, Albert, and Arnold Highfield (eds.). 1980. *Theoretical orientations in creole studies.* New York: Academic Press.

Valdman, Albert, with Sara Yoder, Craige Roberts, Yves Joseph, et al. 1981. *Haitian Creole-English-French dictionary* [2 volumes]. Bloomington: Indiana University, Creole Institute.

Valdman, Albert, Iskra Iskrova, and Benjamin Hebblethwaite. 2007. *Haitian Creole-English bilingual dictionary.* Bloomington: Indiana University, Creole Institute.

Van Coetsem, Frans. 2000. *A general and unified theory of the transmission process in language contact.* Heidelberg: Universitätsverlag, C. Winter.

van de Vate, Marleen Susanne. 2011. Tense, aspect and modality in a radical creole: The case of Saamaka. Doctoral dissertation, University of Tromsø.

Van den Berg, Henk. 1987. A brief note on predicate cleft in Saramaccan. In Alleyne (ed.), 103–111.

van Name, Addison. 1869–1870. Contribution to creole grammar. *Transactions of the American Philological Association, 1869–70*: 123–167.

Van Wijk, Henri L. 1958. Origenes y evolución del Papiamento. *Neophilologus* 42: 169–182.

Védrine, Emmanuel W. 1992. *Dictionary of Haitian Creole verbs (with phrases and idioms).* Cambridge, MA: Soup to Nuts Publishers.

Veenstra, Tonjes. 1996a. *Serial verbs in Saramaccan: Predication and creole genesis.* Dordrecht: Holland Institute of Generative Linguistics.

Veenstra, Tonjes. 1996b. Grammaticalized verbs in Saramaccan. In Baker and Syea (eds.), 95–112.

Veenstra, Tonjes. 2008. Syntaxis pur: expletiva im Papiamentu. *Romanistische Syntax - minimalistisch*, ed. by Eva-Maria Remberger and Guido Mensching, 61–82. Tübingen: Gunter Narr.

Vilsaint, Féquière. 1992. *Diksyonè Anglè Kreyòl/English Kreyòl dictionary.* Temple Terrace, FL: Educa Vision.

Vincent, Diane. 1984. Les ponctuants de la langue. Doctoral dissertation, Université de Montréal, Montreal.

Voorhoeve, Jan. 1973. Historical and linguistic evidence in favor of the relexification theory in the formation of creoles. *Language in Society* 2: 133–145.

Weinreich, Uriel. 1953. *Languages in contact.* The Hague: Mouton de Gruyter.

Westerman, Diedrich. 1930. *A study of the Ewe language*. London: Oxford University Press.

Whinnom, Keith. 1971. Linguistic hybridisation and the "special case" of pidgins and creoles. In Hymes (ed.), 91–115.

Wietz, I. L. van. 1805 [ca 1793]. *Die Apostel Geschichte in die Saramakka Neger Sprache Uebersetzt durch Br. Wietz,* Revedirt und Abgeschrieben 1805. MS no EBGS 632, Moravian Archives Utrecht/MS no H III A 13 (16), Moravian Archives Paramaribo. Transcription published in Schuchardt (ed.), 2–35.

Wijnen, Beppy, and Mervyn Alleyne. 1987. A note on *fu* in Saramaccan. In Alleyne (ed.), 41–45.

Winford, Donald. 1993. *Predication in Caribbean English Creoles* [Creole Language Library 10]. Amsterdam:John Benjamins Publishing.

Winford, Donald. 2007. Processes of creole formation and related contact-induced language change. Paper presented at the Symposium on Language Contact and the Dynamics of Language: Theory and Implications. Max Planck Institute for Evolutionary Anthropology, Leipzig, May 10–13, 2007.

Winford, Donald, and Bettina Migge. 2007. Substrate influence on the emergence of the TMA systems of the Surinamese creoles. *Journal of Pidgin and Creole Languages* 22.1: 73–100.

Wurm, S. A., P. Mühlhäusler, and D. T. Tryon. (eds.). 1996. *Atlas of languages of intercultural communication in the Pacific, Asia, and the Americas*, 3 vols. Berlin: Mouton de Gruyter.

Zagona, Karen. 2002. *The syntax of Spanish*. Cambridge: Cambridge University Press.

INDEX OF SUBJECTS

Adjectives, 18, 24, 37, 70, 140, 141, 143, 146, 147, 172, 173, 174, 183, 192, 194, 196, 199, 232
   deverbal resultative, 167, 172, 194, 196, 197, 198, 199

Case
   semantic, 4, 234, 240–3, 250
   structural, 76
   systems, 228, 234, 240, 241, 242, 251, 254
Calquing, 6, 11, 12, 15, 249, 250, 253, 255, 257
Classifier, 231, 234, 236, 251, 254
Complementizer, 41, 59–61, 65, 77, 81–3, 201–2, 204–8, 210–11
   system, 59–61
Conjunction, 24, 41, 61, 62, 63, 64, 65, 82, 91, 131
   system, 61–4
Creole genesis, 131, 138–9, 142–3, 145, 150, 156, 163, 176–80, 183, 185, 193, 196, 198, 207, 215, 220–2, 225, 257–62, 266–8, 270–1
Creoles
   and language typology, 223–58
   as isolating languages, 34, 100, 256–7, 266, 270

Determiner
   definite, 43–7, 144, 147–8
   system, 42–56
   see also Demonstrative terms; Plural marker; Possessive phrases
Demonstrative terms, 43, 53–5, 78, 91, 140, 150–3, 183
Discourse structures, 228, 234, 248, 254
Double object
   constructions, 105, 221–2
   see also Verbs

Exceptionalism, 258

Full Transfer, 12–13, 16, 222
   as relabeling, 12–13

Grammatical features, 199, 207–8, 212, 214–15, 221–2, 233, 252
Grammaticalization, 7, 25–6, 31–2, 36, 57, 77–84, 89–93, 98–100, 259, 266
   see also Relabeling

Imperfective construction, 108, 113, 115–19, 138, 190–3, 213–14, 261, 268

Leveling, 7, 26, 32, 36, 53, 89, 90–1, 98–9, 229–30, 254, 259, 264–5

Lexicon
  theories of, 103–38, 261–2
Locative constructions, 108, 116, 119,
  120–1, 128, 138, 166, 268

Misascription, 13, 15
Morphological reduplication, 7, 40, 165,
  167, 168, 171, 172, 174, 175, 176,
  184, 191, 197, 198, 266

Negation, 58, 70, 105, 146, 160, 161, 162,
  163, 228, 231, 232, 234, 240, 252,
  253, 254
Number, 6, 7, 9, 18, 23, 29, 30, 43, 44, 47,
  48, 49, 50, 51, 52, 53, 55, 72, 75,
  78, 88, 89, 105, 154, 196, 199, 201,
  207, 210, 213, 230, 232, 242, 259,
  263, 268, 271
  see also Plural

Paralexification, 11, 15
Plural, 22, 25, 38, 42–3, 47, 49–53, 71–6,
  78, 90, 94–5, 140, 142, 148,
  149–50, 152, 181–3, 199, 200–2,
  208–9, 230, 234–6, 264–5
  see also Number
Possessive phrases, 189–90
Postpositions, 7, 18, 24, 37, 115, 119–21,
  128, 139, 142, 146, 154–8, 165–7,
  176, 266, 268
Principles and Parameters, 5, 7, 103–8,
  111, 114–20, 132, 137–8, 261
Pronoun, 16, 38, 53, 58, 71–2, 74–5, 88,
  94–5, 152, 181, 195, 207, 218,
  234–6, 254, 264
Pronominal forms, 72, 94–5, 152, 234–5,
  254, 264

Radical Construction Grammar, 5, 7,
  103–5, 143, 262
Reanalysis, 14–15, 26, 31–2, 36, 89, 91,
  93–5, 98–9, 101, 112, 254, 259
Relexification, 1, 4, 6, 10–11, 13, 15, 19,
  25, 31–3, 99, 176, 212, 250, 252–3,
  255, 257
  as relabeling, 10–11

Reinterpretation, 13, 14, 15, 250
Relabeling
  across language contact situations,
    16–18
  across lexicons, 18–30
  and calquing, 11–12; *see also*
    Calquing
  and diffusion through the lexicon,
    95–8
  and exceptionalism, 258–60
  and full transfer, 12–13; *see also* Full
    Transfer
  and grammaticalizaton, 91–3; *see also*
    Grammaticalization
  and leveling, 89–91; *see also* Leveling
  and misascription, 13
  and other approaches to creole genesis,
    266–71
  and paralexification, 11
  and reanalysis, 14–15, 93–5; *see also*
    Reanalysis
  and reinterpretation, 13
  and relexification, 10–11; *see also*
    Relexification
  and substrate languages, 260–1
  and superstrate languages, 177–222,
    260–1
  and theories of the lexicon, 103–38,
    262–1; *see also* Principles and
    Parameters, Radical Construction
    Grammar
  and types of morphemes, 36–66,
    262–4
  and typological classification of creoles,
    223–57
  and variation among creoles, 264–6
  and word order, 139–63
  consequences of, 100–2
  constraints on, 68–9
  definition of, 1–4
  extent of, 18–30, 88
  in agglutinative languages, 69–72
  in creole genesis, 17, 31–102
  in language death, 18
  in mixed languages, 17
  in New Englishes genesis, 17

in second language acquisition, 16;
   see also Full Transfer
of derivational affixes, 38–41
of functional categories, 41–77
options, 164–76
or grammaticalization, 77–83
predictions of, 85–8

-SELF anaphor, 194–5

Tense-mood-aspect system, 27–59,
   108–19, 236–40
   see also Imperfective construction
Transitivity marker, 234, 243–4, 251,
   254

Typological classification of creoles, 6,
   223–57

Validator, 41, 64, 65
Verb-doubling constructions, 105, 132,
   222, 262
Verbs
   double object, 96–8, 220, 230, 245
   of cutting, 87, 195–6, 199
   serial, 97, 105, 127, 145, 178, 214,
      219, 220–1, 228–9, 230–2, 234,
      246, 254, 262, 264

Word order in creole genesis, 139–64,
   183–93

INDEX OF AUTHORS

Aboh, Enoch O., 43, 46, 60, 68, 141, 183, 189, 205, 255, 267–71
Adam, Lucien, 34, 224
Agbidinoukoun, Cosme Christian, 47
Alleyne, Mervyn C., 32–4, 60, 178
Allsop, Richard, 13
Ameka, Félix K., 196
Andersen, Roger W., 12, 32, 249, 252
Anonymous, 38, 54, 236
Ansaldo, Umberto, ix, 15, 159, 220, 223, 225, 227, 231–7, 239–41, 245–6, 249–50, 253, 256, 267–9, 271
Arends, Jacques, 33–4, 41, 60, 81–2, 101

Baker, Philip, 70, 88
Bakker, Peter, 4, 15, 17, 21–4, 30–1, 60, 78, 81, 174
Bally, Anne-Sophie, 43–5, 48, 51, 55, 57, 64, 76, 96, 111–12, 157, 163, 218, 238
Bao, Zhiming, 4, 18, 28, 112, 177, 180, 211–14, 219–20, 223, 228, 231, 249
Bartens, Angela, 230, 245, 246, 252, 257
Bernabé, Jean, 153, 248
Bickerton, Derek, 33–4, 101–2, 224–5, 271
Blake, Barry J., 245
Bollée, Anegret, 265
Booij, Geert E., 275–6
Boretzky, Norbert, 24–5

Botha, R., 271
Bouchard, Denis, 49
Braun, Maria, 40–1, 168, 172, 175
Brousseau, Anne-Marie, 2–3, 31–2, 38, 40, 43, 47, 51, 56, 59, 62, 64, 73, 76, 83–6, 88, 94–5, 109, 111, 113–14, 119, 124, 127, 135, 140, 145, 157, 167–70, 173, 175, 184, 186–7, 189, 191, 193–4, 201, 228–9, 236, 249, 255, 265
Bruyn, Adrienne, 4, 15, 17, 79, 80, 83–4, 158
Bybee, Joan, 32, 95
Byrne, Francis, 57, 60, 62, 81, 118–19, 193, 238

Cadely, Jean-Robert, 88, 94
Camden, Pastor Bill, 244
Capo, Hounkpati B., 38, 236, 255
Cardoso, Hugo, 155
Chaudenson, Robert, 32, 33, 177–8, 181–2, 224
Chomsky, Noam, 5, 7, 66, 78, 104, 161, 203, 210
Clements, J., 139, 160
Comrie, B., 271
Corne, Chris, 88
Croft, William, 5, 7, 104–6, 143
Crowley, Terry, 243

da Cruz, Maxime, 64, 131–2
d'Ans, André-Marcel, 47
Déchaine, Rose-Marie, 128, 195
DeGraff, Michel A., 40, 47, 54, 85, 87–8, 94, 101, 123, 130, 143, 161, 168, 178–9, 183–4, 203, 205
De Groot, Adrianus H., 79
Denis, Marie-Josée, 40
Déprez, Viviane, 49–50, 79, 88, 94, 143, 202
Detges, Ulrich, 15
Dijkhoff, Marta, 40, 171, 184–5, 208, 211
Dionne, Claude, 31, 96, 218
Dixon, Robert M., 245
Donohue, Mark, 220, 223, 232, 246, 249–50
Dryer, Matthew S., 265
Dubois, Jean, 38
Dumais, Danielle, 31, 50, 202
Dunn, Michael, 27–8, 85

Eades, Diana, 228
Enninger, Werner, 276, 287, 289
Escure, Geneviève, 229, 240, 252
Essegbey, James, 139, 154–5, 158, 166, 196
Étienne, Gérard, 54

Faine, Jules, 47, 67
Fattier, Dominique, 43, 47, 62, 119, 235
Férère, Gérard A., 54
Filipovich, Sandra, 276
Fillmore, Charles J., 104
Foley, William A., 33, 35, 159
Fournier, Robert, 47, 67
Freeman, Bryant C., 170
Furetière, Antoine, 2

Gilbert, Glenn G., 280, 285
Gilles, Rolande, 119, 121, 125
Gisborne, Nikolas, 225
Glock, Naomi, 48, 189
Goldberg, Adele E., 104
Good, Jeff, 33–4, 37, 41, 47, 54, 67, 69, 73, 96, 224, 255

Goodman, Morris F., 33–4, 47, 54, 67, 73, 224
Gougenheim, Georges, 73
Grant, Anthony P., 79, 231, 236, 240, 251
Grimes, Charles E., 220, 223, 232, 246, 249, 250
Güldemann, Tom, 61, 82

Hagège, Claude, 34
Hagemeijer, Tjerk, 154, 220, 229, 246, 248
Hall, Robert A., 15, 33, 40, 42, 77, 83, 97, 102, 177, 224, 250, 256
Ham, William H., 255
Hancock, Ian F., 33, 101, 227
Haspelmath, Martin, 31, 91, 93, 139, 219, 245
Hazoumê, Marc Laurent, 113, 194
Heath, Jeffrey, 71
Hebblethwaite, Benjamin, 293
Heine, Bernd, 31, 81, 83, 92
Hérault, Georges, 54
Hesseling, Dirk Christiaan, 34
Heurtelou, Maude, 117
Highfield, Arnold, 273, 288, 289, 293
Hilaire, Jeannot, 35, 181
Hill, Jane, 18
Hill, Kenneth, 18
Holm, John A., 34, 249
Hopper, Paul J., 101
Hounkpatin, Basile, 142
Huber, Magnus, 280, 286–8, 290
Hudson, Carla L., 101
Hulk, Aafke, 88
Huttar, George L., 4, 37, 85
Hymes, Dell, 33

Igla, Birgit, 24, 25
Iskrova, Iskra, 293

Jacob, June, 220, 232, 246, 249–50
Jaeggli, Osvaldo A., 88
Johnson, Kyle, 105
Joseph, Frantz, 45, 47, 54, 64–5, 119–21, 125, 128

Joseph, Sauveur Joseph, 45, 47, 54, 64–5, 119–21, 125, 128
Joseph, Yves, 45, 47, 54, 64–5, 119–21, 125, 128
Jourdan, Christine, 272, 276, 284, 286, 292

Kaufman, Terrence, 32–3, 35, 101
Kay, Paul, 32, 103–4, 120, 125, 204–5, 218, 232, 240–2
Kaye, Jonathan, 32
Kayne, Richard S., 204–5, 218
Kearns, Lucie, 56, 137, 190, 208, 217, 248
Keesing, Roger M., 11–12, 27–8, 37, 72, 85, 235, 243–4, 249, 252
Kihm, Alain, 66–7, 231, 237, 239, 252–3, 256
Kinyalolo, Kasangati K., 194
Koch, Harold, 4, 15, 17, 69–70, 223, 228, 232–3, 240–2, 244–5, 251–2, 254, 256
Koopman, Hilda, 27, 37, 59, 85, 87, 133, 203, 205–6
Koster, Jan, 158–9
Kouwenberg, Silvia, 33, 58–9, 139, 143, 158, 167, 171, 185, 194, 208, 210, 239
Kramer, Marvin, 118, 166, 174, 192
Kriegel, Sibylle, 15
Kuteva, T., 81, 83

Laberge, Suzanne, 92
Labov, William, 101
Lafage, Suzanne, 16
Lambert-Brétière, Renée, ix, 96–7, 103, 110, 114–16, 120–3, 127, 129–30, 139, 198
Langacker, Ronald, 104
Lang, Jürgen, 139, 155, 223, 229–30, 237, 254
Lardière, Donna, 13, 89
Larson, Richard K., 78, 134
Law, Paul, 70–1, 88, 200, 202–3, 205–7, 235, 240–2
Lefebvre, Claire, 2–6, 15, 17, 26–7, 31–5, 37–68, 72–8, 80–8, 90–4, 96–101, 104–29, 133–7, 140–2, 144, 145, 147, 148, 150–3, 157, 160–2, 168, 171–2,

176–88, 191–5, 199, 200–4, 206, 209, 215–16, 218, 220, 223–4, 227–8, 230, 234, 236–40, 245–7, 249, 250, 252, 254, 256–7, 263, 265, 267, 271
Leland, C., 25
Lenz, Rodolfo, 33
Lightfoot, David, 31
Lim, Lisa, 223, 225, 228, 231, 237
Loranger, Virginie, 56, 57, 59, 60, 61, 81, 82, 83, 85, 112, 238
Lumsden, John S., 4, 5, 15, 17, 27, 32, 33, 34, 35, 37, 47, 56, 66, 76, 77, 78, 85, 88, 90, 92, 93, 99, 100, 140, 144, 179, 183, 189, 190, 195, 205, 218
Lye, Hui Min, 28

Magloire-Holly, Hélène, 283–4, 286
Manfredi, Victor, 195, 205
Marantz, Alec, 167
Massam, Diane, 47, 187, 202
Matthews, Stephen, 223, 251
Maurer, Philippe, 37, 58–9, 137, 154, 189, 208, 217, 219, 248
McWhorter, John H., 37, 60, 81, 96, 98, 102, 225, 270
Merlan, Francesca, 70
Michaelis, Susanne, 139, 154, 178, 219, 225, 245, 265
Migge, Bettina, 4, 13–14, 17, 27, 37–8, 41, 58, 85, 109, 111, 166, 172–5, 178, 181, 229–30, 237–8, 249, 250, 254
Moreau, Marie-Louise, 204–5
Mosel, Ulrike, 243–4
Mous, Maarten, 4, 11, 17, 20–1, 31, 38, 54, 104–5, 186, 236
Mufwene, S., 32, 34, 73, 177, 194, 227, 250, 267, 271
Mufwene, Salikoko S., 32, 34, 73, 177, 194, 227, 250, 267, 271
Mühlhäusler, Peter, 177, 227
Munro, Jennifer, 4, 33, 69–72, 233–7, 240–2, 249, 251–2, 256, 263
Murray, Eric, 33, 171, 185, 194
Muysken, Pieter C., 3–4, 10, 18–19, 24, 31, 33, 58, 60, 77–8, 102, 139, 155, 157–8, 177, 194, 210, 218, 225, 239

Naro, Anthony J., 289
Navarro, Tomás, 33
Neumann-Holzschuh, Ingrid, 178, 181–3, 225
Newport, Elissa L., 101
Nikiema, Emmanuel, 2–3, 83–4, 168–70, 255
Nolasco, Ricardo M., 251

O'Connor, Mary Catherine, 279
Ogie, Ota, 220, 229, 246, 248–9
Olguín, Maribel, 96–7, 208–9, 218–19

Papen, Robert, ix, 21, 24, 265
Parkvall, Mikael, 33, 41, 176
Perl, Matthias, 25, 81, 242
Pienemann, Manfred, 107
Piou, Nanie, 283, 289
Plag, Ingo, 40–1, 107, 139, 141, 143, 168, 172, 175, 269–70
Pollock, Jean-Yves, 58, 105, 160–1
Post, Marike, 154
Potsma, Johannes, 41

Rassinoux, Jean, 14, 38, 54, 97, 113, 127, 151, 191, 199
Rawley, James A., 109
Riemer, Johann Andreas, 55, 79, 80
Ritter, Elizabeth, 47, 52, 134
Rizzi, Luigi, 58
Roberge, Yves, 88
Roberts, Craige, 194, 233, 249
Robertson, Ian, 194
Roberts, Sarah J., 194, 233, 249
Ross, Malcolm, 15
Rountree, Catherine S., 37, 45, 48, 55, 57, 62–3, 65, 79–80, 109, 111–12, 145, 175, 189, 238

Sandefur, John R., 244
Sandefur, Joy L., 244
Sandeman, Barbara, 233, 237, 239, 252
Sankoff, Gillian, 92–3, 101
Schneider, Edgar W., 178, 225
Schuchardt, Hugo, 34, 61, 82
Schumann, Christian Ludwig, 55, 79, 80

Schumann, John H., 32
Schwartz, Bonnie D., 12
Schwegler, Armin, 223, 230, 236, 249
Segal, Gabriel, 78
Segurola, Basilio, 2, 38, 54, 97, 113, 151, 191, 199
Segurola, R., 2, 38, 54, 97, 113, 151, 191, 199
Sharpe, Margaret C., 70, 241
Siegel, Jeff, 4, 14–15, 101, 139, 159, 177, 223, 228, 233, 243–5, 249, 251–4, 256, 267
Singler, John V., 2, 33, 35, 41, 109
Sippola, Eeva, 231, 240
Slobin, D., 271
Slomanson, Peter, 223, 227, 232, 237, 239–40, 250
Smith, Geoff P., 274
Smith, Norval, 4, 8, 33, 41, 82, 85, 109, 111, 112, 118, 142, 155, 165, 168, 174, 177, 181, 192, 225, 255
Sprouse, Rex A., 12–13, 16, 100, 222
Steele, Jeffrey, 2–3
Sterlin, Marie-Denise, 59, 206
Stolz, Thomas, 276
Syea, Anand, 274, 277, 283, 292–3
Sylvain, Suzanne, 34, 47, 54, 59, 73, 119, 224

Terrill, Angela, 4, 27, 28, 85, 234, 249, 252
Therrien, Isabelle, 59, 91, 209, 265
Thomason, Sarah G., 32, 33, 35, 101
Tinelli, Henri, 54
Trask, Robert L., 14
Traugott, Elizabeth C., 101
Tremblay, Mireille, 218
Trudgill, Peter, 32
Tryon, D., 279, 294

Valdman, Albert, 2, 32, 37, 47, 54, 61, 66–7, 88, 96–7, 125–7, 130–1, 170, 181, 196, 201, 235
Van Coetsem, Frans, 15
Van den Berg, Henk, 136, 217, 247
van de Vate, Marleen Susanne, 57, 111

van Marle, Jaap, 275–6, 285
van Name, Addison, 293
Van Wijk, Henri L., 33
Védrine, Emmanuel W., 96, 172
Veenstra, Tonjes, 51, 57, 60, 81, 119, 139, 194, 210, 238
Vilsaint, Féquière, 54, 117
Vincent, Diane, 67
Voorhoeve, Jan, 4, 34, 85

Wee, Lionel, 28
Weinreich, Uriel, 12, 249

Westerman, Diedrich, 52, 73
Whinnom, Keith, 33
White, Lydia, 273, 276, 284, 286, 292
Wietz, I., 43–5, 48, 52, 55, 58, 81
Wijnen, Beppy, 60
Winford, Donald, 15, 58, 61, 111, 238
Wurm, S., 274, 279, 294

Yoder, Sara, 293

Zagona, Karen, 209

INDEX OF LANGUAGES

Alawa, 70, 71, 235, 240–2
Angloromani, 24–6, 259

Belizean Creole, 225–6, 240
Berbice Dutch, 139, 158–9, 194
Bislama, 225–7, 243–4

Casamance Creole, 226
China Coast Pidgin, 225–7, 231, 236–7, 240, 245, 248, 251, 256
Chinese, 28–9, 31, 226, 233
Chinese Pidgin English, 226

Dutch, 33, 139, 158–9, 194

Ewe(gbe), 9, 11, 16, 27, 52–3, 67, 73–4, 84, 90, 97, 113, 14–19, 181, 196, 206, 212, 218, 224, 265

Fiji Hindi, 159
Fijian, 159
Fongbe, 2, 3, 4, 14, 27, 32, 35, 38, 39, 40, 42–90, 94, 96, 97–8, 109, 110–266
French, 2, 3, 4, 16, 21–4, 33–5, 37–8, 40–2, 46, 48, 49–68, 73–6, 79, 83–8, 93–7, 105, 109, 110, 112, 118, 120–1, 124, 126–8, 130–2, 134, 140–2, 144–53, 160–3, 166, 168–72, 176, 178–85, 188, 190–2, 195, 196–9, 201, 202–5, 207–8, 211, 217–19, 224, 229–30, 248, 250, 264–5, 270

Haitian, 2–7, 26–7, 32–5, 37–68, 72–3, 75–8, 83–8, 90–1, 93–8, 100–12, 115–270
Hawai'i Creole, 225–6, 233
Hindi, 159
Hiri Motu, 139, 159

Ijo, 139, 158
Inner Mbugu, 20

Korlai, 160
Kriol, 4, 26, 30, 33, 69–72, 75, 100, 225–7, 233–7, 240–4, 251–2, 256–7, 263–4, 266
Kriyol, 225–6, 230, 237, 239, 252–3
Kwaio, 12, 27, 28, 243, 244

Lavukaleve, 27, 28

Ma'a, 4, 17, 20, 21, 29, 30, 31, 259
Malay, 17, 29, 220, 225, 226, 227, 231, 232, 237, 240, 241, 246, 248, 249, 251, 255, 256
Marra, 71
Marathi, 160
Martinican, 32–3, 53, 61, 74–6, 90, 140–1, 145, 149, 153, 248, 265–6, 269

Media Lengua, 4, 18–21, 24, 26, 29, 78, 259

Michif, 4, 17, 21–4, 26, 29, 30–1, 78, 259

Mindanao Chabacano, 225–6, 231, 236, 240, 251

Ndyuka, 225–6

New South Wales Pidgin, 226

Ngalakgan, 70

Nicaraguan Creole, 226

Normal Mbugu, 20

Palenque(ro), 225, 226

Papiamentu, 4, 5, 7, 32–3, 37, 41, 58–9, 96–8, 109, 136–7, 168, 171, 180, 184–5, 189, 194, 199–220, 225–6, 230, 239, 248

Pidgin Yimas, 159

Portuguese, 5, 33, 41, 55, 57, 59–60, 82, 97, 109–10, 112, 119, 134, 139, 142, 145, 154–7, 159, 160, 165, 174, 180, 225, 233, 238, 248, 253

Providence Creole, 226

Quechua, 18, 19, 21, 25, 78, 218

San Andrés Creole, 226

Santiago Island Creole, 226

Santome, 154, 220, 225–6, 229, 246, 248

Saramaccan, 4–5, 7, 26, 31–3, 37, 40–9, 51–68, 73–85, 90, 96–7, 109–12, 118–19, 136–9, 141–2, 145–50, 153–8, 164–8, 172–6, 180–3, 189–90, 192–4, 198–9, 213–20, 225–6, 230, 238, 247–8, 255, 264–6, 268–70

Singapore English, 4, 17, 28, 29, 112, 220, 225–7, 231

Sinhala, 159, 227, 239–41, 256

Solomon Island's Pijin, 226

Spanish, 5, 18–20, 24–5, 33, 37, 41, 97, 109, 134, 172, 180–1, 184–5, 194, 199, 208–11, 217, 219, 230–1, 248, 251

Sranan Tongo, 226

Sri Lanka Malay, 225–7, 232, 237, 240–1, 251, 256

Sri Lanka Portuguese, 159

St. Lucian Creole, 226, 228, 255

Tamil, 17, 29, 159, 227, 240, 256

Tayo, 225–7, 233, 237, 239

Ternate Chabacano, 225–6, 231, 240

Tok Pisin, 92–3, 101, 225, 226–7, 243

Touo, 27–8

Yoruba, 27, 73

Printed in Great Britain
by Amazon